STUDENTS OF COLOR AND THE ACHIEVEMENT GAP

Students of Color and the Achievement Gap is a comprehensive, landmark analysis of an incontrovertible racialized reality in U.S. K-12 public education—the relentless achievement gap between low-socioeconomic students of color and their economically advantaged White counterparts. Award-winning author and scholar Richard Valencia provides an authoritative and systemic treatment of the achievement gap, focusing on Black and Latino/Latina students. He examines the societal and educational factors that help to create and maintain the achievement gap by drawing from critical race theory, an asset-based perspective, and a systemic inequality approach.

By showing how racialized opportunity structures in society and schools ultimately result in racialized patterns of academic achievement in schools, Valencia shows how the various indicators of the achievement gap are actually symptoms of the societal and school quality gaps. Following each of these concerns, Valencia provides a number of reform suggestions that can lead to systemic transformations of K-12 education. *Students of Color and the Achievement Gap* makes a persuasive and well-documented case that school success for students of color, and the empowerment of their parents, can be fully understood and realized only when contextualized within broader political, economic, and cultural frameworks.

Richard R. Valencia is a professor of educational psychology and faculty associate in the Center for Mexican American Studies at the University of Texas, Austin. Dr. Valencia is a nationally recognized expert on the education of students of color, particularly Mexican Americans. He specializes in historical, social, psychological, measurement, legal, demographic, and reform aspects pertaining to the schooling of students of color. Among his numerous books are: *Chicano School Failure and Success: Past, Present, and Future* (3rd ed., Routledge, 2011)—winner of the American Educational Studies Association 2012 Critics Choice Book Award; *Dismantling Contemporary Deficit Thinking: Educational Thought and Practice* (Critical Educator Series, Routledge, 2010)—winner of the American Educational Research Association 2011 Outstanding Book Award; and *Chicano Students and the Courts: The Mexican American Legal Struggle for Educational Equality* (Critical America Series, New York University Press, 2008)—runner-up winner of the 2010 Robert W. Hamilton Book Award.

STUDENTS OF COLOR AND THE ACHIEVEMENT GAP

Systematic Challenges, Systematic Transformations

Richard R. Valencia

NEW YORK AND LONDON

First published 2015
by Routledge
711 Third Avenue, New York, NY 10017

and by Routledge
2 Park Square, Milton Park, Abingdon, Oxon, OX14 4RN

Routledge is an imprint of the Taylor & Francis Group, an informa business

Library of Congress Cataloging-in-Publication Data
A catalog record for this book has been requested.

ISBN: 978-1-138-01880-8 (hbk)
ISBN: 978-1-138-01881-5 (pbk)
ISBN: 978-1-315-77663-7 (ebk)

Typeset in ApexBembo
by Apex CoVantage, LLC

Printed and bound in the United States of America by Publishers Graphics, LLC on sustainably sourced paper.

This book is dedicated to all students of color and their families in their struggle for equal educational opportunity, equal encouragement, and empowerment.

I also dedicate this volume to all progressive scholars, educators, and policymakers who challenge the ubiquity of educational oppression and devote their time and energy in working for demonstrative school success for children and youths of color.

—Richard R. Valencia

CONTENTS

FIGURES

TABLES

PREFACE

Although the gap in academic achievement between students of color relative to their White peers has been documented going back decades (e.g., White and Mexican American comparisons in Drake, 1927; White and Black comparisons in Whitney, 1923), the usage of the term "achievement gap" is fairly recent. The first time the expression appears in the literature is in a 1963 article in *The Nation* by Walker, who notes that an "educational achievement gap" exists between Black and White elementary school students in Englewood, New Jersey, schools (Salmonowicz, 2009). The term is first seen in an academic journal (*American Economic Review*) in a 1970 article by Gwartney, who reports of a "widening achievement gap" between White and "nonwhite" students (Salmonowicz).

The achievement gap phrase has even worked its way into the landmark national No Child Left Behind (NCLB) Act of 2002 (Public Law 107–110), the federal government's omnibus and ambitious attempt to eliminate academic achievement disparities. On the very first line of the first page of the law, it reads, "An Act: To close the *achievement gap* [italics added] with accountability, flexibility, and choice, so that no child is left behind" (115 Stat. 1425). Later in the NCLB Act, there is reference to Title I of the 1965 Elementary and Secondary Education Act, which cites this goal: "Closing the achievement gap between high- and low-performing children, especially between minority and nonminority students" (115 Stat. 1440 of the NCLB Act).

Certainly, narrowing the achievement gap is a pressing issue of contemporary public education. In regard to African Americans, as a case in point, Rod Paige—former U.S. Secretary of Education in the administration of President George W. Bush—notes, "I have become convinced that the achievement gap is now the most important challenge for African Americans" (2010, p. xviii). In *The Black-White Achievement Gap: Why Closing It Is the Greatest Civil Rights Challenge of Our Time* (with Elaine Witty), Paige continues: "The black-white achievement gap now ranks ahead of our old nemeses of racism and racial discrimination" (p. xviii). This assertion is simply inaccurate. The achievement gap does not trump racism and racial discrimination. Rather, these latter social evils are key forces in the educational system that help to explain, in part, the wide academic chasm between Whites and Blacks, and other students of color. As well, racism and racial discrimination are factors that help shape the deep structural inequality in society, particularly along lines of income, housing, and health—dimensions I refer to in chapter 3 as the "other" gaps, disparities that in themselves help create and maintain the achievement gap.

Currently, there is a voluminous corpus of literature on the school failure of many students of color,[1] particularly low-socioeconomic status (SES) Mexican Americans, Puerto Ricans, other Latinos/Latinas, African Americans, and American Indians.[2] School failure among these students—which is a barometer of the achievement gap—refers to their persistently, pervasively, and disproportionately low academic achievement (Valencia, 2011b). The modifying term "disproportionately" is a key modifier because it denotes comparative performance with White students. This comparison signals an incontrovertible racialized reality in U.S. education: An enormous chasm exists between the aforementioned students of color and their White peers.

This achievement gap demonstrates that *average* group differences in achievement test performance (e.g., reading) are persistent and pervasive between middle- to high-SES Whites and low-SES students of color, with the former consistently outperforming the latter. The achievement gap is not confined to achievement test performance, but it also manifests in other achievement indicators (e.g., high school completion rates). Note that in this operationalization of the achievement gap, the discussion of the academic performance of students of color is typically framed against the White student average (i.e., the normative group). This casting has the danger of interpreting the school performance of students of color from an endogenous locus of explanation via the lens of deficit thinking (e.g., putative cognitive and motivational limitations of the student; see chapter 2, this volume, for an overview of the deficit thinking model). Such an approach to understanding the average academic performance of students of color can lead to a misdirection by and preoccupation of deficit thinkers that there is something about being a student of color that produces low performance (O'Connor, Horvat, & Lewis, 2006). This deficit thinking, a pseudoscientific perspective, must be rejected and more plausible interpretations (e.g., systemic inequalities in schooling, such as curriculum differentiation; see chapter 7, this volume) must be examined in explaining the gulf in achievement. Nonetheless, viewing the achievement gap from a White student/student of color comparison can be quite constructive, as this approach can help in flagging, exploring, and reforming racialized achievement patterns (O'Connor et al.).

Before continuing, it is important to underscore that the persistent and pervasive racialized group differences in achievement are *averages*.[3] That is, noticeable within-racial/ethnic group disparities in achievement exist, and these within-group differences typically exceed between-group differences. As such, the vast proportion of the variability in academic achievement (and measured intellectual ability) lies *within* racial/ethnic groups, not *between* them (Valencia & Suzuki, 2001). As such, within-group analyses are valuable to study because they can unmask the achievement variability that exists, for example, among Puerto Rican students. Notwithstanding the reality that racial/ethnic groups are heterogeneous in their academic performance, it is still vital to be cognizant of the achievement gap, which is measured by a robust collection of indicators informing us that, on the *average,* White students outperform their low-SES students of color peers.

In light of the remarkable enrollment growth of students of color, a crucial question to ask of educators, researchers, and policymakers is: Will workable, comprehensive, and equitable school reform commensurately increase? Given the bankruptcy of the standards-based school reform movement, which has now swept K-12 schooling in the U.S. and is the primary strategy for improving schooling for students of color (especially of low-SES background), I must answer my own question with a resounding "no." The standards-based school reform movement is palliative and bereft of meaningful policy to help realize school success for students of color because the campaign, as I discuss ahead, is structurally misdirected (see Valencia & Pearl, 2010).

In *Students of Color and the Achievement Gap*, three major theses drive my analyses. First, racialized opportunity structures in the larger society and the educational system lead to racialized academic achievement patterns. Second, the various indicators of the achievement gap (especially achievement test performance and school holding power rates) are *symptoms* of the school quality gap between high-enrollment White schools and high-enrollment schools of students of color. As such, the standards-based school reform movement, which is directed toward poor achievement, is structurally misdirected. We need to focus on *causes*—inequalities in society and inferior schools. Third, school success for students of color (particularly low-SES Latino/Latina and Black students) can be understood to a greater extent when analyzed in the broadest political, economic, and cultural contexts. The major aim of *Students of Color and the Achievement Gap* is to integrate the macro-, micro-, and macrolevels of education—which has been done only by a handful of scholars to date (e.g., Ochoa, 2013). The meshing of these three levels establishes the boundaries of possibilities for significantly improving the schooling for students of color.

Students of Color and the Achievement Gap consists of four parts and nine chapters. In Part I, "The Problem," there are two chapters. The first section of chapter 1, "The Achievement Gap," describes and discusses an empirically based overview of the various facets of the achievement gap—for example: (a) achievement test performance, (b) grade retention, (c) school holding power, and (d) matriculation to college. Following this, I provide a brief summary of several approaches authors proffer as useful in diminishing the achievement gap (i.e., via a narrow remedial curricular intervention, an equal opportunity approach, or a systemic analysis). The third section of chapter 1 provides an overview of the extraordinary growth of people and students of color.

Chapter 2, "Competing Models to Explain the Achievement Gap," asks: What best accounts for the persistent and pervasive finding that low-SES students of color perform, on the average, lower than their White peers on the various indicators of the achievement gap that I discuss in chapter 1? Scholars and others have proffered at least four competing explanations. I provide comprehensive reviews of these models and, when appropriate, critiques. The first theory, deficit thinking, is an endogenous model that "blames the victim." This theoretical perspective posits that students of color who experience academic problems do so because they, their cultures, and their families have deficits or deficiencies. Such deficits manifest, it is alleged, in students' limited intellectual abilities and lack of motivation to achieve, dysfunctional cultures, and families in which parents do not value education nor socialize their children for academic competence so they can succeed in school. Given the parsimonious nature of deficit thinking, it is not surprising that advocates of the model fail to look for external attributions why students of color, on the average, experience school failure. Inequalities in society, the hegemonic workings of the political economy of education, and the oppressive policies and practices of local schools are all held exculpatory in helping to create the academic difficulties of students of color.

The second theoretical framework that has been advanced to explain the achievement gap is the cultural-ecological model (CEM), which has been developed by the late educational anthropologist John U. Ogbu. To best understand the CEM in regard to school failure among certain groups of color, one needs to begin with his typology of "minorities" in the U.S., which are "autonomous" (e.g., Mormons; Jews), "immigrant" (e.g., Chinese; Punjabi), and "involuntary or castelike" (e.g., African American; Mexican American; Puerto Rican). Ogbu asserts that members of autonomous groups have a high value for education and demonstrate academic success. Immigrant group members do undergo the experiences of assimilation and acculturation, and students have adjustment problems, but these children and youths do not experience protracted adaptation problems and school failure. On the other hand, students of castelike groups experience chronic school problems in adjustment and academic achievement. The CEM maintains that discrimination in society and school is not adequate in itself to explain the school failure of Blacks, for example. What is also important to include is the assertion of the CEM that Black students eventually internalize, via self-doubt, Whites' perceptions of their alleged cognitive limitations and begin to view school success as the prerogative of Whites. In this section, I undertake an overview of scholarship on the CEM, including a content analysis of six categories of criticism of the CEM that make most sense to me.

The communication process model is discussed next. The earliest variant of this family of models to explain the achievement gap stems from the intense debate of the late 1960s and early 1970s in which the language of children raised in poverty was viewed as "deficient" or "different." In brief, I discuss this early controversy. As the communication process model evolved, it began to underscore that linguistic differences, verbal and nonverbal communication styles, teacher-student conflict, and marked boundaries may affect students' achievement. For example, there is the function of culturally acquired communication styles of students and teachers in creating conflict, which, in turn, helps to explain poor academic achievement among low-SES students of color.

The final theoretical framework I discuss in chapter 2 is the systemic inequality model (SIM). I begin this coverage by unpacking a number of characteristics of the SIM, based on my sense of the literature. These features are: (a) the nature of a system, (b) comprehensiveness, (c) reproduction, (d) hegemony, (e) resistance, and (e) widespread reform. As are the other models I discuss in this chapter, the SIM is not without its detractors. For instance, the model—particularly earlier renditions—has been arraigned as being quite deterministic. Also, some critics comment that the SIM is highly descriptive and lacks prescription for meaningful, democratic school reform. I conclude the chapter by introducing my version of a SIM, which I coin *The Three-M Systemic Model.* The "Three-M" aspect refers to macrolevel, mesolevel, and microlevel factors.

Part II, "Macrolevel Factors," contains chapter 3, which is titled "The 'Other' Gaps: Income, Housing, and Health." A small number of scholars note that the inclusion of the "other" gaps is important to consider in any discourse on school reform vis-à-vis students of color. A shortcoming of this body of work, however, is that most of these authors barely prick the surface of how these gaps negatively affect the academic achievement of students of color, particularly how the "other" gaps exacerbate the academic gulf between White students and students of color. My synthesis of the literature provides a rare overview of how the '"other" gaps are actually related to the lower academic achievement of Latino/Latina and Black students.

In the income gap section of chapter 3, I cover the following across race/ethnicity: (a) drops in median household incomes, resultant of the Great Recession, (b) economic security/insecurity, (c) the wealth gap, and (d) families living in poverty. I conclude the coverage on the income gap by discussing its implications regarding the academic consequences for students of color, especially how variability in family income affects the achievement gap.

The discussion on the housing gap of chapter 3 examines the connection between where a family lives and the quality of schooling the children receive. Given that residential location largely determines the price of particular housing, and such location, in turn, is associated with whether the nearby schools are typically low- or high-performing academically, it is not unforeseen that the housing gap leads to separate and unequal schools. Most of the literature on racial segregation centers on separate housing *or* separate schools, but seldom the interrelation between the two—which I discuss. In my examination of the housing gap, I view it through the lens of the concept "geography of opportunity."

Here, I conceive such opportunity as a process in which residential location is a conduit to high-performing schools—an experience that low-SES students of color are frequently denied.

In the health section of chapter 3, a number of health disparities between students of color and their White counterparts are discussed. Here, I cover select health issues, focusing on those that appear to receive the most attention in the health-related literature—namely, (a) obesity, (b) type 2 diabetes, (c) asthma, (d) lead poisoning, (e) dental caries, and (f) food insecurity and poor nutrition. In addition to discussing these health gaps, I review the literature that has examined how these maladies negatively affect the academic achievement of students of color, thus contributing to the achievement gap. The chapter on the "other" gaps concludes with suggestions for systemic reform regarding race- and class-based differences in income, housing, and health.

Part III, "Mesolevel Factors," consists of four chapters. I conceptualize the topic of each chapter as an institutional process or circumstance that adversely shapes schooling outcomes (i.e., the various indicators of the achievement gap) for low-SES students of color. One can think of these institutional processes as independent variables (e.g., segregation) and the outcomes (e.g., low academic achievement) as dependent variables. It is here, at the mesolevel of schooling, that most scholars have committed their research time. To be sure, this is an important endeavor. Such a preoccupation, however, can be misguided because it often leads to a fragmented and shallow understanding of the schooling of students of color. It is this major shortcoming that has prompted me in *Students of Color and the Achievement Gap* to develop my Three-M Systemic Model, in which I assert that the realization of school success for low-SES students of color can be achieved only by discussing problems and solutions at all three levels—the macrolevel, the mesolevel, and the microlevel.

At the end of each chapter in part III (chapters 4 to 7) and part IV (chapters 8 and 9), I employ my *inversion strategy* for school reform ("Toward Systemic Transformations") when dealing with the various schooling circumstances that shape school failure of students of color. For example, in "Teacher Quality" (chapter 5) I contend that to address the concern of the relation between quality of teachers and student achievement, we have to understand the root cause. Ample research demonstrates that the least qualified and experienced teachers are placed in high-enrollment schools of color. Common sense and research findings inform us that we need to invert matters. Every effort should be undertaken to have the most experienced, best prepared, highly committed, and most qualified teachers work in schools with high enrollments of students of color to dramatically ameliorate their education.

These suggestions I offer for improving the direction of systemic change are designed to serve as roadmaps for informed give-and-take discourse. Three threads run through most of these concluding sections. First, systemic transformations are not doable without serious financial commitment. Systemic reform cannot be done cheaply. Second, these suggestions, for the most part, run counter to the orthodoxy. Given their provocative nature, people need to engage them with an open mind. Third, as often as possible, I base my recommendations on the best evidence I can locate (e.g., grounded in theory; sound methodology; application to the realization of social justice and equality in society and the schools).

"School Segregation, Desegregation, and Integration" is the subject of chapter 4 in part III. School segregation in the U.S. is one of the most studied topics in the field of race relations and education. This is not surprising given the longstanding existence of school segregation and its relation to limited equality of opportunity and as a key mesolevel factor in helping to create the achievement gap. In this chapter, five areas are discussed: (a) current prevalence of school segregation; (b) adverse effects of school segregation—academic and social contexts; (c) historical struggles for school desegregation; (d) period of meaningful school desegregation; and (e) contemporary status of school desegregation.

The topic of chapter 5 is "Teacher Quality." Substantial empirical evidence shows a positive relation between the quality of teachers and student academic performance. Furthermore, numerous research findings report that teacher quality characteristics are inequitably distributed across race/ethnicity and class in the nation's public schools, meaning that low-SES students of color are frequently shortchanged in being taught by the best teachers. This chapter is organized around these topics: (a) inequitable distribution of teacher quality characteristics, and (b) the relation between teacher quality and student academic performance.

Chapter 6 addresses the topic of "Language Suppression and Cultural Exclusion." Given that a group's culture and language capture the very life force of human beings, the language suppression/cultural exclusion issue looms large for students of color. I examine this concern by discussing six areas: (a) the value of bilingualism and multicultural education; (b) students of color and the school curriculum: acts of omission and commission; (c) early language suppression and cultural exclusion: Mexican American students as a case in point; (d) the legal struggle for bilingual education; (e) the politics of demagogic anti-bilingualism and the campaign to eradicate bilingual education; and (f) racism and cultural hegemony in Arizona public schools: the case of House Bill 2281.

The final chapter (7) in part III is "Curriculum Differentiation," which I broadly define as the sorting of students into learning groups based on perceived and/or measured educability. The harm that curriculum differentiation accrues to students (especially low-SES students of color) is quite serious. A particularly deleterious outcome is the curricular tracking that occurs in high schools when many students of color have very limited access to "high-status knowledge," which is the type of knowledge that is a prerequisite for admission to and success in college. I structure chapter 7 around these topics: (a) a brief history of curriculum differentiation; (b) pervasiveness of curriculum differentiation and sorting by race and class; and (c) curriculum differentiation and unequal educational opportunities for students of color.

Part IV, "Microlevel Factors," contains two chapters. Chapter 8, "Parental Engagement and Empowerment," introduces matters by stating that all parents, across different racial/ethnic and SES groups, have aspirations that their children succeed in school. A copious body of quantitative and qualitative research evidence shows that a major predictor of elementary and secondary students' school success is the degree of their parents' engagement in schooling. A *sine qua non* in educational discourse is that the greater parents get involved in their children's schooling, the more successful their offspring will be—particularly in the improvement of academic achievement and the fostering of favorable attitudes toward learning. In chapter 8, several key questions guide my analysis. How does the literature on parental involvement—with respect to theory and practice—apply to low-SES parents of color and the reduction of the achievement gap? Given that many parents of color do not have equal opportunity to partake in school activities germane to their children, how can these barriers be demolished? How can parents of color become further empowered so they can become agents of change? This chapter is organized around four sections: (a) a discussion of the conventional manner in which parental involvement is conceptualized by researchers; (b) a summary of the literature on the value of parental involvement in education; (c) an examination of the myth that parents of color do not value education; and (d) a summary of research findings that demonstrate parents of color do indeed value education and do participate, in various ways, in the education of their children.

"Student Agency and Empowerment" is the topic of chapter 9. The notions of student agency and empowerment stem from various discourses—for example, social capital, democratic education, and resistance theory. The study of student agency and empowerment is somewhat underdeveloped because of the entrenchment of deficit thinking in education: The assertion is that students, particularly of color, are the makers of their own problems. There are some scholars, however, who challenge such deficit thinking and argue for a paradigm shift that examines how students constructively resist oppression in schools. Chapter 9 examines the following: (a) student voice; (b) theoretical perspectives on student agency and empowerment; and (c) narratives on successful initiatives for student agency and empowerment.

Students of Color and the Achievement Gap closes with a very brief "Last Thoughts." These ruminations focus on the need to (a) think broadly and deeply about how to eradicate the achievement gap, (b) conceptualize the achievement gap reduction as both an educational and economic imperative, and (c) embrace and support efforts to empower low-SES students and their parents.

Notes

1. This volume focuses on kindergarten through grade 12 (K-12) public education. At times, however, higher education is covered.
2. See, for example, Darling-Hammond (2010); Ferguson (2007); Gándara & Contreras (2009); García (2001); Irvine (1990); Noguera (2003); Noguera and Wing (2006); Paige

and Witty (2010); Sizemore (2008); Valencia (2011a). In this volume, I omit Asian American students from discussions of school failure and the achievement gap. This exclusion is based on the ubiquitous finding that these students perform, *on the average,* higher than their Latina/Latino, African American, and American Indian peers—and in some cases, higher than their White counterparts. For example, based on SAT scores for the graduating class of 2010, Asian American students were second (M = 519) to Whites (M = 528) on the Critical Reading subtest, and first on Mathematics (M = 591) compared to Whites (M = 526) (College Board, 2010; see Table 1.6 of chapter 1, this volume, to see how Mexican American and African American students performed compared to Whites). It is important to be aware, however, that not all Asian American students are high achievers (see, e.g., Du Phuoc Long, 1996; Kiang, 2002; Lee, 1996; Lew, 2006; Pang, 1990). For example, Lew studied 72 second-generation Korean American youths attending New York City schools (30 of the participants were dropouts attending a GED school; 42 were enrolled in an elite magnet school). Lew found that the magnet school students—in comparison to their peers attending the GED school—came from more economically advantaged families and attended a school that offered a much better education (e.g., more challenging curriculum). Lew notes that to avoid homogenizing Asian American students a la model minority myth (see, e.g., Chou & Feagin, 2008; Lee, 1996), it is important to study the school achievement patterns of these students by examining factors such as family SES and quality of the schools.

3. This paragraph builds on, with modifications, Valencia (2011b, p. 5).

References

Chou, R. S., & Feagin, J. R. (2008). *The myth of the model minority: Asian Americans facing racism.* Boulder, CO: Paradigm.

College Board. (2010). SAT trends: Background on the SAT takers in the class of 2010. New York: Author. Retrieved March 5, 2011, from: http://professionals.collegeboard.com/prof download/2010-sat-trends.pdf.

Darling-Hammond, L. (2010). *The flat world and education: How America's commitment to equity will determine our future.* New York: Teachers College Press.

Drake, R. H. (1927). *A comparison study of the mentality and achievement of Mexican and White children.* Unpublished master's thesis, University of Southern California, Los Angeles.

Du Phuoc Long, P. (with Ricard, L.). (1996). *The dream shattered: Vietnamese gangs in America.* Boston: Northeastern University Press.

Ferguson, R. F. (2007). *Toward excellence with equity: An emerging vision for closing the achievement gap.* Cambridge, MA: Harvard Education Press.

Gándara, P. C., & Contreras, F. (2009). *The Latino education crisis: The consequences of failed social policies.* Cambridge, MA: Harvard University Press.

García, E. E. (2001). *Hispanic education in the United States: Raíces y alas.* Lanham, MD: Roman and Littlefield.

Gwartney, J. (1970). Changes in the nonwhite/white income ratio—1939–67. *The American Economic Review, 60,* 872–883.

Irvine, J. J. (1990). *Black students and school failure: Policies, practices, and prescriptions.* Westport, CT: Praeger.

Kiang, P. N. (2002). K-12 education and Asian Pacific youth development. *Asian American Policy Review, 10,* 31–47.

Lee, S. (1996). *Unraveling the "model minority" stereotype: Listening to Asian American youth.* New York: Teachers College Press.

Lew, J. (2006). *Asian Americans in class: Charting the achievement gap among Korean American students.* New York: Teachers College Press.

No Child Left Behind Act, Pub. L. No (107–110), 115 Stat. 1425 (2002).

Noguera, P. A. (2003). *City schools and the American dream: Reclaiming the promise of public education.* New York: Teachers College Press.

Noguera, P. A., & Wing, J. Y. (Eds.). (2006). *Unfinished business: Closing the racial achievement gap in our schools.* San Francisco: Jossey-Bass.

Ochoa, G. L. (2013). *Academic profiling: Latinos, Asian Americans, and the achievement gap.* Minneapolis: University of Minnesota Press.

O'Connor, C., Horvat, E. M., & Lewis, A. E. (2006). Introduction: Framing the field: Past and future research on the historic underachievement of Black students. In E. M. Horvat & C. O'Connor (Eds.), *Beyond acting White: Reframing the debate on Black student achievement* (pp. 1–24). Lanham, MD: Rowman & Littlefield.

Paige, R., & Witty, E. (2010). *The black-white achievement gap: Why closing it is the greatest civil rights issue of our time.* New York: AMACON.

Pang, V. D. (1990). Asian American students: A diverse population. *Educational Forum, 55,* 1–18.

Salmonowicz, M. (2009, October 3). A short history of the term "achievement gap" (or is it "gaps"?). Retrieved May 25, 2011, from: http://trueslant.com/michaelsalmonowicz/2009/10/03/history-of-the-achievement-gap/.

Sizemore, B. A. (2008). *Walking in circles: The Black struggle for school reform.* Chicago: Third World Press.

Valencia, R. R. (Ed.). (2011a). *Chicano school failure and success: Past, present, and future* (3rd ed.). New York: Routledge.

Valencia, R. R. (Ed.). (2011b). The plight of Chicano students: An overview of schooling conditions and outcomes. In R. R. Valencia (Ed.), *Chicano school failure and success: Past, present, and future* (3rd ed., pp. 3–41). New York: Routledge.

Valencia, R. R., & Pearl, A. (2010). Conclusion: (A) The bankruptcy of the standards-based school reform movement; (B) Toward the construction of meaningful school reform: democratic education. In R. R. Valencia, *Dismantling contemporary deficit thinking: Educational thought and practice* (pp. 148–158). Critical Educator Series. New York: Routledge.

Valencia, R. R., & Suzuki, L. A. (2001). *Intelligence testing and minority students: Foundations, performance factors, and assessment issues.* Series on Racial and Ethnic Minority Psychology. Thousand Oaks, CA: SAGE.

Whitney, F. L. (1923). Intelligence levels and school achievement of the white and colored races in the United States. *Pedagogical Seminary, 30,* 69–86.

ACKNOWLEDGMENTS

It takes the support of many individuals to bring a book to fruition. My deep appreciation goes to Catherine Bernard, Senior Publisher at Routledge, for your unwavering support throughout this project. This is my third book on your watch, and it has been an extraordinarily rewarding experience working with you again. Thank you, Trevor Gori, Editorial Assistant at Routledge, for answering my submission queries and your fine guidance. Special thanks go to the Office of the President at the University of Texas at Austin for awarding me a Subvention Grant to assist with the underwriting of this book. I also extend my appreciation to the Department of Educational Psychology and the Center for Mexican American Studies at UT Austin for providing me with research grants. Very special appreciation is extended to the UT Austin Office of the Vice Provost and Dean of Graduate Studies for awarding me a Faculty Research Assignment, which allowed me to take off a full semester, with pay, so I could work full-time on this book project. A deep thank you goes to my research assistants—Irene Garza, Phoebe Long, and Bruno Villarreal—for their stellar and valuable help.

I extend my affection and gratitude to my wonderful wife, Marta, for allowing me to bounce ideas off you on occasion. Thank you, dear, for your intellectual and moral support during the long process of making this book a reality. Finally, my heartfelt acknowledgment goes to my twin sons, Second Lieutenant Carlos Valencia (U.S. Army) and Second Lieutenant Juan Valencia (U.S. Marines). When I started this book project your academic careers were underway at UT San Antonio (Carlos) and the U.S. Naval Academy at Annapolis (Juan). Now, you are beginning your military careers in the service of your country. Be safe, my sons. You may not be aware of it, but often I looked to you—your commitment to excellence and steadfastness in your goals—for strength and perseverance while I pursued my work on this book. *Mijos*, as I have always said, you are the best sons a father could have.

INTRODUCTION

Understanding and Analyzing the Achievement Gap and School Reform

In order to comprehend and analyze the academic chasm that exists between many White pupils and students of color, it is necessary to examine the educational problems, research findings, and policy/reform implications through various lenses and perspectives. In my probe, I largely draw from four theoretical frameworks: (a) critical race theory, (b) an asset-based perspective, (c) class analysis, and (d) a systemic inequality approach. These models, I believe, have strong explanatory value and provide useful roadmaps to inform practice.

1. *Critical race theory.* This conceptual framework has its origins in the 1970s, when a cadre of legal scholars, lawyers, and activists across the nation realized that the momentum of civil rights litigation had stalled (Delgado & Stefancic, 2001; Taylor, 1998).[1] A form of oppositional scholarship, critical race theory (CRT) questions the experiences of Whites as the norm and bases its conceptual structure in the lives of people of color (Taylor).[2] Some of the issues CRT addresses are campus speech codes, disproportionate sentencing of people of color in the criminal justice system, and affirmative action (Taylor).

Ladson-Billings and Tate (1995) are noted for being among the first scholars to apply CRT to the field of education. Now a growing field of scholarship with a large corpus of literature, CRT has gained widespread popularity in education, especially among scholars of race and ethnicity.[3] Issues studied in CRT and education are diverse and include, for example, the experiences of scholars of color in the academy, student resistance, educational history, families of color, tracking, the Western canon, hierarchy in the schools, and testing. I, for one, have found CRT a very useful tool in my study of Mexican American educational litigation (Valencia, 2005, 2008).

Solórzano (1998), a prominent CRT scholar, has identified five themes, or tenets, that underlie the perspectives, research methods, and pedagogy of CRT in education. I also draw from Yosso's (2006) discussion of these points:

A. *The centrality and intersectionality of race and racism.* CRT begins with the proposition that race and racism are entrenched and enduring in U.S. society. CRT calls for an examination of how race has come to be socially constructed and how the systemic nature of racism serves to oppress people of color while it protects White privilege. Although CRT in education focuses on race and racism, it also seeks to investigate how racism intersects with other manifestations of oppression (e.g., gender; phenotype; class; language; surname).
B. *The challenge to* dominant *ideology.* Heterodoxy is another key element in CRT in education. Here, CRT challenges the orthodoxy, particularly regarding claims of the educational system and its views toward meritocracy, objectivity, color and gender blindness, and equal opportunity. Critical race theorists assert that these conventional and long-established concepts are actually camouflages for the power, self-interest, and privilege of the dominant group.
C. *The commitment to social justice.* CRT in education includes a firm duty to social justice and the elimination of racism. Critical race theorists posit that schools are political institutions, and therefore view education as a vehicle to end various forms of subordination, such as racism and class and gender discrimination.
D. *The centrality of experiential knowledge.* CRT recognizes the great importance of experiential knowledge of people of color and that such knowledge is valid, appropriate, and essential to understanding, analyzing, and teaching about racism in education. CRT considers this experiential knowledge of students of color and their parents as a major strength and draws on various life experiences as communicated, for example, via biographies, family history, and films. Critical race theorists can also participate in this discourse by use of counter-storytelling (alternative or opposing narratives or explanations).
E. *The interdisciplinary perspective.* CRT in education challenges the ahistorical and unidisciplinary preoccupation of most analyses and argues that one can best understand race and racism in education by incorporating interdisciplinary perspectives. Critical race theorists in education frequently work across disciplinary borders, relying on multiple methods of inquiry to provide a sharper eye on the role of race and racism.

2. *Asset-based perspective.* As I (Valencia, 2010), my colleagues and I (Valencia, 1997), and many other scholars have concluded, deficit thinking permeates much of the educational literature on students of color, including their cultures and families. This virulent view of students of color, a perspective that "blames the victim" for her and his educational problems, is explained and critiqued in chapter 2 of this volume. As this tome unfolds, the reader will observe the pervasiveness of deficit thinking in the discourse on the achievement gap. The reader will

also notice in various chapters my continual denouncements of deficit thinking, and my many references to the promises and strengths of students of color and their families. It is refreshing to see that this "asset-based" approach to viewing children, youths, and families of color is seen with growing frequency in the educational, psychological, and community service literature (e.g., Campos, 2013; Lindsey, Karns, & Myatt, 2010; Scanlan, 2007; Shabazz & Cooks, 2014). One major thread that runs through these works is that they reject deficit thinking.

3. *Class analysis.* Much of this book is concerned with race, especially racialized opportunity patterns in society and the schools, which in turn help shape racialized achievement patterns. It is important, however, to be cognizant that class also matters. At least three evidential bases support this assertion. First, there is substantiation that the U.S. is heavily stratified along the lines of class, and that economic, cultural, political, and social psychological factors help create and maintain this class-stratified society (e.g., Beeghley, 2007; Kerbo, 2011; Massey, 2007). Second, in the literature there is the common finding of covariation of SES and race (e.g., LaViest, 2005). That is, students of color, compared to their White counterparts, have a higher probability of being from a lower-SES background. Third, as I note in chapter 3 of the current volume, there is an abundant amount of literature that shows a positive association between SES of origin and children's academic achievement and intellectual performance (e.g., Sirin, 2005; Valencia & Suzuki, 2001; White, 1982), and this relation holds across racial/ethnic groups (Valencia & Suzuki). Considering the saliency of class, I repeatedly refer to *low-SES* students of color—the target population of this book.

4. *Systemic inequality approach.* Of the various competing theories that have been advanced to explain school failure of many low-SES students of color (discussed in chapter 2 of the current volume), I hold that the systemic inequality model has the most promise in understanding the achievement gap, as well as providing robust solutions for societal and school reform. I concur with other scholars (e.g., Noguera, 2009; Pearl, 2002) that the oppression and inequalities experienced by many low-SES students of color in schools represent a microcosm of the oppression and inequalities faced by numerous low-SES people of color in the larger community of the nation. As such, we need to be mindful that the achievement gap is linked to the unceasing, widespread, and deep inequality that is structured in nearly all facets of U.S. society. Therefore, systemic challenges require systemic transformations.

Notes

1. This section on critical race theory builds on, with revisions, Valencia (2005, pp. 392–393) and Valencia (2008, pp. 2–3).
2. For overviews of CRT, see, for example, Araujo (1997); Crenshaw, Gotanda, Peller, and Thomas (1995); Delgado and Stefancic (2001).
3. See, for example, López (2003); Parker, Deyhle, and Villenas (1999); Solórzano and Yosso (2000).

References

Araujo, R. J. (1997). Critical race theory: Contributions to and problems for race relations. *Gonzaga Law Review, 32,* 537–575.

Beeghley, L. (2007). *The structure of social stratification in the United States* (5th ed.). Needham Heights, MA: Allyn & Bacon.

Campos, D. (2013). *Educating Latino boys: An asset-based approach.* Thousand Oaks, CA: Corwin.

Crenshaw, K., Gotanda, N., Peller, G., & Thomas, K. (Eds.). (1995). *Critical race theory: The key writings that formed the movement.* New York: New Press.

Delgado, R., & Stefancic, J. (2001). *Critical race theory: An introduction.* New York: New York University Press.

Kerbo, H. (2011). *Social stratification and inequality: Class conflict in historical, comparative, and global perspective* (8th ed.). Boston: McGraw-Hills Higher Education.

Ladson-Billings, G., & Tate, W. (1995). Toward a critical race theory of education. *Teachers College Record, 97,* 47–68.

LaViest, T. A. (2005). Disentangling race and socioeconomic status: A key to understanding health inequalities. *Journal of Urban Health, 82,* 26–34.

Lindsey, R. B., Karns, M. S., & Myatt, K. (2010). *Culturally proficient education: An asset-based response to conditions of poverty.* Thousand Oaks, CA: Corwin.

López, G. R. (2003). The (racially neutral) politics of education: A critical race theory perspective. *Educational Administrative Quarterly, 39,* 68–94.

Massey, D. S. (2007). *Categorically unequal: The American stratification system.* New York: Russell Sage Foundation.

Noguera, P. A. (2009). The achievement gap: Public crisis in education. *New Labor Forum, 18,* 61–69.

Parker, L., Deyhle, D., & Villenas, S. (Eds.). (1999). *Race is . . . race isn't: Critical race theory and qualitative studies in education.* Boulder, CO: Westview.

Pearl, A. (2002). The big picture: Systemic and institutional factors in Chicano school failure and success. In R. R. Valencia (Ed.), *Chicano school failure and success: Past, present, and future* (2nd ed., pp. 335–364). London: RoutledgeFalmer.

Scanlan, M. (2007). An asset-based approach to linguistic diversity. *Focus on Teacher Education, 7,* 3–5, 7.

Shabazz, D. R., & Cooks, L. M. (2014). The pedagogy of community-service learning discourse: From deficit to asset mapping in the re-envisioning media project. *Journal of Community Engagement & Scholarship, 17,* 71+.

Sirin, S. R. (2005). Socioeconomic status and academic achievement: A meta-analytic review of research. *Review of Educational Research, 82,* 436–476.

Solórzano, D. G. (1998). Critical race theory, race and gender microaggressions, and the experience of Chicana and Chicano scholars. *Qualitative Studies in Education, 11,* 121–136.

Solórzano, D. G., & Yosso, T. (2000). Toward a critical race theory of Chicana and Chicano education. In C. Tejada, C. Martínez, Z. Leonardo, & P. McLaren (Eds.), *Charting new terrains of Chicana(o)/Latina(o) education* (pp. 35–65). Cresskill, NJ: Hampton.

Taylor, E. (1998). A primer on critical race theory: Who are the critical race theorists and what are they saying? *Journal of Blacks in Higher Education, 19,* 122–124.

Valencia, R. R. (Ed.). (1997). *The evolution of deficit thinking: Educational thought and practice.* Stanford Series on Education and Public Policy. London: Falmer Press.

Valencia, R. R. (2005). The Mexican American struggle for equal educational opportunity in *Mendez v. Westminster*: Helping to pave the way for *Brown v. Board of Education. Teachers College Record, 107,* 389–423.

Valencia, R. R. (2008). *Chicano students and the courts: The Mexican American legal struggle for educational equality.* Critical America Series. New York: New York University Press.

Valencia, R. R. (2010). *Dismantling contemporary deficit thinking: Educational thought and practice.* Critical Educator Series. New York: Routledge.

Valencia, R. R., & Suzuki, L. A. (2001). *Intelligence testing and minority students: Foundations, performance factors, and assessment issues.* Racial and Ethnic Minority Psychology Series. Thousand Oaks, CA: SAGE.

White, K. R. (1982). The relations between socioeconomic status and academic achievement. *Psychological Bulletin, 91,* 461–481.

Yosso, T. J. (2006). *Critical race counterstories along the Chicana/Chicano educational pipeline.* New York: Routledge.

PART I
The Problem

1
THE ACHIEVEMENT GAP

Not surprisingly, much has been written about the achievement gap (hereafter referred to as TAG). The extant corpus on TAG ranges in size, depending on the search engine one uses. In June 2014, I conducted a search of the Education Resource Information Center (ERIC) and Psychological Abstracts (PA) databases, using "achievement gap" as the descriptor. Based on a time span from 1962 to 2014, I received 4,177 hits for publications in ERIC and 1,856 in PA. These included publications in which "achievement gap" was in the title or full text. Also, in August 2014, I conducted a Google search with "achievement gap" as the descriptor and received 715,000 hits. Finally, in the summer of 2014, I conducted a computer and hand search for books with the "achievement gap" in the title and located 85 books published between 1954 and 2014.

The following coverage of TAG is organized around three sections: (a) an empirically based overview of eight indicators of TAG (e.g., achievement test performance; school holding power; gifted and talented placement); (b) a summary of several approaches scholars proffer as useful in diminishing TAG; and (c) an overview of the extraordinary growth of people and students of color.

Empirical Overview of TAG

TAG has been well documented, but the literature on it is often scattered and sometimes reports only one achievement indicator in a single document (e.g., reading test performance; as a case in point, see National Center for Education Statistics, 2013a, 2013b). The purpose here is to present data in such a manner that the reader gets a good understanding of the persistent and pervasive nature of TAG as well as a sense of how the data look when all the major indicators of TAG are analyzed in one discussion. I begin by covering the most obvious and frequently reported measure of TAG, achievement test performance. This follows with a presentation of seven other indicators of TAG, which are: (a) grade retention; (b) school holding power; (c) Scholastic Aptitude Test (SAT) scores; (d) matriculation to college; (e) college graduation (baccalaureate and post-baccalaureate); (f) Graduate Record Examination (GRE) scores; and (g) gifted and talented placement. In order to convey the persistent character of TAG, I present, at times, a chronological framing of the data by discussing historical and contemporary information.

1. *Achievement test performance.* For a long time, it has been widely acknowledged that acquiring literacy and numeracy skills are fundamental to students' learning, particularly in the early childhood years. Reading is especially important because it is indispensable as a means for students to progress and succeed in other academic domains (U.S. Commission on Civil Rights, 1971). In a classic article written nearly 5 decades ago, Inkeles (1966) developed his "socialization of competence" model, a framework for understanding how one needs to develop "socialized aptitudes" (i.e., skills) to attain a position in the U.S. middle class. Among these skills is developing a command of language, particularly in the forms of reading and writing—that is, literacy. Another skill Inkeles thinks is important is the acquisition of how to interpret mathematical symbols as seen in arithmetic. Furthermore, Finnie and Meng (2006) find that Canadians who dropped out of school tend to have low functional literacy and numeracy skills and that such skills have significant effects—independent of years of schooling attained—on people's labor market outcomes.

One of the earliest studies on TAG goes back more than 9 decades. Whitney (1923) reports spelling scores (words spelled accurately) by city White and "colored"[1] third- through seventh-grade students in segregated schools in Virginia.[2] Table 1.1 presents the data. Based on the Ayres spelling test, at every grade level (and all grades combined) TAG favors the White students. A historical study on TAG that is germane to Mexican American children is Drake (1927). He conducted his investigation in Tucson, Arizona, in which 108 White and 95 Mexican American seventh- and eighth-grade students attending the same school served as participants. Table 1.2 shows TAG data based on the Stanford Achievement Test (Form A). As noted, the mean and median scores for Whites are greater compared to their Mexican American peers. Although I do not present the data here, 15.4% of the Mexican American students exceed the White median.[3] We need to be mindful of the overlap feature in most studies of TAG. To disregard, or ignore, overlap demeans students of color as it may lead to a stereotype that all such students are low achievers.[4]

For one of my examples of contemporary data on TAG, I have selected a report from the Texas Education Agency (2013a), a state governmental unit that maintains comprehensive achievement performance disaggregated by ethnicity. Table 1.3 shows data and gaps on various achievement indicators (e.g., English Language Arts; Mathematics; Science) for White, Mexican American/Latino and Latina, and African American students (all grades tested) who met the 2012

TABLE 1.1 Percentage Gaps on Ayres Spelling Test for White and Colored Students: Virginia, 1923

Grade and Mean	*Race/Ethnicity*		*W-C Gap (% pts.)*
	White (W)	*Colored (C)*	
Grade 3			
Mean	69.6	62.4	7.2
Grade 4			
Mean	63.8	56.2	7.6
Grade 5			
Mean	68.3	63.5	4.8
Grade 6			
Mean	69.5	59.5	10.0
Grade 7			
Mean	63.1	62.9	0.2
All Grades Combined			
Mean	66.8	60.9	5.9

Source: Adapted from Whitney (1923, p. 84, Table 11).

Note: W = White; C = Colored.

TABLE 1.2 Mean and Median Gaps on Stanford Achievement Test by White and Mexican Students: Tucson, Arizona, 1927

Descriptive Statistic	*Race/Ethnicity*		*Gap (W-M)*
	White (W) (n = 108)	*Mexican (M) (n = 95)*	
Mean	69.4	60.2	9.2
Median	68.9	60.5	8.4

Source: Adapted from Drake (1927, Tables IV and V).

Note: W = White; M = Mexican.

standard[5] on the Texas Assessment of Knowledge and Skills (TAKS).[6] As columns 4 and 5 of Table 1.3 bear out, TAGs for all five subject areas benefit White students. The most consequential TAKS indicator to inspect is "All Tests." TAG between White and Mexican American/Latino and Latina students is the largest of all measures—at 15 percentage points. TAG between White and African American students is also the greatest of all indicators—at 21 percentage points.

TABLE 1.3 Percentage Gaps on Achievement by White, Mexican American/Latino and Latina, and African American Students Who Met the TAKS[a] Standard in 2012: Sum of All Grades Tested, Texas, 2012

TAKS Indicator	*White*	*Mexican American/ Latino and Latina African American*		*W-MA/L*	*W-AA*
	(W) *(%)*	*(MA/L)* *(%)*	*(AA)* *(%)*	*Gap* *(% pts.)*	*Gap* *(% pts.)*
ELA[b]	96	90	89	6	7
Mathematics	89	79	73	10	16
Science	92	80	75	12	17
Social Studies	98	94	93	4	5
All Tests	84	69	63	15	21

Source: Texas Education Agency (2013a).

Note: W = White; MA/L = Mexican American/Latino and Latina; AA = African American.

[a] Texas Assessment of Knowledge and Skills. [b] English Language Arts.

The analyses of local, geographical, and state statistics to document TAG are certainly helpful. Given, however, that these data are microcosms of a much larger picture, a far more comprehensive method to understand the gravity of TAG is to scrutinize national data. As such, the following presentations of TAG are derived from the most recent reports (2013) of the National Assessment of Educational Progress (NAEP), self-dubbed the "Nation's Report Card." I confine this discussion to reading achievement (National Center for Education Statistics, 2013a). To see the data on comparative mathematics achievement, the reader is referred to the National Center for Education Statistics (2013b).[7]

In regard to the most recent NAEP reading data, Figure 1.1 presents a trend analysis of average scores[8] for White and Mexican American/Latino and Latina comparisons from 1992 to 2013 for the eighth-grade cohort (National Center for Education Statistics, 2013a). The observed pattern shows that TAGs are relentless, hovering in the middle 20s over the 21 years. Furthermore, in 2011, nationally, 37% of Mexican American/Latino and Latina students perform "below Basic" on reading—compared to 16% of their White peers (National Center for Education Statistics, 2011, p. 96).

Figure 1.2 shows the NAEP reading scores and gaps for eighth-grade White and Black differentiations from 1992 to 2013. Once again, we see the persistent racialized pattern—TAGs advantage White students. On the whole, TAGs in reading over this 2-decade period linger, generally in the high 20s.[9] Regarding the lowest level of reading performance, NAEP reports that in 2011, 42% of Black eighth graders read "below Basic." By sharp contrast, 16% of White students

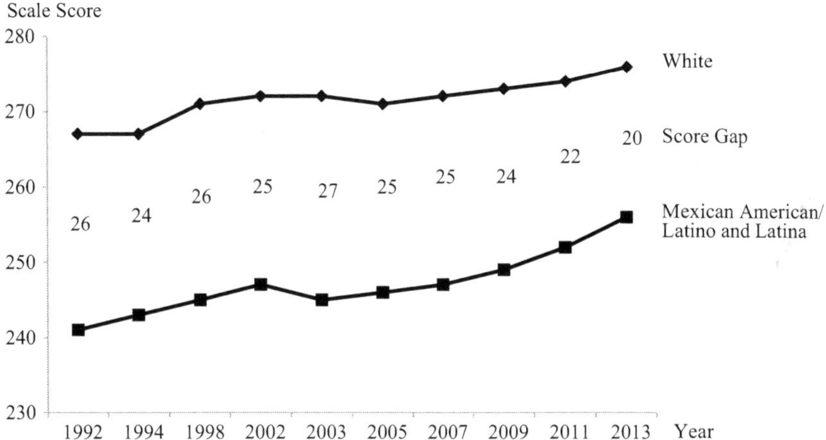

FIGURE 1.1 Trends in Eighth-Grade NAEP Reading Scores and Score Gaps, by White and Mexican American/Latino and Latina Groups

Source: National Center for Education Statistics (2013a).

Note: NAEP = National Assessment of Educational Progress.

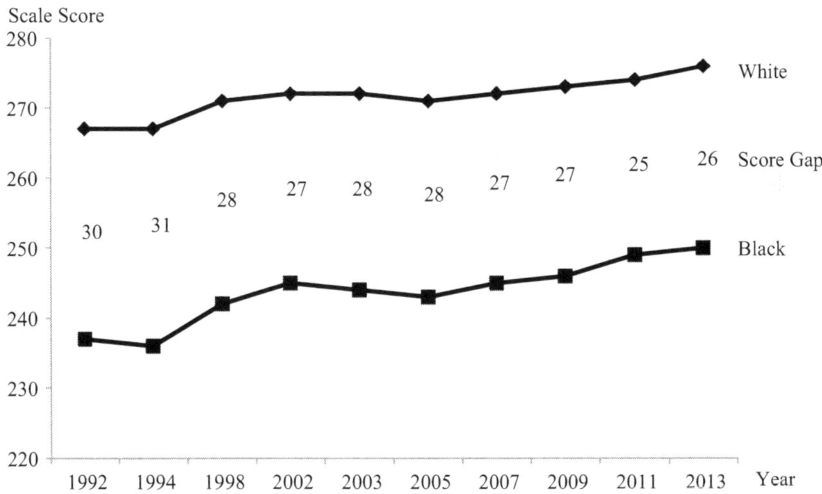

FIGURE 1.2 Trends in Eighth-Grade NAEP Reading Scores and Score Gaps, by White and Black Groups

Source: National Center for Education Statistics (2013a).

Note: NAEP = National Assessment of Educational Progress.

do so (National Center for Education Statistics, 2011, p. 96). In sum, TAG in NAEP performance in all subject matters doggedly persists for Latino/Latina and Black students, notwithstanding billions of dollars spent yearly on remedial and compensatory intervention programs (Ornstein, 2007). In the context of CRT and in light of structural inequality in society and the schools, one can argue that although funding for academic remediation is important, in and of itself financial infusion is simply not enough to dramatically reduce TAG. Given the deep and widespread oppression low-SES students of color and their families regularly experience, systemic transformations at all levels are needed.

2. *Grade retention*. This practice of schooling, a euphemism for a student "flunking" a grade, is certainly not new to U.S. public education. Over 100-plus years ago,[10] Ayers (1909) in *Laggards in Our Schools* reports that 16% of the nation's students were required to "repeat grades." His conclusion was that "slow progress" was the major reason why repeaters needed to be retained. The pedagogical rationale behind retention is that an extra year at the same grade, or a "gift of time" (Jimerson, Woehr, & Kaufman, 2004), will serve as a powerful curative for the student who is experiencing learning difficulties (e.g., reading significantly below grade level). The extant literature on grade retention, however, finds quite strongly that this policy has not fulfilled its promise of remediation. A body of empirical studies and literature reviews reports that students who are retained, compared to matched peers who are promoted, typically fall behind in academic achievement (e.g., mathematics), make fewer or no gains, seldom or never catch up, have socioemotional and behavioral problems, and tend to drop out of school.[11] Another deleterious effect of grade retention is the cost to taxpayers. Writing in 2005, Eide and Goldhaber note that based on an estimate of 2.38 million students retained annually (5%), at a cost of $7,500 per year to educate students, the coffers of public education are drained approximately $17.85 billion dollars per year. Finally, grade retention hits hardest students of color, which I cover next.

The most recent annual report by the Texas Education Agency (2013b) contains TAG grade retention data for AY 2011–2012. Table 1.4 displays the results for K-12 grades, showing a distinct racialized pattern: With the exception of kindergarten, Mexican American/Latino and Latina and Black students have higher retention rates in grade retention relative to their White counterparts.[12] At first glance, the grade retention rates (with the exception of ninth-grade percentages) may appear inconsequential because of their small rates. Yet, when looked at in regard to absolute numbers they inform us of the grave toll on individual students—especially students of color. Of the total K-12 Mexican American/Latino and Latina students (n = 2,337,716) enrolled in Texas public schools in 2011–2012, 91,389 (3.9%) experienced retention. For total K-12 Black students (n = 586,727), 24,485 (4.2%) were retained. With respect to total K-12 White students (n = 1,439,618), 29,333 (2.0%) were held back (Texas Education Agency, 2013b, p. 13, Table 1). These comparisons translate into an odds ratio of about 2.0 for Mexican American/Latino and Latina and Black students.[13]

TABLE 1.4 Percentage Gaps for Grade Retention by Mexican American/Latino and Latina, Black, and White Students: Texas, AY 2011–2012

Grade Level	*Race/Ethnicity*			*Gap*	
	Mexican American/Latino and Latina (MA/L) (%)	*Black (B) (%)*	*White (W) (%)*	*MA-W (% pts.)*	*B-W (% pts.)*
K	2.4	2.2	3.3	−0.9	−1.1
1	5.7	5.6	3.2	2.5	2.4
2	3.7	3.9	1.6	2.1	2.3
3	2.5	2.9	1.0	1.5	1.9
4	1.2	1.4	0.6	0.6	0.8
5	0.6	0.7	0.4	0.2	0.3
6	0.8	0.9	0.5	0.3	0.4
K to 6	2.4	2.5	1.5	0.9	1.0
7	1.2	1.4	0.7	0.5	0.7
8	1.0	0.9	0.6	0.4	0.3
9	12.8	13.1	5.2	7.6	7.9
10	7.1	8.1	3.3	3.8	4.8
11	6.8	7.1	2.7	4.1	4.4
12	7.1	6.3	3.4	3.7	2.9
7 to 12	5.9	6.2	2.6	3.3	3.6

Source: Adapted from Texas Education Agency (2013b, Tables 5 and 6).

Note: MA/L = Mexican American/Latino and Latina; B = Black; W = White.

3. *School holding power.* It appears that the first time the term "holding power" regarding schools is seen in the literature is in a 1924 article, "Holding Power of the Junior High School," by Clayton R. Wise. He sought to examine empirically the impact the relatively new strategy of the junior high (started in 1909) had in facilitating students' matriculation from elementary to high school. The notion of holding power of schools was given prominence in the Mexican American Education Study of 44 years ago (U.S. Commission on Civil Rights, 1971). The commission defined "school holding power" as "a basic measure of a school's effectiveness is its ability to hold its students [in school] until they have completed the full course of study [i.e., K through grade 12]" (p. 8). By placing the main onus on schools for keeping their students in the educational pipeline, the commission championed an anti-deficit thinking perspective. Although the term "school holding power," which refers to the widely used referent of "dropouts," may be unfamiliar to most readers, I prefer to use it here because of its shift of blame from students to schools.

The economic consequences of weak school holding power are dire.[14] For example, in the labor market, students who depart prematurely from school tend to have very low-paying jobs and thus pay fewer taxes, which are the foundation of the country's entitlement programs (e.g., Social Security benefits). Also, early exiting from school is correlated with running afoul of the law and subsequently being incarcerated—a very costly expense for the public, who, through their taxes, pays for the construction and maintenance of local jails and state and federal prisons. These and other adverse effects of poor holding power are discussed, for example, in *The Price We Pay: Economic and Social Consequences of Inadequate Education* (Belfield & Levin, 2007) and Rumberger and Rodríguez (2011).

For contemporary data on TAG for school holding power, I use the most recent information from the National Center for Education Statistics (Snyder & Dillow, 2013). Table 1.5 displays TAGs for years 1980, 1990, 2000, 2010, and 2012.[15] Three interesting trends are discernible. First, all three racial/ethnic groups show school holding power rate increases in each of the 5 years. Second, TAG for Mexican Americans/Latinos and Latinas is fairly stable over the 32-year period, and TAG (in percentage points) in 2012 is nearly identical (27.5) from the baseline of 27.4 in 1980. Third, TAG (in percentage points) for Blacks declines steadily over the 3 decades plus: 20.5 in 1980, 15.2 in 1990, 9.5 in 2000, 7.5 in 2010, and 6.8 in 2012.

4. *Scholastic Aptitude Test (SAT) scores.* The original name of SAT was "Scholastic Aptitude Test." In 1990 it was modified to "Scholastic Assessment Test," and in 1993 it was changed again to "SAT: I Reasoning Test."[16] Despite these changes over time, the acronym "SAT" is entrenched. Thus, I use it here.

For high school students who aspire to go to college, they are quite familiar with the SAT. Likewise, college admissions personnel are very aware of the importance of SAT scores, as they are used as a predictor of college academic success. Together, SAT

TABLE 1.5 Percentage Gaps for School Holding Power (High School) by Whites, Mexican Americans/Latinos and Latinas, and Blacks (Age 25 Years and Older): National, 1980, 1990, 2000, 2010, and 2012

Year	*Race/Ethnicity and School Holding Power Rate*			*Gap*	
	White (W)	*Mexican American/Latino and Latina (MA/L)*	*Black (B)*	*W-MA/L (% pts.)*	*W-B (% pts.)*
1980	71.9	44.5	51.4	27.4	20.5
1990	81.4	50.8	66.2	30.6	15.2
2000	88.4	57.0	78.9	31.4	9.5
2010	92.1	62.9	84.6	29.2	7.5
2012	92.5	65.0	85.7	27.5	6.8

Source: Adapted from Snyder and Dillow (2013, pp. 27–29, Table 8).

Note: W = White; MA/L = Mexican American/Latino and Latina; B = Black.

TABLE 1.6 Score Gaps for SAT Mean Scores by White, Mexican American, and Black Students: National, 2000 and 2010

Year and Subtest	*Race/Ethnicity*			*Gap*	
	White (W)	*Mexican American (MA)*	*Black (B)*	*W-MA*	*W-B*
2000					
Critical Reading	528	453	434	75	94
Mathematics	530	460	426	70	104
Writing	na	na	na	—	—
2010					
Critical Reading	528	454	429	74	99
Mathematics	536	467	428	69	108
Writing	516	448	420	68	96

Source: Adapted from College Board (2010).

Note: W = White; MA = Mexican American; B = Black; na = not available. The scores (scaled) on the three subtests can range from 200 to 800.

scores and high school grades have been found to be the best predictor of success in college (Ramírez, 2008). To be sure, the SAT—which the College Board owns and is developed, administered, and scored by the Educational Testing Serve—is a big business. In the graduating class of 2010, almost 1.6 million students took the SAT at some point in high school through their senior year (College Board, 2010).

Table 1.6 shows mean SAT scores for Critical Reading, Mathematics, and Writing across three groups: White, Mexican American,[17] and Black. Given the racial/ethnic trends previously discussed in the section on "achievement test performance," it is not unexpected that the SAT score patterns in Table 1.6 are also racialized in 2000 and a decade-plus later in 2013. Furthermore, two points are particularly noteworthy. First, TAGs for Mexican American and Black students are relatively stable from 2000 to 2013. Second, TAGs are largest across the SAT subtests for Blacks.

5. *Matriculation to college.* Being admitted to college is a milestone in the academic career of high school students. This continuation in the educational pipeline can eventually lead to a portal to the credential society and some economic success. Over the last 3 decades, the workforce in the U.S. has been transformed into a two-tier workforce, with nearly half of the jobs developed requiring a college degree or more and the other half not necessitating such credentials (Pearl, 2011). Furthermore, there is a strong incentive to go to college and receive a degree: *money.* On the average, an adult, over his or her working life, can expect to earn $1.2 million (high school graduate), $2.1 million (B.A. degree), $2.5 million (M.A. degree), and $3.4 million (Ph.D.) (Longley, 2010).

Lower matriculation rates to college have a long history for Mexican American students, as a case in point. In the 1920s, 1930s, and up to the mid-1940s, a Mexican American presence in colleges and universities was very atypical (San Miguel & Valencia, 1998; Valencia, 2011b). For example, more than 8 decades ago, Manuel (1930) surveyed higher education institutions in Texas and reported that of the 38,538 students enrolled, only 188 (0.49%) were designated as "Mexican." Of these, 34 (18.1%) claimed they resided in Mexico (Valencia, 2011b).

For a contemporary data source on TAGs for college matriculation, I have selected a national report, *The Condition of Education 2012* from the National Center for Education Statistics (Aud et al., 2012). Table 1.7 displays data for years 2000 and 2010 by White, Mexican American/Latino and Latina, and Black high school completers who enrolled in a 2- or 4-year college in the October right after completing high school. There are two points of interest. First, in 2000, TAG for Mexican American/Latino and Latina students (12.8 percentage points) is slightly higher than for Blacks (10.8 percentage points). Second, in 2010 TAG decreases slightly: TAG for college matriculation for Mexican Americans/Latinos is 10.8 percentage points and for Blacks, 8.5 percentage points.

6. *College graduation (baccalaureate and post-baccalaureate).* As I introduce in the previous section on TAG for college matriculation, graduating from high school and enrolling in college is indeed a significant event for young men and women. Yet, entering the higher education pipeline is just the beginning of a challenging journey, in which some students encounter obstacles, such as financial difficulties or personal and academic problems, that force them to drop out or stop out. For other students, the college experience proves successful and eventually they graduate with a baccalaureate (e.g., B.A.) or advanced degree (e.g., M.A. or Ph.D.). In this section, I discuss another indicator of TAG—the chasm in bachelor's and advanced degrees awarded to White students and students of color (i.e., Latinos/Latinas; Blacks).

The national report by Aud et al. (2012) provides a comprehensive contemporary analysis of TAGs for college degrees awarded. Table 1.8 displays these data

TABLE 1.7 Percentage Gaps of High School Completers Enrolled in 2- or 4-Year Colleges by White, Mexican American/Latino and Latina, and Black Students: National, 2000 and 2010

Year	*Race/Ethnicity: Enrollment %*			*Gap*	
	White (W)	*Mexican American/Latino and Latina (MA/L)*	*Black (B)*	*W-MA/L (% pts.)*	*W-B (% pts.)*
2000	65.7	52.9	54.9	12.8	10.8
2010	70.5	59.7	62.0	10.8	8.5

Source: Adapted from Aud et al. (2012, p. 245, Table A-34–2).

Note: W = White; MA/L = Mexican American/Latino and Latina; B = Black.

TABLE 1.8 Percentage Gaps of Degrees Awarded by Whites, Mexican Americans/Latinos and Latinas, and Blacks: National, AY 1999–2000 and 2009–2010

Academic Year and Degree Type	*Race/Ethnicity: Degrees Awarded %*			*Gap*	
	White (W)	*Mexican American/Latino and Latina (MA/L)*	*Black (B)*	*W-MA/L (% pts.)*	*W-B (% pts.)*
1999–2000					
Bachelor's	77.5	6.3	9.0	71.2	68.5
Master's	79.7	4.8	9.0	74.9	70.7
Doctoral[a]	77.9	4.7	6.7	73.2	71.2
2009–2010					
Bachelor's	72.9	8.8	10.3	64.1	62.6
Master's	72.8	7.1	12.5	65.7	60.3
Doctorala	74.3	5.8	7.4	68.5	66.9

Source: Adapted from Aud et al. (2012, p. 285, Table A-47–2).

Note: W = White; MA/L = Mexican American/Latino and Latina; B = Black.

[a] Includes Ph.D.s and Ed.D.s.

for AYs 1999–2000 and 2009–2010[18] for Whites, Mexican Americans/Latinos and Latinas, and Blacks. The patterns are quite clear: Whites, in comparison to Mexican Americans/Latinos and Latinas and Blacks, have the highest percentages of degrees awarded for the three types (bachelor's; master's; doctoral) for AYs 1999–2000 and 2009–2010. For example, in AY 2009–2010, of total bachelor's degrees awarded (N = 1,602,480), Whites earned 72.9% of them and Mexican Americans/Latinos and Blacks earned 8.8% and 10.3%, respectively.[19] TAGs for all degree types decreased from 1999–2000 to 2009–2010, but they remained substantial.

7. *Graduate Record Examination (GRE) scores.* Most students who apply to graduate school programs are expected to take the GRE, which is to graduate school admissions as the SAT is to undergraduate admissions. The scores of the GRE—Verbal, Quantitative, and Analytical Writing—when combined with undergraduate grade point average (GPA) have been found to be generalizably valid statistical predictors of graduate-level GPA (Kuncel, Hezlett, & Ones, 2001). GRE scores, however, should not be used as sole sources of data in making admissions decisions. The Educational Testing Service, developer and administrator of the GRE, strongly advises that the scores be used along with other types of information to make admissions rulings—for example, statement of purpose and letters of recommendation (Educational Testing Service, 2013, pp. 2–3). In regard to the focus of the present chapter, a persistent and pervasive finding of reports on the GRE is the racialized pattern of performance, which I now turn to. Table 1.9 presents GRE scores for the testing year 2011–2012 for a combined

TABLE 1.9 Score Gaps for GRE Mean Scores by White, Mexican American, and Black Students: U.S. Citizens, 2011–2012

Subtest	*Race/Ethnicity*			*Gap*	
	White (W)	*Mexican American (MA)*	*Black (B)*	*W-MA*	*W-B*
Verbal	154.1	149.7	146.7	4.4	7.4
Quantitative	150.4	146.5	143.1	3.9	7.3
Analytical Writing	4.0	3.7	3.4	0.3	0.6

Source: Adapted from Educational Testing Service (2013, pp. 7–8, Table 4).

Note: W = White; MA = Mexican American; B = Black. GRE = Graduate Record Examination. Scores on the Verbal and Quantitative subtests can range from 130 to 170; scores on Analytical Writing can range from 0 to 6.

sample of 257,161 White, Mexican American,[20] and Black examinees(Educational Testing Service, pp. 7–8, Table 4). The data show that TAGs across the three GRE subtests favor Whites. Also, TAGs for White/Black comparisons are larger than for White/Mexican American comparisons.

8. *Gifted and talented placement.* Placement in gifted and talented programs (hereafter referred to as "gifted"[21]) is the pinnacle of achievement for many students, a curricular change that typically occurs in elementary school. When a student is identified as gifted and placed in a program of some sort, such placement can lead to educational advantages that "regular" students often do not experience (e.g., highly challenging curricula; eventual placement in Advanced Placement courses in high school). There is a long history of the gifted movement, internationally and in the U.S. (see, e.g., Valencia & Villarreal, 2011). One major finding that emerges from the literature on the gifted is that students of color (i.e., Mexican Americans/Latinos and Latinas; Blacks; American Indians) have been, and continue to be, underrepresented in gifted programs.[22] This section provides some empirical data on this measure of TAG.

A valuable historical data source on the underrepresentation of gifted students of color is the study conducted nearly 9 decades ago by Lewis Terman, the father of the gifted movement in the U.S.[23] His California study (Terman, 1926) is one of the most ambitious and comprehensive investigations ever conducted in the history of educational psychology. Terman and his research team canvassed parts of California to identify public school children who had IQs that placed them in the top 1% of the population. Based on intelligence test data from over a quarter of a million students, Terman identified 999 students. Here, I restrict the discussion to findings from his main study of 643 gifted children.[24] Regarding the "racial" origins of the 643 children, Terman lists 37 different "racial stocks."[25] In light of the growing populations of school-age students of color at the time of Terman's (1926) study, it is incredulous that only 7 (1.1 %) of the 643 gifted students Terman identified were students of color (Valencia & Villarreal, 2011, p. 238).

When viewed, however, in the elitist Zeitgeist of the 1920s the invisibility of gifted children of color is palpable. Valencia and Villarreal (2011) offer four likely interpretations. First, the use of teacher nominations as a first step to identify gifted children may have resulted in a selection bias (i.e., class bias; see Ceci, 1990).[26] Second, *no* children of color constituted a part of the standardization samples of the Stanford-Binet or the National Intelligence Test (NIT), the two measures that served as the intelligence tests in Terman's (1926) study. Test developers designed these instruments with White, English-speaking, middle-SES children in mind. As such, these highly culturally bound and verbally loaded intelligence tests tended to penalize students of color and children whose mother tongue was not English (see Valencia, 1997). Third, widespread school segregation existed in California (see, e.g., González, 1990; Valencia, 2008, chapter 1); thus students of color had fewer opportunities to learn the school-related content for which the Stanford-Binet and NIT partially tested. Fourth, racial animus entered the picture as documented by Terman's racist views of people of color.[27]

For a contemporary source of data regarding the underrepresentation of students of color (i.e., Mexican American/Latino and Latina and Latina; Black),[28] I turn to Texas. Based on the most recent data from the Texas Education Agency (2013c), I conducted another disparity analysis. Table 1.10 presents this examination for AY 2012–2013. Once more, we see the common racialized pattern: White students are overrepresented in gifted programs (+38.7%), while Mexican American/Latino and Latina and Black students are underrepresented (−20.9% and −48.0%, respectively).

TABLE 1.10 Disparity Analysis of Gifted Enrollment by Race/Ethnicity: Texas, AY 2012–2013

Racial/Ethnic Group	*Total Enrollment (K-12)*		*Gifted Enrollment (K-12)*		*% Disparity*[a]
	No.	*%*	*No.*	*%*	
White	1,521,551	30.0	161,213	41.6	+38.7
Mexican American/Latino and Latina	2,606,126	51.3	157,397	40.6	–20.9
Black	646,182	12.7	25,713	6.6	–48.0

Source: Texas Education Agency (2013c).

[a] A plus sign (+) indicates overrepresentation and a minus sign (-) indicates underrepresentation.

Another contemporary data source showing the all-to-familiar racialized patterns of over- and underrepresentation of gifted students is the most recent national and state information from the U.S. Department of Education, Office for Civil Rights (2012) survey. Based on AY 2009–2010 data for the nation, as a whole, and the 10 states with the largest combined students of color enrollment, I conducted a disparity analysis. These comparisons show that White students are overrepresented (+18.3%) in gifted programs at the national level and in 9 of the 10 listed states (a high of +50.3% in Georgia). For Mexican American/Latino and Latina students, they are underrepresented nationally (–30.9%) and in each of the 10 states, ranging from a high rate (−62.8%) in North Carolina. Black students show a very similar pattern: underrepresentation at the national level (–40.7%) and in 9 of 10 states, with a high underrepresentation rate of −58.7% in North Carolina.

Approaches to Diminish TAG: Remedial Curricular Intervention, Equal Educational Opportunity, and Systemic Analysis Discourses

Because of the extraordinary size of this corpus of publications and space limitations, I refrain from undertaking a comprehensive review. Rather, my focus is to obtain a sense of how various authors communicate their perspectives on how best to diminish TAG. This review of the literature leads me to an understanding that most authors approach the diminution of TAG in either one of three discourses, via: (a) a narrow remedial curricular intervention, (b) an equal educational opportunity approach, or (c) a systemic analysis.

The reductionistic approach tends to be quite simplistic in nature—for example, advocating a narrowly tailored curricular intervention that authors believe can diminish TAG. While these strategies have some merit in providing ideas to help minimize TAG, they usually lack utility due to their quick-fix, singular path approach on how to improve the achievement of students of color. In some cases, these reductionistic strategies are deficit thinking in nature because they place the burden of change on students of color and their families (see Valencia, 2010, for a discussion of the deficit thinking model; also, see chapter 2, this volume). The second approach, equal educational opportunity discourse, identifies reform strategies (e.g., detracking of the curriculum; having the best-qualified teachers) that authors believe can provide students of color with equitable and challenging learning opportunities in order to markedly reduce TAG. Authors of the third approach, a systemic analysis discourse, assert that the narrowing of TAG can best be done by understanding that oppression and inequalities in the educational system are inextricably linked with oppression and inequalities in the larger society. As such, authors of this perspective argue that lasting and equitable school reform (i.e., significant reduction in TAG) can best be achieved by commensurate comprehensive reform in society. In my view, this paradigm has the greatest potential for the realization of meaningful school success and TAG diminution for low-SES students of color. For each of the three approaches, I briefly discuss two representative publications.

1. *Reductionistic discourse.* An example of this category is seen in the book by Akhavan (2007), *Accelerated Vocabulary Instruction: Strategies for Closing the Achievement Gap for All Students.* As a predictor of TAG (particularly in reading achievement),[29] Akhavan zeroes in on what she calls the "vocabulary gap." For empirical evidence of the vocabulary gap, she replies heavily on the research of Hart and Risley (1995, 2003). In her book, Akhavan provides a comprehensive curricular plan for teachers to implement so they can accelerate their students' vocabulary. These lessons are organized around four core principles for vocabulary instruction—"creating a word-rich environment," "making connections to word," "engaging students with explicit instruction," and "accelerating vocabulary development through wide reading" (p. 11).

Given that Akhavan (2007) draws considerably on the work of Hart and Risley (1995, 2003) for the existence of the vocabulary gap, I decided that it was important to review this body of research. Hart and Risley's book *Meaningful Differences in the Everyday Experience of Young American Children* (1995) is the most informative source of the two citations, and thus I refer to it here. The authors' investigation began in 1985 and involved 42 preschool participants and their parents or primary caretakers in Kansas City, Kansas. The children's SES varied, including "professional" (n = 13), "working-class" (n = 23), and "welfare" (n = 6) status; 17 children were African American and 25 were White. Hart and Risley's (1995) research staff conducted home observations of child-family verbal interactions for 1 hour a month over 2.5 years. The primary focus was on vocabulary (e.g., number of words spoken by child and parent/caretaker; quality of vocabulary; growth patterns).

A massive amount of vocabulary data, which took years to analyze, was collected. Three of the major findings of this longitudinal study are: (a) children of professional families had the largest size of vocabulary by age 3 years, with children on welfare the least; children of working-class families were intermediate in vocabulary size; (b) regarding the number of words heard in the home by children spoken by their parents' caretakers, the descending order was: professional, working-class, and welfare families; and (c) vocabulary size was positively correlated with Stanford-Binet Intelligence Scale IQ (Terman & Merrill, 1960) and Peabody Picture Vocabulary Test (PPVT) score (Dunn & Dunn, 1965) at age 9–10 years. Hart and Risley (1995) conclude that the vocabulary size of the average child from welfare families is so limited by age 3 years that these children "would need to be in substitute care 40 hours every week from birth onward" (p. 205) in order to attain the level of vocabulary experienced by the average middle-class child.

What do Hart and Risley (1995) mean by "substitute care"? One strategy they refer to is related to the "Milwaukee Project," a very early intervention program that began in the 1960s (see Garber, 1988). The objective of the project was to prevent mental retardation in children considered at risk because they had low-SES mothers with IQs below 75. According to Hart and Risley (1995), babies (6–8 weeks old) were "enrolled" in full-time child care outside of the home after a paraprofessional spent about 3–5 hours at the home "advising" the mother about "parenting." Hart and Risley (1995) note that the experimental group of children, compared to a control group, were comparable to national norms in "accomplishments" at age 8 years. Yet, the entire Milwaukee Project has been severely criticized for methodological shortcomings, lack of peer review, and questionable integrity of the principal investigator (Allen, Lasater, Farrell, & Reynolds, 1990). For Hart and Risley, in 1995, to rely on a very questionable early intervention study of the 1960s to suggest a "substitute care" program to raise poor children's vocabulary is irresponsible. Furthermore, for the authors to advocate the removal of poor children from their parents from birth onward is inhumane, and via deficit thinking parents are pathologized, as I discuss shortly.

Notwithstanding the comprehensive data collection and analyses undertaken by Hart and Risley (1995), I also have serious reservations about the authors' understanding about cognitive growth and their perceptions of the welfare families. First, the authors note, "Experience and heredity contribute about equally to human functioning" (p. xxiii) and "The differences in vocabulary size we saw at age 4 [years] were undoubtedly influenced by inherited differences in cognitive capacity" (p. 16).[30] These are specious assertions in that intellectual development is much more complex and measured intelligence (a phenotype) can best be understood when we ask the "how" question: How does genotype, *interacting* in myriad ways with the environment, lead to scores on a discrete measure of intelligence, which are mere slivers of observed behavior? For example, the observed number of vocabulary words spoken by a child in a naturalistic setting or measured on the PPVT is a very small sample of behavior of the construct of "intelligence" (see Valencia & Suzuki, 2001, chapter 6). In light of Hart and Risley's (1995) conception of the nature and development of intelligence, it is not surprising that the authors use words like "intractable" (p. 16) and "unalterable" (p. 21) when speaking of the poor children's vocabulary growth patterns at age 4 years. Second, Hart and Risley (1995) appear to view the children and parents/caregivers receiving welfare assistance from a deficit thinking perspective. For example, in reference to poor people, the authors state,

> Competence as a social problem is still with us. American society still sees many of its children enter school ill-prepared to benefit from education. Too many children drop out of school and follow their parents into unemployment or onto welfare, where they raise their children in a *culture of poverty* [italics added]. (p. 2)

The authors' reference to families receiving welfare aid as transmitting a "culture of poverty" across generations is steeped in deficit thinking because the concept rests on class-based bigotry, negative stereotypes, and failure to examine the resiliency of the poor.[31]

In sum, Akhavan's (2007) curricular approach to reduce TAG has some merit. It is, however, myopic in nature because it fails to consider other factors that should be included in discourse about understanding what brings about TAG—that is, (a) gross inequalities in society that lead to race- and class-based stratification and (b) inequalities in schools when young low-SES children enter the educational system (e.g., school segregation; differences in teacher quality; curriculum differentiation). Also of concern to me is that Akhavan's belief in the importance of the vocabulary gap and its predictive utility of TAG relies greatly on the work of Hart and Risley (1995), whose framework rests on misinformed conceptions of the construct of intelligence and deficit thinking perceptions of the poor.

Another example of reductionistic discourse is Larry Bell's (2005) book, *12 Powerful Words That Increase Test Scores and Help Close the Achievement Gap: A Resource for Educators and Parents.* Bell spent 15 years as a classroom teacher, and on his website[32] he notes that he is an "educational consultant, motivational speaker, and author." Bell, an entrepreneur, owns his own company, Multicultural America, Inc. Based on an inspection of his website, I see that Bell devotes much of his time in conducting "Closing the Achievement Gap Seminars" (workshops for preschool to grade 12 teachers) for $595 for a 2-day workshop or $300 for an all-day workshop.[33]

In Bell's (2005) book, which he uses as a major source in his seminars, he introduces and emphasizes that that there are "12 powerful words" that teachers can use in helping their students increase test scores. Furthermore, Bell claims that the curricular use of the "12 powerful words" can assist in closing TAG. These "powerful words" (listed on p. 17) are:

trace	support	formulate
analyze	explain	contrast
infer	summarize	describe
evaluate	compare	predict

Bell discusses many suggestions for using the "12 powerful words" to improve student learning (e.g., using them in daily quizzes; having students create rap songs with the words; incorporating the words in fictitious writing; using them in crossword puzzles).

Do his "12 powerful words," as Bell (2005) asserts, increase students' test scores and help close TAG? Unfortunately, in his 108-page book Bell does not cite a single empirical study to support his claims (nor are any references of any type cited at all). The only semblance of "positive evidence" is in the form of unverified testimonial letters and notes in his website to Bell from various principals and teachers stating that their students' achievement test scores have increased by using "Larry Bell's strategies."[34]

2. *Equal educational opportunity discourse.* An exemplar of a study in this category is by Beecher and Sweeney (2008), who describe an 8-year project in turning around "Central Elementary School" (CES), located, it appears, in the northeastern U.S.[35] CES, 1 of 11 schools, is situated in a high-performing suburban school district. The authors note that CES was considered a "failing" school, with an enrollment of 75% Black, Latino/Latina, and Asian American students; 45% of the students at CES were on the free/reduced lunch program, and 30% were English language learners.

In their article, Beecher and Sweeney (2008) describe the efforts and accomplishments of closing TAG at CES via a school-wide paradigm shift from a remedial approach to an enrichment and differentiated curriculum model. In brief, the new strategic plan had two broad goals: (a) employing the Enrichment Triad Model (Renzulli & Reis, 1985), which is a gifted and talented curricular approach; and (b) implementing a global studies curriculum (e.g., study of West Indies, Japanese, and Mexican cultures). All CES teachers received extensive training in how to meet the school's goals, and a school-wide enrichment team included both teachers and parents.

Beecher and Sweeney report that analyses of scores of state tests showed student academic achievement gains in mathematics, reading, and writing from 1997 to 2004. TAG narrowed from 62 percentage to 10 percentage points for different SES groups. Regarding racial/ethnic comparisons, all groups of students of color improved. For example, in 1997, 21% of the Black students performed at the remedial level, and in 2004, no Black students did. For Latino/Latina students in the remedial band, there were 22% in 1994 and only 7% in 2004.[36] Beecher and Sweeney comment that TAG reduction "resulted from children's active engagement and investment in their own learning, parents' involvement in their children's school lives, and teachers' commitment to their students" (p. 528).

The second example of a publication representative of the equal educational opportunity discourse category is the book by Cheryl Holcomb-McCoy, *School Counseling to Close the Achievement Gap: A Social Justice Framework for Success* (2007). Holcomb-McCoy, a professor of counseling and educational development, specializes, for example, in multicultural school counseling and urban school counselor preparation. In part, she rests her approach on multicultural counseling, which refers to a type of counseling "in which the counselor and client take into account their cultural and personal experiences" (p. 18). As her book's subtitle indicates, Holcomb-McCoy's framework equally draws from the area of "social justice." She offers this broad definition: Social justice has to do with the "*way in which human rights are manifested in the everyday lives of people at every level of society*" (p. 17). A more specific conception of social justice is that it is concerned with addressing and ending the marginalization of certain oppressed groups based on their race, gender, class, disability, language, and sexual orientation (see Theoharis, 2007).[37]

The core of Holcomb-McCoy's (2007) book is what she refers to as the "six C's"—"counseling and intervention planning," "consultation," "connecting schools, families, and communities," "collecting and utilizing data," "challenging bias," and "coordinating student services and support" (p. 22).[38] Her model to close TAG has school counselors using a social justice approach as the driving mechanism of the six functions (i.e., the six C's; see p. 23 of Holcomb-McCoy, 2007). Due to space limitations, I will discuss two of the six functions—(a) connecting schools, families, and communities; and (b) challenging bias. Holcomb-McCoy notes that over the last decade the role and participation of school counselors in building strong relationships among schools, families, and communities have been seriously encouraged (e.g., Bryan & Holcomb-McCoy, 2004; the importance and value of parental engagement in their children's education are covered in chapter 8, this volume). Holcomb-McCoy discusses five principles that can help in realizing effective partnerships among schools, families, and communities: (a) clear *policies* that are developed by schools, parents, and community members; (b) strong and collaborative *leadership* by counselors, school administrators, teachers, parents, and other community stakeholders (e.g., clergy); (c) lines of *communication* between schools and parents that are clear, varied, and frequent; (d) a strong focus on targeting *community* members and agencies in which the schools initiate measures to allow these stakeholders to become fully involved and supportive of the local schools; and (e) an *evaluation* program to assess the objectives and progress of the school-family-community partnership so adjustments can be made, if needed.

Challenging bias is another function of Holcomb-McCoy's (2007) multicultural counseling/social justice framework to help close TAG. She states that counselors need to have the skills and willingness to confront attitudes, behaviors, and policies directed toward students that are biased and oppressive.[39] Holcomb-McCoy offers a number of guidelines for counselors challenging bias. Two examples are: (a) be aware of your own biases and prejudices; to do this, she has an exercise for counselors to take so they can see if they have prejudicial attitudes (e.g., "Latino students tend to . . . "; see p. 97); and (b) be an active and empathetic listener of students' and parents' experiences regarding their accounts of perceived prejudice and discrimination; do not trivialize such concerns.

To sum, Holcomb-McCoy's (2007) multicultural counseling/social justice framework designed to reduce TAG has great potential. We often think of the role of school counselors in a narrow way (e.g., academic guidance in high school). Yet, her approach greatly expands the work of school counselors in helping youths, especially low-SES students of color, to realize school success in psychologically healthy learning environments.

3. *Systemic analysis discourse.* A perspicacious publication on this type of discussion to significantly reduce TAG is an article by Noguera (2009). A central point he stresses is that before policymakers and governmental agencies can

proceed with meaningful and comprehensive school reform, they must come to grips with the fact that the major problems in education (particularly TAG) are inextricably linked to the persistent, pervasive, and profound inequality in practically all facets of U.S. society. Stated succinctly, Noguera (2009) maintains, "The achievement gap is in many respects nothing more than an educational manifestation of social inequality" (p. 64).

Noguera (2009) comments that three critical aspects of educational inequality need to be addressed in order to help close TAG. First, there must be funding equalization for all schools. This long-standing school financing inequity issue between high-enrollment White schools and high-enrollment schools of students of color must be a priority in school reform. Second, the commitment to segregation, desegregation, and integration of our nation's public schools must be renewed. As I discuss in chapter 4, the school segregation of students of color is clearly associated with academic achievement problems (e.g., reading performance). Third, Noguera asserts that current school reform strategies have, for the most part, neglected the unmet (non-academic) needs of poor children and youths of color (e.g., adequate nutrition; health care). These needs, which I refer to as the "other gaps," are covered in chapter 3 of this volume.

Another example of a systemic analysis discourse publication is an article by Mathis (2005), who exposes four fallacies serving the foundation for the position that schools, alone, can significantly diminish TAG. These fallacies are: (a) "successful examples are outliers," (b) "reduction of TAG is a panacea for poor performing schools," (c) "adequate yearly progress [AYP] on test scores decreases the true education gap," and (d) "vouchers bridge achievement gaps." I briefly comment on two of the fallacies.

The occasional successful school being touted as an example of school reform, Mathis (2005) maintains, is a fallacious assertion. The promotion of such schools can lead to the mistaken belief that poorly performing educational institutions can reduce TAG sans any additional resources. It is merely a matter of determination and effort. Although there are indeed examples of successful schools that have demonstrated a diminution of TAG (e.g., Scheurich, Skrla, & Joseph, 2000), Mathis's view is that such schools are "statistical fluke[s]" (p. 591),[40] and thus they give spurious promise of reform.

A second fallacy is that TAG reduction is a panacea for ailing schools. Mathis (2005) refers to the ubiquitous workshops for professional development in which teachers and administrators take home quick-fix curricular approaches designed to close TAG. He remarks that while such training may offer some useful instructional strategies, a paucity of independent evidence exists that these programs, alone, can reduce TAG. A major downside to these workshops is that they can provide a reason for policymakers to disregard inequalities in the larger society. Mathis closes his article by stating that if we truly want our children and youths to succeed in school, we need to tackle a host of factors outside the schools—for example, unemployment, health care, and housing.

The Explosive Growth of People of Color and Students of Color

The 2010 Census report confirmed an ongoing pattern first identified in the early 1980s: Regarding race/ethnicity in the U.S., the proportion of the White-only population (i.e., not Hispanic or Latino/Latina) is shrinking while the percentage of people of color is expanding.[41] Table 1.11 presents U.S. population increases by race/ethnicity from 2000 to 2010. In this decade, the total U.S. population grew from 281,421,906 to 308,745,538—an increase of 27,323,632 people (9.7%). Yet, when this growth of over 27 million is disaggregated by race/ethnicity, Whites accounted for only 8.3% of the total increase. By sharp contrast, Latinos/Latinas made up the majority (55.5%) of the national population growth, and Asians and African Americans accounted for 16.2% and 15.6%, respectively, of the total increase. As such, the percentage of Whites who made up the racial/ethnic pie shrank from 69.1% in 2000 to 63.7% in 2010. In 1980, Whites made up 79.6% of the total U.S. population[42] and in 1990 made up 75.6% of the whole.[43] In sum, from 1980 to 2010, the national White population lost 20% of its share of the total.

Another similar point that can be gleaned from Table 1.11 pertains to inter-racial/ethnic growth patterns. From 2000 to 2010, the White population grew by only 1.2%. By stark contrast, every other group of color outstripped the White increase. The Asian population, a heterogeneous group, grew the most (43.3%), while the Latino/Latina population, also quite diverse in subgroups, increased by a close second at 43.0%. Third, fourth, and fifth places in growth were Native

TABLE 1.11 U.S. Population Increases (in Thousands) by Race/Ethnicity: 2000 to 2010

Racial/Ethnic Group	*2000*		*2010*		*Increase*		
	Total Population		*Total Population*		*Own Group*		*Total Population*
	n	*%*	*n*	*%*	*n*	*%*	*%*
Total	281,422	100.0	308,746	100.0	27,324	9.7	100.0
White	194,553	69.1	196,818	63.7	2,265	1.2	8.3
Latino/Latina	35,306	12.5	50,478	16.3	15,172	43.0	55.5
African American	34,658	12.3	38,929	12.6	4,271	12.3	15.6
Asian	10,243	3.6	14,674	4.8	4,431	43.3	16.2
American Indian/ Alaska Native	2,476	0.9	2,932	0.9	456	18.4	1.7
Native Hawaiian/ Other Pacific Islander	399	0.1	540	0.2	141	35.4	0.5
Two or More Races	6,826	2.4	9,009	2.9	2,183	32.0	8.0

Source: Adapted from Humes, Jones, and Ramírez (2011, p. 4, Table 1).

Hawaiian/other Pacific Islander (35.3%), American Indian/Alaska Native (18.4%), and African American (12.3%). Demographers project that these interracial/ethnic differences in growth will continue well into the future. Passel and Cohn (2008) report that in 2050 the national racial/ethnic diversity will look very different than it does in the present. In mid-century, the total U.S. population is estimated to reach 438 million people—about a 42% increase from 2010. Also, in 2050 a milestone will occur in the history of population demographic history: The White population will further decline and no longer constitute a majority, as it is projected to decrease to 47% (207 million). The Latino/Latina population is expected to increase 2.5 times in size, from 50 million in 2010 to about 127 million in 2050, making up 29% of the total U.S. population. The African American population is projected to grow from 39 million in 2010 to about 60 million in 2050, making up 13% of the total population. Asians are projected to increase from 15 million in 2010 to about 39 million in 2050, constituting 9% of the U.S. population.[44] In sum, if these projections ring true, the year 2050 will indeed signal a landmark event in history, as no single racial/ethnic group will constitute a majority of the total population of the U.S.[45]

Closely related to racial/ethnic shifts in the total U.S. population are the changes in the national K-12 public school enrollment. In light of the dramatic transformations of the overall racial/ethnic makeup of the U.S., the landscape of the K-12 public school enrollment in the nation is also being altered in an appreciable way. As I pen these words on August 1, 2014, public elementary and secondary schools will begin the fall term a mere 3-plus weeks from now, and if projections materialize, a milestone in K-12 schooling will occur. That is, White students will lose their majority status for the first time in the history of U.S. public education. Table 1.12 shows racial/ethnic numerical shifts using four data points—2000, 2010, 2014, and 2020. Note that the White K-12 student population was a strong majority in 2000, making up 61.2% of the total enrollment. In 2010, White students declined to 52.4%, and in 2014 they were projected to be under 50% (Hussar & Bailey, 2014, p. 33, Table 3). Conversely, of course, Table 1.12 reveals that combined students of color are projected to gain an extremely slight, but nonetheless, majority presence (50.3%) in fall 2014. In fall 2020, this majority is predicted to be 53.8%. A major factor accounting for this monumental transformation in the racial/ethnic composition of the K-12 enrollment is the dramatic growth of the Latino/Latina student sector. As shown in Table 1.12, Latino/Latina students made up 16.4% of the total K-12 enrollment in 2000, but in 2014 it was estimated to be 25.8%—a 57.3% increase in 14 years, the largest, by far, of all racial/ethnic groups.

These racial/ethnic patterns of change in the national K-12 population are even more striking in some states. Take the case of California, the most populous state in the country in 2010.[46] Table 1.12 presents public school enrollment by race/ethnicity for California. The White enrollment was only 25% of the total K-12 student body in AY 2013–2014, and all other groups of color combined

TABLE 1.12 Racial/Ethnic K-12 Public School Enrollment (in Thousands): National, 2000, 2010, 2014, and 2020

		Race/Ethnicity							
Year	*Total* *No.*	*White* *No.*	*%*	*Latino/Latina* *No.*	*%*	*Black* *No.*	*%*	*Other* *No.*	*%*
2000	47,204	28,873	61.2	7,733	16.4	8,099	17.2	2,499	5.3
2010	49,484	25,930	52.4	11,442	23.1	7,918	16.0	3,033	6.1
2014[a]	50,018	24,861	49.7	12,883	25.8	7,709	15.4	3,153	6.3
2020[a]	52,124	24,088	46.2	15,062	28.9	7,816	15.0	3,435	6.6

Source: Adapted from Hussar and Bailey (2014, p. 33, Table 3).

[a] Data are projected.

TABLE 1.13 California K-12 Enrollment by Race/Ethnicity: AY 2013–2014

Race/Ethnicity	*No.*	*%*
White	1,559,113	25.0
Latino/Latina	3,321,274	53.3
African American	384,291	6.2
Asian	542,540	8.7
Pilipino	151,745	2.4
American Indian/Alaska Native	38,616	0.6
Pacific Islander	32,821	0.5
Other	206,272	3.3

Source: Adapted from California Department of Education (2014).

made up a strong majority (75%) of the total enrollment. Latino/Latina students were the largest student group, making up a slight majority (53.3%) of the total (Table 1.13).

Conclusion

In light of the persistent and pervasive nature of TAG and the remarkable growth of students of color, a crucial question to ask of educators, researchers, and policymakers is: Will workable, comprehensive, and equitable school reform commensurately increase? Given the bankruptcy of the standards-based school reform movement, which has now swept K-12 schooling in the U.S. and is the primary strategy for improving schooling for students of color (especially of low-SES background), I must answer my own question with a resounding "no."[47] The standards-based school reform movement is palliative and bereft of meaningful policy to help realize school success for students of color because the campaign is structurally misdirected (see Valencia & Pearl, 2010). This movement largely treats the symptoms of school failure (poor academic achievement indicators, such as low reading test scores and high dropout rates from secondary education), rather than identifying and remediating the root causes of school failure, which are societal inequities (e.g., income differentials across SES and racial/ethnic groups; see chapter 3, this volume) and gross inequities in schools (e.g., teacher quality and curriculum differentiation; see chapters 5 and 7, respectively, this volume). As I proceed in this discussion, three major theses drive my analyses. First, racialized opportunity structures in the larger society and the educational system lead to racialized academic achievement patterns. Second, the various indicators of TAG (especially achievement test performance and school holding power rates) are *symptoms* of the school quality gap between high-enrollment White schools and high-enrollment schools of students of color. As such, school reform solely directed toward poor achievement is structurally misdirected. We need to focus on *causes*—inequalities in society and inferior schools. Third, school success for students of color (particularly low SES-Latino/Latina and African American students) can be fully understood when analyzed in the broadest political, economic, and cultural contexts. The integration of macro-, meso-, and microlevel policies establishes the boundaries of possibilities for significantly improving the schooling for students of color.

Notes

1. In my reporting of the historical data on TAG, I follow, with some exceptions, the nomenclature of the times.
2. Whitney (1923) also presents achievement test comparisons of White and colored students for arithmetic, English composition, handwriting, and silent reading.
3. See Valencia (2011b, pp. 18–19) for further discussion of Drake's (1927) study.
4. This sentence is excerpted from Valencia (2011b, p. 19).
5. This note and note 11 are excerpted from Valencia (2011b, p. 31, notes 19 and 20). Beginning in AY 2005–2006, the Texas Education Agency set passing standards via a "panel of educators and other interested citizens" (Texas Education Agency, 2008, p. vi). The actual panel-recommended passing standards are not mentioned.
6. The TAKS is administered for the following subjects and respective grades: reading (3–9); mathematics (3–11); English language arts (10–11); writing (4 and 7); science (5, 8, 10, and 11); and social studies (8, 10, and 11). In the spring of 2012, the State of Texas Assessments of Academic Readiness (STAAR) replaced TAKS. For information on STAAR, see www.tea.state.tx.us/student.assessment/staar/. Retrieved July 18, 2012.
7. For the 2013 NAEP reading assessment, a nationally represented sample of 171,800 eighth graders participated from 6,510 schools (National Center for Education Statistics, 2013a, p. 3), and for the NAEP mathematics assessment a national sample of 170,000 eighth graders enrolled in 6,520 schools served as participants (National Center for Education Statistics, 2013b, p. 3).

8. The NAEP reading results for the eighth-grade sample are reported as average scores on a 0-500 scale (National Center for Education Statistics, 2013a, p. 3). Two cognitive target areas are assessed: comprehension of literacy text and informational text (National Center for Education Statistics, 2013a, p. 3).
9. Such a racialized pattern for Latinos/Latinas and Blacks also appears for 2 decades on mathematics assessment (National Center for Education Statistics, 2013b).
10. This paragraph draws from, with some revisions, Valencia (2002b, p. 14) and Valencia (2011a, p. 21).
11. The literature on the harmful effects of grade retention is quite large. The following are examples of such studies: Holmes (1989); Hong & Yu (2007); Jimerson & Ferguson (2007); Jimerson, Woehr, & Kaufman (2004); Roderick (1994); Shepard & Smithe (1989).
12. In Texas, these racialized retention rates are by no means restricted to AY 2011–2012. For example, Valencia (2002b, p. 16, Figure 1.3) reports such K-12 patterns from 1994–1995 to 1998–1999. Also, in Louisiana, for example, Black students compared to Whites had higher retention rates in grades 4 and 8 from 1997–1998 to 2000–2001 (Valencia & Villarreal, p. 138, Figure 4.5).
13. An odds ratio is a probability. Here, it is calculated by dividing, for example, the Mexican American/Latino and Latina retention rate of 3.9% by the White retention rate of 2.0%. The resultant quotient of 2.0 means: In Texas, K-12 Mexican American/ Latino and Latina students are 2.0 times more likely to be retained in comparison to their White peers.
14. This paragraph draws on, with some revisions, Valencia (2011b, pp. 23–24).
15. Data are also available for 1985–1989, 1991–1999, and 2001–2008. Because of space limitations I present information by decade to examine trends.
16. See en.Wikipedia.org/wiki/SAT. Retrieved March 5, 2011.
17. These scores are also reported for Puerto Rican and "Other Hispanic" students.
18. Aud et al. (2012) also report data for AY 2004–2005. To examine trends, I selected data only for the intermediate AY (1999–2000) and for the most recent AY (2009–2010).
19. The percentages for the three groups for bachelor's degrees awarded (AYs 1999–2000; 2009–2010) presented in Table 1.8 do not total 100% because I did not include the percentages for the other groups: Asian/Pacific Islander and American Indian/Alaska Native. See Aud et al. (2012, p. 285, Table A-47) for these data.
20. GRE scores are also available, separately, for Puerto Rican and "Other Hispanic"—as well as for American Indians and Asian/Pacific Islanders (see Educational Testing Service, 2013, p. 7, Table 4).
21. The following draws from, with a minor revision, Valencia and Villarreal (2011, p. 250, note 2). Often, in the literature the term "gifted" is juxtaposed with the notion of "talented." Gifted children typically score significantly above the norm on measures of intelligence and achievement, and talented children excel in specific areas (e.g., music, art, dance). Although the two labels suggest different denotations, there is no valid justification for such a distinction because both the gifted and talented exhibit three core characteristics: precocity, independence, and a high level of motivation to excel (Winner, 1996). As such, in this section I use the omnibus concept of "gifted."
22. See Valencia and Villarreal (2011) for a discussion of why students of color, on the whole, are underrepresented in gifted programs.
23. This section on Terman (1926) builds on, with revisions, Valencia and Villarreal (2011, pp. 237–239).
24. See Valencia and Villarreal (2011) for a fuller discussion of the methods, findings, and interpretations of Terman's (1926) investigation.

25. During this era, Terman and his contemporaries believed "race" to be a biological entity. As well, they confused "race" with ethnicity and national origin. Presently, there is a consensus that "race" is a social construction (see, e.g., Brace, 1995; Graves, 2001; Templeton, 2002).
26. See Valencia and Suzuki (2001, p. 317, note 14).
27. See Terman (1916, pp. 91–92) and Valencia (2010, pp. 14–16).
28. In the contemporary period, Asian American/Pacific Islander students—as a group—are overrepresented in gifted programs (see Valencia, 2011b, p. 16, Table 1.2) and Valencia and Villarreal (2011, p. 241, Table 11.1).
29. Akhavan cites, for example, Beck, McKeown, and Kucan (2002) and Stahl and Nagy (2006) in providing support that vocabulary size is positively related to reading well.
30. Sulzer-Azaroff (1997), in her review of Hart and Risley (1995), also raises concerns about Hart and Risley's view of intelligence. Sulzer-Azaroff comments,

    > At first blush, those findings might seem to support a strictly hereditary argument: Intellectually limited parents pass on their inferior genes to their offspring. But suppose that parents could be taught to say more to their children and be more reinforcing when their youngsters imitated and embellished upon their examples? (p. 600)

31. See Valencia (2010, chapter 3) for an overview and critique of the concept of "culture of poverty." Also, see chapter 2, this volume.
32. See www.larry-bell.com.
33. *Id.*
34. *Id.*
35. It appears that CES is located in Connecticut, as Beecher is affiliated with the West Hartford Public Schools and Sweeney is affiliated (as of 2008) with the University of Connecticut.
36. Beecher and Sweeney (2008) note that after the intervention, TAG in the school district was substantially larger than at CES.
37. For a brief discussion of the notion of social justice, see Valencia (2010, pp. 138–141).
38. Holcomb-McCoy (2007) devotes one chapter to each of the six C's.
39. For an example of a study that investigates the relation between the racial climate of school and African American high school students' academic achievement and discipline outcomes, see Mattison and Aber (2007).
40. Valencia, Valenzuela, Sloan, and Foley (2001) refer to these successful schools as statistical "outliers" (p. 320). The authors comment, "By focusing exclusively on outlier schools, researchers risk creating an illusion of widespread success and a false sense of security that school reform is in progress" (p. 320). Furthermore, in their essay on public education and accountability in Texas, Valencia et al. (2001) assert that such a circumscribed focus on outlier schools is not a basis for sound educational policy because if anything it diverts attention from the deeply rooted systemic problems in scores of Texas schools.
41. For the purpose of the 2010 Census, the U.S. Office of Management and Budget notes that individuals can self-identify as "Hispanic or Latino and not Hispanic or Latino" and "People who identify as Hispanic, Latino, or Spanish may be any race" (Humes, Jones, & Ramírez, 2011, p. 2). The outcome of such self-identification allows data to be reported for Hispanic or Latino, White alone, and other races (e.g., Black or African American; Asian).
42. Gibson and Jung (2002, p. 18, Table 1).
43. Valencia (2002a, p. 54, Table 2.1).
44. Passel and Cohn (2008, p. 1, Table 1).

45. This projection of no single racial/ethnic group making up a majority of the total U.S. population is 10 years earlier than previously projected (see Valencia, 2002a, p. 56, Table 2.4).
46. Humes et al. (2011, p. 18, Table 1.1).
47. This paragraph builds on, with revisions, Valencia and Pearl (2010).

References

Akhavan, N. (2007). *Accelerated vocabulary instruction: Strategies for closing the achievement gap for all students.* New York: Scholastic.

Allen, L. F., Lasater, L. M., Farrell, D. M., & Reynolds, C. R. (1990). Veracity and vicissitude: A critical look at the Milwaukee project. *Journal of School Psychology, 28,* 285–299.

Aud, S., Hussar, W., Johnson, F., Kena, G., Roth, E., Manning, E., Wang, X., & Zhang, J. (2012). *The condition of education 2012* (NCES 2012–045). Washington, DC: National Center for Education Statistics, Institute of Education Sciences, U.S. Department of Education. Retrieved July 16, 2012, from: http://nces.ed.gov/pubs2012/2012045.pdf.

Ayers, L. P. (1909). *Laggards in our schools: A study of retardation and elimination in city school systems.* New York: Russell Sage.

Beck, I., McKeown, M. G., & Kucan, L. (2002). *Bringing words to life: Robust vocabulary instruction.* New York: Guilford.

Beecher, M., & Sweeney, S. M. (2008). Closing the achievement gap with curriculum and enrichment differentiation. *Journal of Advanced Academics, 19,* 502–530.

Belfield, C. R., & Levin, H. M. (Eds.). (2007). *The price we pay: Economic and social consequences of inadequate education.* Washington, DC: Brookings Institution Press.

Bell, L. I. (2005). *12 powerful words that increase test scores and help close the achievement gap.* Manassas, VA: Multicutural America.

Brace, C. L. (1995). Region does not mean "race": Reality versus convention in forensic anthropology. *Journal of Forensic Sciences, 40,* 29–33.

Bryan, J., & Holcomb-McCoy, C. (2004). School counselor's perceptions of their involvement in school-family-community partnerships. *Professional School Counseling, 7,* 162–171.

California Department of Education. (2014). *Statewide enrollment by ethnicity: 2013–2014.* Sacramento: Author. Retrieved May 21, 2014, from: http://dq.cde.ca.gov/data-quest/.

Ceci, S. J. (1990). *On intelligence . . . more or less: A bio-ecological treatise on intellectual development.* Englewood Cliffs, NJ: Prentice Hall.

College Board. (2010). *SAT trends: Background on the SAT takers in the class of 2010.* New York: Author. Retrieved March 5, 2011, from: http://professionals.collegeboard.com/profdownload/2010-sat-trends.pdf.

Drake, R. H. (1927). *A comparison study of the mentality and achievement of Mexican and White children.* Unpublished master's thesis, University of Southern California, Los Angeles.

Dunn, L. W., & Dunn, L. M. (1965). *Peabody Picture Vocabulary Test.* Circle Pines, MN: American Guidance Service.

Educational Testing Service. (2013). *A snapshot of the individuals who took the GRE revised general test.* Princeton, NJ: Author. Retrieved June 27, 2014, from: www.ets.org/s/gre/pdf/snapshot.pdf.

Eide, E. R., & Goldhaber, D. D. (2005). Grade retention: What are the costs and benefits? *Journal of Education Finance, 31,* 195–214.

Finnie, R., & Meng, R. (2006). *The importance of functional literacy: Reading and math skills and labor market outcomes of high school drop-outs.* Analytical Studies Branch Research

Paper Series. University of Windsor, Ottawa, Canada. Retrieved February 20, 2011, from: www.statcan.gc.ca/pub/11f0019m/11f0019m2006275-eng-pdf.

Garber, H. L. (1988). *The Milwaukee Project: Preventing mental retardation in children at risk.* Washington, DC: American Association on Mental Retardation.

Gibson, C., & Jung, K. (2002). *Historical census statistics on population totals by race, 1790 to 1990, and by Hispanic origin, 1970–1990, for the United States, regions, divisions, and states* (Population Division Working Paper No. 56). Washington, DC: U.S. Department of Commerce, Bureau of the Census. Retrieved May 6, 2011, from: http://www.census.gov/population/www/documentation/twps0056.pdf.

González, G. G. (1990). *Chicano education in the era of segregation.* Philadelphia: Balch Institute Press.

Graves, J. L., Jr. (2001). *The emperor's new clothes: Biological theories of race at the new millennium.* New Brunswick, NJ: Rutgers University Press.

Hart, B., & Risley, T. R. (1995). *Meaningful differences in the everyday experience of young American children.* Baltimore: Brooke.

Hart, B., & Risley, T. R. (2003, Spring). The early catastrophe: The 30 million word gap by age 3. *American Educator.* Retrieved June 2, 2011, from: www.aft.org/pubs-reports/american_educator/spring 2002/catastrophe.html.

Holcomb-McCoy, C. (2007). *School counseling to close the achievement gap: A social justice framework for success.* Thousand Oaks, CA: Corwin Press.

Holmes, C. T. (1989). Grade level retention effects: A meta-analysis of research studies. In L. A. Shepard & M. L. Smith (Eds.), *Flunking grades: Research and policies on retention* (pp. 16–33). London: Falmer Press.

Hong, G., & Yu, B. (2007). Early-grade retention and children's reading and math learning in elementary years. *Educational Evaluation and Policy Analysis, 29,* 239–261.

Humes, K. R., Jones, N. A., & Ramírez, R. R. (2011, March). *Overview of race and Hispanic origin: 2010* (2010 Census Briefs, C2010B2–02). Washington, DC: U.S. Department of Commerce, Economics, and Statistics Administration, Bureau of the Census. Retrieved May 6, 2011, from: www.census.gov/prod/cen2010/briefs/c2010br-02.pdf.

Hussar, W. J., & Bailey, T. M. (2014). *Projections of education statistics to 2022* (NCES 2014–2015). Washington, DC: National Center for Education Statistics, Institute of Education Sciences, U.S. Department of Education. Retrieved August 1, 2014, from: http://nces.ed.gov/pubs2014/201405/.pdf.

Inkeles, A. (1966). Social structure and the socialization of competence. *Harvard Educational Review, 36,* 265–283.

Jimerson, S. R., & Ferguson, P. (2007). A longitudinal study of grade retention: Academic and behavioral outcomes of retained students through adolescents. *School Psychology Quarterly, 22,* 314–339.

Jimerson, S. R., Woehr, S., Kaufman, A. M., & Anderson, G. (2004). Grade retention and promotion: Important information for parents. In A. S. Canter, S. A. Carroll, L. Paige, & I. Romero (Eds.), *Helping children at home and school: Handouts from your school psychologist* (2nd ed., pp. 61–64). Bethesda, MD: National Association of School Psychologists.

Kuncel, N. R., Hezlett, S. A., & Ones, D. S. (2001). A comprehensive meta-analysis of the predictive validity of the Graduate Record Examinations: Implications for graduate student selection and performance. *Psychological Bulletin, 127,* 162–181.

Longley, R. (2010, February 13). Lifetime earnings soar with education. Retrieved March 5, 2011, from: http://usgovinfo.about.com/od/moneymatters/a/edandearnings.htm.

Manuel, H. T. (1930). *The education of Mexican and Spanish-speaking children in Texas.* Austin: Fund for Research in the Social Sciences, University of Texas.

Mathis, W. J. (2005). Bridging the achievement gap: A bridge too far? *Phi Delta Kappan, 86,* 590–593.

Mattison, E., & Aber, M. S. (2007). Closing the achievement gap: The association of racial climate with achievement and behavioral outcomes. *American Journal of Psychology, 40,* 1–12.

National Center for Education Statistics. (2011). *The nation's report card: Reading 2011* (NCES 2012–457). Washington, DC: Institute of Education Sciences, U.S. Department of Education.

National Center for Education Statistics. (2013a). *The nation's report card: Reading 1990–2013* (NCES 2014–451). Washington, DC: Institute of Education Sciences, U.S. Department of Education.

National Center for Education Statistics. (2013b). *The nation's report card: Mathematics 1990–2013* (NCES 2014–451). Washington, DC: Institute of Education Sciences, U.S. Department of Education.

Noguera, P. A. (2009). The achievement gap: Public crisis in education. *New Labor Forum, 18,* 61–69.

Ornstein, A. (2007). *Class counts: Education, inequality, and the shrinking middle class.* Lanham, MD: Rowman & Littlefield.

Passel, J. S., & Cohn, D. (2008, February). *U.S. population projections: 2005–2050.* Pew Hispanic Center, Social and Demographic Trends, Pew Research Center. Retrieved May 7, 2011, from: http://pewhispanic.org/files/reports/85.pdf.

Pearl, A. (2011). The big picture: Institutional and systemic factors. In R. R. Valencia (Ed.), *Chicano school failure and success: Past, present, and future* (3rd ed., pp. 257–272). New York: Routledge.

Ramírez, E. (2008, June 18). High school grades and SAT: Still best predictor of college success, study says. Retrieved March 4, 2011, from: www.usnews.com>Education>On Education.

Renzulli, J. S., & Reis, S. N. (1985) *The Scholastic Enrichment Model: A comprehensive plan for educational excellence.* Mansfield Center, CT: Creative Learning Press.

Roderick, M. (1994). Grade retention and school dropout: Investigating the association. *American Educational Research Journal, 31,* 729–759.

Rumberger, R. W., & Rodríguez, G. M. (2011). Chicano dropouts. In R. R. Valencia (Ed.), *Chicano school failure and success: Past, present, and future* (3rd ed., pp. 76–98). New York: Routledge.

San Miguel, G., Jr., & Valencia, R. R. (1998). From the Treaty of Guadalupe Hidalgo to *Hopwood:* The educational plight and struggle of Mexican Americans in the Southwest. *Harvard Educational Review, 68,* 353–412.

Scheurich, J. J., Skrla, L. & Johnson, J. F. (2000). Thinking carefully about equity and accountability. *Phi Delta Kappan, 82,* 293–299.

Shepard, L. A., & Smith, M. L. (Eds.). (1989). *Flunking grades: Research and policies on retention.* London: Falmer Press.

Snyder, T. D., & Dillow, S. A. (2013). *Digest of education statistics, 2012* (NCES 2014–015). Washington, DC: National Center for Education Statistics, Institute of Education Sciences, U.S. Department of Education. Retrieved June 25, 2014, from: http://nces.ed.gov/pubs2014/2014015.pdf.

Stahl, S. A., & Nagy, W. E. (2006). *Teaching word meaning.* Mahwah, NJ: Lawrence Earlbaum.

Sulzer-Azaroff, B. (1997). Why should I talk to my baby [Review of the book *Meaningful differences in the everyday experiences of young American children*]. *Journal of Applied Behavior Analysis, 30,* 599–600.

Templeton, A. R. (2002). The genetic and evolutionary significance of human races. In J. M. Fish (Ed.), *Race and intelligence: Separating science from myth* (pp. 31–56). Mahwah, NJ: Lawrence Erlbaum.

Terman, L. M. (1916). *The measurement of intelligence.* Boston: Houghton Mifflin.

Terman, L. M. (1926). *Genetic studies of genius: Vol. 1. Mental and physical traits of a thousand gifted children* (2nd ed.). Stanford, CA: Stanford University Press.

Terman, L. M., & Merrill, M. A. (1960). *Stanford-Binet Intelligence Scale: 1960 norms edition.* Boston: Houghton Mifflin.

Texas Education Agency. (2008). *Comprehensive annual report on Texas public schools.* Austin, TX: Author.

Texas Education Agency. (2013a). *2011–2012 Academic Excellence Indicator System: State performance report.* Austin, TX: Author. Retrieved June 23, 2014, from: http://ritter.tea.state.tx.us/perfreport/aeis/2012/state.html.

Texas Education Agency. (2013b). *Grade-level retention in Texas public schools, 2011–12* (Document No. GE14 601 01). Austin, TX: Author.

Texas Education Agency. (2013c). *Enrollment in Texas public schools, 2012–13* (Document No. GE14 601 06). Austin, TX: Author.

Theoharis, G. (2007). Social justice educational leaders and resistance: Toward a theory of social justice leadership. *Educational Administrative Quarterly, 43,* 222–258.

U.S. Commission on Civil Rights. (1971). *Mexican American education study, report 2: The unfinished education. Outcomes for minorities in the five southwestern states.* Washington, DC: Government Printing Office.

U.S. Department of Education, Office for Civil Rights. (2012). *2009–2010 elementary and secondary school civil rights compliance report.* Washington, DC: Author.

Valencia, R. R. (1997). Genetic pathology model of deficit thinking. In R. R. Valencia (Ed.), *The evolution of deficit thinking: Educational thought and practice* (pp. 41–112). Stanford Series on Education and Public Policy. London: Falmer Press.

Valencia, R. R. (2002a). The explosive growth of the Chicano/Latino population: Educational implications. In R. R. Valencia (Ed.), *Chicano school failure and success: Past, present, and future* (2nd ed., pp. 52–69). London: RoutledgeFalmer.

Valencia, R. R. (2002b). The plight of Chicano students: An overview of schooling conditions and outcomes. In R. R. Valencia (Ed.), *Chicano school failure and success: Past, present, and future* (2nd ed., pp. 3–51). New York: RoutledgeFalmer.

Valencia, R. R. (2008). *Chicano students and the courts: The Mexican American legal struggle for educational equality.* Critical America Series. New York: New York University Press.

Valencia, R. R. (2010). *Dismantling contemporary deficit thinking: Educational thought and practice.* Critical Educator Series. New York: Routledge.

Valencia, R. R. (Ed.). (2011a). *Chicano school failure and success: Past, present, and future* (3rd ed.). New York: Routledge,

Valencia, R. R. (Ed.). (2011b). The plight of Chicano students: An overview of schooling conditions and outcomes. In R. R. Valencia (Ed.), *Chicano school failure and success: Past, present, and future* (3rd ed., pp. 3–41). New York: Routledge.

Valencia, R. R., & Pearl, A. (2010). Conclusion: (A) The bankruptcy of the standards-based school reform movement; (B) Toward the construction of meaningful school reform: democratic education. In R. R. Valencia, *Dismantling contemporary deficit thinking: Educational thought and practice* (pp. 148–158). Critical Educator Series. New York: Routledge.

Valencia, R. R., & Suzuki, L. A. (2001). *Intelligence testing and minority students: Foundations, performance factors, and assessment issues.* Series on Racial and Ethnic Minority Psychology. Thousand Oaks, CA: SAGE.

Valencia, R. R., Valenzuela, A., Sloan, K., & Foley, D. E. (2001). At odds—Let's treat the cause, not the symptoms: Equity and accountability in Texas revisited. *Phi Delta Kappan, 83,* 318–321, 326.

Valencia, R. R., & Villarreal, B. J. (2011). Gifted Chicano students: Underrepresentation issues and best-case practices for identification and placement. In R. R. Valencia (Ed.), *Chicano school failure and success: Past, present, and future* (3rd ed., pp. 235–254). New York: Routledge.

Whitney, F. L. (1923). Intelligence levels and school achievement of the white and colored races in the United States. *Pedagogical Seminary, 30,* 69–86.

Winner, E. (1996). *Gifted children: Myths and realities.* New York: Basic Books.

Wise, C. R. (1924). Holding power of the junior high school. *Junior High School Clearinghouse, 2,* 1–5.

2

COMPETING MODELS TO EXPLAIN THE ACHIEVEMENT GAP

What accounts for the persistent and pervasive finding that low-SES students of color[1] perform, on the average, lower than their White peers on the various indicators of TAG that I discussed in chapter 1? Scholars and others have proffered at least four competing explanations. I cover the following models in this chapter: (a) deficit thinking, (b) cultural-ecological, (c) communication process, and (d) systemic inequality.

Deficit Thinking Model

Of the four theories that scholars, educators, and policymakers have advanced to explain the typically lower academic performance of students of color, the deficit thinking model has had the longest currency—having roots in several centuries past.[2] Menchaca (1997) examines the foundation of deficit thinking in the U.S. and delineates how racist discourses impacted race relations and the schooling practices of students of color. The cornerstone of this nascent racism rests, Menchaca comments, in the early 1730s monogenist vs. polygenist debate (Stocking, 1968). She notes that theorists of monogenism asserted, using biblical allegories, that a common origin existed for humankind. By sharp contrast, polygenist theorists argued that humankind had divergent origins, and that "races" (i.e., separate species) evolved at different times. Polygenists thus maintained that there was a racial hierarchy of superiority with Whites (i.e., Europeans) at the top and African Blacks at the bottom. Later, in the early to mid-1800s, craniology "research" in the U.S. began with the work of Samuel G. Morton, physician and natural scientist, who conducted extensive measurements on the cranial capacity of skulls of various "races" (Gould, 1978). He concluded that Whites had the largest cranial capacity (as measured in cubic inches), and Blacks the smallest. According to Morton, cranial volume was an approximate index of brain size, which in turn, was positively correlated with intelligence. As such, the pseudoscientific work of Morton, a prominent polygenist of the times, provided a "scientic" foundation of the belief in separate species of humankind and the advent of scientic racism (Gould 1978; Jackson & Weidman, 2004; Tucker, 1994).[3] Within the framework of CRT, such racism became entrenched.

Another point Menchaca (1997) makes in regard to the early period of deficit thinking is the development of "common sense White racial ideologies," which are beliefs that Whites held. By "common sense," she means "collective views that, for the most part, were unreflective and appeared sound and prudent by most Whites" (p. 32).[4] One such belief, for example, was that the economic exploitation and subordination of people of color via a caste system of employment were justifiable practices. Also, by the end of the 1800s, a commonsense view of Whites is that Blacks, because of their putative inferiority, should not be allowed to mix with Whites. An example: Whites believed Blacks should not be permitted to travel with them in the same railway cars in Louisiana. In 1892, Homer Adolph Plessy (a man of White/Black ancestry) sued the state, questioning the constitutionality of Louisiana's separate but equal railway accommodations (*Ex parte Plessy,* 1892; also, see Irons, 2002). This case eventually reached the U.S. Supreme Court, and in *Plessy v. Ferguson* (1896) the state of Louisiana prevailed. As a result, the "separate but equal" doctrine eventually became codified and led to the de jure segregation of schools and, for example, in public facilities via Jim Crow policies. Apartheid had begun throughout U.S. society. Menchaca remarks that these commonsense views during the early racist discourses assisted in setting the stage for continued articulation of deficit thinking directed toward people and students of color.

With greater relevance and specificity to the present discussion, deficit thinking is an endogenous theory that "blames the victim" (Valencia, 2010, chapter 1). This theoretical perspective posits that students of color who experience academic achievement problems do so because they, their cultures, and their families have deficits or deficiencies. Such deficits manifest, it is alleged, in students' limited intellectual abilities and lack of motivation to achieve, dysfunctional cultures, and in families in which parents do not value education or socialize their children to succeed in school. Given the parsimonious nature of deficit thinking (Valencia, 2010, chapter 1), it is not unexpected that advocates of the model fail to look for external attributions of why students of color, on the average, experience school failure. Inequalities in society, the hegemonic workings of the political economy of education, and the oppressive policies and practices of local schools are all held exculpatory in understanding the academic difficulties of students of color.

Deficit thinking is best thought of as a paradigm consisting of three variants (Valencia, 2010, 2012). In the following sections, I discuss these variations: (a) the genetic pathology model, (b) the culture of poverty model, and (c) the "at-risk" model.

1. *Genetic pathology model.* Of the three variations of deficit thinking, this one injures the target of deficit thinkers in the greatest degree because it alleges that the intelligence of members of specific groups (e.g., African Americans, Mexican Americans) is limited and immalleable. The basis for this assertion among scientific racists is that genetics has a powerfully permanent influence in shaping behavior, particularly in intelligence. The hereditarian doctrine posits that genetics primarily accounts for individual difference in intellectual performance and, most importantly in our discussion, variations among "racial groups" (Valencia, 1997a, 2010, chapter 2).

Given an impetus by earlier polygenist thought, hereditarianism hit its zenith by the early 1920s during the heyday of mass intelligence testing and became entrenched as the orthodoxy in the field of psychology (Valencia, 1997b). Many prominent scholars, researchers, professors, designers of intelligence tests, officers of scholarly organizations, and consultants to governmental agencies held a collective view that intellectual differences favoring Whites over Blacks, Mexican Americans, and American Indians were largely due to an innate basis (Valencia, 1997b). The genetic pathology model of deficit thinking was further fueled by "race psychology" studies (i.e., cross-racial research)[5] during this era (e.g., see Garth, 1925, 1930).

Many of the race psychology studies of measured intelligence in the 1920s were fraught with methodological problems, thus leading researchers to make erroneous conclusions and to not consider rival hypotheses—characteristics of deficit thinking research that carried forward to later decades (Valencia, 1997b, 2010).

To sum, during the genetic pathology era, children of color performed lower than their White peers, it was alleged, largely because of inferiority in native intelligence. This research claim, in and of itself, is indeed a significant social statement of the nature of race relations during the height of the hereditarian era. A scrutiny of the investigations by race psychologists also informs us that many of these researchers who studied intellectual performance across racial/ethnic lines made little effort to take social, cultural, linguistic, and educational factors into consideration in their conceptual frameworks, research designs, and discussions of findings (Valencia, 1997b).

In light of the pervasive racial animus directed toward students of color during the genetic pathology era of deficit thinking, the institutionalization of mass intelligence testing, and homogeneous classroom groupings via curriculum differentiation effectively stratified students along racial/ethnic and SES lines. This low-level, dead-end schooling proved influential in shaping very limited educational and occupational opportunities for many students. A case in point is what happened to Mexican American pupils in the 1920s and early 1930s in Los Angeles (LA) public schools (González, 1974a, 1974b, 1990).

Thus far, this brief historical analysis of the genetic pathology model of deficit thinking has covered the orthodoxy—that is, the established or conventional views of the time. It must be underscored, however, that the status quo did not prevail without contestation during the first 3 decades (particularly the 1920s) of the 20th century. Valencia (1997b) examines this heterodoxy and provides rich examples of this discord. Interestingly, there was no color line among scholars who challenged hereditarianism and who brought to light the methodological shortcomings of race psychologists who did not consider cultural, linguistic, and environmental factors in the intellectual assessment of children and youths of color (Valencia, 1997b).

The arm of regenerated hereditarianism received a potent injection by a 1958 book, *The Testing of Negro Intelligence,* by Audrey M. Shuey—a former doctoral student of Garrett while he was a professor at Columbia University (Valencia, 2010, chapter 2). Her volume is an ambitious undertaking of the literature during 1913–1958. Shuey reviews 240 empirical studies in which examiners administered 60 different measures of intelligence involving 80,000 Black elementary, high school, and college students.[6] Regarding her major explanation for the observed mean differences in intellectual performance between Blacks and Whites, Shuey demonstrates silence throughout her lengthy review. Her conclusion does appear, however, in the *final* sentence on the *final* page. Atavistically, Shuey posits a genetic hypothesis reminiscent of 1920s hereditarian thought: "The remarkable consistency in test results … all point to the presence of *native* [italics added] differences between Negroes and whites as determined by intelligence tests" (p. 318). In light of the attention garnered by Shuey's 1958 book, hereditarianism was reawakened. I refer to this resurgence as "neohereditarianism" (Valencia, 2010, chapter 2). Also, I discern "three temporal waves" of neohereditarianism: Wave I (1958–1982), Wave II (1987–1997), and Wave III (2000–2008).[7]

2. *Culture of poverty model.* As an introduction to this variant of deficit thinking, I need to digress to my previous discussion of the swift decline of the genetic pathology model's dominance, a fall starting around 1930. Predictably so, with a paradigm based on pseudoscience and proselytized by influential researchers and scholars, children of color were losers from the beginning. However, with such an oppressive model serving as the status quo, it was just a matter of time before the genetic pathology model would collapse.

Foley (1997) discusses several factors that led to the downfall of 1920s hereditarianism. First, the eugenics movement—driven by hereditarian thought—became weakened due to the impact of the Great Depression. A number of middle- and upper-class people suffered economic devastation. This was not supposed to occur because eugenicists believed that *subnormal intelligence led to poverty.*[8] Second, the eugenics movement lost many of its followers because of the abominations being committed by Nazi Germany.[9] As Foley (1997) comments, the racial purification measures of Hitler were stimulated, in part, by the U.S. sterilization laws.[10] Therefore, given the ascendancy of Nazism in Germany, many U.S. advocates of eugenics avoided any alignment with racism—which characterized the genetic pathology. Third, drawing from (Valencia, 1997b), Foley (1997) notes that the writings of some anthropologists, particularly Franz Boas, assisted in the debunking of the genetic pathology model of deficit thinking via his position that nurture trumps nature in the explanation of human behavior, including intelligence. Fourth, a contributing factor that led to the disintegration of the genetic pathology model was the mounting corpus of research and writing that called into question the perceived immutable character of intelligence.[11]

In this section, I focus on the culture of poverty model. At its core, this notion is driven by deficit thinking, asserting that the poor are the makers of their own material disadvantagement and deprivation. That is, the poor create their own problems due to insular and deviant cultures, individual shortcomings, and familial dysfunction. Also, it is alleged that poor parents do not value education and fail to socialize their children to succeed academically. Given that SES and race/ethnicity covary, this last assertion has serious implications for students of color and their academic achievement.

Oscar Lewis (1914–1970), cultural anthropologist, coined the term "culture of poverty" in *Five Families: Mexican Case Studies in the Culture of Poverty* (1959). Although Lewis discusses his culture of poverty notion in his other books (e.g., Lewis, 1966a), the phrase became popularized via his *Scientific American* article (1966b), "The Culture of Poverty." Lewis (1966b) asserts that based on his research, 70 "traits" typify the culture of poverty, and the main ones may be framed in four dimensions of the poverty system: (a) the connection between the culture of poverty and the larger society; (b) the makeup of the slum community; (c) the makeup of the family; and (d) the values, attitudes, and character configuration of the individual. A number of culture of poverty traits are quite descriptive and factual of people living in poverty—for example, "lower life expectancy," "lower wages," "and "low level of education and literacy." Other traits (e.g., those dealing with values, character structure, and social/psychological characteristics), however, elicit a strong negative impression of poor people—for example, "wife beating," "personal unworthiness," "frequent use of violence in training children," and "high tolerance for psychological pathology of all sorts" (Leeds, 1971, pp. 239–241). Although Lewis derives the culture of poverty concept from his research in Mexico (the primary site), Cuba, and Puerto Rico (Puerto Ricans in both San Juan and New York City), he asserts that the notion has universal implications. Lewis (1961) claims, "It seems to be that the culture of poverty has some universal characteristics which transcend regional, rural-urban, and even national differences" (p. xxv).

To sum, the insular, autonomous, fatalistic, and dysfunctional nature of Lewis's culture of poverty notion evokes a powerful deficit thinking image of the poor—a depiction of poor people with self-imposed, intractable, transgenerational problems. Note the following:

> The culture of poverty, however, is not only an adaptation to a set of objective conditions of the larger society. *Once it comes into existence it tends to perpetuate itself from generation to generation because of its effect on the children* [italics added]. By the time slum children are age six or seven they have

> usually absorbed the basic values and attitudes of their subculture and are not psychologically geared to take full advantage of changing conditions or increased opportunities which may occur in their lifetime. (Lewis, 1966a, p. xiv)

Lewis formulates his culture of poverty model in such an unequivocal manner that it became effortless for other scholars to appropriate it as a truth claim (Foley, 1997). As the culture of poverty idea penetrated the vocabulary of 1960s scholars, Lewis's notion became redefined as "cultural deprivation" and "cultural disadvantagement" (Katz, 1989). The 1960s gushed with scholarly literature on the "culturally deprived" or "culturally disadvantaged" family, home, and child.[12] The targeted populations of 1960s deficit thinking are all too familiar: "The disadvantaged refer to Whites, Negroes, Puerto Ricans, Mexicans, and all others of the poverty group who basically share *a common design for living* [italics added]" (Marans & Lourie, 1967, p. 20). As well, scholars frequently identify the carrier of the deficit as inadequate parents who "seem to perpetuate their own conditions in their children through their child-rearing patterns . . . [and who] produce a disproportionate incidence of academic failures and of lower socioeconomic memberships among their full-grown offspring" (Marans & Lourie, p. 21). With an eye closer to the alleged home problem, it was not uncommon for deficit thinkers nearly 5 decades past to comment, "Very frequently the unique environment of a given *subculture* [italics added] may not provide the prerequisite learnings or general acculturation essential to school success or to optimal life development" (Edwards, 1967, p. 64).

An example of a contemporary individual who has resurrected the culture of poverty concept is Dr. Ruby K. Payne.[13] She proclaims herself "the leading U.S. expert on the *mindsets* [italics added] of poverty, middle class, and wealth" (Payne, 2005, front cover). Since 1996, she has provided training to hundreds of thousands of educators and other professionals—in 38 states, as well as areas in Canada, Ireland, England, and Australia—as to how poverty impacts "learning, work habits, [and] decision-making."[14] In her training workshops (which number over 200 per year, and for which she charges $295 per person), Payne "teaches rules and mindsets of economic classes" "to positively impact the education and lives of individuals of poverty throughout the world." Payne is the founder and CEO of aha! Process, Inc., a multimillion dollar corporation, and she has self-published several dozen books and videos. Her 1996 seminal work—*A Framework for Understanding Poverty* (revised four times)—has sold over 1 million copies, and is available in Spanish (*Un Marco Para Entender la Pobreza*). Her book (hereafter referred to as *Framework*) is a particular focus here because of the numerous instances in which Payne voices deficit thinking.

Payne notes that among a number of other authors, she draws heavily from the work of Oscar Lewis, particularly his concept of the culture of poverty. For example, in her "Research Notes" section of *Framework*, Payne (2005, p. 147) provides a lengthy quote from Lewis (1971) that describes a litany of culture of poverty traits (e.g., wife beating, machismo, violent behavior, alcoholism, precocious sex, present-time orientation, fatalism). As well, Payne (p. 140) quotes Lewis in regard to his assertion that the culture of poverty contains some universal characteristics.

One of Payne's (2005) premises in *Framework* is "hidden rules," which she asserts are class-bound. These rules originate as follows and serve as survival mechanisms:

> Economic realities create "hidden rules," unspoken cueing mechanisms that reflect agreed-upon *tacit* understandings, which the group uses to negotiate reality. These "hidden rules" come out of cause-and-effect situations. Hidden rules reflect the behaviors and *mindsets* [italics added] that are needed to survive in that economic reality.[15]

In her chapter, "Hidden Rules among Classes," Payne introduces matters by presenting three "quizzes" for the reader, titled "Could You Survive in Poverty?," "Could You Survive in Middle Class?," and "Could You Survive in Wealth?" Examples of an item from each "quiz" are as follows:

> "I know which grocery stores' garbage bins can be accessed for thrown-away food." (poverty)
> "I know which stores are most likely to carry the clothing brands my family wears." (middle class)
> "I have several favorite restaurants in different countries of the world." (wealth) (pp. 38–40)

Payne (2005) then proceeds to ask, "What, then, are the hidden rules?" (p. 41). She responds by providing a 3 × 5 matrix, consisting of 15 categories (e.g., "possessions," "food," "education," "destiny") in which these hidden rules, she claims, describe the behavior of three classes (i.e., poverty, middle class, wealth). It is here that Payne, in her centerpiece of *Framework*, engages in stereotyping of epic proportions. An example is the category of "education." Payne asserts that the hidden rule among people of poverty is: Education is "valued and revered as abstract but not as *reality* [italics added]" (p. 42). By contrast, the hidden rules for middle-class and wealthy people are that education is "crucial for climbing [the] success ladder and making money" and is "[a] necessary tradition for making and maintaining connections," respectively (pp. 42–43). The assertion that low-SES people, particularly of color, do not value, or devalue, education is a long-standing myth,[16] which I discuss in chapter 8.

In *Framework,* Payne (2005) also engages in a discussion maintaining that poor children: (a) lack access to the "formal register" of language (which is frequently used in the classroom), (b) are very disorganized, (c) disrespect teachers, (d) come to school without the "cognitive strategies" necessary to succeed academically, and (e) cheat and steal. Her assertions are empirically baseless, and she is very selective in drawing from certain literature to make her points (Valencia, 2010, chapter 3).

Given Payne's (2005) pathologization and demonization of the poor, it is not surprising that a number of scholars have felt compelled to critique her work. In Valencia (2010, chapter 3), I conducted a content analysis of 13 publications in which authors proffer critical appraisals that largely center on Payne's *Framework*.[17] I identified five themes of criticisms that emerge across this corpus of literature. That is, she: (a) employs a culture of poverty perspective, (b) engages in stereotyping, (c) has a nonscientific research base, (d) applies deficit thinking, and (e) ponders no consideration of alternative explanations. I found that across the 13 independent studies there was a striking consensus among the authors. For example, 77% of the critiques note that Payne frames her discussion of the poor in the context of the culture of poverty. Also 100% of the critiques find her *Framework* to be guided by deficit thinking.

In conclusion, the culture of poverty variant of deficit thinking is a perspective that has no scientific support. Yet, given that the poor are such easy targets of deficit thinkers, the culture of poverty notion needs to be reckoned with and challenged as an explanation for the typically poor academic achievement of many low-SES students of color.

3. *"At-risk" model.* In every epoch over the past four centuries, specific populations of children have been determined to be "at-risk" for having problems.[18] These groups included children, for example, who had severe diseases, physical handicaps, mental retardation, and emotional disturbances. Such groups also included children deemed delinquent, antisocial, indigent, neglected, illegitimate, abused, and destitute (Laosa, 1984).[19] Such children identified as at-risk (then and now) "thus become a major focus of social concern and public responsibility" (Laosa, p. 1).

The modern usage of the term "risk" was given impetus by the release on April 26, 1983, of the powerful report *A Nation at Risk: The Imperative for Educational Reform* (National Commission on Excellence in Education, 1983). In *A Nation at Risk,* the commissioners note that if the U.S. is to maintain and improve its slight competitive edge in global markets, the nation must make a commitment to investing in and reforming its educational system—particularly for the type of learning that is a requirement for success in the "information age" the country is entering (p. 7). The report proposes five recommendations for reform: (a) a basic curriculum (e.g., English, mathematics, computer science); (b) high standards; (c) allocation of more time for learning; (d) higher-quality teachers; and (e) stronger leadership and more fiscal support. A common theme that runs through the proposals is an emphasis on quantity: More is better (Valencia, 2010, chapter 4).

One of the most interesting treatises on the excellence movement, and one that is particularly germane to the focus of the present section on deficit thinking and the at-risk notion, is proffered by Frank Margonis in his article "The Cooptation of 'At-Risk': Paradoxes of Policy Criticism" (1992). Margonis explains that the term "at-risk" was first used by critics of the excellence movement.[20] These critics sought to move educators and policymakers away from "the belief that educational success and failure hinge primarily on individual effort" (p. 343), a view popularized by excellence reforms. Critics contended that school failure was largely systemically based. Margonis further argues that the term was co-opted by the proponents of the excellence movement that it was first used to challenge. He claims that the co-optation of the at-risk notion has done the reverse of what critics of the excellence movement intended. That is, critics sought to use the term "at-risk" to demonstrate the short-sightedness of the movement, arguing that standardization in curricula (tracking) and testing—coupled with large workloads of teachers—created insensitive and impersonal school environments and thus placed students in jeopardy for school failure. Nevertheless, excellence proponents won the semantic war over the terminology. As Margonis notes, "The educational goals embodied in the ideas of excellence became the standard, and students who could not reach these goals came to be at risk" (p. 344). Margonis further notes that the appropriation of the at-risk notion constitutes deficit thinking. He states (p. 344),

> The transformation of the concept *at risk* into a deficit notion has been accomplished as policymakers have conveniently neglected the account of institutional injustice that previously accompanied the term. *What was an alternative to deficit thought—a way of blaming institutions rather than victims—has become a new and potentially more resilient version of deficit thinking* [italics added].

Although the term "at-risk student" sporadically appears in the literature—hitting lows, peaks, and plateaus in frequency[21]—the notion is widely known. In my analysis, the literature tends to view the at-risk concept from one of two vantage points. First, there is a student-centered perspective via an inventory of factors believed to predispose some students for school failure (e.g., having experienced grade retention or failing a course; as examples, see Baker & Sansone, 1990; Frymier & Gansneder, 1989; Solberg, Carlstrom, Howard, & Jones, 2007). I assert that this student-centered perspective is a form of deficit thinking, as it overlooks any strengths and promise of the students labeled, while drawing attention to the presumed personal and familial shortcomings of the individual (Valencia, 2010, chapter 4).

The other perspective of the at-risk notion is proffered by authors who frame their discussion around a systemic or structural analysis. A penetrating example of this view is Beth B. Swadener and Sally Lubeck's (1995a) edited book, *Children and Families "at Promise": Deconstructing the Discourse of Risk.*[22] Swadener and Lubeck (1995b) note that the at-risk concept is based on a deficit model, frequently taking the embodiment of blaming the victim, in which the systemic societal practices of exclusion and oppression are ignored. That is, the use of the "at-risk" label is very troublesome because it is a classist, racist, ableist, and sexist term—a 1990s rendering of the 1960s cultural and familial deficit framework that locates alleged pathologies in the individual, family, and community, rather than focusing on institutional arrangements (e.g., White privilege, political conservatism, class stratification) that generate and perpetuate inequality. As is the case of deficit thinking in general, the notion of at-risk fails to acknowledge the strengths, competencies, resiliencies, and promise of low-SES children and parents.[23] The contributors in Swadener and Lubeck's volume speak forcefully to this point of "at promise" regarding African American, Latino/a, Asian American, and American Indian children and their families.

In Valencia (2010, chapter 4), I argue that there needs to be a major paradigm shift about the at-risk notion via-à-vis students who are experiencing academic problems. I help advance the suggestion that rather than referring to "at-risk students" we need to focus on "at-risk schools"—that is, those educational institutions that are organized along lines that make it very difficult for many students of color to attain school success. In later chapters, I discuss a number of aspects regarding inequities in schools—for example: (a) school segregation and its adverse effects (covered in chapter 4), and (b) inequities in the distribution of teacher quality characteristics and student academic performance (covered in chapter 5).

In conclusion, deficit thinking as a competing theory to explain TAG is certainly a system of assertions of which to be aware. Based on our discussion thus far, there are six characteristics of deficit thinking (Valencia, 2010, chapter 1).[24]

1. *Victim blaming.* Deficit thinking is a person-centered explanation of school failure among individuals as linked to group membership (typically, the combination of racial minority status and economic disadvantagement). The endogenous nature of the deficit thinking framework roots students' poor schooling performance in their alleged cognitive and motivational deficits, and absolves institutional structures and inequitable schooling arrangements that exclude students from optimal learning. Finally, the model is largely based on imputation and little documentation.

2. *Oppression.* In light of the "victim-blamers/victims" nature of deficit thinking and the lopsided power arrangements between deficit thinkers and low-SES students of color, the model can oppress its victims. As such, the deficit thinking paradigm holds little hope for addressing the possibilities of school success for such students.

3. *Pseudoscience.* The deficit thinking model is a form of pseudoscience in which researchers approach their work with deeply embedded negative biases toward people of color, pursue such work in methodologically flawed ways, and communicate their findings in proselytizing manners.

4. *Temporal changes.* Depending on the historical period, alleged low-grade genes, inferior culture and class, or inadequate familial socialization transmit the supposed deficits.

5. *Educability.* Not only does the deficit thinking model contain descriptive, explanatory, and predictive elements, but it is also—at times—a prescriptive model based on educability perceptions of students of color.

6. *Heterodoxy.* Historically, the deficit thinking model has rested on orthodoxy—reflecting the dominant, conventional scholarly and ideological climates of the time. Through an evolving discourse, heterodoxy has come to play a major role in the scholarly and ideological spheres in which deficit thinking has been situated. CRT informs us that these counternarratives have been essential in debunking deficit thinking.

Cultural-Ecological Model

The late educational anthropologist John U. Ogbu (1939–2003) developed the cultural-ecological model (CEM).[25] Born—son of farmers—in Umudomi, Onicha, Onicha Government Area, Ebonyi State, Nigeria, Ogbu received his Ph.D. in anthropology from the University of California at Berkeley in 1971, and taught there until his death.[26] He is well known for his groundbreaking and controversial scholarship on the education of students of color. In her foreword to Ogbu's last book, *Minority Status, Oppositional Culture, and Schooling* (Ogbu, 2008d), Roslyn A. Mickelson, who took on the laborious task of bringing the volume to fruition after Ogbu's death, writes, "Virtually every serious scholarly monograph or article on the race gap and minority education published in the last 20 years has cited John" (2008, p. xvi).

In this section, I briefly cover: (a) Ogbu's conception of his CEM, (b) a number of scholars' criticisms of Ogbu's work, and (c) Ogbu's responses to his critics.

1. *CEM.* To best understand Ogbu's CEM in regard to the educational problems (i.e., school failure; see Valencia, 2011b, pp. 4–6) of certain groups of students of color, one needs to begin with his typology of "minorities": "autonomous," "immigrant," and "involuntary or castelike" (e.g., Ogbu, 1978, 1990, 1991, 2003; Ogbu & Simons, 1998).

Autonomous minorities are Mormons and Jews, for example, residing in the U.S. Such groups are mainly characterized as minorities in a numerical way. Although autonomous minorities may be victimized by prejudice and denigration, they are not, according to Ogbu, stratified in society. Furthermore, members of this group typically have a "cultural frame of reference which demonstrates and encourages academic success" (Ogbu, 1990, p. 46). Autonomous minorities in Ogbu's CEM serve as comparative groups, but not as subjects of his research.

Immigrant minorities consist of people who emigrated from their homeland to another country (e.g., U.S.) in search of improved economic prospects, higher-quality opportunities in general, and/or greater freedom in the political realm. Immigrant minorities undergo the typical experiences of assimilation and acculturation, and students have adjustment problems, but these children and youths generally do not experience protracted adaptation issues and school failure. Examples of immigrant minorities are the Chinese that Ogbu (1974) studied in Stockton, California, and the Punjabi that Gibson (1988) researched in Valleyside, California.[27]

Involuntary or castelike minorities[28] are persons who, at the onset, did not select to come to a particular country (e.g., U.S.) and become members. The more powerful incorporated such groups via slavery (e.g., African Americans; see Kolchin, 2003; Ogbu, 2008a), conquest (e.g., American Indians; see Jennings, 2010; Stannard, 1993), and colonization (e.g., Mexican Americans; see Acuña, 2007; Perea, 2003). These minority groups construe the barriers built against them (e.g., economic, political, educational, and social obstacles) as racially discriminatory, and often these people will engage in extended civil rights struggles against their oppressors (e.g., Valencia, 2008; Weisbrot, 1990). Ogbu notes that in the U.S. involuntary minorities perceive their subjugation in ways that influence "the ways that they respond to White Americans and to the societal institutions which Whites control" (Ogbu, 1990, p. 47). Finally, involuntary or castelike groups are the minorities that experience chronic school problems in adjustment and academic achievement. It is these students, particularly African Americans, that Ogbu studied over many years.

Ogbu's CEM maintains that there are two separate and major parts (Ogbu, 2003, 2008b; Ogbu & Simons, 1998). The first component, the "system," comprises three groups of factors:

> (a) the educational policies of local, state, and national educational agencies (e.g., segregation, school funding, and staffing). . . . ; (b) treatment of minority children within the school and classroom, including teacher expectations, the breadth and depth of curriculum, assessment tools and practices, and tracking; (c) the rewards that society gives or does not give to minorities for their educational accomplishments, such as employment and wages. (Ogbu, 2008b, pp. 11–12)

Ogbu (2008b) contends that these schools and societal factors are part of the history of discrimination against minorities, and that such forces shape involuntary minority students' academic performance. The oppressive schooling conditions Ogbu refers to in parts "a" and "b" are not new in the discourse of school failure of students of color. I, for example, have discussed a number of these conditions (e.g., segregation, curriculum differentiation) vis-à-vis Mexican American students for nearly 25 years (see Valencia, 1991, chapter 1; 2002, chapter 1; 2011b, chapter 1). Furthermore, I discuss most of these conditions in this volume (chapters 4–7).

Discrimination in school and society, Ogbu (2008b) asserts, is not adequate in itself to explain the school failure and success of involuntary minority students. As such, this is where part two—"community forces"—of his CEM comes into play. These forces are dominant forms (i.e., behavior, beliefs, and attitudes) about and toward education that exist in communities of involuntary minorities. In brief, Ogbu's CEM covers four components of these community forces (Ogbu, 2008b):

A. "Frame of reference": Here, Ogbu uses a comparative frame of reference of immigrant and involuntary minorities. Members of the former group compare their educational and occupational opportunities in the U.S. more favorably than in their home countries. By contrast, involuntary minorities use the White middle class as their point of reference, and they frequently deduce that they are in less-advantageous positions only because of their minority status.

B. "Instrumental beliefs about schooling": These include minorities' beliefs about (a) folk theory about advancing via education, (b) alternative means of moving forward and how education can help, and (c) the effect of education in developing one's role models.

C. "The relational domain": This component includes the following aspects affecting the education of minorities: (a) enduring conflicts—for example, group struggles to attain equal educational opportunities; (b) level of trust or mistrust in regard to education (e.g., schooling, teachers); (c) amount of pragmatic trust; and (d) belief regarding the function of schooling in the oppression of minorities.

D. "Expressive factors": This element includes what Ogbu (2008b, p. 13) refers to as (a) "collective identity" and (b) "cultural and language frames of reference." Ogbu (2008b) explains:

> This is where the issue of oppositional collective identity and oppositional culture arises. That is, for some minorities, usually non-immigrants [i.e., involuntary or castelike], their collective identity and cultural frame of reference may be oppositional to what the minorities perceive as White American collective identity and cultural frame of reference. (pp. 13–14)

It is the component "expressive factors," or, more precisely, "oppositional culture," that has attracted considerable attention from Ogbu's critics (which I discuss in the next section). It is important, however, first to unpack the construct of oppositional culture. In 1986, Signithia Fordham and John Ogbu published the article "Black Students' School Success: Coping with the 'Burden of "Acting White."'" In the authors' conceptual framework, they assert that over time Whites in the U.S. refused to accept that Blacks are intellectually capable of achievement. Furthermore, Blacks eventually internalized, via self-doubt, Whites' perceptions of their alleged cognitive limitations and started to view school success as the prerogative of Whites. This led Black students to dissuade their peers from following Whites in academic endeavors—that is, "acting White." Fordham and Ogbu note, "Because of the ambivalence, affective dissonance, and social pressure, many black students who are academically able do not put forth the necessary effort and perseverance in their schoolwork and, consequently, do poorly in school" (p. 177). Later, the oppositional culture construct—along with discrimination in school and society and instrumental factors in the Black community (e.g., perceptions and responses to the job ceiling)—is what Ogbu (2008b) coins the "Fordham-Ogbu Thesis" (pp. 14–16).

Evidence for the "acting White" notion is highlighted in Fordham and Ogbu (1986).[29] The setting for this 1-year ethnography is Capital High School (pseudonym), a 99% Black school located in a rather low-SES Black section of Washington, D.C. The participants were 33 11th-grade students. Fordham and Ogbu comment that Black students at the high school identified a number of attitudes and behaviors that characterize "acting White," which is not acceptable—for example, "speaking standard English," "working hard to get good grades," "listening to white music," "getting good grades," and "being on time" (p. 186). The authors discuss various ways in which "underachieving" and "high-achieving" students cope and adapt to the "burden of acting White"—all behaviors that can be considered counterproductive.

2. *Ogbu's critics.* To be sure, the groundbreaking and controversial work of John Ogbu has not gone unnoticed. In light of his 3-decade plus record of scholarly publications and theorizing on the school failure of certain student groups of color, he is considered by many of his peers as one of the nation's premier educational anthropologists (e.g., see Foley, 2005; Foster, 2008). Notwithstanding Ogbu's important scholarship on the academic disengagement of students of color (with a primary focus on African American students), a substantial corpus of publications exists that provides critiques of Ogbu's CEM. In this section, I present a brief overview of this criticism. Based on my review of a fairly large, but not exhaustive, body of work, I have placed these publications in six categories of criticism that make most sense to me (see Table 2.1). All of the categories are not mutually exclusive (e.g., sampling problems, ignores student heterogeneity). Given space limitations, I briefly discuss, in ascending order of frequency, representative publications of each of the six categories of criticism.

A. *Ahistorical.* In this category of critique, several authors (e.g., Foster, 2005; Perry, 2003) listed in Table 2.1 assert that the history of the African American community Ogbu incorporates in his CEM is somewhat selective and at times is simply inaccurate. For example, Perry maintains that had Ogbu known of the rich and long-standing history and courageous struggle for educational opportunity and equality of African Americans, he would not have based, in part, his CEM on an anti-achievement ideology.[30] In making her case, Perry draws upon the works of historians (Anderson, 1988; Weinberg, 1977) and other writers (Angelou, 1969; Malcolm X, 1975) to demonstrate this powerful and uplifting history of African American history vis-à-vis education. In summing this up, Perry states that the "effort optimism" and epistemological views of education among African Americans are sustained in the historical tenet of "freedom for literacy and literacy for freedom" (p. 77).

TABLE 2.1 Categorical Analysis of Ogbu's Critics

Category of Criticism	*Publication*
Ahistorical	Cousins (2008); Foster (2005, 2008); Perry (2003); Spencer & Harpalani (2008)
Sampling Problems	Ainsworth-Darnell & Downey (1998); Bobbit-Zehner (2004); Downey (2008); Downey & Ainsworth-Darnell (2002)
Deterministic	Erickson (1987); Foster (2004, 2005); Gibson (2005); O'Connor (1997); Spencer et al. (2001); Trueba (1988)
Deficit Thinking	Flores-González (2005); Foley (1991, 2004, 2005); Foster (2005, 2008); Gould (1999); Hamann (2004); Lundy (2003); Spencer et al. (2001); Spencer & Harpalani (2008)
Ignores Student Heterogeneity	Ainsworth-Darnell & Downey (1998); Akom (2003); Conchas (2001); Datnow & Cooper (1996); Downey, (2008); Flores-González (1999, 2005); Ford et al. (2008); Foster (2004, 2005); Horvat & Lewis (2003); Hubbard (2005); Spencer & Harpalani (2008); Trueba (1988); Tyson (2002); Valenzuela (2008)
Counterevidence of Oppositional Culture	Ainsworth-Darnell & Downey (1998); Akom (2003); Bergin & Cooks (2002); Conchas (2001); Cook & Ludwig (1997, 2008); Cousins (2008); Datnow & Cooper (1996); Deyhle (2008); Downey (2008); Downey & Ainsworth-Darnell (2002); Ferguson (2001); Flores-González (1999, 2005); Foley (1991); Ford & Harris (1996); Hemmings (1996); Horvat & Lewis (2003); Hubbard (2005); Lundy (2003); Mehan et al. (1994); O'Connor (1997, 1999); Spencer & Harpalani (2008); Spencer et al. (2001); Tyson (2002); Tyson et al. (2005)

B. *Sampling problems.* Table 2.1 lists several studies that maintain the methodology Ogbu employs in his CEM has serious sampling problems. For example, Downey (2008) argues that a major limitation of Ogbu's work is that he *describes* the educational values of African American students, when a more appropriate sampling technique would have been to *compare* such values of both African American and similarly placed White students. As such, the results of this method could possibly address the question of whether African American students hold greater anti-academic achievement sentiment compared to their White peers. Downey frames this issue around Coleman's (1961) book, *The Adolescent Society,* which reports that students of all ethnic groups tend to demonstrate a lack of interest in school.

Another criticism raised against Ogbu regarding his sampling of participants is that he fails to examine SES as a factor in his CEM[31] (Bobbit-Zeher, 2004; Downey, 2008). To address this, in one of his latest studies, *Black Students in an Affluent Suburb: A Study of Academic Disengagement,* Ogbu (2003) sought to study

"White and Black social classes [that] are not too dissimilar" (p. 36). Yet, Bobbitt-Zeher, in a review of his 2003 book, notes that the SES of the Black and White families in the study were far from being close on material conditions. For example, based on 2000 U.S. Census data, the median home value for White families in Shaker Heights, Ohio (the site of Ogbu's study), was $238,000, and the median home value for Blacks was $131,330.

C. *Deterministic.* A central concept in the field of anthropology of education is culture—a dynamic, learned, fluid, highly complex, and multidimensional notion (González, 2004; Gutiérrez, 2002). Yet, a number of authors (see Table 2.1) claim that Ogbu, in his CEM, uses culture in such a way that it is viewed as static and demarcated, and thus a deterministic factor of behavior.

D. *Deficit thinking.* As seen in Table 2.1, there are 11 publications in which the authors contend that Ogbu's CEM is characterized as being guided by deficit thinking, a major theoretical position that has been advanced as an explanation for the school failure of many students of color. How part of the CEM is viewed as a form of deficit thinking stems from Ogbu's assertion that oppressed involuntary minority students (e.g., African Americans) try to solve their status problems by developing a "new sense of self" by opposing the dominant group (i.e., White students; Ogbu, 2008a). Thus, the persistent academic failure of many African American students, for example, is brought about by alleged ineffective strategies, such as an anti-achievement ideology. In sum, this premise of the CEM smacks of deficit thinking because it views castelike students of color as being unmotivated to achieve, and thus they are dysfunctional in the schooling context (see, e.g., Foster, 2005; Lundy, 2003).

A prime example of the perspective that Ogbu's CEM is shaped by deficit thinking is presented in the essay by Gould (1999), who makes the point that Ogbu's deficit thinking implies that African American students suffer from poor motivation—not cognitive limitations (also, see Lundy, 2003). The failure of African American and Mexican American students, for example, to do well in school is because of a "low-effort syndrome" (e.g., not taking their schoolwork seriously; see Ogbu, 1974). As such, Gould claims that Ogbu slips into a type of cultural deprivation posturing that results in culture of poverty arguments and, in turn, characterizes African American students as having intractable, negative cultural orientations.

The deficit thinking perspective imbedded in Ogbu's CEM has been appropriated by some other scholars. For example, Thernstrom and Thernstrom (2003), in *No Excuses: Closing the Racial Gap in Learning,* who rely heavily on a cultural explanation for the school failure of many students of color, note in part, "The low expectations of their [Black students'] parents may also explain why they [Black teenagers] are willing to settle for low grades" (p. 147). Furthermore, such deficit thinking appropriations have even entered the print media. Reid, (2003) in a book review of *No Excuses* published in *Education Week*, also refers to Ogbu's (2003) book, *Black Students in an Affluent Suburb: A Study of Academic*

Disengagement. Reid writes, "John H. Ogbu found that black students avoided the behavior conducive to getting good grades" (p. 5).

Finally, it is noteworthy to point out that the putative anti-achievement ideology ascribed to castelike students of color by Ogbu has also entered the popular literature (e.g., McWhorter, 2000, 2005; Williams, 2006). For example, McWhorter (2000) in a reference to Ogbu's (2003) investigation of Shaker Heights, Ohio, comments that this is a "case study that shows *very clearly* [italics added] that black students' aversion to school is brought to school from the outside rather than learned from the inside" (p. 123). As I discuss earlier in this chapter, given the parsimonious nature of deficit thinking as an explanation of human behavior and the reductionism it leads to, it is quite easy for deficit thinkers to blame the student of color and his or her culture and family for school failure (see Valencia, 2010, chapter 1).

E. *Ignores student heterogeneity*. Well over a dozen publications fall into this category of critique of Ogbu's CEM (see Table 2.1). Ogbu was primarily interested in explaining school failure of many castelike students. Yet, some castelike youngsters have and do experience school success (e.g., Conchas, 2001; Horvat & Lewis, 2003; Hubbard, 2005). This lack of attention by Ogbu to the range of academic achievement of these students is a concern among a number of scholars (see Foster, 2004, 2005). More specifically, some critics assert that Ogbu, in his CEM, fails to look at factors that play roles in shaping academic achievement outcomes. These variables include, for example, the sociocultural context and opportunity structure of the school (e.g., Flores-González, 2005), SES background of students (e.g., Downey, 2008), gender (e.g., Hubbard, 2005), ethnic identity formation (e.g., Flores-González, 1999), generational status (e.g., Conchas), ethnic composition of the school (e.g., Datnow & Cooper, 1996), and religious affiliation (e.g., Akom, 2003).

F. *Counterevidence of oppositional culture*. This category contains, by far, the most critiques—numbering over two dozen publications (see Table 2.1).[32] As I discuss earlier in the overview of the CEM, Ogbu and his associates (e.g., Fordham & Ogbu, 1986) assert that African Americans, for example, over time internalize the White-initiated stereotype that they are not very bright. Subsequently, African American students develop an affective dissonance, believing that school success is the domain of *only* White students. The CEM posits that this self-doubt of African American students, along with societal and school discrimination directed toward them, eventually leads to "oppositional culture." A major manifestation of this oppositional stance is "acting White," in which low- and high-achieving African American students forsake their ethnic identity and take on a number of attitudes and behaviors deemed "White" (e.g., working industriously to earn good grades, being punctual; see Fordham & Ogbu). This oppositional culture, the CEM explains, is counterproductive and sets in motion among many African American students—who are unable or unwilling to wrestle with the "burden of acting White" (Fordham & Ogbu)—an anti-achievement ideology.

In light of the deficit thinking, pathological, self-degradation orientations, and anti-achievement ethos that the construct of oppositional culture imbues—and its significance in partially explaining African American school failure—it is not at all surprising that the notion has caught the attention of many scholars. The main question these researchers are asking is: Is there ample and valid evidence to support the construct of oppositional culture? As listed in Table 2.1, there are a number of investigations that conclude there is little evidence to support the existence of oppositional culture.

For example, Ainsworth-Darnell and Downey (1998) examined information from the initial follow-up of the National Education Longitudinal Study (NELS), in which the National Center for Education Statistics collected self-reported data on 17,000 high school sophomores in 1990. The NELS sample Ainsworth-Darnell and Downey investigated included the following racial/ethnic groups and their respective sizes: White students (13,942), African American students (2,197), and Asian American students (653). In their test of the oppositional culture notion of the CEM, which attempts to explain ethnic differences in academic achievement, the authors note the following findings that are especially pertinent to the present discussion: (a) compared to their White peers, African American students' responses to the NELS questionnaire showed they were significantly more likely to report that education is of great value to obtain a job later in their life, and to have greater optimism about procuring a job; (b) compared to their White counterparts, African American students were more likely to try hard in their classes; and (c) relative to White students, African American students were particularly popular when they were commensurately viewed as extremely good students.[33] Upon close examination of the NELS data, Ainsworth-Darnell and Downey conclude that the oppositional culture construct of the CEM fails in its predictions.[34]

Flores-González (1999) conducted a year-long ethnography in an inner-city Chicago secondary school, Hernandez High School (a pseudonym). This large school (2,600 students) had an enrollment of 55% Puerto Rican students; the balance of the student body was ethnically diverse. Her sample included 33 low-SES Puerto Rican students, consisting of 11 high achievers (as determined by being in good academic standing and having at least a "B" GPA) and 22 low achievers ("C" GPA or less). Based on intensive observations and in-depth life history interviews, Flores-González (1999) reports that the participants (both low and high achievers) did not imply that "being White" meant doing well academically. Also, students of neither achievement group associated achievement success with any ethnic group. Furthermore, the low achievers reported that subpar academic performance had nothing to do with a disinclination to acting White. Also, none of the high achievers perceived strong achievement as being "less Puerto Rican" or acting White. Finally, the high achievers failed to report that when they received good grades they were accused by their peers of being "less Puerto Rican" or acting White. Flores-González (1999) concludes that her findings run counter to what one would predict under the CEM for two major reasons. First, the Puerto Rican students in her study were quite proud of their ethnicity, as evidenced, for example, in use of the Spanish language, food eaten, and celebration of holidays. Second, the structure of the school allowed opportunities for student success, such as taking challenging courses and engaging in meaningful extracurricular activities.

3. *Ogbu's responses to his critics.* Given the volume of criticism leveled against Ogbu's CEM, it is not unexpected that he has countered his critics. Earlier in his writings, some of his replies were born of sheer frustration that some authors misinterpreted his scholarship. Ogbu's replies to his critics, as well as a fuller explication of his CEM, are comprehensively addressed in his last book, an edited volume (Ogbu, 2008d) that I referred to earlier in this chapter. Mickelson, who wrote the foreword to the book, comments that Ogbu's commitment to the book was motivated by his "expectation that the record would be set straight" (p. xvii). In this section, I draw from Ogbu's chapters in Ogbu (2008d) and provide capsule discussions of his major responses to his critics.[35]

A. *The CEM and acting White are not the same.* This appears to be Ogbu's most serious concern. He chastises those many critics who confuse his CEM and the acting White thesis (see Fordham & Ogbu, 1986, for an explication of this line of reasoning) by lumping the two and considering them as the same (Ogbu, 2008b). Specifically, Ogbu (2008b) comments that a pattern of confusion has arisen over the years. That is, a number of detractors have failed to differentiate among his CEM, the Fordham-Ogbu acting White thesis, and Fordham's own position (e.g., Fordham, 1996).

B. *The history of Blacks is complex and integral to the CEM.* Here, Ogbu focuses on those critics who state the history of Blacks he presents is ahistorical and inaccurate. Also, Ogbu (2008a) remarks that his critics disregard the historical and the community circumstances of Black students' behaviors and center near exclusively on what transpires between students and their schools. He clarifies matters by offering an overview of "oppositional collective identity" of Blacks. Ogbu (2008a) covers the periods of slavery, post-emancipation, post–civil rights, and the contemporary era. He notes, underscoring the intricacy of the Black experience, that a number of "culturally patterned strategies or coping responses" (Ogbu, 2008a, p. 46) were used by Blacks (e.g., assimilation, acculturation without assimilation, resistance or opposition). His principal argument is that throughout these eras, Blacks had to deal with the "burden of acting White" (Ogbu, 2008a). Detractors, he notes, fail to understand that the oppositional culture of the CEM—only one aspect of the framework—has to be understood within a dynamic and elaborate historical foundation of the Black experience in the U.S. (Ogbu, 2008a).

C. *Ethnographic research is the most appropriate methodology.* In the investigation by Ainsworth-Darnell and Downey (1998), which I previously discussed in the section on "Counterevidence of Oppositional Culture," the authors assert that the CEM's "key claims have not received *empirical* verification" [italics added] (p. 537). As such, it appears that this concern prompted Ainsworth-Darnell and Downey to assess the validity of the oppositional culture construct by using the NELS, a large national database. As I discussed earlier, based on this non-qualitative (i.e., survey) data, Ainsworth-Darnell and Downey fail to support the CEM's predictions—leading to their conclusion that Ogbu's work is not "scientific" (Ogbu, 2008f). Ogbu underscores that the methodology employed by Ainsworth-Darnell and Downey, and some other scholars who fault him, is in the long-standing tradition of logical positivism (Ogbu, 2008f). It is a paradigm that many of us outside anthropology are all too familiar with via our training, which includes the following sequence: the definition of a research problem, hypothesis formulation, design (e.g., sampling, instruments), data gathering, data analysis and reporting, confirmation or rejection of hypothesis, and discussion of theoretical implications and/or practical applications.[36] Ogbu (2008f) criticizes the survey work of scholars like Ainsworth-Darnell and Downey because this methodology (as well as rigid interview protocols) is unable to capture the nuances of students' behaviors and attitudes and the complex set of interconnecting factors of the CEM.

In the final analysis, what can we say about the efficacy of the CEM as a competing model to explain TAG? I share the perspective of some of my fellow scholars (e.g., Foley, 2004, 2005; Foster, 2004, 2005; Mickelson, 2008) who note that Ogbu's work, over a period of 30-plus years, has certainly changed the landscape of research and theorizing on the schooling experiences of castelike minorities (i.e., specific groups of students of color, particularly African Americans, Mexican Americans, and Puerto Ricans). Ogbu's research has forced us to examine TAG with a much more careful analysis by looking at the larger context of schooling—for example, societal discrimination; schooling (institutional) inequalities; and student attitudes and behaviors, especially how castelike minorities confront the arduous task of coping with a society and school system that favors White privilege. Furthermore, although there are dangers of overgeneralizations, his typology of minorities (i.e., autonomous, immigrant, and castelike; Ogbu, 1990, 2003) is, in my view, a valuable heuristic in studying the education of students of color. In my own work (as well as scholarship with colleagues) on Mexican American education (e.g., Valencia, 2005, 2008, 2011a; Menchaca & Valencia, 1990; San Miguel & Valencia, 1998), I find his concept of castelike minority particularly fruitful in understanding the plight of Chicana/Chicano students in light of the oppressive colonization of the Mexican American people. This maltreatment and injustice began with the Treaty of Guadalupe Hidalgo of 1848, which brought an end to the imperialistic Mexican American War (1846–1848). The treaty's signing and the U.S. annexation of the present Southwest marked the onset of decades of prejudice and discrimination against the Mexican American community, including its children and youths, who were forced to attend inferior, unequal schools (Valencia, 2008, chapter 1).

I also appreciate Ogbu's CEM in that he provides a systemic analysis of the education of castelike minorities (Ogbu, 2008b). Attention to local, state, and national realities, such as school segregation and curriculum and how they have negative consequences for students of color, is highly regarded in any model that attempts to explain TAG.

It should be clear by now, however, that Ogbu and his CEM are not without detractors, and there are many (see Table 2.1). Given my work over the years on the construct of deficit thinking (Valencia, 1997a, 2010), I have developed rather sensitive antennae discerning the presence of deficit thinking in scholarship, and in mundane discourse and events. I am in agreement with a number of scholars who find that Ogbu's work is shaped by deficit thinking, as articulated by Ogbu's belief that castelike students adopt an anti-achievement ideology (e.g., see critiques by Gould, 1999; Lundy, 2003; see Table 2.1). This is unfortunate, given that a number of scholars, including myself, have strongly debunked the myth that students of color and their parents (e.g., Mexican Americans) do not value education (e.g., Moreno & Valencia, 2011; Valencia, 2008; Valencia & Black, 2002; also, see chapter 8, this volume). It must be mentioned, however, that although Ogbu is not a conventional deficit thinker (i.e., defects are believed to be inherent), his preoccupation with putative dysfunctional behaviors and attitudes among Blacks made Ogbu "a prisoner of deficit thinking discourse" (Foley, 2005, p. 654). Another problem with the CEM is that Ogbu in his writing, which underscores the predominance of race, shows an exclusive avoidance of class stratification and analysis, either in the context of Marxist or Weberian camps (see Foley, 1991, 2004). In conclusion, notwithstanding some limitations, Ogbu's CEM is a provocative framework for understanding and explaining TAG, and his model has made a major contribution to the literature. Foster (2008) wraps up matters most appropriately: "[Ogbu's work] encourages a dynamic approach to ideas, where we see a seminal body of work not as the final answer to a question or set of questions, but rather as an important and lasting contribution to ongoing and vitally important discussions" (p. 590).

Communication Process Model

The earliest variant of this family of models to explain TAG stems from the intense debate of the late 1960s and early 1970s in which the language of children raised in poverty was viewed as "deficient" or "different."[37] Frederick Williams, editor of *Language and Poverty: Perspectives on a Theme* (1970), commented more than 4 decades ago, "The deficit-difference issue is one of the most fundamental questions challenging our society" (p. 1). Examples of individuals who posited that poor children's language (mainly children of color) was deficient include Blank (1970), Engelmann (1970), and Daniel (1967). For example, Blank, drawing from child development literature, maintains that poor children—compared to their middle-class peers—have not developed adequate language structures and thus possess restricted linguistic codes.[38] The intervention Blank develops for the "disadvantaged" child is a "language-based tutorial program" (pp. 73–76), predicated on the belief that because poor children have not experienced adequate language stimulation, they need concerted one-on-one tutoring, such as vocabulary development. The assertion of the alleged language deficiency of low-SES children is part of the larger camp of the 1960s deficit thinking paradigm in which it was claimed that these children suffered not only from linguistic deprivation but also from such limitations as inadequate familial socialization (e.g., Marans & Lourie, 1967) and accumulated environmental deficits (e.g., Deutsch & Brown, 1964), particularly cognitive shortcomings (see Pearl, 1997, for a comprehensive discussion).

By noticeable contrast, advocates of the language difference perspective are seen in the work of such sociolinguists as Baratz (1970), Baratz and Baratz (1970), Cazden (1970), Labov (1970), and Shuy (1970). A case in point is the work of Baratz (1970). She does not deny that many inner-city Black children fail in schools, but these students do so because schools are unable to teach them how to read, which sets in motion a vicious cycle of teachers' low expectations, unfavorable teacher-student interactions (e.g., failure to call upon a child), low self-esteem of the children, and continued school failure. In debunking the fallacy of linguistic deficiencies, Baratz maintains that the research of psychologists was sophisticated, but it was also quite naive regarding the conclusions made about poor children's language (e.g., the assertion that a system of language could not be fully developed).

As the communication process model evolved,[39] it began to underscore that linguistic differences, verbal and nonverbal communication styles, teacher-student conflict, and marked boundaries may affect students' academic achievement. Given that no single individual can be identified as the prime mover of this model, I believe that the best way to get a sense of this diverse literature is to discuss the work and thinking of some of the prominent scholars in this area, which I briefly do next.

1. *Frederick Erikson.* I begin with Erikson, as it appears that he coined the term "communication process" in an article intended to expand our understanding of various explanations of school failure among students of color, particularly of low-SES background (Erikson, 1987). The communication process model, he states, underscores the function of culturally acquired communication styles of students and teachers in creating conflict that helps to explain poor academic achievement among students of color. In his perspective of the communication process model, Erikson draws from sociolinguistics, as did his predecessors (e.g., Baratz, 1970; Labov, 1970). Erikson comments that teachers and students, mainly in the lower grades, have differences in perceptions of what is appropriate verbal and nonverbal behavior. In general, members of different speech networks have different assumptions about the intentions of various communications (e.g., irony; disinterest; sincerity). In the classroom, Erikson maintains, based on supporting evidence (e.g., Au & Mason, 1981; Erickson & Mohatt, 1982; Heath, 1983;

Michaels & Collins, 1984), that cultural differences sometimes exist between teachers and students in the ways they speak and listen. These dissimilarities in speech networks trigger routine and repeated classroom miscommunication. An example Erikson provides is the case of a child who is raised in a speech network in which direct eye contact is considered impolite. By comparison, if the teacher is socialized in a speech network in which direct eye contact is considered paying attention, miscommunication may ensue. As a result, the teacher, who may interpret this communicative event from a deficit thinking perspective, concludes that the child is unmotivated—rather than accurately perceiving the event as a cultural difference.

2. *Jacqueline Jordan Irvine.* Irvine's theorizing is also worthy of discussion because she lays out a basic rendition of a communication process model particular to African American students, which she labels "cultural synchronization" (hereafter referred to as CS). Irvine (1990) states that CS has its roots in the notion of Afrocentricity (see Asante, 1988; cited in Irvine) and African American life. She maintains that the confluence of children who are Afrocentric and schools that are Eurocentric often leads to conflict due to lack of sync between the two cultural entities. When CS is lacking, Irvine notes that teachers wrongly interpret, disparage, or ignore Black children's behavior—for example, spoken language, nonverbal cues, style (e.g., walking; dress), and cognitive styles (sometimes referred to as learning styles). By contrast, when CS is present, communication between teachers and African American students is intensified, and favorable teacher affect is seen. Via the self-fulfilling prophecy, teachers' expectations become positive, leading to effective teacher-student interactions, which result in increased student learning and academic achievement (Irvine).[40]

3. *Janice E. Hale.* Hale's (1986) theorizing is similar to what Irvine (1990) posits. Hale (1986), however, offers a more elaborated framework in which Afrocentricity plays a major role in shaping the child-rearing practices of parents (especially mothers) and the learning styles of Black youngsters. She asserts that Black children are raised in a distinct culture—one that is rooted in West Africa (Hale, 1986). In her model, Hale (1986) includes language (i.e., nonverbal communication, conversational style, and speech) as a prominent component. Based on studies from the 1970s (e.g., Lein, 1975; Newmeyer, 1970), Hale (1986) concludes that Black children have culturally shaped communicative styles that are important to consider in the schooling of these students. Lein, as a case in point, reports that young, Black migrant children's speech patterns are quite complex and situational-specific. Her findings note quite a few incompatibilities between cultures of the home and school. For example, in the home, Black children often participate in general conversations with adults and others, which is not in harmony with teacher-directed and -dominated speech events in the classroom. Lein urges that teachers need to be aware by carefully listening to Black children's speech across various classroom contexts to encourage the students' best skills.

In a later book (Hale, 2001), her major call is for schools to revise and strengthen traditional instruction for Black children, especially from low-SES background. The model Hale (2001) proffers—which goes beyond language—is what she coins "culturally appropriate pedagogy" (chapter 6). In short, the framework has three components: classroom instruction (the foundation), and two support systems of such instruction—cultural enrichment and an instructional accountability infrastructure.

4. *Lisa Delpit.* Her approach is different from, for example, Irvine (1990) and Hale (1986), in that it provides an analysis of power relationships between students and teachers. Delpit's (1995) communication process model—one that underscores cultural conflict in the classroom—draws from her experiences as a school teacher, graduate student, and a professor of teacher education (i.e., pre-professional teacher training). Delpit delves deeply into communication blocks between students of color and teachers (predominately White), focusing on what she refers to as "the culture of power" (p. 24). She proposes that five premises need to be considered in regard to an understanding of how teachers have power over students. To wit:

- Issues of power are enacted in the classroom.
- There are codes or rules for participating in power; that is, there is a "culture of power."
- The rules of the culture of power are a reflection of the rules of the culture of those who have power.
- If you are not already a participant in the culture of power, being told explicitly the rules of that culture makes acquiring power easier.
- Those with power are frequently least aware of—or least willing to acknowledge—its existence. Those with less power are often most aware of its existence. (pp. 24–26)

With these postulations in mind, Delpit (1995) contends that instructional methodology, centering on different perspectives concerning disagreements over "skill" versus "process" methods of teaching, can lead to an awareness of student detachment and miscommunication, and thus to a comprehension of what she refers to as the "silenced dialogue" (p. 24). Rather than a "skill" versus "process" instructional pedagogy, she asserts that the attested practice of accomplished teachers of all ethnicities generally incorporates an array of pedagogical orientations.

5. *Susan U. Philips.* Finally, I briefly cover an often cited and discussed study on communication process. Philips (1983) explores classroom and community communication of "Indian" (her word choice) children attending school on the Warm Springs Indian Reservation in Central Oregon.[41] In her approximately 2-year ethnography of communication, Philips primarily uses a participant observation method. For her data gathering, she observed two classrooms at the Warm Springs Reservation elementary school (first and sixth grades; 95%

Indian students), and two grade school classrooms (also first and sixth grades; 95% "Anglo" students)[42] in schools located in the close-by town of Madras. In regard to the community (reservation and Madras), Philips also employed a participant observation approach—for example, informal interviews, home visitations, attending events open to the public, and travel around the reservation.

Philips's (1983) major objective was to investigate whether cultural differences in the use of language were a significant factor in contributing to the generally poorer academic performance of the Indian children, compared to their Anglo counterparts. She asserts that the early communicative skills and behaviors of the children acquired on the reservation become incompatible with the classroom environment once the children begin school. Philips maintains that the verbal messages communicated in the classroom are organized around Anglo, middle-SES modes—creating a cultural discontinuity for the Indian children and thus thwarting their academic growth. Based on her observations of reservation speakers, she finds that adult Indians—compared to their Anglo peers—can be characterized as having, for example, these language behaviors: not speaking as loud, speaking at a slower rate, nodding and gazing less, being stiller when listening, having less control over turns when communicating with others, and having a more even distribution of turn-taking in communication with others. In regard to Philips's observations of the classrooms (first and sixth grades), she reports that the Indian children, relative to their Anglo counterparts, exhibit the following communicative behaviors: speaking less in teacher-controlled talk, responding less to their teachers, paying less attention, being disinclined to choose themselves as next speaker, and having tendencies to maintain interactions with a greater number of children.

In her analysis, Philips (1983) claims that the communicative practices of the Indian children learned in their early preschool years on the reservation carry on to the classroom, leading to a discontinuity and conflict that eventually result in the poor academic achievement among many of the children. She also states that many of the Indian children's language behavior leads the teacher to conclude that the children are inattentive (which some appear to be); thus they are deemed to be less interested in learning. This is a deficit thinking perspective. A more accurate assessment of matters is that inequality exists in the classroom because the teachers are unaware of the cultural differences in communicative practices between individuals on the reservation and in the schools. To correct this, Philips remarks that teacher training programs at universities must prepare, through concerted specialized training, those teachers who plan to teach in schools of high-enrollment students of color with ways to adapt their traditional modes of teaching to culturally different children. These "agents of change [must] be structurally linked with and responsive to the minority communities' goals for their children, and their knowledge of what their children need in order to grow and learn" (p. 135).

The communication process model has some theoretical import and empirical support in advancing our understanding of how to explain TAG. Given the frequency of communication in our daily lives and in the classroom, this is a field of study that certainly needs more research. It is estimated that about 70% of our time awake is spent engaging in some type of communication. Of that time, the greatest length is spent listening (42% to 57%), followed by talking (30%), reading (16%), and writing (9%) (Simonds & Cooper, 2011). Some data indicate that, in general, the vast majority of communication is sent nonverbally (about 65% to 93%).[43] In the classroom, students are expected to listen to a great extent, ranging from 53% to 90% of their total communication duration (Galvin, 1985; cited in Simonds & Cooper).

Notwithstanding the importance of the communication process model, the framework is not without limitations. First, this model can be perceived as somewhat insular when considered in view of the many aspects that create schooling inequalities for children of color, such as school segregation, teacher quality, and curriculum differentiation (discussed in part III, this volume). Often, the model fails to discuss factors such as these that clearly play a role in thwarting the academic success of students of color (e.g., Oakes, 2005; Valencia, 2008, chapter 1; Valencia, 2011b, chapter 2). To sum, some teachers when teaching culturally different students may engage in deficit thinking by believing that the children's inattentiveness is their own fault, rather than seeing that unaccommodated cultural differences are the basis for the children not paying attention, which leads to their incomprehensibility of the lessons and poor academic performance (as reported in Philips, 1983).

Systemic Inequality Model

Of the various models advanced to help explain TAG, the systemic inequality model (hereafter referred to as the SIM) is the most difficult to pin down as to its constitution and workings. Given that this theoretical framework is systemically based, what is meant by "system"? How is "inequality" conceptualized, and where does it manifest? What is "reproduction," and how does the educational system contribute to it? Given that some scholars who discuss this model underscore, in a somewhat deterministic manner, that the "correspondence principle" explains how students are channeled into a stratified workforce in society, is there room for student agency and resistance to the oppressive forces in schools that lead to such economic stratification? These and other questions surround the SIM. In light of these insightful queries and the inability to corral this model into a confined space, I prefer to think of the SIM as a family of theories. In this section, I discuss a number of characteristics of the SIM, based on my sense of the literature. By no means am I assuming that all scholars who write about and subscribe to the SIM cover all these features in their rendition of the theory. My discussion of the following six characteristics is meant to capture the configuration of the SIM in a broad, not exclusive, manner. I close by introducing my rendition of a SIM.

1. *System.* A useful starting point to understand the character of the SIM is to analyze what a "system" is. In light of the ubiquitousness of systems (e.g., solar system, family system, health care system), it is not surprising that scholars have spent considerable time conceptualizing the nature of a system. For example, Rozycki (1999) defines, in a colloquial way, a system as being a set of variables that are mutually dependent. In a more logical and more precise manner, Rozycki defines a system as having a set of variables, suggesting that each variable remains a function of each variable in the group. In a similar fashion, Harary and Batell (1981) note that common to all conceptions of a system is that the various components are interrelated and there exists some type of hierarchical structure among the units. For our purposes, a conception of a system discussed by Pearl (2002), noted for his writings on the SIM, is also quite helpful. "Systemic refers to established processes whereby values, traditions, hierarchies, styles, and attitudes are deeply embedded into the political, economic, and cultural structures of any society" (p. 336). He continues by stating that contemporary systems are strongly influenced by historical forces, and this history establishes—often via muted or masked forms—the ways by which certain groups of people (e.g., African Americans, Puerto Ricans) are incorporated or excluded from positions of control and dominance (also, see Brantlinger, 2003).

2. *Comprehensiveness.* As just discussed, the SIM is a systemically based paradigm. Thus, by design, the model covers an appreciable area in its analysis of understanding how and where inequality becomes embedded within and across interrelated systems—most importantly the economic system, the political system, and, of course, the educational system. Because schools are not neutral grounds (e.g., Anyon, 2011; Apple, 1979), and due to the inextricable connections between economic forces and what transpires in schools (e.g., Bowles & Gintis, 1976, 2011; Rothstein, 2004), SIM scholars assert that a comprehensive approach must be employed to fully understand TAG and the racialized and class-based nature of public education in the U.S.

3. *Reproduction.* Debate over how societies and cultures carry on and preserve themselves is long-standing, appearing to have roots 2 millennia ago in the writings of Aristotle (Barker, 1962). A major mechanism believed to assist in societal and cultural perpetuation has been, and continues to be, the educational system. The main question here is: Do schools serve as the "great equalizer," enthusiastically expressed by Horace Mann in 1848 (Cremin, 1957, p. 8)? Mann, considered the "father of public education" in the U.S., believed that education was a valuable means, especially for the poor, to gain upward mobility. As the "great equalizer," Mann proclaimed that schools are the "balance-wheel of the social machinery" (Cremin, p. 8). But do schools truly equalize opportunities between the poor and the economically advantaged? Or do schools reproduce and reinforce the existing economic inequalities in society (Collins, 2009)? Social reproduction theory, a key aspect of the SIM, answers the latter question with a resounding "yes." The analyses of the notion of reproduction, which has its origins in Marxist thought (Anyon,

2011; Collins, 2009), surfaced in the 1960s and held theoretical import until the 1990s (Collins, 2009). Currently, there are three perspectives of social reproduction, as discussed by Collins (2009): economic (e.g., Bowles & Gintis, 1976, 2002, 2011; Willis, 1977), cultural (e.g., Bourdieu & Passeron, 1977; Foley, 1990), and linguistic (e.g., Cazden, Hymes, & John, 1972; Collins, 1989; Phillips, 1983).

In regard to economic reproduction, the foundational scholarship in this area is credited to Bowles and Gintis (1976), who coauthored the influential *Schooling in Capitalist America: Educational Reform and the Contradictions of Economic Life.* The authors advanced the perspective that via the "correspondence principle," schools prepare some future workers to function compliantly in the workplace. Bowles and Gintis (1976) largely focus on the explicit curriculum that socializes students, via differential teacher-student interactions and rewards based on social class, in a structure that is remarkably similar to the arrangement of a stratified world of work. The authors (Bowles & Gintis, 1976, 2002, 2011) also demonstrate that parents' SES is transmitted to their children, and that this class-based intergenerational inequality is largely due to the socializing influences of schooling and familial economic advantages, and is explained only in part by the cognitive abilities the students acquire in schools. Later in chapter 7 (this volume), I explore how "implicit" or "official" curriculum (Oakes, 1985, 2005) contributes to the reproductive nature of schooling inequalities.

4. *Hegemony.* Hegemonic ideologies and practices are oppressive, which refers to the ruthless and unfair use of authority intended to keep a group of people in a dominated and subaltern position. With respect to economic reproduction, Italian revolutionary Antonio Gramsci originated the concept of hegemony in his description of the dominance of capitalism (Hoare & Nowell-Smith, 1971; cited in Anyon, 2011).[44] Later scholarship argued that capitalism was not the only form of hegemony. As such, sexism became a focal point of study (e.g., Weis, 1990, 2004; also, see Collins, 1992, 2009). Furthermore, some believe that racism is an important hegemony to include in any analysis of the SIM. Writers who draw from CRT in their analysis of the systemic inequality in education, as I do in this volume, are examples of scholars advancing the important role of racism in understanding racialized opportunities in education, White privilege, and the subordination of students of color (e.g., Ladson-Billings & Tate, 1995; Solórzano & Yosso, 2000; Valencia, 2008; Yosso, 2006). Notwithstanding the power of hegemonies of class, gender, and race, schools can be sites of resistance by students, teachers, and administrators—which I turn to next.

5. *Resistance.* This feature does not characterize all of the SIMs. As a case in point, it principally does not describe the highly deterministic theories (e.g., Bowles & Gintis, 1976). The notion of resistance has become a valuable heuristic in the discourse on critical pedagogy and cultural/social reproduction (e.g., Darder, 1991; De Jesús, 2005; Giroux, 1983b; Morrow & Torres, 1995). Giroux (1983b), for example, remarks that resistance has come to mean a type of intellectual discussion that shuns conventional views on why students, especially

low-SES youngsters of color, experience school failure (e.g., explanations fueled by deficit thinking, oppositional culture).[45] He continues, noting that resistance has do to with ethical and political umbrage, challenge to ideological dominance, dispute, struggle, and self-emancipation. Darder (1991) points out that schools are dynamic sites in which hegemonic practices must be constantly defended by those in power. When there are openings for contestation, however, oppressed students' counter-ideologies and counternarratives can break through the dominant shield, and via resistance insist on equality and liberation. In chapter 9 of this volume, I further discuss student resistance.

6. *Widespread reform.* Given that the SIM has "comprehensiveness" as a characteristic, it is logical that scholars who advance this paradigm to understand TAG advocate sweeping reform. Individuals who write about and advocate widespread systemic reform maintain that improving the schools is simply not enough (e.g., Anyon, 1997, 2005; Noguera, 2009; Ornstein, 2007; Rothstein, 2004). Although scholars such as these vary in the breadth and targets of their reform proposals, what they appear to have in common is that TAG is inextricably connected to the unrelenting and pervasive inequality deeply and systemically structured in nearly all spheres of U.S. society. CRT informs us that school reform is indeed essential to accomplish, but it needs to be done in tandem with other types of improvement—particularly the dramatic diminution of inequalities in income, housing, and health care. Contemporary school reform initiatives have paid little attention to the unmet (i.e., non-academic) needs, such as acceptable nutrition and dental care, of low-SES students of color (Noguera). In chapter 3 of this volume, I provide some discussion of these unfulfilled needs.

As are the other models I have discussed here, the SIM is not without its detractors. First, the model—especially earlier renditions (e.g., Bowles & Gintis, 1976)—has been criticized as being quite deterministic. For example, Collins (2009) comments that some critics have argued that schools are more than reproductive factories of class stratification (e.g., Apple, 1982; Giroux, 1983b). Schools are also sites of resistance by students—and in some cases, teachers (Marx, 2006) and administrators (McKenzie & Scheurich, 2004), who employ their agency to contest the oppressive nature of schooling and struggle for needed change. In sum, critics have found the determinism in the earlier SIMs unpalatable because the authors were far removed from the actual day-to-day life of what transpired in many classrooms and schools (i.e., agency and transformation). I return to this topic in chapter 9 of this volume. Second, some detractors comment that the SIM is highly descriptive and lacks prescription for meaningful, democratic school reform. Even some of the scholars who denounce schools as institutions of oppression and espouse "critical pedagogy" as an emancipatory curriculum have come under fire. Pearl (2002), for example, asserts that such scholars—who agree that schools are maintained and perpetuated around systemic inequality—are themselves far removed from the classroom they want to transform (e.g., McLaren, 1995, 1998). Such individuals, Pearl (2002) notes, are imprecise in their reform strategies and use language that is inaccessible and elitist. Furthermore, Morrow and Torres (1995) concur, noting that scholars who write about resistance discourse (e.g., Giroux, 1983a, 1983b) suffer from considerably high degrees of abstraction and sweeping generalizations. Pearl, a noted SIM scholar, advocates "democratic education" (Pearl, 2002; Pearl & Knight, 1999) as one means to transform schools. In chapter 9 of this volume, I discuss his work.

To close this section and chapter, I further discuss my version of a SIM, which I introduce in the book's preface. I coin my theoretical framework the *Three-M Systemic Model*. The "Three-M" aspect refers to macrolevel, mesolevel, and microlevel factors. I am not the first scholar to utilize this terminology. Two months before I submitted this volume's manuscript to my publisher, I discovered that Ochoa (2013) uses "a tripartite macro-meso-micro framework" (p. 11) in her book on TAG. Her focus on each of the aspects, however, differs from how I structure my model. As to the macrolevel, I confine my factors to what I call the "other" gaps—chasms between Whites and people of color in income, housing, and health. For her macrolevel, Ochoa has a wider focus, concentrating mainly on ideologies and the economic structure of the U.S. My mesolevel analysis covers four schooling conditions (e.g., segregation, teacher quality) that help shape TAG. Ochoa's mesolevel also covers some of these school policies and practices, but she also discusses differential power arrangements among White pupils and students of color and assimilationist policies of schools. At the microlevel, I confine my discussion to parental engagement and empowerment, as well as student agency and empowerment. For her microlevel, Ochoa largely focuses on differential teacher attitudes and behaviors toward students. In sum, although Ochoa and I use the same terminology (i.e., macro, meso, and micro) in describing our conceptual frameworks, we have, for the most part, different emphases in these dimensions of analysis.

In my Three-M Systemic Model, TAG is not confined to the most examined indicator of the academic chasm between White students and their peers of color—achievement test performance. Among TAG measures, I also incorporate the seven indicators I cover in chapter 1 of this volume (e.g., grade retention, school holding power, matriculation to college, gifted and talented placement). Table 2.2 illustrates the Three-M Systemic Model.

TABLE 2.2 Three-M Systemic Model

Level	*Factor*
I. Macrolevel	• The "Other" Gaps: Income, Housing, and Health
II. Mesolevel	• School Segregation, Desegregation, and Integration • Teacher Quality • Language Suppression and Cultural Exclusion • Curriculum Differentiation
II. Microlevel	• Parental Engagement and Empowerment • Student Agency and Empowerment

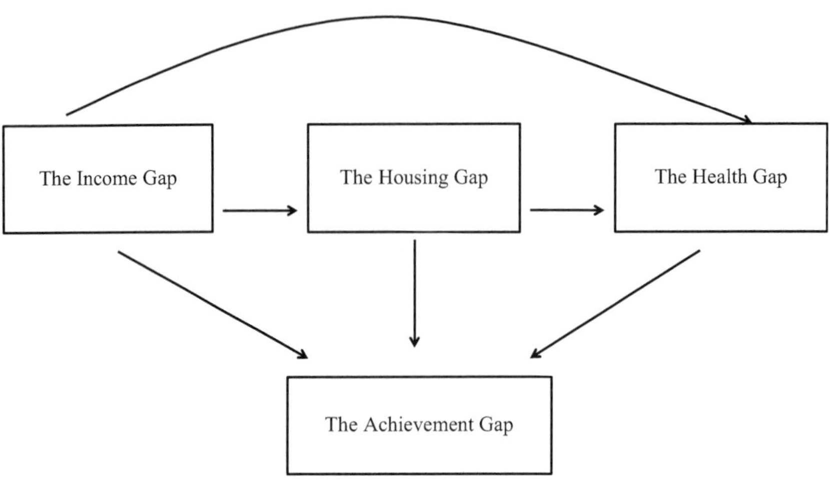

FIGURE 2.1 Level I (Macrolevel Factors) of the Three-M Systemic Model: Interrelations among the "Other" Gaps—Income, Housing, and Health

Level I, macrolevel factors, consists of what I refer to as the "other gaps." These are racialized gulfs between middle- and upper-class Whites and low-SES people of color as evidenced in income, housing, and health (discussed in greater detail in chapter 3, this volume). Figure 2.1 shows a graphic presentation of the interrelation of the "other gaps" and how they impinge on TAG. These interconnections of the macrolevel factors are explicated in chapter 3.

Level II of the Three-M Systemic Model is shown in Table 2.2. These mesolevel factors comprise four schooling conditions that help shape deleterious academic outcomes (i.e., the various TAG indicators, such as achievement test performance and school holding power) for students of color (see Valencia, 2011b, chapter 1). Each of the mesolevel factors listed in Table 2.2 is discussed in detail in chapters to follow. For example, the condition of school segregation, desegregation, and integration is covered in chapter 4, teacher quality is discussed in chapter 5, and so forth.

Level III, the microlevel factors of the model, is composed of two facets: parental engagement and empowerment and student agency and empowerment. Each of these factors is treated in separate chapters (8 and 9, respectively).

A final note on the Three-M Systemic Model: The framework, in addition to having an *explanatory* feature (e.g., how poor teacher quality contributes to TAG), has also been designed to have a *prescriptive* function. At the end of each of the macro-, meso-, and microlevel chapters, I have a section on "Toward Systemic Transformations." In these concluding parts of chapters 3 through 9, I employ what I call an *inversion strategy* for systemic school reform. For example, in chapter 7, I first discuss how curriculum differentiation (CD), via the sorting of unequal educational opportunities for low-SES students of color, helps, in part, to explain TAG. At the chapter's end, I discuss how we can invert CD, by detracking strategies, to help promote equal educational opportunities and diminish TAG.

Conclusion

To be sure, scholars have not been reticent in proffering a number of competing models to assist in explaining why a substantial number of low-SES students of color, compared to their economically advantaged White counterparts, experience school failure. While each of these explanatory frameworks has specific strengths and weaknesses, the deficit thinking model is clearly the least instructive in helping us understand TAG. This theoretical sphere has had the longest currency of the models because of its simplicity. Fueled by the law of parsimony, the apocryphal deficit thinking theory blames the victim—while holding societal forces and the schooling process exculpatory in explaining TAG. Although the CEM and the communication process models, albeit with some weaknesses, are meritorious and have advanced our understanding of the school failure of many students of color, in my view the SIM holds the most promise in explaining and comprehending the forces shaping TAG, and as well as offering strong solutions for societal and school reform. In the remainder of this book, my charge is to explicate these forces and reform suggestions.

Notes

1. Previously in this volume, I note that TAG refers to the achievement problem of *low-SES* students of color. In the remainder of the book, "low-SES" is implied when I refer to students of color, or when other authors refer to "minority" students.
2. This section on deficit thinking draws from, with revisions, Valencia (1997b, pp. 2, 63, and 71); Valencia (2010, pp. 6, 18, 37–38, 78–79, 101, 105, 110–111, and 114); Valencia and Suzuki (2001, pp. 14 and 17).
3. See Gould (1978) for a debunking of Morton's research design and findings regarding cranial capacity.
4. Menchaca (1997) draws on Forgacs (1988).
5. Garth (1925), as well as a number of other race psychologists of this period, used "race" in a biological sense. Also, Garth confused "race" with national origin and national identity. Furthermore, many later scholars assert there is no scientific evidence to conclude that objectively measureable races exist (Graves, 2002). Also see, for example, Cavalli-Sforza, Menozzi, and Piazza (1994), Nei and Livshits (1989), and Templeton (2002).
6. See Valencia (2010, pp. 33–37) for a discussion and critique of Shuey (1958).
7. See Valencia (2010, p. 34, Table 2.1) for a listing of the three waves and accompanying authors and their respective publications. See Valencia (2010, chapter 2) for critiques of these scholars. Also, see Valencia (2013) for the most recent example of a neohereditarian scholar.
8. See Blum (1978).

9. See Chase (1977).
10. See Kühl (1994).
11. See, for example, Hunt (1961) and Piaget (1929).
12. See, for example, Frost and Hawkes (1966) and Hellmuth (1967). For a critique of the 1960s literature on the "culturally deprived" child, family, and home environment, see Pearl (1997).
13. This is an abridged version of a discussion and critique of Payne's work. See Valencia (2010, chapter 3) for a comprehensive coverage.
14. I culled this biographical information of Ruby Payne from her website (www.ahaprocess.com/About_Us/Ruby_Payne.html), the back cover of Payne (2005), Dworin and Bomer (2008), Gorski (2008), and Kunjufu (2006).
15. See www.ahaprocess.com/School_Programs/Research_&_Development/Research _Base.html.
16. For discussions of this myth as well as evidence that low-SES parents of color value and do get involved in their children's education, see, for example, Jackson and Remillard (2005); Lott (2003); Moreno and Valencia (2011); Valencia and Black (2002). Also, see chapter 8, this volume.
17. See Valencia (2010, p. 92, Table 3.2) for a listing of the 13 publications.
18. Some scholars consistently place the term "at-risk" in quotation marks, indicating they question the validity of the construct (e.g., Fine, 1995; Swadener, 1995). I also raise serious concerns about the soundness of the at-risk notion, but to avoid repetitiveness I do not place the term in quotation marks.
19. For further discussion of the historical origins of the at-risk notion, see Cuban (1989); Horn (2003); Swadener (1990).
20. This discussion of Margonis (1992) draws from, with revisions, Ronda and Valencia (1994, p. 366).
21. A number of years ago, I conducted an ERIC search for the years 1983 to 2008, delimiting the search to "at-risk students" and "academic achievement" (Valencia, 2010, p. 111). The number of citations that appear after the release of *A Nation at Risk* (National Commission on Excellence in Education, 1983) is scant. The citation count peaks between 1990 and 1993 and plateaus from 1994 to 2008 (see Valencia, 2010, p. 111, Figure 4.1).
22. For other examples of the systemic analysis, see Sanders (2000) and Stringfield and Land (2002).
23. See, for example, Edin and Lien (1997); Piven and Cloward (1979); Willie (1976).
24. For an explication of these six characteristics, see Valencia (2010, pp. 7–18).
25. Ogbu coined the acronym "CEM" (see Ogbu, 2008d, p. xxiv).
26. Biography of John U. Ogbu, retrieved August 5, 2011, from: www.ogbu.coml.
27. Valleyside, a pseudonym, is an agricultural community in the Sacramento Valley—approximately 100 miles east of San Francisco (Gibson, 1988, pp. ix).
28. Ogbu's conception of caste builds on the earlier works of scholars, such as Berreman (1960) and De Vos and Wagatsuma (1972).
29. The ethnographic research presented in Fordham and Obgu (1986) is based on Fordham (1981).
30. A parallel case can be made for Mexican Americans, who are also included as a "caste-like" minority in Ogbu's CEM. Although there are allegations that Mexican Americans do not value education (see, e.g., Valencia & Black, 2002, for a discussion of this myth), there exists ample evidence that Mexican Americans have fought long and hard for educational equality (see, e.g., Valencia, 2008, for a legal history) and have socialized their children for academic competence (see, e.g., Moreno & Valencia, 2011).

31. The issue of omitting students' SES overlaps somewhat with the problem discussed earlier regarding the critique of "sampling problems."
32. There are, however, a handful of studies that support the oppositional culture of the CEM (e.g., Farkas, Lleras, & Maczuga, 2002; Irving & Hudley, 2008; Matute-Bianchi, 1986; Taylor, 2008).
33. For a critique of Ainsworth-Darnell and Downey (1998), see Farkas et al. (2002). See Downey and Ainsworth-Darnell (2002) for a response.
34. In an earlier investigation of the NELS data, Cook and Ludwig (1997) also report counterevidence of the oppositional culture notion of the CEM.
35. See Ogbu (2008a, 2008b, 2008c, 2008e, and 2008f). In addition to these publications, Ogbu—in his earlier writings—responded to or clarified some of the critic's concerns (see citations listed in Ogbu, 2008b, p. 4).
36. See Ogbu (2008f, p. 66, Figure 3.2) for a rendition of the linear sequence of social science research.
37. Parts of this section of the communication process model draw from, with revisions, Valencia (2010, 3–5).
38. For a contemporary discussion of what the authors refer to as "linguistic deficit theory," see MacSwan and Rolstad (2006).
39. For a reader who first wants an introduction to the nature of a communicative event, see Hymes (1974), who discusses the various components of such an occurrence (e.g., participants; modes of communication; shared codes; attitudes and contents; pp. 9–10).
40. For the work of other scholars who have contributed to this theoretical framework, see, for example, Boykin (1986); Hale (1986); Pasteur and Toldson (1982); Shade (1982)—all cited in Irvine (1990).
41. Warm Springs Reservation is the home of nearly 4,000 members of the Warm Springs, Paitue, and Wasco Confederated Tribes; most of the reservation members reside around or in the town of Warm Springs, located on the reservation. Information retrieved on June 13, 2012, from: www.warmsprings.com/warmsprings/Tribal_Community/.
42. Philips (1983) prefers to use "Anglo" (a "cultural" term she notes) instead of "White" (p. 16). She asserts that because her study is concerned with cultural differences, Anglo is more appropriate than White, which denotes race.
43. Information retrieved on June 15, 2012, from: www.hrepic.com/Teaching/GenEducation/nonverbcom/nonverbcom.htm.
44. For a short discussion of the role of hegemony in capitalism in several countries, see Greenberg (1980, pp. 398–405).
45. Regarding oppositional culture, see the earlier section on the CEM in this chapter.

References

Acuña, R. F. (2007). *Occupied America: A history of Chicanos* (6th ed.). New York: Longman.

Ainsworth-Darnell, J. W., & Downey, D. B. (1998). Assessing the oppositional culture explanation for racial/ethnic differences in school performance. *American Sociological Review, 63,* 536–553.

Akom, A. A. (2003). Reexamining resistance as oppositional behavior: The Nation of Islam and the creation of a black achievement ideology. *Sociology of Education, 76,* 305–325.

Anderson, J. (1988). *The education of Blacks in the South, 1860–1935.* Chapel Hill: University of North Carolina Press.

Angelou, M. (1969). *I know why the caged bird sings.* New York: Random House.

Anyon, J. (1997). *Ghetto schooling: A political economy of urban educational reform.* New York: Teachers College Press.

Anyon, J. (2005). *Radical possibilities: Public policy, urban education, and a new social movement.* New York: Routledge.

Anyon, J. (2011). *Marx and education.* New York: Routledge.

Apple, M. (1979). *Ideology and education.* New York: Routledge.

Apple, M. (1982). *Education and power.* Boston: Routledge & Kegan Paul.

Asante, M. K. (1988). *Afrocentricity.* Trenton, NJ: Africa World Press.

Au, K. H., & Mason, J. (1981). Social organizational factors in learning to read: The balance of rights hypothesis. *Reading Research Quarterly, 17,* 115–152.

Baker, J., & Sansone, J. (1990). Interventions with students at risk for dropping out of school: A high school responds. *Journal of Educational Research, 83,* 181–186.

Baratz, J. C. (1970). Teaching reading in an urban Negro school system. In F. Williams (Ed.), *Language and poverty: Perspectives on a theme* (pp. 11–24). Chicago: Markham.

Baratz, S. S., & Baratz, J. C. (1970). Early childhood intervention: The social science base of institutional racism. *Harvard Educational Review, 40,* 29–50.

Barker, E. (1962). *The politics of Aristotle.* (E. Barker, Trans.). New York: Oxford University Press.

Bergin, D. A., & Cooks, H. C. (2002). High school students of color talk about accusations of "acting white." *Urban Review, 34,* 113–134.

Berreman, G. D. (1960). Caste in India and the United States. *American Journal of Sociology, 66,* 120–127.

Blank, M. (1970). Some philosophical influences underlying preschool intervention for disadvantaged children. In F. Williams (Ed.), *Language and poverty: Perspectives on a theme* (pp. 62–80). Chicago: Markham.

Blum, J. (1978). *Pseudoscience and mental ability: The origins and fallacies of the IQ controversy.* New York: Monthly Review Press.

Bobbitt-Zeher, D. F. (2004). [Review of the book *Black students in an affluent suburb: A study of academic disengagement*]. *Contemporary Sociology, 33,* 414–416.

Bourdieu, P., & Passeron, J-C. (1977). *Reproduction in education, society and culture.* London: Sage.

Bowles, S., & Gintis, H. (1976). *Schooling in capitalist America: Educational reform and the contradictions of economic life.* New York: Basic Books.

Bowles, S., & Gintis, H. (2002). *Schooling in capitalist America revisited. Sociology of Education, 75,* 1–18.

Bowles, S., & Gintis, H. (2011). *Schooling in capitalist America: Educational reform and the contradictions of economic life* (Rev. ed.). Chicago: Haymarket Books.

Boykin, A. W. (1986). The triple quandary and the schooling of Afro-American children. In U. Neisser (Ed.), *The school achievement of minority children* (pp. 57–92). Hillsdale, NJ: Lawrence Erlbaum.

Brantlinger, E. (2003). *Dividing classes: How the middle class negotiates and rationalizes school advantage.* New York: RoutledgeFalmer.

Cavalli-Sforza, L. L., Menozzi, P., & Piazza, A. (1994). *The history and geography of human genes.* Princeton, NJ: Princeton University Press.

Cazden, C., Hymes, D., & John, V. (Eds.). (1972). *Functions of language in the classroom.* New York: Teachers College Press.

Cazden, C. B. (1970). The neglected situation in child language research and education. In F. Williams (Ed.), *Language and poverty: Perspectives on a theme* (pp. 81–101). Chicago: Markham.

Chase, A. (1977). *The legacy of Malthus.* New York: Knopf.

Coleman, J. S. (1961). *The adolescent society.* New York: Free Press.

Collins, J. (1989). Hegemonic practice: Literacy and standard language in public education. *Journal of Education, 171,* 9–35.

Collins, J. (1992). [Review of the book *Learning capitalist culture: Deep in the heart of Tejas*]. *Latin American Anthropology Review, 4,* 83–84.

Collins, J. (2009). Social reproduction in classrooms and schools. *Annual Review of Anthropology, 38,* 33–48.

Conchas, G. Q. (2001). Structuring failure and success: Understanding the variability in Latino school engagement. *Harvard Educational Review, 71,* 475–504.

Cook, P. J., & Ludwig, J. (1997). Weighing the "burden of 'acting white'": Are there race differences in attitudes toward education? *Journal of Policy Analysis and Management, 16,* 256–278.

Cook, P. J., & Ludwig, J. (2008). The burden of "acting White": Do Black adolescents disparage academic achievement? In J. U. Ogbu (Ed.), *Minority status, oppositional culture, and schooling* (pp. 276–297). New York: Routledge.

Cousins, L. (2008). Black students' identity and acting White and Black. In J. U. Ogbu (Ed.), *Minority status, oppositional culture, and schooling* (pp. 167–189). New York: Routledge.

Cremin, L. A. (1957). *The republic and the school: Horace Mann on the education of free man.* New York: Teachers College Press.

Cuban, L. (1989). The "at risk" label and the problem of urban school reform. *Phi Delta Kappan, 70,* 780–784, 800–801.

Daniel, W. G. (1967). Some essential ingredients in educational programs for the socially disadvantaged. In J. Hellmuth (Ed.), *Disadvantaged child* (Vol. 1, pp. 205–221). New York: Brunner/Mazel.

Darder, A. (1991). *Culture and power in the classroom: A critical foundation for bicultural education.* New York: Bergin & Garvey.

Datnow, A., & Cooper, R. (1996). Peer networks of African American students in independent schools: Affirming academic success and racial identity. *Journal of Negro Education, 65,* 56–72.

Deyhle, D. (2008). Navajo youth and Anglo racism: Cultural integrity and resistance. In J. U. Ogbu (Ed.), *Minority status, oppositional culture, and schooling* (pp. 433–480). New York: Routledge.

De Jesús, A. (2005). Theoretical perspectives on the underachievement of Latino/a students in United States schools: Toward a framework for culturally additive schooling. In P. Pedroza & M. Rivera (Eds.), *Latino education: An agenda for community action research* (pp. 343–371). Mahwah, NJ: Lawrence Erlbaum.

Delpit, L. (1995). *Other people's children: Cultural conflict in the classroom.* New York: New Press.

Deutsch, M., & Brown, B. (1964). Social influences in Negro-white intelligence differences. *Journal of Social Issues, 20,* 24–35.

De Vos, G., & Wagatsuma, H. (Eds.). (1972). *Japan's invisible race: Caste in culture and personality* (Rev. ed.). Berkeley: University of California Press.

Downey, D. B. (2008). A funny thing happened on the way to confirming oppositional culture theory. In J. U. Ogbu (Ed.), *Minority status, oppositional culture, and schooling* (pp. 298–311). New York: Routledge.

Downey, D. B., & Ainsworth-Darnell, J. W. (2002). The search for oppositional culture among black students. *American Sociological Review, 67,* 156–164.

Dworin, J. E., & Bomer, R. (2008). What we all (supposedly) know about the poor: A critical discourse analysis of Ruby Payne's "Framework." *English Education, 40,* 101–121.

Edin, K., & Lein, L. (1997). *Making ends meet: How single mothers survive welfare and low-wage work.* New York: Russell Sage Foundation.

Edwards, T. J. (1967). Pedagogical and psycho-social adjustment problems in cultural deprivation. In J. Hellmuth (Ed.), *Disadvantaged child* (Vol. 1, pp. 161–171). New York: Brunner/Mazel.

Engelmann, S. (1970). How to construct effective language programs for the poverty child. In F. Williams (Ed.), *Language and poverty: Perspectives on a theme* (pp. 102–122). Chicago: Markham.

Erickson, F. (1987). Transformation and school success: The politics and culture of educational achievement. *Anthropology and Education Quarterly, 18,* 335–356.

Erickson, F., & Mohatt, G. (1982). Cultural organization of participation structures in two classrooms of Indian students. In G. D. Spindler (Ed.), *Doing ethnography of schooling: Educational anthropology in action* (pp. 132–175). New York: Holt, Rinehart & Winston.

Ex parte Plessy, 11 So. 948 (La. 1892).

Farkas, G., Lleras, C., & Maczuga, S. (2002). Does oppositional culture exist in minority and poverty peer groups? *American Sociological Review, 67,* 148–155.

Ferguson, R. F. (2001). A diagnostic analysis of black-white GPA disparities in Shaker Heights, Ohio. In D. Ravitch (Ed.), *Brookings Papers on Educational Policy 2001* (pp. 347–414). Washington, DC: Brookings Institution.

Fine, M. (1995). The politics of who's "at risk." In B. B. Swadener & S. Lubeck (Eds.), *Children and families "at promise": Deconstructing the discourse of risk* (pp. 76–94). Albany: State University of New York Press.

Flores-González, N. (1999). Puerto Rican high achievers: An example of ethnic and academic identity compatibility. *Anthropology and Education Quarterly, 30,* 343–362.

Flores-González, N. (2005). Popularity versus respect: School structure, peer groups and Latino academic achievement. *International Journal of Qualitative Studies in Education, 18,* 625–642.

Foley, D. E. (1990). *Learning capitalist culture: Deep in the heart of Texas.* Philadelphia: University of Pennsylvania Press.

Foley, D. E. (1991). Reconsidering anthropological explanations of ethnic school failure. *Anthropology and Education Quarterly, 22,* 60–86.

Foley, D. E. (1997). Deficit thinking models based on culture: The anthropological protest. In R. R. Valencia (Ed.), *The evolution of deficit thinking: Educational thought and practice* (pp. 113–131). Stanford Series on Education and Public Policy. London: Falmer Press.

Foley, D. E. (2004). Ogbu's theory of academic disengagement: Its evolution and its critics. *Intercultural Education, 15,* 385–397.

Foley, D. E. (2005). Elusive prey: John Ogbu and the search for a grand theory of academic disengagement. *International Journal of Qualitative Studies in Education, 18,* 643–657.

Ford, D. Y., Grantham, T. C., & Whiting, G. W. (2008). Another look at the achievement gap: Learning from the experience of gifted Black students. *Urban Education, 43,* 216–239.

Ford, D. Y., & Harris, J. J., III (1996). Perceptions and attitudes of Black students toward school, achievement, and other educational variables. *Child Development, 67,* 1141–1152.

Fordham, S. (1981). *Black student school success as related to fictive kinship: A study in the Washington, D.C., public school system.* Unpublished doctoral dissertation, American University, Washington, DC.

Fordham, S. (1996). *Blacked out: Dilemmas of race, identity, and success at Capital High*. Chicago: University of Chicago Press.

Fordham, S., & Ogbu, J. U. (1986). Black students' school success: Coping with the "burden of 'acting white.'" *Urban Review, 18,* 176–206.

Forgacs, D. (Ed.). (1988). *An Antonio Gramsci reader: Selected writings, 1916–1935*. New York: Shocken Books.

Foster, K. M. (2004). Coming to terms: A discussion of John Ogbu's cultural-ecological theory of minority academic achievement. *Intercultural Education, 15,* 369–383.

Foster, K. M. (2005). Narratives of the social scientist: Understanding the work of John Ogbu. *International Journal of Qualitative Studies in Education, 18,* 565–580.

Foster, K. M. (2008). Forward-looking criticism: Critiques and enhancements for the next generation of the cultural-ecological model. In J. U. Ogbu (Ed.), *Minority status, oppositional culture, and schooling* (pp. 577–592). New York: Routledge.

Frost, J. F., & Hawkes, G. R. (Eds.). (1966). *The disadvantaged child: Issues and innovations*. New York: Houghton Mifflin.

Frymier, J., & Gansneder, B. (1989). The Phi Delta Kappa Study of Students at Risk. *Phi Delta Kappan, 71,* 142–146.

Galvin, K. (1985). *Listening by doing*. Lincolnwood, IL: National Textbook.

Garth, T. R. (1925). A review of race psychology. *Psychological Bulletin, 22,* 343–364.

Garth, T. R. (1930). A review of race psychology. *Psychological Bulletin, 27,* 329–356.

Gibson, M. A. (1988). *Accommodation without assimilation: Sikh immigrants in an American high school and community*. Ithaca, NY: Cornell University Press.

Gibson, M. A. (2005). Promoting academic engagement among minority youth: Implications from John Ogbu's Shaker Heights ethnography. *International Journal of Qualitative Studies in Education, 18,* 581–603.

Giroux, H. A. (1983a). Theories of reproduction and resistance in the new sociology of education: A critical analysis. *Harvard Educational Review, 53,* 257–293.

Giroux, H. A. (1983b). *Theory and resistance in education: A pedagogy for the opposition*. South Hadley, MA: Bergin & Hadley.

González, G. G. (1974a). Racism, education and the Mexican community in Los Angeles, 1920–1930. *Societas, 4,* 287–301.

González, G. G. (1974b). *The system of public education and its function within the Chicano communities, 1910–1930*. Unpublished doctoral dissertation, University of California, Los Angeles.

González, G. G. (1990). *Chicano education in the era of education*. Philadelphia: Balch Institute Press.

González, N. (2004). Disciplining the discipline: Anthropology and the pursuit of quality education. *Educational Researcher, 33,* 17–25.

Gorski, P. C. (2008). Peddling poverty for profit: Elements of oppression in Ruby Payne's *Framework*. *Equity & Excellence in Education, 41,* 130–148.

Gould, M. (1999). Race and theory: Culture, poverty, and adaptation to discrimination in Wilson and Ogbu. *Sociological Theory, 17,* 171–200.

Gould, S. J. (1978). Morton's ranking of races by cranial capacity. *Science, 200,* 503–509.

Graves, J. L., Jr. (2002). The misuse of life history theory: J. P. Rushton and the pseudoscience of racial hierarchy. In J. M. Fish (Ed.), *Race and intelligence: Separating science from myth* (pp. 57–94). Mahwah, NJ: Lawrence Earlbaum.

Greenberg, S. B. (1980). *Race and state in capitalist development: Comparative perspectives*. New Haven, CT: Yale University Press.

Gutiérrez, K. D. (2002). Studying cultural practices in urban learning communities. *Human Development, 45,* 312–321.

Hale, J. E. (1986). *Black children: Their roots, culture, and learning styles* (Rev. ed.). Baltimore: John Hopkins University Press.

Hale, J. E. (2001). *Learning while Black: Creating educational excellence for African American children.* Baltimore: Johns Hopkins University Press.

Hamann, E. T. (2004). Lessons from the interpretation/misinterpretation of John Ogbu's scholarship. *Intercultural Education, 15,* 399–412.

Harary, F., & Batell, M. F. (1981). What is a system? *Social Networks, 3,* 29–40.

Heath, S. B. (1983). *Ways with words: Language, life and work in communities and classrooms.* Cambridge, MA: Cambridge University Press.

Hellmuth, J. (Ed.). (1967). *Disadvantaged child* (Vol. 1). New York: Brunner/Mazel.

Hemmings, A. (1996). Conflicting images? Being black and a model high school student. *Anthropology and Education Quarterly, 27,* 20–50.

Hoare, Q., & Nowell-Smith, G. (1971). *Antonio Gramsci: Selections from the prison notebooks* (Q. Hoare & G. Nowell-Smith, Trans.). New York: International Publishers.

Horn C. (2003). High-stakes testing and students: Stopping or perpetuating a cycle of failure. *Theory into Practice, 42,* 30–41.

Horvat, E. M., & Lewis, K. S. (2003). Reassessing the "burden of 'acting white'": The importance of peer groups in managing academic success. *Sociology of Education, 76,* 265–280.

Hubbard, L. (2005). The role of gender in academic achievement. *International Journal of Qualitative Studies in Education, 18,* 605–623.

Hunt, J. McV. (1961). *Intelligence and experience.* New York: Ronald Press.

Hymes, D. (1974). *Foundations in sociolinguistics: An ethnographic approach.* Philadelphia: University of Pennsylvania Press.

Irons, P. (2002). *Jim Crow's children: The broken promise of the Brown decision.* New York: Penguin Books.

Irvine, J. J. (1990). *Black students and school failure: Policies, practices, and prescriptions.* Westport, CT: Praeger.

Irving, M. A., & Hudley, C. (2008). Oppositional identity and academic achievement among African American males. In J. U. Ogbu (Ed.), *Minority status, oppositional culture, and schooling* (pp. 374–394). New York: Routledge.

Jackson, J. P., Jr., & Weidman, N. M. (2004). *Race, racism, and science: Social impact and interaction.* New Brunswick, NJ: Rutgers University Press.

Jackson, K., & Remillard, J. (2005). Rethinking parental involvement: African mothers construct their roles in the mathematics education of their children. *School Community Journal, 15,* 51–73.

Jennings, F. (2010). *The invasion of America: Indians, colonialism, and the cant of conquest.* Chapel Hill: University of North Carolina Press.

Katz, M. B. (1989). *The undeserving poor: From the war on poverty to the war on welfare.* New York: Pantheon Books.

Kolchin, P. (2003). *American slavery: 1619–1877.* New York: Hill and Wang.

Kühl, S. (1994). *The Nazi connection: Eugenics, American racism, and German national socialism.* New York: Oxford University Press.

Kunjufu, J. (2006). *An African centered response to Ruby Payne's theory.* Chicago: African American Images.

Labov, W. (1970). The logic of nonstandard English. In F. Williams (Ed.), *Language and poverty: Perspectives on a theme* (pp. 153–189). Chicago: Markham.

Ladson-Billings, G., & Tate, W. F., IV (1995). Toward a critical race theory of education. *Teachers College Record, 97,* 47–68.

Laosa, L. M. (1984). Social policies toward children of diverse ethnic, racial, and language groups in the United States. In H. W. Stevenson & A. E. Siegel (Eds.), *Child development research and social policy* (Vol. 1, pp. 1–109). Chicago: University of Chicago Press.

Leeds, A. (1971). The concept of the "culture of poverty": Conceptual, logical, and empirical problems, with perspectives from Brazil and Peru. In E. B. Leacock (Ed.), *The culture of poverty: A critique* (pp. 226–284). New York: Simon and Schuster.

Lein, L. (1975). Black American migrant children: Their speech at home and school. *Council on Anthropology and Education Quarterly, 6,* 1–11.

Lewis, O. (1959). *Five families: Mexican case studies in the culture of poverty.* New York: Basic Books.

Lewis, O. (1961). *The children of Sánchez: Autobiography of a Mexican family.* New York: Random House.

Lewis, O. (1966a). *La Vida: A Puerto Rican family in the culture of poverty—San Juan and New York.* New York: Random House.

Lewis, O. (1966b). The culture of poverty. *Scientific American, 215,* 19–25.

Lewis, O. (1971). The culture of poverty. In E. Penchef (Ed.), *Four horsemen: Pollution, poverty, famine, violence* (pp. 135–141). San Francisco: Canfield Press.

Lott, B. (2003). Recognizing and welcoming the standpoint of low-income parents in the public schools. *Journal of Educational and Psychological Consultation, 14,* 91–104.

Lundy, G. F. (2003). The myths of oppositional culture. *Journal of Black Studies, 33,* 450–467.

MacSwan, J., & Rolstad, K. (2006). How language proficiency tests mislead us about ability: Implications for English language learner placement in special education. *Teachers College Record, 108,* 2304–2328.

Malcolm X. (1975). *The autobiography of Malcolm X.* New York: Random House.

Marans, A. E., & Lourie, R. (1967). Hypotheses regarding the effects of child-rearing patterns on the disadvantaged child. In J. Hellmuth (Ed.), *Disadvantaged child* (Vol. 1, pp. 17–41). New York: Brunner/Mazel.

Margonis, F. (1992). The cooptation of "at risk": Paradoxes of policy criticism. *Teachers College Record, 94,* 343–364.

Marx, S. (2006). *Revealing the invisible: Confronting passive racism in education.* New York: Routledge.

Matute-Bianchi, M. E. (1986). Ethnic identities and patterns of school success and failure among Mexican-descent and Japanese-American students in a California high school. *American Journal of Education, 95,* 233–255.

McKenzie, K. B., & Scheurich, J. J. (2004). Equity traps: A useful construct for preparing principals to lead schools that are successful with racially diverse students. *Educational Administration Quarterly, 40,* 601–632.

McLaren, P. (1995). *Critical pedagogy and predatory culture: Oppositional politics in a postmodern age.* New York: Routledge.

McLaren, P. (1998). *Life in schools: An introduction to critical pedagogy in the foundations of education.* White Plains, NY: Longman.

McWhorter, J. (2000). *Losing the race: Self-sabotage in black America.* New York: Harper Perennial.

McWhorter, J. (2005). *Winning the race: Beyond the crisis in black America.* New York: Gotham Books.

Mehan, H., Hubbard, L., & Villanueva, I. (1994). Forming academic identities: Accommodation without assimilation among involuntary minorities. *Anthropology and Education Quarterly, 25,* 91–117.

Menchaca, M. (1997). Early racist discourses: The roots of deficit thinking. In R. R. Valencia (Ed.), *The evolution of deficit thinking: Educational thought and practice* (pp. 13–40). Stanford Series on Education and Public Policy. London: Falmer Press.

Menchaca, M., & Valencia, R. R. (1990). Anglo-Saxon ideologies and their impact on the segregation of Mexican students in California, 1920s–1930s. *Anthropology and Education Quarterly, 21,* 222–249.

Michaels, S., & Collins, J. (1984). Oral discourse styles: Classroom interaction and the acquisition of literacy. In D. Tannen (Ed.), *Coherence in spoken and written discourse* (pp. 219–244). Norwood, NJ: Ablex.

Mickelson, R. A. (2008). Foreword. In J. U. Ogbu, (Ed.), *Minority status, oppositional culture, and schooling* (pp. xv–xxi). New York: Routledge.

Moreno, R. P., & Valencia, R. R. (2011). Chicano families and schools: Challenges for strengthening family-school relationships. In R. R. Valencia (Ed.), *Chicano school failure and success: Past, present, and future* (3rd ed., pp. 197–210). New York: Routledge.

Morrow, R. A., & Torres, C. A. (1995). *Social theory and education: A critique of theories of social and cultural reproduction.* Albany: State University of New York Press.

National Commission on Excellence in Education. (1983). *A nation at risk: The imperative for educational reform.* Washington, DC: U.S. Government Printing Office.

Nei, M., & Livshits, G. (1989). Genetic relationships of Europeans, Asians and Africans and the origins of modern Homo sapiens. *Human Heredity, 39,* 276–281.

Newmeyer, J. A. (1970). *Creativity and nonverbal communication in preadolescent White and Black children.* Unpublished doctoral dissertation, Harvard University, Cambridge, MA.

Noguera, P. A. (2009). The achievement gap: Public crisis in education. *New Labor Forum, 18,* 61–69.

Oakes, J. (1985). *Keeping track: How schools structure inequality.* New Haven, CT: Yale University Press.

Oakes, J. (2005). *Keeping track: How schools structure inequality* (2nd ed.). New Haven, CT: Yale University Press.

Ochoa, G. L. (2013). *Academic profiling: Latinos, Asian Americans, and the achievement gap.* Minneapolis: University of Minnesota Press.

O'Connor, C. (1997). Dispositions toward (collective) struggle and educational resilience in the inner city: A case analysis of six African-American high school students. *American Educational Research Journal, 34,* 593–629.

O'Connor, C. (1999). Race, class, and gender in America: Narratives of opportunity among low-income African Americans youths. *Sociology of Education, 72,*137–157.

Ogbu, J. U. (1974). *The next generation: An ethnography of education in an urban neighborhood.* New York: Academic Press.

Ogbu, J. U. (1978). *Minority education and caste: The American system in cross-cultural perspective.* New York: Academic Press.

Ogbu, J. U. (1990). Minority education in comparative perspective. *Journal of Negro Education, 59,* 45–57.

Ogbu, J. U. (1991). Immigrant and involuntary minorities in comparative perspective. In M. A. Gibson & J. U. Ogbu (Eds.), *Minority status and schooling: A comparative study of immigrant and involuntary minorities* (pp. 3–33). New York: Garland.

Ogbu, J. U. (2003). *Black students in an affluent suburb: A study of academic disengagement.* Mahwah, NJ: Lawrence Erlbaum.

Ogbu, J. U. (2008a). Collective identity and the burden of "acting White" in Black history, community, and education. In J. U. Ogbu (Ed.), *Minority status, oppositional culture, and schooling* (pp. 29–63). New York: Routledge.

Ogbu, J. U. (2008b). The history and status of a theoretical debate. In J. U. Ogbu (Ed.), *Minority status, oppositional culture, and schooling* (pp. 3–28). New York: Routledge.

Ogbu, J. U. (2008c). Language and collective identity among adults and students in a Black community. In J. U. Ogbu (Ed.), *Minority status, oppositional culture, and schooling* (pp. 112–129). New York: Routledge.

Ogbu, J. U. (Ed.). (2008d). *Minority status, oppositional culture, and schooling.* New York: Routledge.

Ogbu, J. U. (2008e). Multiple sources of peer pressures among African American students. In J. U. Ogbu (Ed.), *Minority status, oppositional culture, and schooling* (pp. 89–111). New York: Routledge.

Ogbu, J. U. (2008f). Ways of knowing: The ethnographic approach to the study of collective identity and schooling. In J. U. Ogbu (Ed.), *Minority status, oppositional culture, and schooling* (pp. 64–88). New York: Routledge.

Ogbu, J. U., & Simons, H. D. (1998). Voluntary and involuntary minorities: A cultural-ecological theory of school performance with some implications for education. *Anthropology and Education Quarterly, 29,* 155–188.

Ornstein, A. (2007). *Class counts: Education, inequality, and the shrinking middle class.* Lanham, MD: Rowman & Littlefield.

Pasteur, A. B., & Toldson, I. L. (1982). *The roots of soul: The psychology of black expressiveness.* New York: Anchor Press.

Payne, R. K. (2005). *A framework for understanding poverty* (4th rev. ed.). Highlands, TX: aha! Process.

Pearl, A. (1997). Cultural and accumulated environmental deficit models. In R. R. Valencia (Ed.), *The evolution of deficit thinking: Educational thought and practice* (pp. 132–159). Stanford Series on Education and Public Policy. London: Falmer Press.

Pearl, A. (2002). The big picture: Systemic and institutional factors in Chicano school failure and success. In R. R. Valencia (Ed.), *Chicano school failure and success: Past, present, and future* (2nd ed., pp. 335–364). London: RoutledgeFalmer.

Pearl, A., & Knight, T. (1999). *The democratic classroom: Theory to inform practice.* Cresskill, NJ: Hampton Press.

Perea, J. F. (2003). A brief history of race and the U.S.-Mexican border: Tracing the trajectories of conquest. *UCLA Law Review, 51,* 283–312.

Perry, T. (2003). Competing theories of group achievement. In T. Perry, C. Steele, & A. G. Hillard III, *Young, gifted, and Black: Promoting high achievement among African-American students* (pp. 52–86). Boston: Beacon Press.

Philips, S. U. (1983). *The invisible culture: Communication in classroom and community on the Warm Springs Indian Reservation.* New York: Longman.

Piaget, J. (1929). *The child's conception of the world* (J. Tomlinson & A. Tomlinson, Trans). New York: Harcourt, Brace, & World. (Original work published 1926).

Piven, F. F., & Cloward, R. (1979). *Poor people's movements: Why they succeed and how they fail.* New York: Vintage Books.

Plessy v. Ferguson, 163 U.S. 537 (1896).

Reid, K. (2003). Book cites role of culture in achievement. *Education Week,* October 29, p. 5.

Ronda, M. A., & Valencia, R. R. (1994). "At-risk" Chicano students: The institutional and communicative life of a category. *Hispanic Journal of Behavioral Sciences, 16,* 363–395.

Rothstein, R. (2004). *Class and schools: Using social, economic, and educational reform to close the black-white achievement gap.* Washington, DC: Economic Policy Institute.

Rozycki, E. G. (1999). What is a system? A "top-down" explanation following von Bertalanffy. Retrieved June 22, 2012, from: www.newfoundations.com/EGR/system.html.

Sanders, M. G. (Ed.). (2000). *Schooling students placed at risk: Research, policy, and practice in the education of poor and minority students.* Mahwah, NJ: Lawrence Erlbaum.

San Miguel, G., Jr., & Valencia, R. R. (1998). From the Treaty of Guadalupe Hidalgo to *Hopwood:* The educational plight and struggle of Mexican Americans in the Southwest. *Harvard Educational Review, 68,* 353–412.

Shade, B. J. (1982). Afro-American cognitive style: A variable in school success? *Review of Educational Research, 52,* 219–244.

Shuey, A. M. (1958). *The testing of Negro intelligence.* Lynchburg, VA: J. P. Bell.

Shuy, R. W. (1970). The sociolinguists and urban language problems. In F. Williams (Ed.), *Language and poverty: Perspectives on a theme* (pp. 335–350). Chicago: Markham.

Simonds, C. J., & Cooper, P. J. (2011). *Communication for the classroom teacher* (9th ed.). Boston: Allyn & Bacon.

Solberg, V.S.H., Carlstrom, A. H., Howard, K.A.S., & Jones, J. E. (2007). Classifying at-risk high school youth: The influence of community violence and protective factors on academic and health outcomes. *Career Development Quarterly, 55,* 313–327.

Solórzano, D. G., & Yosso, T. (2000). Toward a critical race theory of Chicana and Chicano education. In C. Tejada, C. Martínez, Z. Leonardo, & P. McLaren (Eds.). *Charting new terrains of Chicana(o)/Latina(o) education* (pp. 35–65). Cresskill, NJ: Hampton.

Spencer, M. B., & Harpalani, V. (2008). What does "acting White" actually mean? In J. U. Ogbu (Ed.), *Minority status, oppositional culture, and schooling* (pp. 222–239). New York: Routledge.

Spencer, M. B., Noll, E., Stolzfus, J., & Harpalani, V. (2001). Identity and school adjustment: Revisiting the "acting White" assumption. *Educational Psychologist, 36,* 21–30.

Stannard, D. E. (1993). *American holocaust: The conquest of the new world.* New York: Oxford University Press.

Stocking, G. W., Jr. (1968). *Race, culture, and evolution.* New York: Free Press.

Stringfield, S., & Land, D. (Eds.). (2002). *Educating at-risk students: One hundred-first yearbook of the National Society for the Study of Education, Part II.* Chicago: National Society for the Study of Education.

Swadener, B. B. (1990). Children and families "at risk": Etiology, critique, and alternative paradigms. *Educational Foundations, 4,* 17–39.

Swadener, B. B. (1995). Children and families "at promise": Deconstructing the discourse of risk. In B. B. Swadener & S. Lubeck (Eds.), *Children and families "at promise": Deconstructing the discourse of risk* (pp. 17–49). Albany: State University of New York Press.

Swadener, B. B., & Lubeck, S. (Eds.). (1995a). *Children and families "at promise": Deconstructing the discourse of risk.* Albany: State University of New York Press.

Swadener, B. B., & Lubeck, S. (1995b). The social construction of children and families "at risk": An introduction. In B. B. Swadener & S. Lubeck (Eds.), *Children and families "at promise": Deconstructing the discourse of risk* (pp. 1–14). Albany: State University of New York Press.

Taylor, A. (2008). A quantitative examination of oppositional identity among African American and Latino middle-school students. In J. U. Ogbu (Ed.), *Minority status, oppositional culture, and schooling* (pp. 481–495). New York: Routledge.

Templeton, A. R. (2002). The genetic and evolutionary significance of human races. In J. M. Fish (Ed.), *Race and intelligence: Separating science from myth* (pp. 31–56). Mahwah, NJ: Lawrence Earlbaum.

Thernstrom, A., & Thernstrom, S. (2003). *No excuses: Closing the racial gap in learning.* New York: Simon & Schuster.

Trueba, H. T. (1988). Culturally based explanations of minority students' academic achievement. *Anthropology and Education Quarterly, 19,* 270–287.

Tucker, W. H. (1994). *The science and politics of racial research.* Urbana: University of Illinois Press.

Tyson, K. (2002). Weighing in: Elementary-age students and the debate on attitudes toward school among black students. *Social Forces, 80,* 1157–1189.

Tyson, K., Darrity, W., Jr., & Castellino, D. R. (2005). It's not a "black thing": Understanding the burden of acting white and other dilemmas of high achievement. *American Sociological Review, 70,* 582–605.

Valencia, R. R. (1991). The plight of Chicano students: An overview of schooling conditions and outcomes. In R. R. Valencia (Ed.), *Chicano school failure and success: Research and policy agendas for the 1990s* (pp. 3–26). Stanford Series on Education and Public Policy. London: Falmer Press.

Valencia, R. R. (Ed.). (1997a). *The evolution of deficit thinking; Educational thought and practice.* Stanford Series on Education and Public Policy. London: Falmer Press.

Valencia, R. R. (1997b). Genetic pathology model of deficit thinking. In R. R. Valencia (Ed.), *The evolution of deficit thinking: Educational thought and practice* (pp. 41–112). Stanford Series on Education and Public Policy. London: Falmer Press.

Valencia, R. R. (2002). The plight of Chicano students: An overview of schooling conditions and outcomes. In R. R. Valencia (Ed.), *Chicano school failure and success: Past, present, and future* (2nd ed., pp. 3–51). London: RoutledgeFalmer.

Valencia, R. R. (2005). The Mexican American struggle for equal educational opportunity in *Mendez v. Westminister*: Helping to pave the way for *Brown v. Board of Education. Teachers College Record, 107,* 389–423.

Valencia, R. R. (2008). *Chicano students and the courts: The Mexican American legal struggle for educational equality.* Critical America Series. New York: New York University Press.

Valencia, R. R. (2010). *Dismantling contemporary deficit thinking: Educational thought and practice.* Critical Educator Series. New York: Routledge.

Valencia, R. R. (Ed.). (2011a). *Chicano school failure and success: Past, present, and future* (3rd ed.). New York: Routledge.

Valencia, R. R. (2011b). The plight of Chicano students: An overview of schooling conditions and outcomes. In R. R. Valencia (Ed.), *Chicano school failure and success: Past, present, and future* (3rd ed., pp. 3–41). New York: Routledge.

Valencia, R. R. (2012). Deficit thinking paradigm. In J. A. Banks (Ed.), *Encyclopedia of educational diversity* (Vol. 2, pp. 611–613). Thousand Oaks, CA: Sage.

Valencia, R. R. (2013). Jason Richwine's dissertation, *IQ and Immigration Policy:* Neohereditarianism, pseudoscience, and deficit thinking. *Teachers College Record.* Retrieved November 1, 2013, from: http://tcrecord.org ID Number: 17134.

Valencia, R. R., & Black, M. S. (2002). "Mexican Americans don't value education!": On the basis of the myth, mythmaking, and debunking. *Journal of Latinos and Education, 2,* 81–103.

Valencia, R. R., & Suzuki, L. A. (2001). *Intelligence testing and minority students: Foundations, performance factors, and assessment issues.* Series on Racial and Ethnic Minority Psychology. Thousand Oaks, CA: Sage.

Valenzuela, A. (2008). Ogbu's voluntary and involuntary hypothesis and the politics of caring. In J. U. Ogbu (Ed.), *Minority status, oppositional culture, and schooling* (pp. 496–530). New York: Routledge

Weinberg, M. (1977). *A chance to learn: The history of race and education in the United States.* New York: Cambridge University Press.

Weis, L. (1990). *Working class without work: High school students in a de-industrialized economy.* New York: Routledge.

Weis, L. (2004). *Class reunion: The remaking of the American white working class.* New York: Routledge.

Weisbrot, R. (1990). *Freedom bound: A history of American's civil rights movement.* New York: W. W. Norton.

Williams, F. (1970). Some preliminaries and prospects. In F. Williams (Ed.), *Language and poverty: Perspectives on a theme* (pp. 1–10). Chicago: Markham.

Williams, J. (2006). *Enough: The phony leaders, dead-end movements, and culture of failure that are undermining black America—and what we can do about it.* New York: Three Rivers Press.

Willie, C. V. (1976). *A new look at Black families.* New York: General Hall.

Willis, P. (1977). *Learning to labor: How working class kids get working class jobs.* New York: Teachers College Press.

Yosso, T. (2006). *Critical race counterstories along the Chicana/Chicano educational pipeline.* New York: Routledge.

PART II

Macrolevel Factors

3

THE "OTHER" GAPS

Income, Housing, and Health

About 80 years ago, Horace Mann Bond, the renowned scholar of African American educational issues and history and author of *Education of the Negro in the American Social Order* (1934), wrote these prescient words in his now-classic book:

> Along with educational improvements, there should go far-reaching coordinations between other agencies of social betterment in the extension of these services to the masses of Negroes and whites. *Housing, health, wages and working conditions* [italics added] need to be synchronized with educational reforms as objectives of attack. (p. 460)

Bond (1934) was an activist scholar (see earlier discussion, chapter 2, of the genetic pathology variant of the deficit thinking model) and tenacious critic of oppressive schooling conditions faced by African American students (Fultz, 1996). I daresay he would be frustrated if he were still alive, knowing that his call for close and careful attention to be paid to the "other" racialized gaps has made little progress 8 decades later. On the other hand, Bond may have been pleased that some contemporary scholars, particularly those who draw from CRT, have followed in his tracks by calling for systemic reform, asserting that educational improvement must be executed in tandem with other transformations that bear upon school success for all students—namely, equitable reforms in the existing racialized and class-based gaps in income, housing, and health. In this chapter, I make the case, as did Bond 80 years ago, that advancements in education (i.e., TAG reduction) are not enough. Accompanying systemic reform in income, housing, and health gaps is also essential to accomplish.[1]

In the remainder of this chapter, I provide some of the most recent statistics in regard to the gaps in income, housing, and health care in the U.S. Following each of these presentations, I discuss the academic consequences (e.g., of the income gap) for students of color. In closing, I offer a brief discussion of systemic reform suggestions that can serve as diminutions to the harmful effects of the "other" gaps on TAG.

The Income Gap

The U.S. economy has certainly seen its best and worst of times. Notwithstanding a slow recovery, the nation currently remains in the midst of one of the worst economic crises in its history (Heffner, 2014). Prompted by many different factors—e.g., far too much questionable investment in areas like housing, failure to regulate the financial system, maintaining interest rates at low levels, and greed (see, e.g., Domitrovic, 2012; Weisberg, 2010)—the U.S. experienced the Great Recession that occurred within the time frame of December 2007 and June 2009. This tumultuous period has the unfortunate distinction of being the most severe economic recession since the Great Depression of 1929–1933 (Center on Budget and Policy Priorities, 2012). The Great Recession is analogous to Hurricane Katrina of 2005 in that the former tempest brought to light the fragile nature and weaknesses of the U.S. economy, while the latter storm dramatically exposed the shortcomings of the country's infrastructure in not being able to keep people safe from physical wrath (Bhargava et al., 2009).

Following the Great Recession, it became evident that the effects of the economic downturn were deep and wide. This seemingly cavernous hole produced many serious problems: a drop in the nation's gross domestic product, unprecedented job losses, a sharp rise in the unemployment rate, historic peaks in the long-term unemployment rates, millions added to the ranks of the poor—and an issue which I discuss soon—declines in the median household income (Center on Budget and Policy Priorities, 2012; DeNavas-Walt, Proctor, & Smith, 2012). Some scholars assert that the consequences of the Great Recession would have been even more severe had the federal government not intervened with policies of financial stabilization and fiscal stimulus, including the American Recovery and Reinvestment Act, signed by President Barack Obama in 2009 (Center on Budget and Policy Priorities).

Not unexpectedly, median household income dwindled during the Great Recession.[2] Also, it is not surprising that these declines indicate a racialized pattern—as seen in Table 3.1. These data show that all racial/ethnic groups experienced drops in median household income from 2007 to 2009, but Asian Americans and Whites had smaller declines compared to Blacks and Latinos/Latinas (e.g., Blacks declined in median income by 5.5%, compared to Whites, who decreased by 4.1%). Table 3.1 also underscores the income gap when median household incomes are compared across groups: In 2009, the differences in White/Black and White/Latino and Latina were $30,584 and $25,586,

TABLE 3.1 Changes in Median Income for Households with Children: By Race/Ethnicity, 2007 to 2009

Race/Ethnicity	*Median Household Income in 2009 (in dollars)*	*Change in Dollars from 2007*	*Change in Percent from 2007*
White	64,566	−2,752	−4.1
Black	33,982	−1,991	−5.5
Latino/Latina	38,980	−2,042	−5.0
Asian American	81,957	−87	−0.1

Source: Adapted from Annie E. Casey Foundation (2011, p. 11, Table 2).

TABLE 3.2 Middle-Class Financial Security

Race/Ethnicity (of Families	*Security in Middle Class (%)*	*In-Between (%)*	*Risk of Slipping Out of Middle Class (%)*
National Average	31	44	25
Black	26	42	33
Latino/Latina	18	40	41

Source: Adapted from Wheary, Shapiro, Draut, and Meschede (2008, p. 5).

respectively. Median household income gaps 2 years later (i.e., 2011) for the various racial/ethnic groups are smaller, but still evident, compared to the 2009 data. For example, in 2011 the White/Black difference was $23,183, and the White/Latino and Latina gap was $16,788 (DeNavas-Walt et al., 2012, p. 5, Figure 1).

Another way of looking at the income gap is to examine economic security across groups. Table 3.2 presents data for financial security among middle-class Blacks, Latinos/Latinas, and Whites (using the national average as a proxy). These data point to findings that Whites are the most likely to be securely in the middle class, or in-between classes, and the least likely to slip out of the middle class.[3] By contrast, Blacks have a lower probability of securely being in the middle class or in-between classes, and a higher probability of exiting the middle class. Latinos/Latinas by comparison have the bleakest financial security. They have the lowest likelihood of securely being in the middle class or in-between classes, and the highest probability of slipping out of the middle class. Numerous statistical predictors indicate that financial vulnerability is connected to income levels (DeNavas-Walt et al., 2012).

Another aspect of the income gap I discuss is a sublevel—the wealth gap.[4] In a very current report, an analysis of Internal Revenue Service data shows that the income gap in the U.S. is the largest since 1928 (Neuman, 2013). In regard to economic recovery from the Great Recession, the richest income earners (top 1%) swelled by 31.4% compared to the rest (bottom 99%), who gained a minuscule 0.4% in income from the period of 2009 to 2012. All told, the richest are near full recovery, and the rest of families have barely begun their upturn (Saez, 2013).

Given the ubiquitous racialized pattern of the income gap in the U.S., it should not be unexpected that what follows is a racialized arrangement of the wealth gap. In a recent report by the Pew Research Center (Kochlar, Fry, & Taylor, 2011), it is strikingly clear that the median wealth of White households vastly surpasses the median wealth of Latinos/Latinas and Blacks. The data in this report should not be taken lightly, as the findings by Kochlar et al. (2011) are derived from the Survey of Income and Program Participation (SIPP), which is an economic-based questionnaire administered by the U.S. Census Bureau to tens of thousands of U.S. households. The SIPP is deemed to be the most sweeping data source on wealth of households in the U.S. in which race/ethnicity is treated as an independent variable (Kochlar et al.). Table 3.3 displays data on median net worth and median change in net worth for U.S. households from 2005 to 2009. This is a crucial time frame to examine as it allows a penetrating probe of the impact of the Great Recession, before and after. The wealth gaps are enormous. In 2009, the median wealth of U.S. White households was 18 times greater than that of Latino/Latina households, and even larger than that of Black households—20 times. Table 3.3 also indicates that the financial fallout of the Great Recession was more calamitous for households of color. In regard to percentage change in median net worth from 2005 to 2009, the negative change was over 4 times greater for Latina/Latino households compared to Whites, and such change was about 3.5 times larger for Black households compared to Whites.

Aside from the racialized pattern of wealth accumulation in the U.S., findings from international analyses are noteworthy. In comparison to other wealthy countries (e.g., Canada, Denmark, Finland, Japan, Norway, Sweden), the U.S. is different in a way that has garnered little attention: It has the dubious distinction of being the most unequal, economically (Condron, 2011). Namely, both wealth and income are distributed in a greater pattern of unevenness in the U.S. relative to other affluent nations (also, see Smeedling, 2005; Wolff, 2002).

TABLE 3.3 Median Net Worth and Change in Median Net Worth of Households: 2005 and 2009

Race/Ethnicity (of households)	*Median Net Worth (in 2009 dollars)*		*Percentage in Median Net Worth (2005 to 2009)*
	2005	*2009*	
White	134,992	113,149	−15.6
Latino/Latina	12,124	5,677	−53.2
Black	18,359	6,325	−56.5

Source: Adapted from Kochlar, Fry, and Taylor (2011, pp. 1–2).

This section on the income gap would be incomplete without a discussion of one of the nation's most vulnerable groups—the poor. How does the federal government define poverty and how widespread is it? The U.S. Census Bureau uses a number of monetary income thresholds to measure poverty. These thresholds, of which there are 48 possibilities, are determined by total family income (before taxes), family size, and family members' ages. If the total income of the family is less than the assigned threshold, then the family is deemed to be in poverty (U.S. Department of Commerce, Bureau of the Census, 2012). Suffice it to say, a family that falls below a particular poverty threshold simply does not have enough to cover its basic needs. An example: For a family of 4 to be considered living in poverty, it would have to earn a gross yearly income of less than $23, 021, which is $1,918 per month. Some basic arithmetical budgeting informs us that such a family would find it impossible to make ends meet. Notwithstanding some assistance from the federal government (e.g., food stamps), a gross monthly income of about $1,900 is not nearly enough to cover expenses for rent or a home mortgage, food, health insurance, clothing, utilities, transportation, vehicle maintenance, recreation, and so on. Such a struggle is underscored by Barbara Ehrenreich in *Nickel and Dimed: On (Not) Getting By in America* (2001). Ehrenreich, who has a Ph.D. in biology, took time out to go undercover (spring 1998 to summer 2000) and work for minimum wage in a variety of low-skill jobs (e.g., server in a restaurant, housekeeping in a hotel, "associate" [i.e., clerk] at Wal-Mart). At the book's end, she describes her experiences, and those of the poor, as a "lifestyle of chronic deprivation and relentless low-level punishment" (p. 214).

Table 3.4 displays data on the degree of contemporary poverty calculated by the U.S. Census Bureau and presented in a report by DeNavas et al. (2012). Although I do not show trend patterns, it is important to mention them (see DeNavas et al., p. 13, Figure 4). In 1959, the number of people living in poverty

TABLE 3.4 People in Poverty by Total, Race/Ethnicity, and by Related Children under 18 Years of Age in Families, by Race/Ethnicity: 2011 (in thousands)

Children under 18						
Race/Ethnicity	*Number*	*Percent*	*Relative Risk Ratio*	*Number*	*Percent*	*Relative Risk Ratio*
Total of All Groups	46.2[a]	15.0	—	15.5	21.4	—
White	19.2	9.8	—	4.9	12.5	—
Latino/Latina	13.2	25.3	2.6	5.8	33.7	2.7
Black	10.9	27.6	2.8	4.3	38.6	3.1
Asian American	2.0	12.3	1.3	.5	13.0	1.0

Source: Adapted from DeNavas et al. (2012, p. 14, Table 3; pp. 56–61, Table B.2).

[a] The total number for the four racial/ethnic groups does not equal 46.2 million because of rounding.

numbered about 40 million—one of the highest numbers ever. Soon after, the number declined to 35 million in the early 1960s, and plateaued to approximately 25 million in the mid-1960s to 1980 (likely due to the War on Poverty). Soon after, the number of people in poverty soared to 35 million in the early 1980s (certainly influenced by the extensive recession of the time) and plateaued out. Around 1990, the number began to rise and hit 40 million a few years later. The figure began to drop, and around the year 2000 the number living in poverty was about 32 million. The estimate of people in poverty began to rise, and in 2007, the beginning of the Great Recession, the number dramatically shot up. In 2011, 46.2 million people (15% of the total population) were judged to be in poverty (see Table 3.4).

The data in Table 3.4 also illustrate the number of people, as well as related children under 18 years of age, living in poverty when the total of 46.2 million is disaggregated by race/ethnicity. Once again, the ever-present pattern of racialization is revealed. Although Whites have the highest number of people living in poverty at 19.2 million, compared to each of the classifications of color, every one of the latter groups has a higher representation (i.e., percentage) among the poor. To provide a closer sense of this racialization, I quantified it by calculating relative risk ratios.[5] Table 3.4 shows, for example, that Latinos/Latinas are 2.6 times at risk and Blacks are 2.8 times at risk, compared to Whites, for being in poverty. What is particularly distressing about the data in Table 3.4 is the large numbers of children under 18 years of age who live in poverty.[6] For the nation as a whole, about 1 in 5 children (15.5 million) are poor, and approximately 1 in 8 White children reside in poverty. The poverty rates, however, for Latino/Latina and Black children are even more disturbing: Approximately 2 in 5 of Latino/Latina children live in poverty and 1 in 4 of Black youngsters reside in poverty. The relative risk ratios are 2.7 and 3.1 for Latino/Latina and Black children, respectively.

A further point on poverty: What is the likeliness of being in poverty across the life span of U.S. adults? In a somewhat dated but impressive study, Rank and Hirschl (1999) present an informative analysis of the enduring nature of poverty. In their investigation, one of the most comprehensive of its kind, the authors draw from the Panel Study of Income Dynamics (PSID), a nationally representative sample in a longitudinal design (interviewed each year beginning in 1968). The PSID is the longest continuing panel of data in the U.S. designed to trace income forces over years. Respondents were first interviewed when they were 20 years old. In sum, Rank and Hirschl found that poverty over the life span was fairly common, meaning that by age 65 years the slight majority (51.4%) of people have spent at least 1 year in poverty. Yet, when poverty rates were disaggregated by race/ethnicity,[7] the results were shocking. For Whites, by age 75 years, Rank and Hirschl estimated that a little more than half (52.6%) of them had endured at least 1 year being poor. By sharp contrast, *91%* of Blacks, by the time they reached 75 years of age, had undergone at least 1 year living in poverty. Rank and Hirschl continue, noting that by the time the Black population is 28 years of age, the accumulative level of its life span in poverty that is reached is what the White population attains at age 75 years. Stated a bit differently, "Black Americans have experienced in nine years the same risk of poverty that white Americans do in 56 years" (p. 209). Given the finding that nearly every Black in the U.S. is touched by poverty at some time in the course of his or her life as an adult, the authors conclude that such an alarming fact says a great deal about the economic significance of being Black in the U.S.

I conclude this section on the income gap by discussing its implications regarding the academic consequences for students of color, especially in understanding how family income affects TAG. There is a voluminous corpus of literature that finds a positive association between SES of origin and the performance of children on measures of academic achievement, as well as intelligence (e.g., Sirin, 2005; Valencia & Suzuki, 2001, chapter 3; White, 1982). It is surprising, however, that only a paucity of research has been conducted on one of the main aspects of SES—parental income, particularly how much parents actually *spend* on their children's education. Furthermore, even less is known about whether such spending is positively correlated with children's learning outcomes (we assume it is). The relation between parental spending and children's education is grounded in the *investment hypothesis* (e.g., Furstenberg, 2011; Kausal, Magnuson, Waldfogel, 2011; Mayer, 1997), which asserts that more economically advantaged parents—compared to their economically disadvantaged counterparts—are able to spend more money on educationally valuable services (e.g., private preschools), tools (e.g., computers), and the paramount investment—paying in full or part for their children's higher education.[8] Furthermore, parental investment via monetary expenditures is thought to help build human capital (a la Becker, 1991, 1994) and its "material" effects—for example, future income and economic security (also, see Kornrich & Furstenberg, 2012).

An example of an investigation of the investment hypothesis is that of Kausal et al. (2011). The authors used two sizable data sets with nationally representative samples: the Consumer Expenditure Survey (CEX) and the Early Childhood Longitudinal Study, Kindergarten Cohort (ECLS-K). The CEX, a repeated cross-sectional survey (1997–2006), contains comprehensive data on family income, as well as expenditures. Of the thorough analyses Kausal et al. report, the results for spending on education (e.g., books, school supplies, electronics, computers, college tuition) are the most germane here. For example, as family budgets increase by $1,000 increments, their children benefit in increased enrichments via parental spending. More specifically, based on quintile analyses, families in quintile 1 (the bottom) allot 3% of the total spending to educationally enriching items, while families in quintile 4 and 5 (the top) allocate 9% of their expenditures for educational enrichment. A limitation of the CEX data set is that children's achievement outcomes are not available. The ECLS-K, however, contains mathematics and reading achievement scores for the children in this longitudinal investigation (kindergarten and grades 1, 3, and 5). Kausal et al. report that overall, as income quintile increases, so does the spending on educational enrichment (e.g., lessons [such as foreign language instruction and music], books, compact disks, computers). Furthermore, the authors report that as income gradients increase, achievement does likewise. For example, kindergarteners in quintile 1 for family income have mathematics and reading scores of 45 (based on a mean of 50 and a standard deviation of 10). Children in quintile 3 have mathematics and reading scores of about 50, and children in quintile 5 perform at approximately 55 in achievement scores. In sum, although Kausal et al. did not disaggregate their analyses by race/ethnicity, the results still have relevance for low-SES children of color and their families. As the authors note, this economic inequality is so pervasive among families that, if uncorrected, it is quite likely to be instrumental in the continuation of such inequality, and by extension, the maintenance of TAG.

In a related investment hypothesis study of the association between family income and children's academic achievement, Reardon's (2011) main research query is: Given that the income chasm between high- and low-income families has widened, has the achievement gap between children from such families concomitantly expanded? In investigating this question, Reardon utilized data from 19 nationally representative surveys (e.g., ECLS-K, NAEP, Project Talent), and analyzed trend patterns over a number of decades (1943 to 2001 cohorts). A principal aspect of this study is the examination of what Reardon terms the "90/10 income achievement gap," which he operationalizes by comparing the average mathematics and reading scores of children whose families are at the 90th percentile of income distribution (approximately $160,000 in 2008) and children in families at the 10th percentile of income distribution (around $17,500 in 2008). In brief, Reardon reports that the 90/10 achievement gap trend before the 1970s is not too clear, but the trend from around the mid-1970s to 2001 is quite discernible: That is, the 90/10 achievement gap has increased approximately 40% to 50%, for the population altogether (see Reardon, pp. 95–96, Figures 5.1 and 5.2). When disaggregated by race/ethnicity, the 90/10 achievement gap for Whites and Latinos/Latinas resembled the national trend from 1943 to 2001, while for Blacks the pattern seemed to grow in a steady manner from the mid-1940s to 2001.

In an attempt to explain why the 90/10 achievement gap has widened, Reardon (2011) proffers several interpretations. For example, there is the rise in income inequality, particularly over the last 40 years. Although this is a plausible hypothesis, Reardon notes that the 90/10 achievement gap cannot be explained exclusively by rising income equality. He comments that perhaps a contributing factor is that each dollar of income seems to be able to purchase more educational enrichment than it did a few decades ago. Another hypothesis is that parents' investment patterns in their children's education have changed over time. Drawing from Wrigley's (1989) article on the type of parenting advice provided in journal articles and popular magazines from 1900 to 1985, Reardon remarks that prior to 1930 physicians provided the most advice, suggesting that parents should concentrate on keeping their children quiet and healthy. In the 1960s, however, parenting advice shifted to suggestions centered around the cognitive stimulation of children. A related aspect of transformations regarding parental investments is the likely influence of the standards-based school reform movement, which had its origins in the early 1980s publication of *A Nation at Risk: The Imperative for Educational Reform* (National Commission on Excellence in Education, 1983; see Valencia, 2010, chapter 4). Reardon proposes that in light of the importance of high-stakes testing, which is the driver of the standards-based school reform movement, parents have become more cognizant of the consequences of such testing and therefore have invested more in services and tools for their children's academic development, with these investments being more affordable for higher-income families. In closing, Reardon—in a manner similar to the conclusions Kausal et al. (2011) draw—maintains that as the offspring of the affluent perform better in school and subsequently have a greater probability of becoming wealthy, the U.S. is further placed at risk of perpetuating a society that is economically unequal and polarized.

The Housing Gap

Most of us are familiar with the mantra of the real estate housing industry—"location," "location," "location." This paramount principle helps to guide potential buyers to a house that they deem important in terms of safety, comfort, and convenience. More specifically, prospective home buyers strive for a location that is relatively close to, for example, work, a hospital and family medical clinic, a dentist, a church, diverse restaurants, a mall, a grocery store, and public parks. Furthermore, for likely home buyers who have school-age children or plan to have offspring, a nearby school with a fine academic reputation is desirable.[9] In light of these coveted features, it is well known that location is a major determinant of the price of a house (Kiel & Zabel, 2008).

In this section, I focus on the housing gap by examining the connection between where a family lives and the quality of schooling the children receive. Given that residential location largely determines the price of particular housing, and such location is associated with whether the nearby schools are typically low- or high-performing academically, it is not unforeseen that the housing gap leads to separate and unequal schools (Frankenberg, 2013; Logan, 2002). Most of the literature on segregation centers on separate housing *or* separate schools, but seldom the interrelation between the two (see Powell, Kearney, & Kay, 2001). Furthermore, existing social science scholarship on racial isolation in U.S. society—as well as the courts' decisions on school segregation cases—fails to consider the function residential segregation has in producing school segregation (Kearney, 2001). I examine the housing gap through the lens of the concept "geography of opportunity" (e.g., Briggs, 2005a; Galster & Killen, 1995). Here, I view such opportunity as a process in which residential location is a conduit to high-performing schools—an experience that low-SES students of color, because of where they live, are denied. In chapter 4, "School Segregation, Desegregation, and Integration," I extend this section's discussion by covering the deleterious academic and social effects on students of color who attend segregated schools.

In light of the previously discussed income gap, most families of color are not financially capable of either renting or purchasing housing in neighborhoods (typically in the suburbs) where high-performing schools are generally located. Though very important, the income gap is not the only factor that has played a role in the formation and entrenchment of racialized housing segregation. Drawing from the typology developed by Cutler, Glaeser, and Vigdor (1999) to help explain the likely bases of racial residential segregation, Boustan (2011) discusses three factors: (a) collective action by Whites, (b) individual action by Whites, and (c) self-segregation by Blacks. Due to space limitations, I confine this discussion to White collective action. Given that most of the scholarship on residential segregation is on Blacks, I add to this discourse by covering—when the literature permits—such segregation apropos to Latinos/Latinas.

Historically, one of the most common methods collectively used by Whites to prevent people of color (especially Blacks) from moving into and living in White neighborhoods was racially restrictive housing covenants, which were memorialized in home deeds across the nation. Such covenants mushroomed during the Great Migration between 1915–1970, when about 6 million Blacks moved from the South to the Midwest, North, and West in search of a better life (Wilkerson, 2010; also, see Ocen, 2012). At their core, these covenants were driven by White racial animus and served as "social signals" to the incoming Blacks that they were not welcome (Brooks & Rose, 2013). During the heyday of these covenants (from the 1920s to the 1940s), Mexican Americans were also excluded from such White racialized spaces. For example, racially restrictive covenants were regularly employed in San Antonio, Texas (Ramos, 2001), and in Los Angeles, California (Garrison, 2008). In a little known case, *Doss v. Bernal* (1943), Mexican Americans Alex and Esther Bernal, of Fullerton, California, paid a down payment of $750 on a house the owners, Joe and Velda Johnson, agreed to sell to the Bernals for $4,250. Shortly before the Bernals were to move in, the Johnsons informed them that there may be a problem because the deed restriction forbade the selling of the house to Mexicans. The White residents (Ashley Doss et al.) of the neighborhood brought suit against the Bernals, seeking enforcement of the racially restrictive housing covenant. In this Superior Court case, Judge Albert F. Ross ruled in favor of the Bernals, opining that the restrictive housing covenant in question was, in part, violative of the 5th and 14th Amendments of the U.S. Constitution (Romero & Fernández, 2012).

In *Shelley v. Kraemer* (1948), racially restrictive covenants suffered a major blow in a landmark U.S. Supreme Court decision. The case involved a plaintiff Black family (the Shelleys) who bought a home in St. Louis, Missouri. It was unknown to them that a restrictive covenant, which had been operative since 1911, prohibited "Negroes" and "Mongolians" from possessing the property. As such, White neighbors joined in a lawsuit to block the Shelleys from closing on the ownership.[10] In brief, the High Court ruled: (a) private parties are allowed to engage, voluntarily, in restrictive housing covenants, but (b) states (including the courts) cannot enforce such covenants, as this would be deemed discriminatory and thus a violation of the Equal Protection Clause of the 14th Amendment. Notwithstanding the Supreme Court's judgment, the pervasive use of racially restrictive covenants persisted, but states could not enforce them, legally.[11] In some cases, such covenants changed, however, by the use of agreements among neighborhood associations that allowed owners to not rent or sell, on an individual basis, to Blacks. As a case in point, 200-plus neighborhoods were established to practice racial exclusion in Detroit, Michigan, in the decades of the 1940s and 1950s (Sugrue, 1996; cited in Boustan, 2011). Another major blow to racialized space in housing came in 1968 with the Fair Housing Act (1968; also known as Title VII of the Civil Rights Act of 1968), which prohibits discrimination based on color, race, religion, national origin, and sex.

Although it is not discussed by Boustan (2011), another significant White collective action historically used to create residential segregation by race was the role of the federal government in its discriminatory lending policies for home mortgages (Bryant, 2001; Seitles, 1998). The Federal Housing Administration (FHA), which is under the Department of Housing and Urban Development, was established in 1934 and is the world's largest mortgage insurer, having insured more than 34 million properties since its establishment.[12] It has been documented, however, that the FHA in its early years was instrumental in the creation and perpetuation of all-White neighborhoods via its lending practices (Bryant; Seitles). The FHA's policy of tightly linking race to loan eligibility ipso facto viewed neighborhoods of color as being serious monetary risks. From 1934 to 1962, the FHA underwrote $120 billion of home mortgage loans—with greater than 98% going to White borrowers (*Race: The Power of an Illusion*, 2003). In sum, the FHA therefore has the dubious distinction of being the initial federal agency to overtly advise and support societal segregation (Bryant; Seitles).

Unfortunately, the issue of institutional racism in home mortgage continues in contemporary times (Gane-McCalla, 2011; Rothstein, 2012). For example, Countrywide Financial, owned by mega Bank of America, was sued by the Department of Justice for racial discrimination and had to pay $335 million to over 200,000 *qualified* Blacks and Latinos/Latinas. Bank of America was found to practice discriminatory lending practices from 2004 to 2008 in 41 states (and Washington, DC) and 180 geographic markets (Gane-McCalla).

To what degree does racial segregation in housing exist? A convenient way to quantify such segregation is by use of the dissimilarity index (DI), which is generally utilized to calculate racial segregation in cities and metropolitan statistical areas.[13] DI values range from 0 to 100, with a DI of 60 or greater considered very high. A moderate level of segregation ranges from 40 to 50, and a DI of 30 or less is considered relatively low.[14] Furthermore, the DI refers to the percentage of a particular group's population (e.g., Black, White) that would need to change residence from each neighborhood to derive the same percentage of that racial/ethnic group that exists in the larger residential unit (e.g., city).[15] For example, for a DI of 70, 70% of one group (e.g., Latinos/Latinas) would have to change neighborhoods for both groups to be equally distributed (Whites are the other group in this instance).

To provide a sense of contemporary racial segregation in housing, I provide DIs[16] for the 10 largest cities by population in the U.S.[17] based on 2010 data. Table 3.5 presents these data. Two major points can be gleaned from the table. First, given that a DI of 60 or more is deemed considerably high, 6 of the top 10 cities listed suggest intense housing segregation (i.e., New York, Los Angeles, Chicago, Houston, Philadelphia, and Dallas). The other four cities (i.e., Phoenix, San Antonio, San Diego, and San Jose) show DIs of moderate segregation. Second, with the exception of the four latter cities mentioned, the DIs for White-Black comparisons are greater than for White-Latino/Latina comparisons. In sum, racial housing segregation appears to be quite common in the 10 largest cities in the U.S. as of 2010. Furthermore, in the country, as a whole, it stubbornly persists (e.g., Adelman & Gocker, 2007; Briggs, 2005b). It follows that such segregation does not bode well for school integration (e.g., Denton, 2001).

An effective way to gain further insight into the housing gap is through the notion of "geography of opportunity" (e.g., Briggs, 2005a; Galster & Killen, 1995). Although some scholars do not use the term, they certainly imply it in

TABLE 3.5 Racial Segregation in Housing for Top 10 Cities by Population in U.S.: 2010

Top 10 Cities (descending order)[a]	*Dissimilarity Index*[b]	
	White-Black	*White-Latino/Latina*
New York, NY	81.4	65.8
Los Angeles, CA	66.9	65.2
Chicago, IL	82.5	60.9
Houston, TX	68.6	60.4
Philadelphia, PA	73.4	62.0
Phoenix, AZ	49.9	57.7
San Antonio, TX	43.1	46.8
San Diego, CA	54.6	57.8
Dallas, TX	66.1	61.1
San Jose, CA	36.8	48.8

[a] See note 17, this chapter. [b] See note 14, this chapter.

their work (e.g., see *Place Matters: Metropolitics for the Twenty-First Century*, by Dreier, Mollenkopf, & Swanstrom, 2004). Here, I primarily conceptualize the geography of opportunity in the context of education—as a means by which a family's residential location can provide a channel to high-performing schools, which is a process often denied to low-SES families of color because very limited finances restrict where they can rent or purchase housing. An insightful way to view the limitations of geography of opportunity is to examine it in the context of "unevenness." Uneven geography of opportunity—especially how boundaries in choice of housing are sharply linked to race and income—produces the "geographic concentration" of educational failure of many low-SES students of color via highly segregated schools (Briggs, 2005b). The connection between segregated housing and segregated schools is powerful. It is important to ask, however: What factors are involved in shaping the geography of opportunity in regard to the starting point of the link—the housing gap?

One critical facet is the formation of the "dual mortgage market" and its driver, the continuing discrimination in mortgage lending (Apgar & Calder, 2005). Apgar and Calder note that the term "dual mortgage market" was coined by Immergluck and Wiles (1999) in their extensive analysis of lending patterns in Chicago neighborhoods in the late 1990s. Immergluck and Wiles found that mainstream lenders often provided prime loans to borrowers in upper-SES White areas, and subprime and FHA lending occurred in lower-SES areas and in communities of color. The authors conclude that these class-based and racialized patterns were too robust to be accounted for by disparities in the borrowers' quality of credit. The primary explanation Immergluck and Wiles proffer is that conventional lenders failed to proceed assertively in seeking out borrowers in communities of color, especially of low SES.

The unevenness of geography of opportunity is not merely influenced by the limited financial resources of people of color and discrimination in mortgage lending. This terrain is also "color coded," in that White attitudes toward people of color inform racialized housing patterns in the U.S. (e.g., Charles, 2005; Turner & Ross, 2005). Based on his synthesis of survey research, Charles (2005) concludes that across racial groups, quite discernible ranking patterns emerge for preferences of racial compositions of neighborhoods. Most Whites prefer to live in predominantly or near exclusive White neighborhoods. The majority of Blacks are the most forthcoming in preferring considerable housing integration, and the least probable to want to live in exclusively all-Black neighborhoods. Finally, Latinos/Latinas and Asians have neighborhood housing preferences that fall between those of Whites and Blacks.

In a related vein, outright racial discrimination plays a significant role in the geography of opportunity. In their synthesis, Turner and Ross (2005) summarize the results of the comprehensive U.S. Department of Housing and Development study of 2000 that yields rich data on racial discrimination in the housing and rental markets (see Turner, Ross, Galster, & Yinger, 2002). Some key findings are:

(a) discrimination toward Blacks and Latinos/Latinas who strive to buy homes or rent dwellings has, on the average, decreased since 1989; but (b) substantial discrimination in housing against Blacks and Latinos/Latinas continues, which is a national problem; (c) in their search for housing, Latino/Latina renters are more likely to encounter discrimination compared to Blacks; (d) a growing and major type of housing discrimination is "geographic steering," which occurs when a real estate agent shows people of color more housing options in mixed or highly populated neighborhoods of people of color, and Whites are steered to housing in predominantly or exclusively White neighborhoods.

Any discussion of the housing gap through the lens of the geography of opportunity would be unfinished without a brief mention of the role of the federal policies in helping maintain the housing chasm between economically advantaged Whites and low-SES people of color. Historically, there is considerable evidence that the policies of the federal government in regard to home ownership were appallingly racist, leading to the concentration of Blacks in ghettoes and Latinos/Latinas in barrios (e.g., Dreier et al., 2004; Massey & Denton, 1993; Seitles, 1998).

The current unevenness of the geography of opportunity has also been deeply shaped by the racialization of federally subsidized housing, more commonly known as "public housing" or "projects."[18] The origin of public housing can be traced to immediate post-WWII years as the nation was experiencing a housing shortage. The thousands of isolated and inexpensive apartments were largely built with Black renters in mind (Turner, Popkin, & Rawlings, 2009).[19] Housing developers, hired by the federal government, built massive high-rise buildings with designs that cut costs. Careless construction, insufficient funding, and unabating mismanagement played a part in the acute distress of projects in a number of U.S. cities (National Commission on Severely Distressed Public Housing, 1992; cited in Turner et al., 2009). The perils of living in projects became aggravated and were ignored by subsequent administrations and their public housing policies (e.g., the Urban Renewal policies of the 1950s and 1960s; see Turner et al., 2009).

Continued decline in the quality of public housing occurred in the 1980s. By the decade's end, public housing in the nation's largest cities was heavily concentrated with overwhelmingly Black renters of very-low SES background. Many projects were described as having residents who suffered from constant joblessness and dependency on welfare. Single parents typically ran families, and children and youths, who attended nearby segregated schools, often experienced school failure—particularly low academic achievement and high dropout rates (e.g., Popkin, Buron, Levy, & Cunningham, 2000; Spence, 1993; cited in Turner et al., 2009). To sum, as the 1980s came to an end, public housing had the dubious distinction of being the largest and most conspicuous failure of social welfare plans in the nation (National Commission on Severely Distressed Public Housing, 1992). Furthermore, and especially germane to this discussion, is that we need to be mindful of how public housing contributed to the segregation of schools (e.g., Powell et al., 2001; Turner et al., 2009).

Health Gap

Of the three gaps—income, housing, and health—physical health status is the most palpable. Its face is quite recognizable, expressing the pangs of hunger and the unhealthy consequences of malnutrition, the pain resulting from a decayed tooth, the gasps for air brought on by an asthma attack, or the numbness of neuropathy (nerve damage), a complication of type 2 diabetes. A wealth of data demonstrates that these health issues, and others, are more pronounced among low-SES children and youths of color, relative to their more economically favorable White peers. In this section, I explore this significant health gap and discuss how the health problems experienced by many economically disadvantaged students of color negatively affect their academic achievement, thus contributing to TAG.

There are a number of health disparities between students of color and their White counterparts. Here, I cover select health issues, focusing on those that appear to receive the most attention in the health-related literature.

1. *Obesity.* It seems as if nary a day goes by without the media mentioning the obesity epidemic in the U.S. Overweight, a related term, signifies an increase in body weight in the context of one's height, which in turn is compared to a standard of what is considered a reasonable weight. Obesity, on the other hand, has a more precise and quantifiable definition. It refers to an amount of adipose tissue (body fat) that is excessive, compared to lean body mass. In an adult, he or she is deemed obese if the body mass index (BMI) is 30 or greater (Levi, Segal, St. Laurent, Lang, & Rayburn, 2012).[20] In children, the BMI is also calculated, but the index is compared to percentiles for the child's age and sex. Having a BMI percentile of 85 to 94 is considered overweight, and a percentile of 95 or higher is deemed obese (Levi et al.).

Much has been written about the obesity epidemic in the U.S. and its health consequences (e.g., Finkelstein, Trogdon, Cohen, & Dietz, 2009; Levi et al., 2012; Ogden, Carroll, Kit, & Flegal, 2012; Wang & Beydoun, 2007). A particularly alarming finding is that obesity can lead to acute diseases. The top five are: type 2 diabetes (which I discuss later), hypertension, coronary heart disease and stroke, arthritis, and cancers related to obesity (Levi et al.; Seo & Sa, 2010). Another disconcerting point about obesity is the widespread nature and growth of the condition. If the current prevalence rates of obesity go unabated in the U.S., in all 50 states more than 44% of individuals are likely to be obese by 2030. Furthermore, by 2030 about 60% of people in 13 states may be obese (Levi et al.). It follows that if the prevalence of obesity continues on its current track, then the diseases associated with obesity will rise. For example, by 2030, for every 100,000 people, new cases of coronary heart disease and stroke will increase by 35,519 in West Virginia alone; the average increase for each state is projected to be 26,573 (Levi et al.).

TABLE 3.6 Child Obesity Rates by Race/Ethnicity and Age: National, 2009–2011

Age Interval (in years)	*White*	*Black*	*Mexican American*
2 to 5	6.0	17.0	11.9
6 to 11	10.7	27.8	22.4
12 to 19	14.7	24.8	18.6

Source: Adapted from Ogden et al. (2012, p. 487, Table 2).

Note: Obesity is indicated by a BMI ≥ 95th percentile.

In light of the data for adult obesity (e.g., Levi et al., 2012; Pan et al., 2009), it is not unforeseen that racialized patterns of obesity exist among children.[21] Ogden et al. (2012), drawing from 2009–2010 data from the National Health and Nutrition Examination Survey (NHANES), report that at all age levels children of color (especially of low-SES background) are more likely to be obese compared to their White counterparts. Table 3.6 present data from Ogden et al. (2012) for child obesity percentages for three age intervals across White, Black, and Mexican American children (boys and girls combined).[22] Several points are noteworthy. First, in each of the three age groups, White children have the lowest obesity rates. Second, the Black children have the highest rates of obesity in all age groups. Third, in each of the three age groups the rates for the Mexican American children fall intermediate between the obesity percentages of their White and Black peers. In an earlier study of NHANES data (2007–2008), Ogden et al. (2010) also found these racialized patterns. Furthermore, in an even more recent investigation (of 2011 data), Levi et al. (2012) report the following obesity rates for U.S. high school students by race/ethnicity: White (11.5%), Latino/Latina (14.1%), and Black (18.2%).

In addition to the major finding that obesity is a health condition affecting children and youths of color more frequently than their White peers, another central concern is that obesity is associated with diminished academic performance (e.g., Byrd, 2007; Daniels, 2008; García & Park, 2012; Gurley-Calvez & Higginbotham, 2010; Story, Kaphingst, & French, 2006). In their review of germane literature, Story et al. (2006) note that very overweight children and adolescents are about four times more probable, compared to their peers with healthy weight, to state they have diminished school functioning. Story et al. also report that in one study of over 11,000 kindergartners, children who were overweight, in comparison to children who were not overweight, scored significantly lower on reading and mathematics tests—and the differences carried into the first grade (see Datar, Sturm, & Magnabosco, 2004). In an investigation especially pertinent to the present discussion, García and Park (2012) found that obese Latino high school students in Texas (most likely Mexican Americans) scored lower than their normal-weight and overweight Latino counterparts on the Reading and

Mathematics sections of the Texas Assessment of Knowledge and Skills, a state-mandated test. No differences between level of weight and achievement were found for the Latina group. In sum, a consistent connection has been established between obesity and academic achievement. Yet, the "cause" is not known. What is suggested by researchers, however, is that children's physical activity level and fitness are positively related to children's cognitive abilities, and hence academic performance (e.g., Efrat, 2011). I will discuss this further at the chapter's end.

2. *Type 2 diabetes.* In type 1 diabetes (T1D), one's body cannot produce insulin—a hormone that helps the body utilize and store blood sugar (glucose) in order to provide energy via the body's metabolism. By contrast, in type 2 diabetes (T2D) the body does make insulin, but not at adequate levels to keep a person healthy (Isley, Molitch, & Vigersky, 2004). Approximately 95% of all people with diabetes have T2D, greatly outnumbering those with T1D (Centers for Disease Control and Prevention, 2012). Historically, T2D very seldom struck children and adolescents. Now, however, T2D most often strikes youths during puberty (i.e., coinciding with the second decade of life).[23] Regarding older children, worldwide prevalence rates show that around the year 2000, T2D constituted about 3% of all new cases of T2D in adolescents. A decade later, 45% of onset diabetes is attributed to T2D for this age group (D'Adamo & Caprio, 2011). Much has been written about the epidemic of T2D in the U.S. (e.g., Dabelea, Pettitt, Jones, & Arslanian, 1999; Imperatore et al., 2012; Vivian, Carrel, & Becker, 2011). In 2010, of U.S. youths younger than 20 years of age, 22,820 had T2D. After applying an annual incidence rate of 2.3%, it is projected that by 2050 there will be 84,131 cases of T2D in the younger than 20-years-old population—an increase of 269% (Imperatore et al.). If not medically treated, diabetes (both types) can lead to critical consequences—for example, end-stage renal (kidney) disease requiring dialysis, neuropathy causing loss of legs or digits, heart attack, and blindness (Isley et al.). Because obesity is a major risk factor for T2D, children and youths of color have higher rates of T2D in comparison to their White peers (e.g., Caballero, 2007; Dabelea et al., 1999; Imperatore et al., 2012; Lipton, Keenan, Onyemere, & Freels, 2002).

In regard to the relation between T2D (as well as T1D) and academic achievement/cognitive functioning, a small but informative corpus of literature reports that diabetes has adverse effects (e.g., Jameson, 2006; Kodi & Seaquist, 2008; McCarthy, Lindgren, Mengeling, Tsalikian, & Engvall, 2003; Yau et al., 2010). As a case in point, Yau et al. (2010) compared 18 obese adolescents (race/ethnicity not noted) with T2D to a control group (obese, non-diabetic) residing in New York City. The authors report that on all measures—IQ, academic achievement, memory, attention/psychomotor efficiency, and executive functions—the participants with T2D performed lower (in some cases significantly so) in comparison to the control group. Yau et al. hypothesize that T2D may lead to brain complications, particularly in regard to a merging of vascular changes and metabolic abnormalities in glucose and lipids (fatty acids). In a comprehensive literature review, Kodi and Seaquist (2008) underscore that T2D has negative effects on cognitive function—for example, memory (verbal, visual, immediate and delayed recall), executive function, verbal fluency, and attention. Although the precise pathophysiology of cognitive impairment of diabetes (both types) is not fully comprehended, Kodi and Seaquist suggest such dysfunction may be related to hyperglycemia (excessive glucose in the blood system), hypoglycemia (deficient glucose), and vascular disease.

3. *Asthma.* This is a persistent respiratory disease marked by spasms of the bronchi (air passages) of the lungs. Major symptoms include coughing, wheezing, tightness of the chest, and dyspnea (shortness of breath), and it is one of the most prevalent chronic diseases affecting children, adolescents, and adults in the U.S. (Nguyen, Peng, & Boulay, 2010). According to the Centers for Disease Control and Prevention, in 2010 nationally there were 7 million children (1 in 11, 9.1%) and 18.7 million adults (1 in 12, 8.3%) who had asthma[24]—and the rate is surging (Silvers & Lang, 2012). Studies have found that Black youngsters are struck by asthma at higher rates of prevalence, relative to their White counterparts (e.g., Akinbami, Rhodes, & Lara, 2005; Pham, Teitelbaum, & Ortiz, 2006; Silvers & Lang; Stewart et al., 2010). For example, in their review of germane medical literature Silvers and Lang (2012) conclude that Blacks, compared to Whites, have not only higher prevalence rates of asthma but also higher percentages of hospitalization and mortality due to asthma. The authors note that these elevated rates of prevalence, morbidity, and mortality may be accounted for by such factors as genetics, cockroach allergen, tobacco smoke, living in poverty, and obesity.

Assessing prevalence rates of asthma among Latinos/Latinas is more complicated (e.g., Canino et al., 2006; Lara, Akinabami, Flores, & Morgenstern, 2006). Lara et al. (2006) utilized data (1997 to 2001) from the National Health Interview Survey. Based on 46,511 responses, the authors report the following asthma prevalence rates across race/ethnicity for children 2–17 years of age (in descending order): Puerto Rican (26%), Black (16%), White (13%), and Mexican American (10%). Other investigations (e.g., Canino et al.) corroborate higher rates for Puerto Rican children. Furthermore, other studies (e.g., Bloom, Cohen, Vickerie, & Wondimu, 2003) confirm the Lara et al. finding that Mexican America children (under 18 years of age) have asthma prevalence rates that are lower compared to Blacks and Whites. Lara et al. conclude that when asthma is investigated among Latino/Latina children, it is important to not treat them as a homogeneous group.

Given that asthma is a debilitating disease affecting one's breathing, it is not surprising that this chronic condition is associated with a diminution in children's academic performance (e.g., Joe, Joe, & Rowley, 2009; Moonie, Sterling, Figgs, & Castro, 2008; Taras & Potts-Datema, 2005). Yet, this body of research should be interpreted with caution (see, e.g., Taras & Potts-Datema). A case in point is the investigation by Moonie et al. (2008), who studied the relation between children's asthma status, absence from school, and academic test performance.

The participants were 3,812 children (5% White, 95% Black) aged 8–17 years old. Of these, 397 (10.4%) were determined to have asthma. The achievement measure was the Missouri Assessment Program (MAP), a state-mandated test. Asthma symptom severity consisted of four classifications: "mild intermittent," "mild," "moderate," and "severe persistent" (p. 141). The authors found that severity level of asthma was the key factor predictive of diminished test performance: Students with asthma performed, as a group, the same on the MAP as their peers sans asthma. Students with severe persistent asthma, however, scored lower on MAP compared to the students who did not have asthma. Moonie et al. also report that the students with asthma, in comparison to those without asthma, were absent from school more often. The link between asthma and high rates of absenteeism has been documented in other studies (e.g., Grant & Brito, 2010; Joe et al.; Taras & Potts-Datema). In sum, the association between asthma and academic achievement is indeed complex. Research designs that fail to take into account such confounding variables as the trigger for absenteeism, SES, poor control and management of asthma, possible side effects of medicine, how asthma is conceptualized, severity level of the disease, and chronic stress make it difficult to have a fuller understanding of the relation between asthma and academic performance (e.g., Joe et al.; Moonie et al.; Taras & Potts-Datema).

4. *Lead poisoning.* In the mid-1970s to the late 1980s, a number of changes were made in U.S. federal laws designed to reverse the growing prevalence of elevated blood lead levels (EBLLs) in young children. Such statutes prohibited the adding of lead in, for example, gasoline for road vehicles, house paint, plumbing parts, public water networks, and beverage and food cans (Levin et al., 2008). Although these governmental interventions and policies have proved successful in lowering the rate of EBLLs in young children (Pirkle et al., 1998), lead poisoning remains a major public health concern. Based on the most recent data from the Centers for Disease Control and Prevention, Wheeler and Brown (2013), using data from the NHANES, extrapolate that in the period 2007–2010 there were 535,000 children (2.6%), aged 1–5 years, nationwide with EBLLs—operationalized as levels of ≥5 μg/dL. Most of the literature on lead poisoning reports the all-too-familiar pattern of racialization of health maladies: Black and Latino/Latina children are at greater risk for lead poisoning and demonstrate higher rates in comparison to their White counterparts (e.g., Levin et al., 2008; McIlvaine, Mosammat, & Prum, 2004; Miranda, Kim, Reiter, Overstreet Galeano, & Maxson, 2009; Pham et al., 2006; Warniment, Tsang, & Galazka, 2010; Wheeler & Brown).[25] Pham et al. (2006), for example, drawing from NHANES data, note the following EBLLs for children aged 1–18 years: Black (7.0%), Latino/Latina (2.8%), and White (2.5%). The sources of lead poisoning number in the thousands of applications. Yet, the primary origins are lead in paint chips (in older homes) ingested by youngsters, and in polluted soil and dust (Levin et al.).

A number of studies have discussed the findings that lead poisoning leads to impaired cognitive functioning and diminished academic achievement (e.g.,

Gould, 2009; Levin et al., 2008; Miranda et al., 2009; Warniment et al., 2010). The investigative question by Miranda et al. is especially appropriate to the present discussion: Is lead poisoning an environmental contributor to TAG? The authors' sample consisted of 57,678 fourth-grade children (56.9% White, 43.1% Black) attending North Carolina public schools. Participants' fourth-grade reading test scores were compared to their respective blood lead levels. Miranda et al. (2009) report that the Black children, compared to their White peers, had a lower mean reading score and a higher mean lead level.[26] The authors conclude that given this observed relation, "[a higher than average level of] lead does in fact explain part of the achievement gap" (p. 1023).

5. *Dental caries.* This oral disease, dental caries (hereafter referred to as caries), is reported to be the most common chronic childhood health concern (see Bugis, 2012; Mouradian, Wehr, & Crall, 2000). Caries affects 5 to 8 times as many youngsters as does asthma; by the middle of childhood (age 8 years) about 52% of children have discernible caries, and by the end of adolescence (age 17 years) approximately 78% of youths have the disease (Pham et al., 2006). The consequences of not treating caries are indeed dire. Good oral health is a microcosm of general good health, and given that the oral cavity is a gateway for organisms that are infectious, untreated caries can lead to serious health problems (Jackson, Vann Jr., Kotch, Pahel, & Lee, 2011). Oral infections have been known to be associated with, for example, such diseases and illnesses as: pain in the mouth, leading to difficulty in eating, which in turn can cause malnutrition and stunted growth; heart disease; stroke; diabetes; periodontal (gum) disease; and brain infection (Fox, 2011; Jackson et al.; Pham et al.; Touger-Decker & van Loveren, 2003).

Childhood caries is disproportionately distributed in the U.S. The vast majority (75%–80%) of caries among children is found in a small sector (20%–25%) of the childhood population, and this segment can be characterized as being low-SES, immigrant status, and of color (Eckert, Jackson, & Fontana, 2010). In regard to the prevalence of caries by race/ethnicity, numerous studies report that children of color have higher rates relative to their White counterparts (e.g., Bugis, 2012; Eckert et al., 2010; Mouradian et al., 2000; Pham et al., 2006; Vargas & Ronzio, 2006). As a case in point, Vargas and Ronzio (2006) note the following national prevalence rates by race/ethnicity for children 2–5 years of age who had caries: Mexican American (40%), Black (29%), and White (18%). Furthermore, Pham et al. report the following national rates for children 6–8 years of age with untreated caries: Latino/Latina (43%), Black (36%), and White (26%). Regarding SES, it has also been found to be statistically predictive of childhood caries. Youngsters of low-SES background are twice as likely as children of higher-SES families to have untreated caries (Pham et al.).

A small number of empirical investigations and literature reviews note that caries is linked to children's increased school absences and diminished academic achievement (e.g., Blumenshine, Vann Jr., Gizlice, & Lee, 2008; Fox, 2011; Jackson et al., 2011; Pham et al., 2006; Seirawan, Faust, & Mulligan, 2012). Caries and other health issues related to dental problems are associated with a considerable amount of absences from school—about 52 million lost hours annually (Jackson et al.; Pham et al.). The assumption is that such missed time from school can lead to academic problems (Fox). With respect to empirical research that has investigated the impact of poor oral health on academic achievement, Jackson et al., using data from a parental questionnaire, examined the relation between children's oral health (i.e., condition of the teeth: "excellent," "very good," "fair," or "poor") and poor school performance (operationalized as mostly "Cs," "Ds," or "Fs"). Participants were 1,782 K-12 students attending public schools in North Carolina; the sample was racially/ethnically diverse (63.1% White, 23% Black, and 10.1% Latino/Latina). The authors found that children who had poor oral health were more likely to do poorly in school, as measured by grades.

In another empirical study, Seirawan et al. (2012) investigated the association between caries and academic performance in 1,495 students in the mega Los Angeles Unified School District (LAUSD). The sample included Latino/Latina (61.3%), Black (23.8%), Asian (9.7%), and White (5.2%) students. Two age groups of students were recruited: 6–8 years and 14–16 years; these groups were sought as they coincide with the dentition stages of mixed and permanent teeth, respectively. Examination of the participants' oral health status was conducted, at the school sites, by two general dentists. The LAUSD, cooperating closely with the researchers, provided achievement test data and GPAs of the students (the latter available only for the high school students). Seirawan et al. report that participants who had a toothache in the last six months were nearly 4 times more probable to have earned a GPA below the median of 2.8, compared to a control group sans a recent toothache. Also, students who had a toothache missed school at a rate 6 times greater than the control group.

6. *Food insecurity and poor nutrition.* Based on the gross domestic product, in 2012 the U.S. was the wealthiest nation in the world.[27] Yet, as of 2011 there were 17.9 million U.S. households (14.9% of total households) that had experienced "food insecurity," affecting about 50 million people (Coleman-Jensen, Nord, Andrews, & Carlson, 2012). In the mid-1990s, the U.S. Department of Agriculture began to measure the concept of food insecurity (hereafter referred to as FI) via the U.S. Food Security Scale, administered yearly by the U.S. Census Bureau in the Current Population Survey (Cook & Frank, 2008). In brief, FI is the "lack of consistent access to adequate food" (Wright, Thampi, & Briggs, 2010, p. 5). An extended conception notes that FI "is an economic and social condition characterized by reduced or unknown access to sufficient healthful and safe food or the limited ability to acquire fare in ways deemed appropriate by society" (Nalty, Sharkey, & Dean, 2013, p. 1).[28]

In addition to being the richest country in the world, the U.S. is also one of the leading producers of food. For example, in 2010 the U.S. ranked number one in corn and soybean production and third in wheat.[29] It is ironic that in light of the abundance of food in the U.S., there are millions and millions of children and adults who experience FI. This unfortunate situation has been referred to as "a paradox of plenty" (Debusmann, 2009). As such, the primary basis of FI in the U.S. is not food scarcity. The chief predictor of such FI is living in poverty (Cook & Jeng, 2009), a societal inequality. For example, Wright et al. (2010), drawing from 2008 national data, note that 28.9% of poor households (defined as families with an income 100% beneath the poverty line) reported that their children experienced FI. In stark comparison, 7.5% of nonpoor households had children who faced FI.

Given the covariation of poverty and race/ethnicity (see Table 3.4), it is not surprising at all that children of color are disproportionately represented among the ranks of having experienced FI (e.g., Agénor, Ettinger de Cuba, Rose-Jacobs, & Frank, 2006; Coleman-Jensen et al., 2012; Cook & Frank, 2008; Nord, 2009).[30] FI has affected Black and Latino/Latina children at high rates for some time now. Several years after the concept of FI was developed and the instrument to measure it was used in surveys, data from 1999 show a pattern of racialization. In U.S. households with FI, Black and Latino/Latina families were 3 times more likely to experience FI in comparison to White households (Cook & Frank, p. 4, Figure 2). More than a decade ago (2004), in households with children under 18 years of age, the following FI racial/ethnic rates were: Black (29.2%), Latino/Latina (26.8%), and White (12.7%) (Agénor et al., p. 8, Table 1). In a very recent report on FI, the racialized pattern of FI persists. In 2011, FI was more prevalent in households of color, as follows: Latino/Latina (26.2%), Black (25.1%), and White (11.4%) (Coleman-Jensen et al., p. 11, Table 2).

Because FI involves inconsistent access to adequate amounts of food and healthy nourishment, FI has caught the attention of medical researchers and practitioners. Childhood FI has been found to be associated with, for example, iron deficiency and iron deficiency anemia, protein-calorie deficiency, proneness to infections because of a compromised immune system, obesity (due to ingestion of "empty" calories—i.e., solid fat and excess sugar), and diminished cognition (e.g., Cook & Jeng, 2009; Nyberg, Ramírez, & Gallion, 2011a; Taras, 2005). It is this latter issue, a decline in cognitive functioning, that is of particular interest here—specifically, is FI in children associated with deleterious effects on academic performance? A corpus of literature exists that has investigated this relation, and it reports that FI does indeed have negative effects on children's academic achievement (e.g., Alaimo, Olson, & Frongillo, 2001; Jyoti, Frongillo, & Jones, 2005; Ross, 2010; Winicki, 2003).[31] By way of illustration, Winicki (2003) drew from the Early Childhood Longitudinal Study-Kindergarten Cohort (ECLS-K), which includes a nationwide representative sample of 21,260 kindergarten children from 1,592 schools. The author compared the relation between FI and mathematics test scores and reports that the children in families with any indicators of FI scored lower in achievement compared to their food-secure peers. Furthermore, the mean gain score (from fall to spring) in mathematics scores was less for children in households with FI.

In another insightful study, Alaimo et al. (2001) used data from the NHANES and compared the relation between FI and cognitive and academic achievement outcomes. The cognitive measures were two subsets (Block Design and Digit Span) of the Wechsler Intelligence Scale for Children–Revised; achievement was measured by two subsets (Reading and Mathematics) of the Wide Range Achievement Test–Revised. Children with FI, compared to those without it, had significantly lower scores on both cognitive measures and both achievement measures. Also, the former group of children had significantly more grade retentions and days absent.

Researchers do not have an unequivocal explanation of why FI is associated with impaired academic achievement. There are, however, hypotheses; two appear to have some merit. Alaimo et al. (2001) note that one possibility has to do with the affective consequences of food deprivation. FI, the authors suggest, can lead a child to be distractible, irritable, or experience emotional changes. Alaimo et al. base their hypothesis on the theoretical framework proffered by Strupp and Levitsky (1995), who reappraised the literature on the lasting cognitive consequences of early malnutrition. Strupp and Levitsky note that research based on early malnutrition (either pre- or postnatal) in laboratory rats shows that such animals, compared to controls, have some impairments in cognitive flexibility, attention, and motivation. The authors comment that research on early malnutrition in laboratory animals may hold some promise for understanding the effects of poor nutrition in children, but we should be very mindful that such deleterious effects do not happen in isolation. Factors such as environmental insults (e.g., lead poisoning, iron deficiency anemia), SES circumstances (e.g., dearth of medical care for the poor), and institutional arrangements (e.g., inferior schools) must be considered. A second hypothesis that has been advanced to explain how FI negatively affects academic achievement is similar to the theory offered by Strupp and Levitsky, but it has a much stronger emphasis on the role of nutrition in cognition in young children. Ross (2010), in a literature review, notes that the following, for example, are very important for optimal brain functioning and learning: protein, complex carbohydrates (e.g., grains; fruits), Omega-3 fatty acids, minerals and vitamins (e.g., iron; zinc; vitamins A, B6, B12, and C).

Toward Systemic Transformations

Here, and in the closing of each chapter to follow (i.e., 4–9), I offer suggestions for moving in the direction of systemic transformations in the exigent pursuit of TAG diminution and educational equality. My comments are not intended to serve as comprehensive proposals, but rather as outlines that can serve as roadmaps for informed give-and-take discourse. Three threads run through most of these concluding sections. First, systemic transformations are not achievable without serious financial commitment. Systemic reform cannot be done cheaply. Second, these suggestions, for the most part, run counter to the orthodoxy. Given their provocative nature, people need to engage them with an open mind. Third, as often as possible, I base my recommendations on the best evidence I can locate (e.g., grounded in theory, sound methodology, and application to the realization of social justice and equality in society and the schools).

1. *The income gap.* Clearly, one of the most profound markers of class stratification in the U.S. is the marked chasm in income and wealth between the economically advantaged and disadvantaged. In light of the persistent and pervasive covariation of race and class, and in the context of the investment hypothesis, parents of color are less able to spend on the education of their children, including the payments (in full or part) for their children's higher education. How can the income gap in the U.S. be reduced so that parents of color can have increased financial means to make investments in their children's education?

A. *Living wage.* What is a living wage? A consensus: It is an adequate remuneration, permitting workers and their families to be self-reliant in meeting basic, frills-free needs, such as housing, food, transformation, and clothing (Brooks, 2007). The campaign for a living wage originated over 100 years ago when the Women's Educational and Industrial Union lobbied the Boston City Council in 1911 to pass an ordinance calling for a "self-sufficiency standard." In the ensuing year, Massachusetts became the initial state to adopt a law guaranteeing a minimum wage (Luce, 2002). In modern times, the living wage movement has its beginnings in Baltimore, Maryland, in 1994 when the mayor signed a bill mandating that all firms with city contracts pay their employees a living wage. This new wage of $6.10 per hour was nearly $2.00 per hour more than the prevailing federal minimum wage of $4.25 (Brooks; Luce, 2012). The movement for a living wage in the U.S. quickly propagated, and by 2012 there were living wage decrees in over 140 counties, cities, and universities (Luce, 2012). One of the campaign's striking accomplishments was what transpired in Santa Fe, New Mexico. In February 2006, all businesses in the city were mandated to pay a minimum wage of $9.50 an hour, the highest rate in the nation (Brooks; Gertner, 2006). The new wage amounted to a dramatic 84.5% increase over the New Mexico minimum wage of $5.15 per hour.[32]

Living wages in the U.S. can be quantified. Dr. Amy Glasmeier, professor of urban studies and planning at the Massachusetts Institute of Technology, has developed a "Living Wage Calculator" that provides an estimate of a wage rate that is needed to meet *minimum* standards, based on the local cost of living expenses (Glasmeier, 2013). For example, in Austin, Texas, the hourly living wage for a family of two adults and two children is $19.85. The corresponding poverty wage and minimum wage are, respectively, $10.60 and $7.25.[33] In regard to the question of whether a living wage has made an impact, either positively or negatively, the available literature concludes that living wage ordinances have not resulted in the dire consequences predicted by opponents (e.g., greater unemployment, declines in the number of companies making bids for city contracts; see Luce, 2012). On the contrary, living wage ordinances have helped to promote the growth of economic justice (e.g., Brenner, 2004; Brooks, 2007; Chapman & Thompson, 2006; Luce, 2012; Neumark, Thompson, & Koyle, 2012).

B. *Minimum wage.* A major concern with living wage ordinances is that, on the whole, they advantage only a minuscule fraction of workers (e.g., Brenner, Wicks-Lim, & Pollin, 2002; Holzer, 2008; Luce, 2012). As a case in point, take the Los Angeles-Long Beach metropolitan statistical area (MSA). In 1999, 2 years after the Los Angeles City Council passed its living wage law, the MSA had 4.6 million residents in the labor market. Of these, the living wage ordinance covered about 7,600 workers, or .17% of the work force (Brenner et al.). The number of workers who have benefitted has not appreciably increased. Based on data from 2001–2003, about 10,000 workers (22% of the labor force) were covered by the living wage ordinance in the city of Los Angeles (Fairris, 2007). Given the very small number of workers assisted by living wage ordinances, it is not unexpected that the backers of the campaign for living wage laws have lent their support in efforts to raise the federal minimum wage, as well as at the state level (Luce, 2012).

The debate over whether substantially raising the federal minimum wage is beneficial or harmful to the U.S. economy continues ad nauseam. In the remainder of this section, I note only, in the briefest fashion, the arguments on both sides of this important issue. One aspect of this dispute on which most people—pundits and scholars alike—would likely agree is that the current federal minimum wage of $7.25 (as of 2014) is nearly not enough to meet the basic financial needs of a family. At this wage, an individual (e.g., retail store clerk, security guard) who works full-time earns about $15,080 per year (Riley, 2012). If that retail clerk is the sole breadwinner in a family of four, his or her annual salary is about $8,470 below the federal poverty level of $23,021 for a family of four (see page 95, this chapter). It is estimated that a single mother with two children would have to earn, working full-time, between $17.50 and $31.60 per hour (variation is due to geographic differences in costs of living) in order to meet the essential needs of her family (Vohra-Gupta, 2012).

Proponents of raising the federal minimum wage (and state minimum wages) assert, based on research findings, that there would be some positive consequences, such as: stimulation of the economy, no job losses, reduction of turnovers in businesses, and a lessening of burdens on taxpayers (e.g., due to the working poor not having to rely as much on food stamps) (e.g., Baiman, Doussard, Mastracci, Persky, & Theodore, 2003; Lester, Madland, & Bunker, 2011; Vohra-Gupta, 2012). Opponents of increasing the minimum wage contend that such a policy will raise business costs, forcing firms to reduce workers' hours and to downsize their work force—leading to less or no take-home pay, thus increasing poverty (Saltsman, 2013). Another assertion is that an increase in the minimum wage results in no corresponding reduction of people living in poverty (Saltsman). On this latter point, Sabia and Nielsen (2012) agree: Increasing the minimum wage has not been successful in lessening poverty and material hardship. One reason for the ineffectiveness of minimum wage hikes in reducing poverty is that the majority of poor people (55%) do not work, and thus cannot benefit from minimum wage increases. As an alternative, Sabia and Nielsen argue that the Earned Income Tax Credit (EITC) needs to be greatly expanded. The EITC is a refundable federal income tax credit designed for individuals and families who earn low to moderate incomes.[34] It is estimated that for every 1% increase in a state add-on to the EITC, the poverty rate falls by 1% (Sabia & Nielsen).

C. *The digital divide.* The expression "digital divide" entered the U.S. vocabulary in the mid-1990s. It refers to the "disparity between individuals who have and do not have access to information technology" (Eamon, 2004, p. 91)—particularly access to computers and the Internet. I include the digital divide as an issue under "The Income Gap" because of the relatively high costs of a computer for families with limited financial means. My focus here is on the racialization of the digital divide, which has been well documented (e.g., Clotfelter, Ladd, & Vigdor, 2008; DeBell & Chapman, 2006; Eamon; Vigdor & Ladd, 2010). In one of the most comprehensive analyses to date on the digital divide, DeBell and Chapman (2006) used 2003 Current Population Survey data, which is representative of national households in the U.S. The authors report that White, Black, and Latino/Latina K-12 public school students use computers at school at quite comparable rates: White (85%), Black (82%), and Latino/Latina (80%). By sharp contrast, the percentages of K-12 students who use computers at *home* vary significantly by race/ethnicity: White (78%), Latino/Latina (48%), and Black (46%).[35] In sum, White students are about 1.7 times more likely to use home computers in comparison to their Latino/Latina and Black peers. These racialized differences persist in the present (Vigdor & Ladd). In light of the high costs of purchasing a computer, the digital divide also exists along SES lines. DeBell and Chapman (2006) note, for example, that 37% of children from families with annual incomes of less than $20,000 use home computers. On the other hand, 88% of children from families who earn $75,000 a year or more engage in home computer use.[36]

A germane question regarding the digital divide remains: Is home computer and Internet use positively associated with students' academic achievement? Intuitively, one would expect this query to be answered with a resounding "yes." The available literature, however, offers mixed findings. Some studies report that home computer use is positively correlated with students' academic achievement (e.g., Drain, Grier, & Sun, 2012; Subrahmanyam, Kraut, Greenfield, & Gross, 2000; Tsikalas, Lee, & Newkirk, 2007), while some investigations find no effects (e.g., Fairlie & Robinson, 2013; Vigdor & Ladd, 2010). These equivocal findings may be due to methodological issues dealing with differences in: geographic locations, sample sizes, academic achievement measures, and student time spent on computers. Regarding this last variable, a few researchers have noted that students, while on the computer, sometimes spend time on "non-productive activities" (Vigdor & Ladd). There is some evidence for this. DeBell and Chapman (2006) report that the most prevalent (56%) computer activity in which K-12 students engage is playing games; second most common (47%) is completing school assignments.[37]

Even if research studies eventually find that home computer use by students has no effect on academic achievement, learning how to operate a computer does have collateral advantages, such as learning how to run advanced programming and becoming proficient at hardware maintenance, skills which can prepare students for a career in computer technology (Vigdor & Ladd, 2010). Also, for the college-bound student, becoming skilled at computer use (i.e., word processing, Internet searches) will prove invaluable in his or her classes. In any event, I feel strongly that we need serious relief for the digital divide. All low-SES students of color should have access to a home computer. Although this will be a very expensive venture, perhaps the state or federal government—working closely with philanthropic organizations (such as One Laptop at a Time)[38]—can make this a reality.

D. *Forgivable student college loans.* One of the most effective pathways a young, low-SES man or woman of color can travel to increase his or her eventual earning power is to matriculate to college and earn a bachelor's degree, or beyond. As I note in chapter 1, an adult with a bachelor's degree can earn, over his or her lifetime, close to 1 million dollars more than an individual with only a high school diploma (Longley, 2010). A disincentive, however, to attend college is the very heavy indebtedness a graduate can accrue. For the class of 2013, the mean student loan debt for someone who earned a bachelor's degree was $30,000—and for those graduates who have credit card debt and loans due to family members, the indebtedness was $35,200 (Izzo, 2013). And the indebtedness of earning a college degree keeps climbing. The class of 2014 has the dubious distinction of accruing the highest indebtedness of college graduates in the history of the U.S.—with an average of $33,000 per graduate (Klahn, 2014). That unfortunate record likely will be broken by the class of 2015.

One way college-bound low-SES students of color can avoid this enormous loan debt is to consider applying for forgivable student loans. Some loan forgivable programs exist through the federal government. For example, the Teacher Loan Forgiveness Program offers such loans for those who are willing to teach in elementary and secondary schools that serve low-SES students. If a graduate teaches in a select school full-time for five consecutive years, he or she is eligible for loan forgiveness up to $17,500.[39] Forgivable student college loans are also available in some states. For example, California has a loan forgiveness program for students pursuing a bachelor's degree in nursing.[40] One of the most comprehensive forgivable student college loan programs is in North Carolina. Approved career areas are: allied health (e.g., chiropractic care; dental hygiene; radiology; social work), nursing, medicine (doctorate only—e.g., dentistry), and teaching (e.g., mathematics, special education).[41]

It would be ideal to have comprehensive forgivable college loan programs (as in North Carolina) in every state. For the state and low-SES students of color, in particular, such programs would have win-win consequences. First, the state would benefit by having jobs filled in areas where there are shortages (e.g., nursing, teaching of mathematics). Second, the state would profit by filling jobs in underserved areas (e.g., teaching positions in low-SES schools). Third, institutions and firms in the state would benefit by diversifying their workforce along lines of race/ethnicity. In sum, for students of color, forgiveness programs would allow them to begin their careers sans the financial burden of hefty student loan repayments. Moreover, not being saddled with considerable indebtedness when they launch their careers, young men and women of color, once they begin to have offspring, will be better able to invest in their children's education.

2. *The housing gap.* Earlier in this chapter, I underscore that housing segregation and school segregation are inextricably linked. As I discuss, scholars seldom focus on the interrelation between two types of isolation. Therefore, a fitting place to elaborate on this connection is in the concluding section of the next chapter, "School Segregation, Desegregation, and Integration."

3. *The health gap.* Although there are a number of serious health issues that affect the quality of life of students of color, as well as their academic achievement, these matters of concern are not insurmountable. In my view, two major aspects appear to be the most viable in scaling the health gap: prevention and intervention. Next, I briefly provide examples from these two domains of health care.

A. *Prevention.* A case in point is preventive medical care. Regular visits by children and youths to the family's primary care provider are essential for optimal health care (e.g., Pham et al., 2006). These appointments can prove invaluable in screening (and follow-up care if necessary) for the health problems I discuss earlier in this chapter. Screening can be done, for example, to gather data on: BMI measurement, blood glucose level, lung function, lead poisoning, and poor nutrition (via a blood test). Another example of prevention is dental care. Fox (2011) suggests that preventive dental care can be done at schools, at no cost to the low-SES student. She asserts that dental therapists, who have undergone extensive training, are competent to do teeth cleaning, apply sealants, treat cavities, and do fluoride rinses. For treatment beyond the range of the therapist's expertise, the child should be referred to a dentist.

The bulk cost of preventive medical and dental care would be paid by health insurance. This does, however, present a problem for some low-SES children of color. In 2011, 10.2% of Black children and 15.1% of Latino/Latina children were uninsured—compared to 6.8% of White children. Furthermore, children living in poverty were more likely to be uninsured (DeNavas et al., 2012). In sum, to attain the best preventive medical and dental care for low-SES children of color in the U.S., there has to be universal coverage. Matters were likely to improve when the Affordable Care Act—signed by President Barack Obama on March 23, 2010—went into effect in 2014.[42] Furthermore, part of the Affordable Care Act maintains the Children's Health Insurance Program (CHIP) through 2019, and extends its funding until October 1, 2015—a point in time where CHIP's funding will be substantially increased. CHIP currently provides coverage to almost 8 million children whose families' incomes are too high to be eligible for Medicaid but too low to pay for private health insurance coverage.[43]

B. *Intervention*. There are many ways to intervene to promote better health care for students of color. Here I briefly note several. One of the most common breakfasts children eat is cereal with milk. Yet, for some students of color this prevalent morning staple presents a problem. Research shows that cereal designed for children is not a very nutritious food (Harris et al., 2012). Cereals that are marketed to youngsters have 60% more sodium, 85% more sugar, and 65% less fiber compared to those cereals geared for the adult market. Also, cereal firms target their advertisements more assertively toward Black and Latino/Latina children, compared to Whites. Sharp rises have been seen particularly on Spanish-language television (Harris et al.). Given that the cereal industry is self-regulating (Harris et al.), governmental intervention is needed. As well, parents of color need to help their children make healthier cereal choices (e.g., far less sugar, more fiber). The milk that goes into cereal, or is consumed as a beverage, is also a concern. Nutrition experts recommend that children drink low-fat milk to help promote good bone health. Yet, it has been reported that in regard to low-fat milk consumption, 28% of White children and adolescents drink the healthier milk, compared to 10% of Latinos/Latinas and 5% of Blacks (Kit, Carroll, & Ogden, 2011).

In regard to obesity, a number of studies conclude that interventions work. Yet, none of these investigations have focused on children of color. One exception, however, is the meta-analysis of obesity interventions by Seo and Sa (2010). The authors analyzed 40 studies containing 10,725 participants aged 6–19 years; 6,602 (62%) of the children were Black, Mexican American and other Latino/Latina, American Indian, and Asian American. Seo and Sa primarily focused on the participants of color. Among the authors' conclusions, two points are of particular importance. First, the most efficacious interventions in the prevention or treatment of childhood obesity are those that use three or more components (e.g., nutrition; exercise; counseling). Second, parental involvement as an intervention, compared to no parental engagement, proved to be successful. The authors underscore that the most effective obesity interventions with children of color are those with multicomponents.

One of the interventions that have received considerable attention is the need to strengthen and improve school programs and policies for physical activity and physical education. These recommendations are comprehensively covered in the recent National Academies Press book, *Educating the Student Body: Taking Physical Activity and Physical Education to School,* by Harold Kohl and Heather Cook (2013). Physical activity is not the panacea for a healthy life, but its benefits are enormous—for example, improved cardiovascular health and metabolism, enhanced muscular strength, sturdier bones, improved cognition, less body fat, and better mental health (Kohl & Cook). In a nutshell, Kohl and Cook are calling for a systemic transformation in the way our schools view physical activity. The authors recommend that students should devote 60 minutes a day to vigorous to moderate-intensity exercise, of which 50% should be done during school hours. For physical activity before or after school, all students should be given opportunities to participate in intramural and extramural sports. To be successful, this paradigm shift will require cooperative and coordinative efforts and resources from, for example, state and local governments, school boards, parent teacher organizations, and local businesses. Furthermore, given that physical education is the cornerstone for a lifelong commitment to optimal health, Kohl and Cook recommend that the U.S. Department of Education classify physical education as a core curricular subject.

To sum, the "other" gaps—in income, housing, and health—all contribute to TAG. The empirical evidence of this association is quite convincing. Why is it, then, that the "other" gaps do not receive the full attention they deserve in discourse on the education of low-SES students of color? I offer at least two explanations. First, many people, because they view society through a narrowly focused lens, fail to see that the U.S. is rife with societal inequalities along lines of class and race. Given that public schools are microcosms of the larger society, such myopia leads to a perception that externally based inequalities (e.g., in housing) are unrelated to what transpires in schools. CRT, on the other hand, helps us to challenge the ahistoricism and narrow views of these analyses. Second, a good number of educational researchers and policymakers view schools in highly compartmentalized ways—for example, teacher quality, student assessment, and curricular matters. These individuals fail to see the nested and complex interrelations of the "other" gaps and the academic achievement of low-SES students of color.

Notes

1. Also, see Duncan and Murnane (2011), Ornstein (2007), and Rothstein (2004).
2. Researchers typically use *total* household income, rather than *family* income. This index allows a more accurate assessment of who earns what (McKernan, Ratcliffe, & Cellini (2009).
3. To ascertain whether a family's profile justifies a status of middle-class security or an in-between category, or places them at risk of slipping out of the middle class, the authors developed a Middle-Class Security Index using five areas (e.g., educational attainment; assets; health insurance; see Wheary, Shapiro, Draut, & Meschede, 2008, pp. 1–3).
4. Here, wealth—or household "net worth"—is defined as "the sum of the market value of assets owned by every member of the household minus their liabilities (debt)" (Kochlar, Fry, & Taylor, 2011, p. 7). Examples of assets are: financial institution savings; U.S. savings bonds; owned home; motor vehicles. Instances of liabilities are: motor vehicle loans; home mortgages; credit card balances; student loans (Kochlar et al.).

5. A relative risk ratio is used to express the degree of disproportionality of a particular condition. In Table 3.4, the ratio is calculated by dividing the poverty percentage of a group of color (e.g., Blacks) by the poverty percentage of the White group. A relative risk ratio of 1.0 indicates equal representation, while a value more than 1.0 points to overrepresentation. See Coutinho and Oswald (2004) for further discussion.
6. For a discussion of childhood poverty trends (from about the late 1930s to the early 1990s), see Hernández (1997).
7. Due to small sample sizes, Rank and Hirschl (1999) were unable to include Latinos/Latinas and other groups of color in their analysis.
8. In regard to the investment hypothesis, another principal way in which parents direct activities that promote cognitive development and favorable academic outcomes is in the quantity of quality of *time* spent with their children (Philips, 2011). Researchers primarily rely on interviews with or observations of the mother, in which questions of frequency or actual dyadic interactions are recorded (e.g., frequency of mother: reading to child, providing positive reinforcement to child, consulting child's teacher to discuss his or her progress, and so forth). Although parental time investment has been shown to be a valid predictor of children's cognitive development and academic achievement (for White children and their peers of color), I do not discuss this literature here (see, e.g., Philips, 2011; Valencia & Suzuki, 2001, chapter 4).
9. See "Location, location, location: How to find a home of your own." Retrieved December 12, 2012, from: www.cmhc.ca/newcomers/pdfs/English/B9.pdf.
10. 1948: *Shelly v. Kraemer*. Fair Housing Center of Boston. Retrieved December 27, 2012, from: www.bostonfairhousing.org/timeline/1948-Shelley-v-Kramer.html.
11. *Id.*
12. "Federal Housing Administration (FHA)." Retrieved December 28, 2012, from: http://portal.hud.gov:80/hudportal/HUD?src=/program_offices/housing/fhahistory.
13. "US2010: Discover American in a new century: Residential segregation." Providence, RI: Brown University. Retrieved January 20, 2013, from: www.s4.brown.edu/us2010/segregation2010/city.aspx?cityid=668000.
14. The DI can also be represented by values between 0 to 1.0, where 0 is considered complete integration and 1.0 is complete segregation. See "Segregation calculator." Retrieved January 20, 2013, from: http://ryandenos.com/teaching/segregation_calculator.html.
15. *Id.*
16. See note 14, this chapter.
17. "Top 50 cities in the U.S. by population and rank." Retrieved January 20, 2013, from: www.infoplease.com/ipa/A0763098.html.
18. Most of the scholarship on public housing is concerned with Black families. For a discussion of Mexican Americans, for example, see Vigil's (2007) case study of the Pico Rivera public housing in East Los Angeles.
19. Also, see Hirsch (1998, 2000; cited in Turner et al., 2009).
20. The BMI is calculated as follows (Levi et al., 2012, p. 15):

$$\text{BMI} = \frac{\text{weight in pounds}}{(\text{height in inches}) \times (\text{height in inches})} \times 703$$

21. See, for example, Flegal, Ogden, and Carroll (2004); Levi et al. (2012); Nyberg, Ramírez, and Gallion (2011b); Joe, Joe, and Rowley (2009); Ogden, Carroll, Curtin, Lamb, and Flegal (2010); Ogden et al. (2012); Wang and Beydoun (2007); Wang, Orleans, and Gortmaker (2012).

22. It is atypical in health-related literature to report data on disaggregated Latino/Latina groups. Most of the time, data are reported for the Latino/Latina aggregate.
23. This is not to imply that T2D is not seen in older segments of the population. In truth, the rate of T2D rises dramatically with age. For adults aged 65 years or older, the prevalence rate of T2D is approximately seven times higher than people aged 20–44 years (Centers for Disease Control and Prevention, 2012).
24. See *Asthma's impact on the nation: Data from the CDC National Asthma Control Program*. (2012). Atlanta, GA: Centers for Disease Control and Prevention. Retrieved April 20, 2013, from: www.cdc.gov/asthma/impacts_nation/AsthmaFactSheet.pdf.
25. There are, however, exceptions to this racialized pattern. In this corpus of literature, there is one study in which Latino/Latina children did not have an EBLL, in comparison to Black children, who did (see Kemp et al., 2007). Also, in at least one national study, Mexican American children had a lower rate of lead poisoning, compared to their White peers (see Wheeler & Brown, 2013).
26. Miranda et al. (2009) also found an SES effect. Children who participated in the free/reduced lunch program and had parents with lower educational attainment had lower reading scores and higher blood lead levels.
27. "Top 10 richest countries in the world 2012." Retrieved May 1, 2013, from: http://toptenpk.com/top-10-richest-countries-in-the-world-2012/.
28. "Hunger," a related term, is conceived as "the uneasy or painful sensation caused by a lack of food. The recurrent and involuntary lack of access to food. Hunger may produce malnutrition over time. . . . Hunger . . . is a potential, although not necessary consequence of food insecurity" (Cook & Frank, 2008, p. 1). In sum, hunger is a physiological state. It should be distinguished from FI, which is concerned with the availability of and access to food (Coleman-Jensen et al., 2012, p. 4, note 6).
29. "Top agricultural producing countries." Retrieved May 1, 2013, from: www.investopedia.com/ financial-edge/0712/top-agricultural-producing-countries.aspx.
30. It should be noted that with respect to *absolute* numbers, White households with children experience the largest amount of FI—because Whites make up the greatest proportion of the total population.
31. For an extensive annotated bibliography on the relation between food security/nutrition and learning/behavior, see *Role of nutrition and learning and behavior: A resource list for professionals* (2011). Washington, DC: U.S. Department of Agriculture, Food and Nutrition Information Center. Retrieved April 30, 2013, from: www.nal.usda.gov/fnic/pubs/learning.pdf.
32. The information on the 2006 minimum wage rate in New Mexico came from U.S. Department of Labor, "Wage and Hour Division," retrieved May 8, 2013, from: www.dol.gov/whd/minwage/america.htm.
33. Glasmeier's (2013) "poverty wage" is in reference to the federal poverty guidelines. In 2013, the federal poverty standard for a family of four was designated at an annual income level of $23,550 (see Amadeo, 2013).
34. See www.irs.gov/Individuals/EITC-Home-Page—It's-easier-than-ever-to-find-out-if-you-qualify-for-EITC.
35. See DeBell and Chapman (2006, p. 15, Table 3).
36. *Id.*
37. See DeBell and Chapman (2006, p. 21, Table 5).
38. See "Saving the world, One Laptop at a Time." *News USA*. Retrieved May 28, 2013, from: www.voanews.com/content/saving-the-world-1-laptop-at-a-time-85032157/161757.html.

39. See http://studentaid.ed.gov/repay-loans/forgiveness-cancellation/charts/teacher.
40. See http://nursezone.com/student-nurses/student-nurses-featured-articles/ Innovative-Loan-forgiveness-Program-Encourages-California-Nursing-Students_18576.aspx.
41. See www.cfnc.org/FELS.
42. See www.healthcare.gov/law/timeline/.
43. See www.medicaid.gov/CHIP/CHIP-program-information.html.

References

Adelman, R. M., & Gocker, J. C. (2007). Racial residential segregation in urban America. *Sociology Compass, 1,* 404–423.

Agénor, M., Ettinger de Cuba, S., Rose-Jacobs, R., & Frank, D. A. (2006). *The impact of food insecurity on the development of young low-income Black and Latino children.* Washington, DC: Joint Center for Political and Economic Studies Health Policy Institute. Retrieved April 30, 2013, from: www.hungercentter.org/ publications/the-impact-of-food-insecurity-on-the-development-of-young-low-income-black-and-latino-children-2/.

Akinbami, L. J., Rhodes, J. C., & Lara, M. (2005). Racial and ethnic differences in asthma diagnosis among children who wheeze. *Pediatrics, 115,* 1254–1260. Retrieved April 16, 2013, from: http://pediatrics.aappublications.org/content/115/5/1254.full.html.

Alaimo, K., Olson, C. M., & Frongillo, E. A., Jr. (2001). Food insufficiency and American school-aged children's cognitive, academic, and psychosocial development. *Pediatrics, 108,* 44–53. Retrieved April 30, 2013, from: http://pediatrics.aappublications.org/content/108/1/44.full.html.

Amadeo, K. (2013). Federal policy level. *About.com Guide.* Retrieved May 24, 2013, from: http://useconomy.about.com/od/glossary/g/Federal_Poverty_Level.htm.

Annie E. Casey Foundation. (2011). *Promoting opportunity for the next generation: America's children, America's challenge: 2011 KIDSCOUNT data book: State profiles of child well-being.* Baltimore: Author. Retrieved October 19, 2012, from: www.kidscount.org/datacenter.

Apgar, W., & Calder, A. (2005). The dual mortgage market: The persistence of discrimination in mortgage lending. In X. de Souza Briggs (Ed.), *The geography of opportunity: Race and housing choice in metropolitan America* (pp. 101–123). Washington, DC: Brookings Institution Press.

Baiman, R., Doussard, M., Mastracci, S., Persky, S., & Theodore, N. (2003). *Raising and maintaining the value of the state minimum wage: An economic impact study of Illinois.* Chicago: University of Illinois, Center for Urban Economic Development. Retrieved May 26, 2013, from: www.urbaneconomy.org/node/43.

Becker, G. S. (1991). *A treatise on the family.* Cambridge, MA: Harvard University Press.

Becker, G. S. (1994). *Human capital: A theoretical and empirical analysis, with special reference to education* (3rd ed.). Chicago: University of Chicago Press.

Bhargava, D., Casey, T., Cavanagh, J., Dolan, K., Edelman, P., Ehrenreich, B., Gupta, S., Muhammad, D., Pearce, D., Savner, S., & Shih, K. (2009). *Battered by the storm: How the safety net is failing Americans and how to fix it.* December. Washington, DC: Institute for Policy Studies, the Center for Community Change, Jobs with Justice, and Legal Momentum. Retrieved October 27, 2012, from: www.ips-dc.org/reports/battered-by-the-storm.

Bloom, B., Cohen, R. A., Vickerie, J. L., & Wondimu, E. A., (2003). *Summary health statistics for U.S. children: National health interview survey, 2001.* Hyattsville, MD: National Center for Health Statistics, Centers for Disease Control and Prevention. Retrieved April 21, 2013, from: www.cdc.gov/nchs/data/senes/sr_10/sr10_216.pdf.

Blumenshine, S. L., Vann, W. F., Jr., Gizlice, Z., & Lee, J. Y. (2008). Children's school performance: Impact of general and oral health. *Journal of Public Health Dentistry, 68,* 82–87. Retrieved April 29, 2013, from: www.ncbi.nlm.nih.gov/pubmed/18221320.

Bond, H. M. (1934). *The education of the Negro in the American social order.* New York: Prentice-Hall.

Boustan, L. P. (2011). Racial residential segregation in American cities. In N. Brooks, K. Donaghy, & G.-J. Knapp (Eds.), *The Oxford handbook of urban economics and planning* (pp. 318–339). New York: Oxford University Press.

Brenner, M. D. (2004). *The economic impact of living wage ordinances* (Working Paper Series No. 80). Amherst: University of Massachusetts, Political Economy Research Institute. Retrieved May 24, 2013, from: www.peri.umass.edu/fileadmin/pdf/working_papers/working-papers-51-100/WP80.pdf.

Brenner, M. D., Wicks-Lim, J., & Pollin, R. (2002). *Measuring the impact of living wage laws: A critical appraisal of David Neumark's How Living Wage Laws Affect Low-Wage Workers and Low-Income Families* (Working Paper Series No. 143). Amherst: University of Massachusetts, Political Economy Research Institute. Retrieved May 25, 2013, from: scholarworks.umass.edu/peri_workingpapers/11/.

Briggs, X. de Souza (Ed.). (2005a). *The geography of opportunity: Race and housing choice in metropolitan America.* Washington, DC: Brooking Institution Press.

Briggs, X. de Souza (2005b). More *pluribus,* less *unum*? The changing geography of race and opportunity. In X. de Souza Briggs (Ed.), *The geography of opportunity: Race and housing choice in metropolitan America* (pp. 17–41). Washington, DC: Brookings Institution Press.

Brooks, F. (2007). The living-wage movement: Political implications for the working poor. *Families in Society, 88,* 437–442. Retrieved May 8, 2013, from: http://digitalarchive.gsu.edu/ssw_facpub/31/.

Brooks, R. W., & Rose, C. M. (2013). *Saving the neighborhood: Racially restrictive covenants, law, and social norms.* Cambridge, MA: Harvard University Press.

Bryant, M. L. (2001). Combating school resegregation through housing: A need for a reconceptualization of American democracy and the rights it protects. In J. A. Powell, G. Kearney, & V. Kay (Eds.), *In pursuit of a dream deferred: Linking housing and education policy* (pp. 49–87). New York: Peter Lang.

Bugis, B. A. (2012). Early childhood caries and the impact of current U.S. Medicaid: An overview. *International Journal of Dentistry, 2012,* 1–7. Retrieved April 25, 2013, from: www.hindawi.com/journals/ijd/2012/348237/.

Byrd, J. (2007, March 30). *The impact of physical activity and obesity on academic achievement among elementary children.* Rice University, TX: Connexions Project. Retrieved April 15, 2013, from: http://cnx.org/content/m14420/1.1/.

Caballero, A. E. (2007). Type 2 diabetes in the Hispanic or Latino population: Challenges and opportunities. *Current Opinion in Endocrinology, Diabetes and Obesity, 14,* 151–157. Retrieved April 13, 2013, from: www.ncbi.nlm.nih.gov/pubmed/17940434.

Canino, G., Koinis-Mitchell, D., Ortega, A. N., McQuaid, E. L., Fritz, G. X., & Alegria, M. (2006). Asthma disparities in the prevalence, morbidity, and treatment of Latino children. *Social Science & Medicine, 63,* 2926–2937. Retrieved April 16, 2013, from: www.sciencedirect.com/science/article/pii/S0277953606003807.

Center on Budget and Policy Priorities. (2012, October 26). *Chart book: The legacy of the Great Recession.* Retrieved October 27, 2012, from: www.cbpp.org/cms/index.cfm?fa=view&id=3252.

Centers for Disease Control and Prevention. (2012). *Diabetes report card 2012.* Atlanta, GA: Author, U.S. Department of Health and Human Services. Retrieved April 10, 2013, from: www.cdc.gov/diabetes/pubs/pdf/DiabetesReportCard.pdf.

Chapman, J., & Thompson, J. (2006). *The economic impact of local living wages.* Washington, DC: Economic Policy Institute. Retrieved May 24, 2013, from: www.epi.org/publication/bp170/.

Charles, C. Z. (2005). Can we live together? Racial preferences and neighborhood outcomes. In X. de Souza Briggs (Ed.), *The geography of opportunity: Race and housing choice in metropolitan America* (pp. 45–80). Washington, DC: Brookings Institution Press.

Clotfelter, C. T., Ladd, H. F., & Vigdor, J. L. (2008). *Scaling the digital divide: Home computer technology and student achievement. CiteSeerX.* Retrieved May 27, 2013, from: citeseerx.ist.psu.edu/viewdoc/summary?doi=10.1.1.172.8466.

Coleman-Jensen, A., Nord, M., Andrews, M., & Carlson, S. (2012). *Household food security in the United States in 2011* (ERR-141). Washington, DC: U.S. Department of Agriculture, Economic Research Service. Retrieved April 30, 2013, from: www.ers.usda.gov/media/884525/err141.pdf.

Condron, D. J. (2011). Egalitarianism and educational excellence: Compatible goals for affluent societies? *Educational Researcher, 40,* 47–55.

Cook, J., & Jeng, K. (2009). *Child food insecurity: The economic impact on our nation: A report on the impact of food insecurity and hunger on child health, growth, and development.* Chicago: Feeding America. Retrieved April 30, 2013, from: feedingamerican.org/SiteFiles/child-economy-study.pdf.

Cook, J. T., & Frank, D. A. (2008). Food security, poverty, and human development in the United States. *New York Academy of Sciences, 40,* 1–16. Retrieved April 30, 2013, from: www.childrenhealthwatch.org/upload/ resource/cook_frank_annals_08.pdf.

Coutinho, M. J., & Oswald, D. P. (2004). Disproportionate representation of culturally and linguistically diverse students in special education: Measuring the problem. *LD Online.* Retrieved November 3, 2012, from: www.ldonline.org/article/5603/.

Cutler, D. M., Glaeser, E. L., & Vigdor, J. L. (1999). The rise and decline of the American ghetto. *Journal of Political Economy, 107,* 455–506.

Dabelea, D., Pettitt, D. J., Jones, K. L., & Arslanian, S. A. (1999). Type 2 diabetes mellitus in minority children and adolescents: An emerging problem. *Endocrinology and Metabolism Clinics of North America, 28,* 709–729. Retrieved April 7, 2013, from: www.ncbi.nlm.nih.gov/pubmed/10609116.

D'Adamo, E., & Caprio, S. (2011). Type 2 diabetes in youth: Epidemiology and pathophysiology. *Diabetes Care, 34,* 161–165. Retrieved April 10, 2013, from: http://care.diabetesjournals.org/content/34/Supplement_2/S161.full.

Daniels, D. Y. (2008). Examining attendance, academic performance, and behavior in obese adolescents. *Journal of School Nursing, 24,* 379–387. Retrieved April 15, 2013, from: http://jsn.sagepub.com/content/24/6/379.abstract.

Datar, A., Sturm, R., & Magnabosco, J. L. (2004). Childhood overweight and academic performance: National study of kindergartners and first-graders. *Obesity Research, 12,* 58–68. Retrieved April 15, 2013, from: www.ncbi.nim.nih.gov/pubmed/14742843.

DeBell, M., & Chapman, C. (2006). *Computer and internet use by students in 2003: Statistical analysis report* (NCES 2006–065). Washington, DC: Institute of Education Sciences, U.S. Department of Education. Retrieved May 26, 2013, from: http://nces.ed.gov/pubs2006/2006065.pdf.

Debusmann, B. (2009, November 24). A paradox of plenty—hunger in America. *Reuters.* Retrieved April 30, 2013, from: http://blogs.reuters.com/great-debate/2009/11/24/a-paradox-of-plenty-hunger-in-america/.

DeNavas-Walt, C., Proctor, B. D., & Smith, J. C. (2012). *Income, poverty, and health insurance coverage in the United States: 2011.* Current Population Reports (P60–243), U.S. Census

Bureau. Washington, DC: U. S. Government Printing Office. Retrieved October 16, 2012, from: www.census.gov/hhes/www//poverty.

Denton, N. A. (2001). The persistence of segregation: Links between residential segregation and school integration. In J. A. Powell, G. Kearney, & V. Kay (Eds.), *In pursuit of a dream deferred: Linking housing and education policy* (pp. 89–119). New York: Peter Lang.

Domitrovic, B. (2012, May 7). The weak dollar caused the Great Recession. *Forbes Magazine.* Retrieved October 28, 2012, from: www.forbes.com/forbes/2012/0507/capital-flows-crisis-weak-dollar-great recession.html.

Doss v. Bernal, Civil Action No. 41466 (Superior Court, Orange County, California, November 1943).

Drain, T. S., Grier, L. E., & Sun, W. (2012). Is the growing use of electronic devices beneficial to academic performance? Results from archival data and a survey. *Issues in Information Systems, 13,* 225–231. Retrieved May 27, 2013, from: iacis.org/iis/2012/50_iis_2012_225–231.pdf.

Dreier, P., Mollenkopf, J., & Swanstrom, T. (2004). *Place matters: Metropolitics for the twenty-first century.* Lawrence: University Press of Kansas.

Duncan, G. J., & Murnane, R. J. (Eds.). (2011). *Whither opportunity?: Rising inequality, schools, and children's chances.* New York: Russell Sage Foundation.

Eamon, M. K. (2004). Digital divide in computer access and use between poor and non-poor youths. *Journal of Sociology and Social Welfare, 31,* 91–112. Retrieved May 27, 2013, from: imet.csus.edu.imet8/leu/251/articles/Article_Eamon_PoorYouth.pdf.

Eckert, G. J., Jackson, R., & Fontana, M. (2010). Sociodemographic variation of caries risk factors in toddlers and caregivers. *International Journal of Dentistry, 2010,* 1–17. Retrieved April 15, 2013, from: www.hindaul.com/journals/ijd/2010/593487/.

Efrat, M. (2011). The relationship between low-income and minority children's physical activity and academic-related outcomes: A review of the literature. *Health Education & Behavior, 38,* 441–451. Retrieved April 15, 2013, from: http://heb.sagepub.com/content/38/5/441.

Ehrenreich, B. (2001). *Nickel and dimed: On (not) getting by in America.* New York: Metropolitan Books.

Fair Housing Act. (1968). 42 U.S.C.A. §§ 3601–3631.

Fairlie, R. W., & Robinson, J. (2013). *Experimental evidence on the effects of home computers on academic achievement among schoolchildren* (Discussion Paper No. 7211). Bonn, Germany: IZA. Retrieved May 27, 2013, from: ftp.iza.org/dp7211.pdf.

Fairris, D. (2007). The effects of living wages on workers and firms: Evidence from the Los Angeles ordinance. *Policy Matters, 1,* 1–11. Retrieved May 25, 2013, from: policy.matters.ucr.edu/.

Finkelstein, E. A., Trogdon, J. G., Cohen, J. W., & Dietz, W. (2009). Annual medical spending attributable to obesity: Payer-and service-specific estimates. *Health Affairs, 28,* 822–831. Retrieved March 23, 2013, from: http://content.healthaffairs.org/content/28/5/w822.full.html.

Flegal, K. M., Ogden, C. L., & Carroll, M. D. (2004). Prevalence and trends in overweight in Mexican-American adults and children. *Nutrition Reviews, 62,* 144–148. Retrieved March 31, 2013, from: onlinelibrary.wiley.com/doi/10.1111/j.1753-4887.2004.tb00085.x/pdf.

Fox, J. (2011). The epidemic of children's dental diseases: Putting teeth into the law. *Yale Journal of Health Policy, Law, and Ethics, 11,* 225–266. Retrieved April 27, 2013, from: http://digitalcommons.law.yale.edu/yjhple/vol11/iss2/1.

Frankenberg, E. (2013). The role of residential segregation in contemporary school segregation. *Education and Urban Society, 45,* 548–570.

Fultz, M. (1996). Horace Mann Bond. In F. C. Jones-Wilson, C. A. Asbury, M. Okazawa-Rey, D. Kamili Anderson, S. M. Jacobs, & M. Fultz (Eds.), *Encyclopedia of African-American education* (pp. 59–60). Westport, CT: Greenwood Press.

Furstenberg, F. (2011). The challenge of finding causal link between family educational practice and schooling outcomes. In G. J. Duncan & R. J. Murnane (Eds.), *Wither opportunity?: Rising inequality, schools, and children's life chances* (pp. 465–482). New York: Russell Sage Foundation.

Galster, G. C., & Killen, S. P. (1995). The geography of metropolitan opportunity: A reconnaissance and conceptual framework. *Housing Policy Debate, 6,* 7–43.

Gane-McCalla, C. (2011, December 28). Home loan company pays $335 million for racial discrimination. *NewsOne for Black America.* Retrieved December 27, 2012, from: http://newsone.com/2000695/home-loan-company-pays-335-million-for-racial-discrimination/#0_undefined,0_.

García, A., & Park, K-S. (2012). Effects of obesity and physical fitness on academic achievement in Hispanic high school students. *International Journal of Exercise Science: Conference Abstract Admissions, 2,* Article 5. Retrieved April 15, 2013, from: http://digitalcommons.wku.edu/ijesab/vol2/iss4/55/.

Garrison, J. (2008, July 27). Living with a reminder of segregation. *Los Angeles Times.* Retrieved December 27, 2012, from: http://articles.latimes.com/2008/jul/27/local/me-covenant27.

Gertner, J. (2006, January 15). What is a living wage? *New York Times Magazine.* Retrieved May 8, 2013, from: www.nytimes.com/2006/01/15/magazine/15wage.html?pagewanted=all.

Glasmeier, A. (2013). *Poverty in America: Living wage calculator.* Cambridge, MA: Massachusetts Institute of Technology. Retrieved May 24, 2013, from: http://livingwage.mit.edu/.

Gould, E. (2009). Childhood lead poisoning: Conservative estimates of the social and benefits of lead hazard control. *Environmental Health Perspectives, 117,* 1162–1167. Retrieved April 16, 2013, from: www.ncbi.nlm.nih.gov/pmc/articles/PMC2717145/.

Grant, R., & Brito, A. (2010). *Chronic illness and school performance: A literature review focusing on asthma and mental health conditions.* New York: Children's Health Fund. Retrieved April 12, 2013, from: www.childrenshealthfund.org/ sites/default/files /chronic-illness-and-school-performance.pdf.

Gurley-Calvez, T., & Higginbotham, A. (2010). Childhood obesity, academic achievement, and school expenditures. *Public Finance Review, 38,* 619–646. Retrieved April 15, 2013, from: http://pfr.sagepub.com/content/38/5/619.abstract.

Harris, J. L., Schwartz, M. B., Brownell, K. D., Sarda, V., Dembek, C., Mausell, C., Shin, C., Ustjanauskas, A., & Weinberg, M. (2012). *Cereal FACTS 2012: Limited progress in the nutrition quality and marketing of children's cereals.* New Haven, CT: Yale University, Rudd Center for Fool Policy & Obesity. Retrieved March 7, 2013, from: www.cerealfacts.org/media/Cereal_FACTS_Report_2012_7.12.pdf.

Heffner, T. (2014, June 12). Economic problems facing the U.S. *Economy in Crisis: America's Economic Report-Daily.* Retrieved July 1, 2014, from: http://economyincrisis.org/content/major-economic-problems-facing-united-states.

Hernández, D. J. (1997). Poverty trends. In G. J. Duncan & J. Brooks-Gunn (Eds.), *Consequences of growing up poor* (pp. 18–34). New York: Russell Sage Foundation.

Hirsch, A. R. (1998). *Making the second ghetto: Race and housing in Chicago, 1940–1960.* Cambridge: Cambridge University Press.

Hirsch, A. R. (2000). Searching for a "sound negro policy": A racial agenda for the housing acts of 1949 and 1954. *Housing Policy Debate, 11,* 393–441.

Holzer, H. J. (2008). *Living wage laws: How much do (can) they matter?* (Discussion Paper No. 1358–08). Washington, DC: Georgetown University, Institute for Research on Poverty. Retrieved May 25, 2013, from: www.irp.wisc.edu/publications/dps/pdfs/dp135808.pdf.

Immergluck, D., & Wiles, M. (1999). *Two steps back: The dual mortgage market, predatory lending, and the undoing of community development.* Chicago: Woodstock Institute.

Imperatore, G., Boyle, J. P., Thompson, T. J., Case, D., Dabelea, D., Hamman, R. F., Lawrence, J. M., Liese, A. D., Liu, L. L., Mayer-Davis, E. J., Rodríguez, B. L., & Standiford, D. (2012). Projections of type 1 and type 2 diabetes burden in the U.S. population aged < 20 years through 2050. *Diabetes Care, 35,* 2515–2520. Retrieved April 7, 2013, from: http://care.diabetesjournals.org/content/35/12/2515.full.pdf+html.

Isley, W. L., Molitch, M. E., & Vigersky, R. A. (2004). Type 2 diabetes and A1c. *Journal of Clinical Endocrinology & Metabolism, 89,* 1–2. Retrieved April 10, 2013, from: http://jcem.endojournals.org/content/89/2/0.2.full.

Izzo, P. (2013, May 18). Number of the week: Class of 2013, most indebted ever. *Wall Street Journal.* Retrieved May 28, 2013, from: http://blogs.wsj.com/economics/2013/05/18/number-of-the-week-clas…er-of-the-week-class-of-2013-most-indebted-ever%253Fmod%253De2tw.

Jackson, S. L., Vann, W. F., Jr., Kotch, J. B., Pahel, B. T., & Lee, J. Y. (2011). Impact of poor oral health on children's school attendance and performance. *American Journal of Public Health, 101,* 1900–1905. Retrieved April 20, 2013, from: www.colorado.gov/cs/Satellite?blobcol=urldata&blobheadernamel=Content-Disposition&blob.

Jameson, P. L. (2006, May). Diabetes, cognitive function, and school performance. *School Nurse News, 23,* 34–36. Retrieved April 12, 2013, from: www.ncbi.nlm.nih.gov/pubmed/16736993.

Joe, S., Joe, E., & Rowley, L. L. (2009). Consequences of physical health and mental illness risks for academic achievement in grades K-12. *Review of Research in Education, 33,* 283–309.

Jyoti, D. F., Frongillo, E. A., Jr., & Jones, S. J. (2005). Food insecurity affects school children's academic performance, weight gain, and social skills. *Journal of Nutrition, 135,* 2831–2839. Retrieved May 4, 2013, from: http://jn.nutrition.org/content/135/12/2831.

Kausal, N., Magnuson, K., & Waldfogel, J. (2011). How is family income related to investments in children's learning? In G. J. Duncan & R. J. Murnane (Eds.), *Whither opportunity? Rising inequality, schools, and children's life chances* (pp. 187–205). New York: Russell Sage Foundation.

Kearney, G. (2001). Introduction. In J. A. Powell, G. Kearney, & V. Kay (Eds.), *In pursuit of a dream deferred? Linking housing and education policy* (pp. 1–9). New York: Peter Lang.

Kemp, F. W., Neti, P.V.S.V., Howell, R. W., Wenger, P., Louria, D. B., & Bogden, J. D. (2007). Elevated blood level concentrations and vitamin D deficiency in winter and summer in young urban children. *Environmental Health Perspectives, 115,* 630–635. Retrieved April 16, 2013, from: www.ncbi.nlm.nih.gov/pmc/articles/PMC1852643/.

Kiel, K. A., & Zabel, J. E. (2008). Location, location, location: The 3L approach to house price determination. *Journal of Housing Economics, 17,* 157–190.

Kit, B. K., Carroll, M. D., & Ogden, C. L. (2011). *Low-fat milk consumption among children and adolescents in the United States, 2007–2008* (NCHS data brief No. 75). Hyattsville,

MD: National Center for Health Statistics. Retrieved March 7, 2013, from: www.cdc.gov/nchs/data/databriefs/db75.htm.

Klahn, K. (2014, June 25). 5 questions to ask before you borrow to pay student loans. *Wall St. Cheat Sheet.* Retrieved July 1, 2014, from: http://wallstcheatsheet.com/personal-finance/should-you-borrow-money-to-pay-off-student-loans.htm./?a=viewall.

Kochlar, R., Fry, R., & Taylor, P. (2011). *Twenty-to-one: Wealth gaps rise to record highs between Whites, Blacks, and Hispanics.* Washington, DC: Pew Research Center. Retrieved July 27, 2012, from: www.pewsocialtrends.org/2011/07/26/wealth-gaps-rise-to-record-highs-between-whites-blacks-hispanics/.

Kodi, C. T., & Seaquist, E. R. (2008). Cognitive dysfunction and diabetes mellitus. *Endocrine Reviews, 29,* 494–511. Retrieved April 12, 2013, from: http://edrv.endojournals.org/content/29/4/494.full.pdf+html.

Kohl, H. W., III, & Cook, H. D. (Eds.). (2013). *Educating the student body: Taking physical activity and physical education to school.* Washington, DC: National Academies Press.

Kornrich, S., & Furstenberg, F. (2012). Investing in children: Changes in parental spending on children, 1972 to 2007. *Demography.* Retrieved November 27, 2012, from: link.springer.com/article/10.1007%2Fs13524-012-0146-4.

Lara, M., Akinbami, L., Flores, G., & Morgenstern, H. (2006). Heterogeneity of childhood asthma among Hispanic children: Puerto Rican children bear a disproportionate burden. *Pediatrics, 117,* 43–53. Retrieved April 16, 2013, from: http://pediatrics.aappublications.org/content/117/1/43.full.html.

Lester, T. W., Madland, D., & Bunker, N. (2011). *An increased minimum wage is good policy even during hard times.* Washington, DC: Center for American Progress Fund. Retrieved May 25, 2013, from: www.americanprogressaction.org/issues/labor/news/2011/06/07/9747/an-increased-minimum-wage-is-good-policy.

Levi J., Segal, L. A., St. Laurent, R., Lang, A., & Rayburn, J. (2012). *F as in fat: How obesity threatens America's future 2012.* Washington, DC: Trust for America's Health. Retrieved March 11, 2013, from: www.healthyamericans.org/assets/files/TFAH2012FasinFatFnlRv.pdf.

Levin, R., Brown, M. J., Kashtock, M. E., Jacobs, D. E., Whelan, E. A., Rodman, J., Schock, M. R., Padilla, A., & Sinks, T. (2008). Lead exposure in U.S. children, 2008: Implications for prevention. *Environmental Health Perspectives, 116,* 1285–1293. Retrieved April 24, 2013, from: www.ncbi.nlm.nih.gov/pmc/articles/PMC2569084/.

Lipton, R., Keenan, H., Onyemere, K. U., & Freels, S. (2002). Incidence and onset features of diabetes in African-American and Latino children in Chicago, 1985–1994. *Diabetes Metabolism Research and Reviews, 18,* 135–142. Retrieved April 7, 2013, from: www.ncbi.nlm.nih.gov/pubmed/11994905.

Logan, J. R. (2002). *Separate and unequal: The neighborhood gap for blacks and Hispanics in metropolitan America.* Albany, NY: Lewis Mumford Center for Comparative Urban and Regional Research. (ERIC Document Reproductive Service No. ED 471 515)

Longley, R. (2010, February 13). Lifetime earnings soar with education. Retrieved March 5, 2011, from: http://usgovinfo.about.com/od/moneymatters/a/edandearnings.htm.

Luce, S. (2002). "The full fruits of our labor": The rebirth of the living wage movement. *Labor History, 43,* 401–409. Retrieved May 24, 2013, from: www.tandfonline.com/doi/abs/10.1080/0023656022000030218?journalCode=clah20#preview.

Luce, S. (2012). Living wage policies and campaigns: Lessons from the United States. *International Journal of Labour Research, 4,* 11–26. Retrieved May 8, 2013, from: international.vlex.com/vid/living-policies-campaigns-united-states-420104422.

Massey, D., & Denton, N. A. (1993). *American apartheid: Segregation and the making of the underclass.* Cambridge, MA: Harvard University Press.

Mayer, S. E. (1997). Trends in the economic well-being and life chances of America's children. In G. J. Duncan & J. Brooks-Gunn (Eds.), *Consequences of growing up poor* (pp. 49–69). New York: Russell Sage Foundation.

McCarthy, A. M., Lindgren, S., Mengeling, M. A., Tsalikian, E., & Engvall, J. (2003). Factors associated with academic achievement in children with Type 1 diabetes. *Diabetes Care, 26,* 112–117. Retrieved April 12, 2013, from: http://care.diabetesjournals.org/content/26/1/112.pdf+html.

McKernan, S.-M., Ratcliffe, C., & Cellini, S. R. (2009, September). *Transitioning in and out of poverty.* Washington, DC: Urban Institute. Retrieved September 5, 2012, from: www.urban.org/url.cfm?ID=411956.

Mcllvaine, M., Mosammat, F., & Prum, N. (2004). Lead poisoning: The silent epidemic affecting poor and minority children in urban areas. *Traprock, 3,* 33–36. Retrieved April 15, 2013, from: www.trincoll.edu/~cgeiss/tr/tr3/tr_3_p8.pdf.

Miranda, M. L., Kim, D., Reiter, J., Overstreet Galeano, M. A., & Maxson, P. (2009). Environmental contributors to the achievement gap. *NeuroToxicology, 30,* 1019–1024. Retrieved April 24, 2013, from: www.sciencedirect.com/science/article/pii/S0161813X09001661.

Moonie, S., Sterling, D. A., Figgs, L. W., & Castro, M. (2008). The relationship between school absence, academic performance, and asthma status. *Journal of School Health, 78,* 140–148. Retrieved April 12, 2013, from: www.ncbi.nlm.nih.gov/pubmed/18307609.

Mouradian, W. E., Wehr, E., & Crall, J. J. (2000). Disparities in children's oral health and access to dental care. *Journal of American Medical Association, 284,* 2625–2631. Retrieved April 25, 2013, from: jama.jamanetwork.com/article.aspx?articleid=193312.

Nalty, C. C., Sharkey, J. R., & Dean, W. R. (2013). Children's reporting of food insecurity in predominantly food insecure households in Texas border *colonias. Nutrition Journal, 12,* 1–9. Retrieved April 30, 2013, from: www.nutritionj.com/content/12/1/15.

National Commission on Excellence in Education. (1983). *A nation at risk: The imperative for educational reform.* Washington, DC: U.S. Government Printing Office.

National Commission on Severely Distressed Public Housing. (1992). *Final report to Congress and the Secretary of Housing and Urban Development.* Washington, DC: Author.

Neuman, S. (2013, September 10). Study says America's income gap widest since Great Depression. *The Two-Way: NPR.* Retrieved September 11, 2013, from: www.npr.org/blogs/the two-way/2013/09/10/221124533/study-says-americas-income-gap-widest-since-great-depression.

Neumark, D., Thompson, M., & Koyle, L. (2012). The effects of living wage laws on low-wage workers and low-income families: What do we know now? *IZA Journal of Labor Policy, 1,* 1–12. Retrieved May 8, 2013, from: www.izajolp.com/content/1/1/11.

Nguyen, K., Peng, J., & Boulay, E. (2010). Effect of smoking on the association between environmental triggers and asthma severity among adults in New England. *Journal of Asthma & Allergy Educators, 1,* 210–218. Retrieved April 20, 2013, from: http://jaa.sagepub.com/content/early/2010/08/19/2150129710377348.

Nord, M. (2009). *Food insecurity in households with children: Prevalence, severity, and household characteristics* (EIB-56). Washington, DC: U.S. Department of Agriculture, Economic Research Service. Retrieved April 30, 2013, from: www.ers.usda.gov/media/155368/eib56_1_pdf.

Nyberg, K., Ramírez, A., & Gallion, K. (2011a). *Addressing nutrition, overweight and obesity among Latino youth.* San Antonio, TX: Salud America!: The Robert Wood Johnson

Research Network to Prevent Obesity among Latino Youth. Retrieved May 3, 2013, from: www.rwjf.org/en/research-publications/find-rwjf-research/2011/12/addressing-nutrition-overweight-and-obesity-among-latino-youth.html.

Nyberg, K., Ramírez, A., & Gallion, K. (2011b). *Influence of media on overweight and obesity among Latino youth.* San Antonio, TX: Salud America! The Robert Wood Johnson Foundation Research Network to Prevent Obesity among Latino Children. Retrieved March 31, 2013, from: www.rwjf.org/content/dam/web-assets/2011/12/influence-of-media-on-overweight-and-obesity-among-latino-youth.

Ocen, P. A. (2012). The new racially restrictive covenant: Race, welfare, and the policing of Black women in subsidized housing. *UCLA Law Review, 59,* 1540–1582.

Ogden, C. L., Carroll, M. D., Curtin, L. R., Lamb, M. M., & Flegal, K. M. (2010). Prevalence of high body mass index in US children and adolescents, 2007–2008. *Journal of the American Medical Association, 303,* 242–249, Retrieved March 31, 2013, from: jama.jamanetwork.com/article.aspx?articleid=185233.

Ogden, C. L., Carroll, M. D., Kit, B. K., & Flegal, K. M. (2012). Prevalence of obesity and trends in body mass index among US children and adolescents, 1999–2010. *Journal of the American Medical Association, 307,* 483–490. Retrieved March 23, 2013, from: http://jama.jamanetwork.com/article.aspx?volume=307&issue=5&page=483.

Orstein, A. (2007). *Class counts: Education, inequality, and the shrinking middle class.* Lanham, MD: Rowman & Littlefield.

Pan, L., Galuska, D. A., Sherry, B., Hunter, A. S., Rutledge, G. E., & Dietz, W. H. (2009). Difference in prevalence of obesity among black, white, and Hispanic adults—United States, 2006–2008. *Morbidity and Mortality Weekly Report, 58,* 740–744. Retrieved March 24, 2013, from: www.cdc.gov/mmwr/preview/mmwrhtml/mm5827a2.htm?s_cid=mm5827a2_e.

Pham, E., Teitelbaum, M., & Ortiz, M. (2006). *Improving children's health: Understanding children's health disparities and promising approaches to address them.* Washington, DC: Children's Defense Fund. Retrieved March 21, 2013, from: www.childrensdefense.org/child-research-data-publications/data/Childrens-Health-Disparities-Report-2006.html.

Philips, M. (2011). Parenting, time use, and disparities in academic outcomes. In G. J. Duncan & R. J. Murnane (Eds.), *Wither opportunity?: Rising inequality, schools, and children's life chances* (pp. 207–228). New York: Russell Sage Foundation.

Pirkle, J. L., Kaufmann, R. B., Brody, D. J., Hickman, T., Gunter, E. W., & Paschal, D. C. (1998). *Environmental Health Perspectives, 106,* 745–750. Retrieved April 24, 2013, from: www.ncbi.nlm.nih.gov/pmc/articles/PMC1533471/.

Popkin, S. J., Buron, L. F., Levy, D. K., & Cunningham, M. K. (2000). The Gautreaux legacy: What might mixed-income and dispersal strategies mean for the poorest public housing tenants? *Housing Policy Debate, 11,* 911–942.

Powell, J. A., Kearney, G., & Kay, V. (Eds.). (2001). *In pursuit of a dream deferred? Linking housing and education policy.* New York: Peter Lang.

Race: The power of an illusion. (2003). *Episode three: The house we live in.* Retrieved December 28, 2012, from: http://newsreel.org/transcripts/race3.htm.

Ramos, C. (2001). The educational legacy of racially restrictive covenants: Their long term impact on Mexican Americans. *Scholar: St. Mary's Law Review and Minority Issues, 4,* 149–184.

Rank, M. R., & Hirschl, T. A. (1999). The likelihood of poverty across the American adult life span. *Social Work, 44,* 201–216.

Reardon, S. F. (2011). The widening academic achievement gap between the rich and the poor: New evidence and possible explanations. In G. J. Duncan & R. J. Murnane

(Eds.), *Wither opportunity?: Rising inequality, schools, and children's life chances* (pp. 91–115). New York: Russell Sage Foundation.

Riley, T. (2012, August 24). What is a living wage? *Moyers & Company*. Retrieved May 25, 2013, from: http://billmoyers.com/2012/08/24/what-is-a-living-wage/.

Romero, R. C., & Fernández, L. F. (2012). *Doss v. Bernal:* Ending Mexican apartheid in Orange County (Report No. 14). Los Angeles: University of California at Los Angeles, Chicano Studies Research Center.

Ross, A. (2010). *Nutrition and its effects on academic performance: How can our schools improve?* Unpublished master's thesis, Northern Michigan University, Marquette. Retrieved April 30, 2013, from: www.nmu.edu/sites/DrupalEducation/files/UserFiles/Files/Pre-Drupal/SiteSelections/Students/GradPapers/Projects/Ross_Amy_MP.pdf.

Rothstein, R. (2004). *Class and schools: Using social, economic, and educational reform to close the black-white achievement gap.* Washington, DC: Economic Policy Institute.

Rothstein, R. (2012, January 23). *A comment on Bank of American/Countrywide's discriminatory mortgage lending and its implications for racial segregation.* Economic Policy Institute. Retrieved December 28, 2012, from: http://www.epi.org/publication/bp335-boa-countrywied-discriminatory-lending.

Sabia, J. J., & Nielsen, R. B. (2012). *Can raising the minimum wage reduce poverty and hardship: New evidence from the Survey of Income and Program Participation.* Washington, DC: Employment Policies Institute. Retrieved May 26, 2013, from: www.epionline.org/study/r141/.

Saez, E. (2013). Striking it richer: The evolution of top incomes in the United States. Retrieved September 11, 2013, from: http://emi.berkeley.edu/-saez/saez-UStopincomes-2012.pdf.

Saltsman, M. (2013). The record is clear: Minimum wage hikes destroy jobs. *Forbes.* April 17. Retrieved May 24, 2013, from: www.forbes.com/sites/realspin/2013/04/17/the-record-is-clear-minimum-wage-hikes-destroy-jobs/.

Seirawan, H., Faust, S., & Mulligan, R. (2012). The impact of oral health on the academic performance of disadvantaged children. *American Journal of Public Health, 102,* 1729–1734. Retrieved April 25, 2013, from: www.ncbi.nih.gov/pubmed/22813093.

Seitles, M. (1998). The perpetuation of residential racial segregation in America: Historical discrimination, modern forms of exclusion, and inclusionary remedies. *Journal of Land Use & Environmental Law, 14.* Retrieved December 29, 2012, from: www.law.fsu.edu/journas/landuse/Vol141/seit.htm.

Seo, D.-C., & Sa, J. (2010). A meta-analysis of obesity interventions among U.S. minority children. *Journal of Adolescent Health, 46,* 309–323.

Shelley v. Kraemer, 334 U.S.1 (1948).

Silvers, S. K., & Lang, D. M. (2012). Asthma in African Americans: What can we do about the higher rates of disease? *Cleveland Clinical Journal of Medicine, 79,* 193–201. Retrieved April 20, 2013, from: www.ccjm.org/content/79/3/193.full.

Sirin, S. R. (2005). Socioeconomic status and academic achievement: A meta-analytic review of research. *Review of Educational Research, 82,* 436–476.

Smeedling, T. M. (2005). Public policy, economic inequality, and poverty: The United States in comparative perspective. *Social Science Quarterly, 86,* 955–983.

Spence, L. H. (1993). Rethinking the social role of public housing. *Housing Policy Debate, 4,* 355–372.

Stewart, K. A., Higgins, P. C., McLaughlin, C. G., Williams, T. V., Granger, E., & Croghan, T. W. (2010). Differences in prevalence, treatment, and outcomes of asthma among a diverse population of children with equal access to care. *Archives of Pediatrics &*

Adolescent Medicine, 164, 720–726. Retrieved April 20, 2013, from: jamanetwork.com/article.aspx?articleid=383574.

Story, M., Kaphingst, K. M., & French, S. (2006). The role of schools in obesity prevention. *Childhood Obesity, 16,* 110–142. Retrieved April 15, 2013, from: http://futureofchildren.org/publications/journals/article/index.xml?journalid=36&articleid=98§ionid=607.

Strupp, B. J., & Levitsky, D. A. (1995). Enduring cognitive effects on early malnutrition: A theoretical reappraisal. *Journal of Nutrition, 125,* 2221–2232. Retrieved May 4, 2013, from: jn.nutrition.org/content/125/8_Suppl/2221.full.pdf.

Subrahmanyam, K., Kraut, R. E., Greenfield, P. M., & Gross, E. F. (2000). The impact of home computer use on children's activities and development. *Children and Computer Technology, 10,* 123–144. Retrieved May 27, 2013, from: www.princeton.edu/futureofchildren/org/publications/journals/article/index.xml?journalid=45.

Sugrue, T. (1996). *The origins of the urban crisis: Race and inequality in postwar Detroit.* Princeton, NJ: Princeton University Press.

Taras, H. (2005). Nutrition and student performance at school. *Journal of School Health, 75,* 199–213. Retrieved May 3, 2013, from: www.ncbi.nlm.nih.gov/pubmed/16014126.

Taras, H., & Potts-Datema, W. (2005). Childhood asthma and student performance at school. *Journal of School Health, 75,* 296–312. Retrieved April 16, 2013, from: www.highbeam.com/doc/1G1–137407209.html.

Touger-Decker, R., & van Loveren, C. (2003). Sugars and dental caries. *American Journal of Clinical Nutrition, 78,* 881–892. Retrieved April 25, 2013, from: ajcn.nutrition.org/content/ 78/4/881S.full.

Tsikalas, K., Lee, J., & Newkirk (2007). *Home computing, school engagement and academic achievement of low-income adolescents: Findings from year one of a three year study of the CFY intervention.* New York: Computers for Youth Foundation. Retrieved May 27, 2013, from: www.givewell.org/files/Cause4/Computers%20for%20Youth/EIN%2013–3935309%20Cause%204%20CFY%20Test%20Score%20Study%20Attach.

Turner, M. A., Popkin, S. J., & Rawlings, L. (2009). *Public housing and the legacy of segregation.* Washington, DC: Urban Institute Press.

Turner, M. A., & Ross, S. L. (2005). How racial discrimination affects the search for housing. In X. de Souza Briggs (Ed.), *The geography of opportunity: Race and housing choice in metropolitan America* (pp. 81–100). Washington, DC: Brookings Institution Press.

Turner, M. A., Ross, S. L., Galster, G. C., & Yinger, J. (2002). *Discrimination in metropolitan housing markets: National results from Phase 1 of the Housing Discrimination Study (HDS).* Washington, DC: U.S. Department of Housing and Urban Development.

U.S. Department of Commerce, Bureau of Census. (2012). *How the Census measures poverty.* Washington, DC: Author. Retrieved November 3, 2012, from: http://www.census.gov/hhes/www/poverty/about/overview/measure.html.

Valencia, R. R. (2010). *Dismantling contemporary deficit thinking: Educational thought and practice.* Critical Educator Series. New York: Routledge.

Valencia, R. R., & Suzuki, L. A. (2001). *Intelligence testing and minority students: Foundations, performance factors, and assessment issues.* Racial and Ethnic Minority Psychology Series. Thousand Oaks, CA: SAGE.

Vargas, C. M., & Ronzio, C. R. (2006). Disparities in early childhood caries. *BMC Oral Health, 6,* 1–4. Retrieved April 25, 2013, from: www.biomedcentral.com/1472–6831/6/S1/S3.

Vigdor, J. L., & Ladd, H. F. (2010). *Scaling the digital divide: Home computer technology and student achievement.* (Working Paper 48). Washington, DC: Urban Institute. Retrieved May 27, 2013, from: www.urban.org/UploadedPDF/1001433-digital-divide-pdf.

Vigil, J. D. (2007). *The projects: Gang and non-gang families in East Los Angeles.* Austin: University of Texas Press.

Vivian, E. M., Carrel, A. L., & Becker, T. (2011). Identifying children at risk for type 2 diabetes in underserved communities. *Diabetes Educator, 37,* 519–527. Retrieved April 7, 2013, from: www.ncbi.nlm.nih.gov/pubmed/21617176.

Vohra-Gupta, S. (2012). *Women of color and minimum wage: A policy of racial, gender, and economic discrimination* (Policy Brief). Austin: University of Texas, Institute for Urban Policy Research and Analysis. Retrieved May 22, 2013, from: www.utexas.edu/cola/insts/iupra/about-us/staff.php.

Wang, Y. C., & Beydoun, M. A. (2007). The obesity epidemic in the United States—gender, age, socioeconomic, racial/ethnic, and geographic characteristics: A systematic review and meta-regression analysis. *Epidemiologic Reviews, 29,* 6–28. Retrieved March 23, 2013, from: http://epirev.oxfordjournals.org/content/29/1/6.full.

Wang, Y. C., Orleans, C. T., & Gortmaker, S. L. (2012). Reaching the healthy people goals for reducing childhood obesity: Closing the energy gap. *American Journal of Preventive Medicine, 42,* 437–444. Retrieved March 31, 2013, from: www.hsph.harvard.edu/prc/files/2012/11/wang_yc_orleans_ct_gortmaker_sl._2012.pdf.

Warniment, C., Tsang, K., & Galazka, S. S. (2010). Lead poisoning in children. *American Family Physician, 81,* 751–757. Retrieved April 16, 2013, from: www.aafp.org/afp/2010/0315/p751.html.

Weisberg, J. (2010, January 8). What caused the Great Recession? *Daily Beast.* Retrieved October 28, 2012, from: www.thedailybeast.com/newsweek/2010/01/08/what-caused-the-great-recession-html.

Wheary, J., Shapiro, T. M., Draut, T., & Meschede, T. (2008). *Economic (in)security: The experience of the African-American and Latino middle classes.* New York: Dēmos: A Network for Ideas and Action and The Institute on Assets and Social Policy at Brandeis University. Retrieved October 16, 2012, from: iasp.brandeis.edu/pdfs/byathreadlatino.pdf.

Wheeler, W., & Brown, M. J. (2013). Blood lead levels in children aged 1–5 years—United States, 1990–2010. *Morbidity and Mortality Weekly Report, 62,* 245–248. Retrieved April 9, 2013, from: www.cdc.gov/mmwr/preview/mmwrhtml/mm6213a3.htm?s_cid=mm6213a3_e.

White, K. R. (1982). The relation between socioeconomic status and academic achievement. *Psychological Bulletin, 91,* 461–481.

Wilkerson, I. (2010). *The warmth of other sons: The epic story of America's Great Migration.* New York: Random House.

Winicki, J. (2003). Food insecurity and hunger in the kindergarten classroom: Its effects on learning and growth. *Contemporary Economic Policy, 21,* 145–147. Retrieved April 30, 2013, from: ddr.nal.usda.gov/bitstream/10113/14599/1/IND44053524.pdf.

Wolff, E. N. (2002). *Top heavy: The increasing inequality of wealth in America and what can be done about it.* New York: New Press.

Wright, V. R., Thampi, K., & Briggs, J. (2010). *Who are America's poor children? Examining food insecurity among children in the United States.* New York: National Center for Children in Poverty. Retrieved April 30, 2013, from: http://nokidhungry.org/sites/default/files/text_958.pdf.

Wrigley, J. (1989). Do young children need intellectual stimulation? Experts' advice to parents, 1900–1985. *History of Education Quarterly, 29,* 41–75.

Yau, P. L., Javier, D. C., Ryan, C. M., Tsui, W. H., Ardekani, B. A., Ten, S., & Convit, A. (2010). Preliminary evidence for brain complications in obese adolescents with type 2 mellitus. *Diabetologia, 53,* 2298–2306. Retrieved April 12, 2013, from: www.ncbi.nlm.nih.gov/pmc/articles/PMC3116653/.

PART III

Mesolevel Factors

4

SCHOOL SEGREGATION, DESEGREGATION, AND INTEGRATION

School segregation in the U.S. is one of the most studied topics in the field of race relations and education. This is not surprising given the long-standing existence of school segregation and its relation to limited equality of opportunity for students of color, and as a key mesolevel factor in creating and maintaining TAG. Parents of color did not sit idly by as their children were forced to attend segregated, inferior schools. The Black struggle against school segregation commenced 166 years ago in *Roberts v. City of Boston* (1849), which laid a pathway to the monumental U.S. Supreme Court ruling over 100 years later in *Brown v. Board of Education of Topeka* (1954).[1] Other groups of color have also been quite active in desegregation litigation. Mexican Americans, for example, mounted a vigorous campaign for school desegregation. Beginning with the case of *Romo v. Laird* (1925) in Tempe, Arizona, and through *Santamaria v. Dallas Independent School District* (2006) in Texas, Mexican Americans have brought forth 36 school desegregation lawsuits (Valencia, 2008, chapter 1 and pp. 306–309).

In the remainder of this chapter, I cover the following: (a) current prevalence of school segregation, (b) adverse effects of school segregation—academic context and social context, (c) historical struggles for school desegregation, (d) period of meaningful school desegregation, (e) contemporary status of school desegregation, and (f) suggestions for systemic reform.

Current Prevalence of School Segregation

With the demise of court-ordered school desegregation and the severe setback of even voluntary desegregation plans (discussed later), we now live in a time of hypersegregated public schools. Chief Justice Earl Warren's powerful words in the *Brown* opinion, "Separate educational facilities are inherently unequal,"[2]

TABLE 4.1 Percentage of Students by Race/Ethnicity in Minority Schools: National, AY 2009–2010

Race/Ethnicity	*% of Racial/Ethnic Group in 50–100% Minority School*	*% of Racial/Ethnic Groups in 90–100% Minority School*	*% of Racial/Ethnic Group in 99–100% Minority Schools*
Black	74.1	38.1	15.5
Latino/Latina	79.5	43.1	14.1

Source: Adapted from Orfield, Kucsera, and Siegel-Hawley (p. 19, Table 2), with permission of G. Orfield.

Note: Minority school enrolls Latino/Latina, Black, Asian American, and American Indian students.

continue to have grave consequences for contemporary students of color. In regard to current racial/ethnic isolation, Table 4.1 shows national public school (K-12) segregation data for AY 2009–2010 based on three density levels of student enrollment (Orfield, Kucsera, & Siegel-Hawley, 2012). For schools with 50%–100% combined students of color, about 3 of 4 Black students attend such schools, and 4 of 5 Latino/Latina students are enrolled in these schools. With respect to the intermediate level of enrollment (90%–100% students of color), which Orfield et al. refer to as "intensely segregated" (p. 18), 38.1% of Blacks and 43.1% of Latinos/Latinas, respectively, attend such schools. These schools have a White student body of less than 10%. For the most segregated schools (99–100% students of color), which Orfield et al. term "apartheid schools" (p. 19), approximately 1 of 7 Black and 1 of 7 Latino/Latina students are enrolled. About 1% of White students attend apartheid schools.

Several conclusions can be drawn from Table 4.1, and the Orfield et al. (2012) report as a whole. First, although some success in school desegregation occurred from the 1960s through the 1980s, public school segregation is on the rise in the U.S.[3] Second, school segregation has escalated dramatically for Latino/Latina students (also see Kucsera & Flaxman, 2012). From 2001–2002 to 2009–2010, the number of Latino/Latina students enrolled in 50%–100% schools of color in the nation increased by 2,117,752. By contrast, during this same time frame Black students in 50%–100% schools of color grew by 204,320 (Orfield et al., p. 19, Table 3). This pattern and the data in Table 4.1 show a remarkable development: Latinos/Latinas in public schools are the most segregated group of students of color in the country. Third, a finding that does not receive the attention it deserves is that White students are the least likely to be exposed in their schooling to other racial/ethnic groups (see Orfield et al., p. 20, Table 4; Valencia, 2011, p. 64, Table 2.3). In sum, *Whites are the most isolated racial/ethnic student group in the nation.*

Another finding is worth noting. Mitchell and Mitchell (2010), using mathematical modeling, investigated segregation in 551 public schools in 53 school districts from 1968 to 2007 in the Riverside-San Bernardino MSA in California.

The authors report that most of the regional segregation was between districts, not within districts (also, see Clotfelter, 2004, chapters 2 and 7). Although interdistrict school segregation may be greater than intradistrict segregation, it remains important not to lose sight of the severity of school segregation that occurs within an individual school district. Such school segregation is the face that scores of students, parents, teachers, administrators, and school board members across the country witness every day—though they may not internalize the depth of this racial/ethnic isolation in their respective school districts.

To illustrate this localized intradistrict school segregation, I have selected the Austin Independent School District (AISD) as exhibit A. The city of Austin is a multiracial/ethnic community of 790,390 people based on the 2010 Census (48.7% White; 35.1% Latino/Latina; 8.1% Black; 6.3% Asian American).[4] Notwithstanding the racial/ethnic diversity in the population of this Central Texas city, AISD is intensely segregated at the elementary, middle school, and high school levels. This pattern is a microcosm of the K-12 public school system in Texas, one of the most segregated states in the nation in public school K-12 education.[5] With respect to the segregation of Latino/Latina students, Texas ranks number 3 nationally in percentage (87.4%) of Latinos/Latinas enrolled in 50%–100% minority schools and number 2 (52.7%) in 90%–100% minority schools. For Black students in Texas, the state ranks number 5 nationally in percentage (82.4%) of Blacks attending 50%–100% minority schools and number 5 (47.6%) in 90%–100% minority schools (Orfield et al., 2012, pp. 46–47, Tables 18 and 19).

To estimate the degree of racial/ethnic segregation in the AISD, I utilized the "±15%" rule of thumb formula.[6] One takes the percentage of the *combined* enrollment of students of color in a school district, and then adds 15 percentage points to obtain the *upper limit* of the band and also subtracts 15 percentage points to obtain the *lower limit* of the band. Individual schools that fall *within* the band's upper and lower limits in combined students of color percentage are deemed racially/ethnically "balanced." Schools that fall *outside* the lower or upper limits are considered "imbalanced."[7]

Table 4.2 presents the results of my analysis of school segregation in the AISD based on data for AY 2012–2013. Although the AISD is a singular school district, I artificially created three districts (elementary, middle, and high school) for the sake of a finer-grained examination of racial/ethnic segregation. In regard to the elementary school level, the total enrollment is 43,869 students in the 82 schools.[8] The total enrollment of students of color is 34,633 (79%). By use of the ±15% formula, the upper limit and the lower limit of the band are 64% and 94%, respectively. Further calculations indicate that of the 82 elementary schools, 20 (24%) are racially/ethnically balanced, while 62 (76%) are considered imbalanced. Of the 62 imbalanced elementary schools, 20 (32%) are deemed predominantly White and 42 (68%) are considered to be predominantly

TABLE 4.2 Segregation of Austin Independent School District: AY 2012–2013

School Level			*Segregation Status (racial/ethnic mix) of School*				*Race/Ethnicity of Imbalanced Schools*			
			Balanced		*Imbalanced*		*Predominantly White*		*Predominantly Students of Color*	
			n	*%*	*n*	*%*	*n*	*%*	*n*	*%*
Elementary										
Total Schools	82		20	24%	62	76%	20	32%	42	68%
Total Enrollment	43,869									
White Enrollment	9,236	(21%)								
Students of Color Enrollment	34,633	(79%)								
Middle										
Total Schools	18		4	22%	14	78%	5	36%	9	64%
Total Enrollment	14,804									
White Enrollment	4,083	(28%)								
Students of Color Enrollment	10,721	(72%)								
High										
Total Schools	12		3	25%	9	75%	3	33%	6	67%
Total Enrollment	19,198									
White Enrollment	5,568	(29%)								
Students of Color Enrollment	13,630	(71%)								

Source: Texas Education Agency (2013a).

Note: Prepared by Richard R. Valencia and Bruno J. Villarreal.

students of color (i.e., Latino/Latina and Black). Table 4.2 also contains data on the degree of segregation at the middle school level. Of the 18 schools, 4 (22%) are balanced and 14 (78%) are imbalanced. For the 12 high schools, 3 (25%) are found to be balanced and 9 (75%) imbalanced. In sum, the AISD is a reflection of the statewide pattern of school segregation along lines of race/ethnicity: Latino/Latina and Black students have little opportunity to attend the same schools with White students, and, vice versa, White students have only a slight chance of having exposure to Latino/Latina and Black students in their schooling experience.

Adverse Effects of School Segregation

The literature on school segregation in the U.S. is voluminous, covering such aspects as litigation, prevalence rates, desegregation plans, and suggestions for school integration. A thread that ties this corpus of research together is: School segregation is equivalent, for the most part, to inferior education and thus has a detrimental impact on students of color, particularly Latino/Latina and Black pupils. In this section, I discuss the two major circumstances in which school segregation adversely affects students of color, and to some extent, White students: the academic context and the social context.

1. *Academic context.* A common research finding, whether it be from historical or contemporary investigations, is that many students of color who attend segregated schools experience, on the average, school failure. In chapter 1, I conceptualize school failure as the persistently, pervasively, and disproportionately low academic achievement of low-SES students of color. Low academic achievement includes, for example, poor achievement test performance, weak school holding power, high grade retention rates, and low matriculation rates to college (see chapter 1, this volume). The adverse effects of segregation in the academic context do not occur in a vacuum. They are inextricably linked to the other mesolevel factors discussed in later chapters—for example, teacher quality and curriculum differentiation.

The connection between school segregation and poor academic outcomes for students of color is deeply rooted in history. Black students' academic achievement, for example, was negatively affected by school segregation. Bond (1934) reports Stanford Achievement Test performance (collected from 1929–1931) for 15 counties in heavily segregated Alabama, Louisiana, and North Carolina. Compared to national norms (which meant standards for White children), Black students in third and sixth grade scored below the standardization norm in each of the 15 counties (Bond, p. 342, Table L).

Subsequent to historical observations, many empirical studies have been conducted on the relation between school segregation and the academic achievement of students of color. Some of these investigations go back 3 decades (e.g., Espinosa & Ochoa, 1986; Jaeger, 1987; Orfield, 1988; Valencia, 1984), while some are more current (e.g., Ready & Silander, 2011; Valencia, 2000, 2011; Vasquez Heilig & Holme, 2013). The basic design researchers use in these studies is to correlate the density of students of color in the various schools of a district against an aggregate measure of academic achievement. The typical finding is that as the percentage of students of color rises (i.e., as school segregation increases), academic achievement decreases.[9]

For a more recent example of the adverse effects of school segregation in the academic context, I turn again to the AISD. In my investigation, I conducted a correlational analysis based on AY 2012–2013 data for fifth graders from 78 of the 82 elementary schools of the district (4 schools are either pre-K or primary schools with no fifth grades). The percentage of failure rates of all grade 5 students (in each school) on the State of Texas Assessments of Academic Readiness (STAAR) Reading test was correlated with the percentage of combined Latino/Latina and Black students in each of the 78 schools. Figure 4.1 graphically illustrates that as the percentage of students of color increases in the elementary schools, the percentage of students who fail the Reading test likewise increases. The observed *r* of .62 is large and statistically significant and suggests a discernible pattern of racialized academic achievement in the AISD elementary schools.[10]

It needs to be emphasized, however, that this achievement configuration is a generalization, and not a characteristic of *all* high-enrollment elementary schools of students of color in the AISD. Note that there are a small number of schools in the Figure 4.1 scatterplot that can be considered outliers. For example, the two schools on the horizontal axis to which the arrow is pointed—both indicating a combined Latino/Latina and Black enrollment of 70%—have *no* fifth graders who failed the STAAR Reading test. Another set of outliers is observed in the bottom right corner of the scatterplot, where the arrow is pointing to five schools. These elementary schools have very high combined enrollments of Latino/Latina and Black students (92%–98%), but the STAAR grade 5 Reading test failure rates are some of the lowest in the AISD, ranging from about 5% to 11%. Researchers need to pay more attention to outlier schools, as they defy the typical negative association seen in the literature—namely, when the concentration of students of color increases in schools, achievement scores tend to decline. An important question emerges: What processes, structures, and climates are being implemented in outlier schools that lead to the high achievement of many students of color? Much of the present book is designed to see how we can transform schools so students of color can achieve at high levels on a regular basis. In sum, how can high-achieving schools (outliers) become the norm? What systemic transformations are necessary?

2. *Social context*. In addition to the adverse effects of school segregation as documented in the academic context, there are also negative consequences shaped by the social context of segregated schooling—frequently referred to as intergroup relations research (Wells, Holme, Revilla, & Atanda, 2004). The premise that the social climate of segregation can lead to harmful effects for both students of color and their White counterparts is that such isolation disallows children and youths of diverse racial/ethnic backgrounds to commingle, which often leads to negative consequences. First, school segregation prevents these students from attending schools and classes together, offers very limited classroom discourse about each groups' heritage and history, and allows few opportunities for students to get to know one another and become friends. Second, the social context of school segregation poorly prepares both students of color and their White peers to live and work in a multiracial/ethnic U.S. Finally, the social context of school segregation does little in helping to bring about the process of debunking racial/ethnic stereotypes and the means for prejudice reduction. In the remainder of

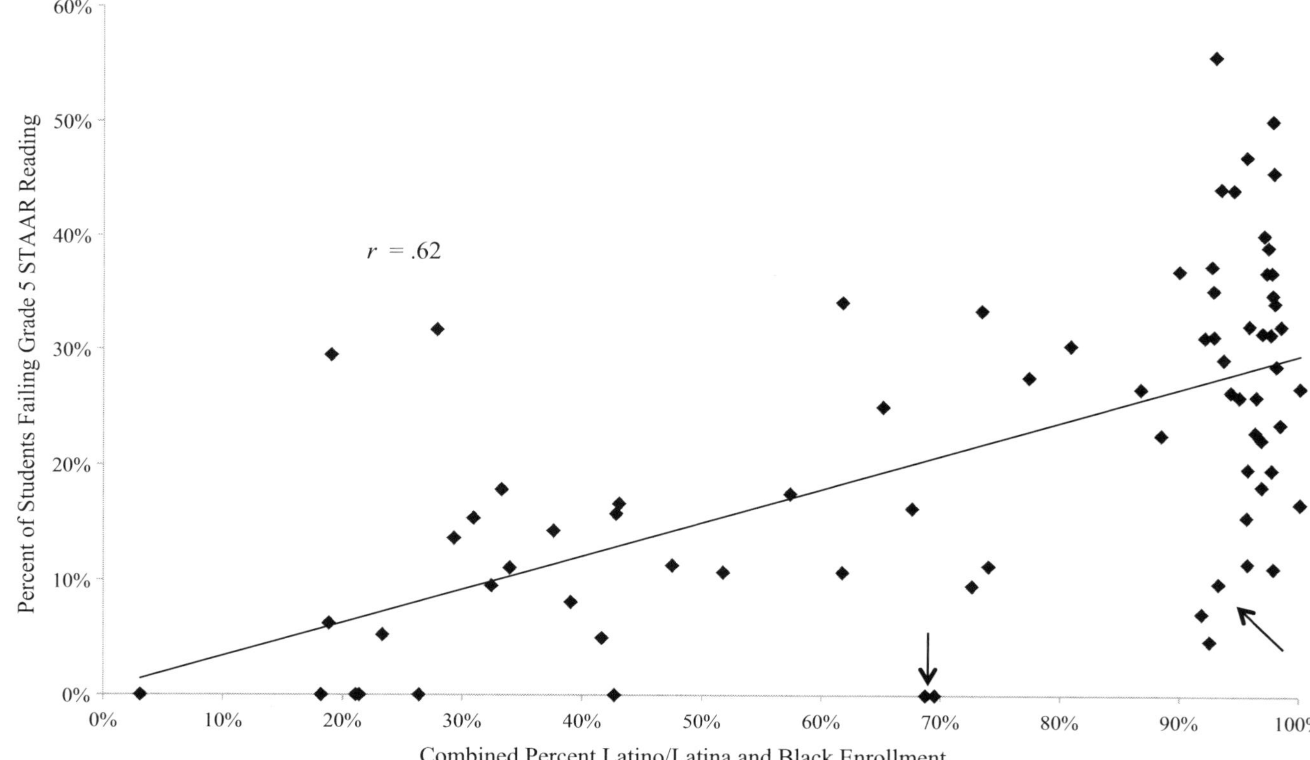

FIGURE 4.1 Scatterplot of Correlation between AISD Elementary Schools' Combined Percentage of Latino/Latina and Black Enrollment and Percentage of Students Failing Grade 5 STAAR Reading, 2012–2013 (*N* = 78 schools)

Source: Texas Education Agency (2013a).

Note: AISD = Austin Independent School District. STAAR = State of Texas Assessments of Academic Readiness.

this section on the social context, I focus on the latter point—intergroup contact and prejudice reduction.

In his classic 1954 book, *The Nature of Prejudice*, renowned social psychologist Gordon Allport is credited with introducing, at the time, the most authoritative analysis of intergroup contact theory. Early in his chapter 16, "The Effect of Contact," he underscores that one cannot just assemble people together and expect a reduction in prejudice. There are, he asserts, a number of variables that the researcher must study singularly or in different combinations. The types of contact Allport identifies are: (a) quantitative aspects (e.g., frequency, duration); (b) status aspects (e.g., minority person has inferior or equal status); (c) role aspects (e.g., competitive, cooperative); (d) social atmosphere (e.g., voluntary or involuntary); (e) personality of the individual (e.g., high or low prejudice); and (f) area (e.g., occupational, residential). Allport summarizes matters by articulating his now well-known contact hypothesis:

> Prejudice . . . may be reduced by equal status contact between majority and minority groups in the pursuit of common goals. The effect is greatly enhanced if this contact is sanctioned by institutional supports (i.e., by law, custom or local atmosphere), and provided it is of a sort that leads to the perception of common interest and common humanity between members of the two groups. (p. 281)

Stated in another way, Allport's contact hypothesis holds that a significant means of reducing intergroup prejudice can be achieved by having frequent contact between diverse groups under four propitious conditions, to wit: equal status between in-group and out-group members, common objectives, no competition between the groups, and authority sanction for the intergroup contact.

Allport's (1954) intergroup contact theory, particularly his contact hypothesis, has generated a voluminous corpus of research over the last 60-plus years. The main question investigators have asked is: Does the contact hypothesis, as framed by Allport, reduce prejudice held by the in-group toward the out-group? To empirically address this critical query, Pettigrew and Tropp (2006) undertook the most comprehensive analysis to date on the contact hypothesis. The authors employed a meta-analytic approach of the extant literature, covering 713 independent samples across 515 investigations.

For their findings, Pettigrew and Tropp (2006) report that the *r*s range from −.205 to −.214 (M = .21). Given the fairly large number of samples, the effect size is highly statistically significant (p > .001). The authors also report that in 94% of the samples, an inverse relation between intergroup contact and prejudice is observed. Pettigrew and Tropp (2006) also sought to examine whether Allport's (1954) four conditions (i.e., equal status, common goals, cooperation, authority sanction) could be empirically demonstrated to reduce prejudice. In complex analyses, the authors find that although greater intergroup contact is, in general, linked to reduced levels of prejudice, the four conditions are not crucial for bringing about prejudice diminution. Rather, it appears that the conditions function as facilitators in producing favorable contact outcomes. That is, the "conditions are best conceptualized as an unrelated bundle rather than as independent factors" (p. 751).

Historical Struggles for School Desegregation

Before discussing the contemporary state of school desegregation efforts, it would be informative to take a brief look at some historical endeavors to bring students of color and their White counterparts together in the same schools. During the pre-*Brown* era, litigative attempts to desegregate U.S. public schools proved, for the most part, futile. In the nation's first desegregation lawsuit, *Roberts v. City of Boston* (1849), Benjamin F. Roberts, a Black man, brought forth a lawsuit on behalf of his 5-year-old daughter, Sarah. She was forced to attend Smith Grammar School, the "colored school," which was badly run down. The classrooms were very small, the walls had defaced paint, and the equipment was in disrepair. On her way to school, Sarah had to pass five White schools, which were far superior to hers (Kluger, 2004, p. 74). The Roberts attorneys, Charles Sumner (White) and Robert Morris (Black), argued a number of points in their complaint—for example: (a) Massachusetts law does not establish school segregation, and thus such racial separation is unconstitutional; (b) the local school committee does not have the power to discriminate by race; and (c) segregation of Black children imposes a stigma of inferiority upon them.[11] The Massachusetts Supreme Court ruled in favor of the defendants, noting that the local school committee is already exercising its power in a prudent manner (e.g., separation of boys and girls, hiring of only female teachers, special schools for poor and neglected children). Thus, they have the right to maintain separate primary schools for Black and White children.[12]

I would dare say that many scholars of race relations and education are unaware that Asian Americans also fought for school desegregation during the pre-*Brown* era. In *Gong Lum v. Rice* (1927), Chinese American Gong Lum filed a lawsuit in 1924 on behalf of his 9-year-old daughter, Martha, who was born in the U.S. in 1915. Martha was enrolled at Rosedale Elementary School, an all-White school, located in Bolivar County, Mississippi. During the noon recess, the district superintendent, acting on behalf on an order from the Board of Trustees, who in turn was following instructions from the state superintendent of education, informed Martha she had to leave school and not return. The exclusion of Martha was based solely on the argument that she was Chinese, and not "Caucasian." Plaintiff Lum asserted that section 207 of Mississippi's Constitution of 1890 required "separate schools shall be maintained for children of white and colored races." He further argued that Martha was not colored, nor was she of mixed ancestry. She was "pure Chinese," and thus her 14th Amendment rights were being violated.[13] The local court ruled for the plaintiffs, stating that Martha's rights indeed had been infringed. Furthermore, the judge ruled that she was not colored.[14] Defendants appealed to the Supreme Court of Mississippi, and the justices overruled the decision of the lower court,[15] writing that the segregationist section of the Constitution of Mississippi was intended to "preserve the integrity and purity of the white race" and that the term "white" refers strictly to the "Caucasian race," while the term "colored" is not exclusively "limited to negroes or persons having negro blood."[16] Lum appealed to the U.S. Supreme Court (*Gong Lum v. Rice*, 1927), and it affirmed the ruling of the lower court. What we learn from *Gong Lum*, in the context of CRT, is that White school authorities will go to great lengths to protect their privilege, even using the pseudoscience of White racial superiority.

Not all the school desegregation lawsuits initiated by plaintiffs during the pre-*Brown* epoch of color were fruitless.[17] For example, in *Mendez v. Westminister* (1946) not only did Mexican Americans prevail in their first attempt in the federal courts, but also the decision had widespread impact (Valencia, 2005). First, the *Mendez* ruling helped bring about public pressure on the state of California to revoke its sections of the Education Code that allowed school boards to establish separate schools for certain American Indian students and pupils of Chinese, Japanese, and "Mongolian" ancestry.[18] Second, *Mendez* prompted two other Mexican American–initiated school desegregation cases in the Southwest: *Delgado v. Bastrop Independent School District of Bastrop County* (1948) in Texas, and *Gonzales v. Sheely* (1951) in Colorado (see Valencia, 2005). Plaintiffs triumphed in these federal court cases. Third, *Mendez* helped to lay some of the important groundwork for the landmark *Brown* case. Attorneys in *Mendez* used expert witnesses to argue that school segregation imposed stigma and inferiority among the Mexican American children, where none existed in the first place. The experts also argued that the isolation of Mexican American students from their White peers based on language needs had no sound pedagogical rationale. In sum, these arguments by the expert witnesses demonstrated the power of social science evidence and helped to bolster the integrationist theory of the *Mendez* attorneys. This integrationist strategy, which proved so useful in *Mendez*, would also serve as the linchpin in *Brown* (Valencia, 2005).

CRT provides a compelling theoretical framework for understanding and analyzing *Mendez* and other Mexican American–initiated school segregation litigation, as all five tenets of CRT apply (see preface of this volume for a discussion of the five principles). First, the *Mendez* case and the earlier Mexican American–initiated desegregation lawsuits insisted, in their legal arguments, on the centrality of race and racism in the lives of Mexican American schoolchildren. Second, *Mendez* challenged the dominant belief that segregation of Mexican American children was in their best interests, thereby exposing this traditional claim of White self-interest and privilege.

Third, *Mendez* represents a commitment beyond the boundaries of Orange County, California. In this way, the ruling in *Mendez* helped to end the de jure segregation of Asian Americans and American Indians in California's public schools. As well, *Mendez* lent force to desegregation lawsuits in other states, including Texas and Arizona. Fourth, *Mendez* wisely used the centrality of experiential knowledge of victimized Mexican American children and adults, as seen in trial testimony. Lastly, *Mendez* used interdisciplinary perspectives and considerable collaboration. Mexican American plaintiffs, White expert witnesses, and diverse organizations—including the National Association for the Advancement of Colored People, the American Jewish Council, and the American Civil Liberties Union at the appellate level—all worked together to help plaintiffs prevail in *Mendez* (Valencia, 2005).

By all accounts, the 1954 ruling of the U.S. Supreme Court in the *Brown* case was the watershed case in school desegregation, and, as well, it helped to launch the modern civil rights movement. *Brown* has been extensively covered by many scholars (see note 1, this chapter), and thus I will not replow this ground. What I do briefly, however, is draw from CRT and discuss the fierce resistance by Whites to enforce the desegregation edict of the *Brown* court. A major problem with *Brown* was the U.S. Supreme Court's failure to establish a deadline for dismantling segregated public schools. This omission gave segregationists time to pressure federal officials to delay its enforcement. On May 31, 1955, the High Court justices passed *Brown II*,[19] which required segregated states to comply fully and with all deliberate speed with the 1954 ruling. The Supreme Court delegated the responsibility of determining the pace of desegregation to federal judges. This created the mechanism to retain segregated school systems as most judges throughout the country did not favor immediate and total desegregation (Salomone, 1986).

Vergon (1988) discusses a number of ways White citizens and state officials, during the period from 1955 to 1967, attempted to nullify the U.S. Supreme Court's orders in *Brown II*. These measures included interposition statutes, circumvention, minimal plans of desegregation, and phased-in plans. A popular strategy in southern states was the use of interposition statutes, designed to argue that states' rights trump the supremacy of the U.S. Constitution and the jurisdiction of the role of the federal government in interpreting and enforcing laws and court orders. An example of the use of interposition laws was seen in 1957 in the attempt to block the desegregation of Central High School in Little Rock, Arkansas—which created a showdown between President Dwight Eisenhower and Governor Orval Faubus (Irons, 2002, chapter 10). An example of circumvention is what transpired in Virginia. In Prince Edward County, school authorities closed the public schools and transferred resources to private, racially isolated White schools (Irons; Vergon).

To Vergon's (1988) discussion of the strategies school officials utilized to challenge the *Brown II* orders, I would add the use of "expert" witnesses who testified against desegregation in certain lawsuits, such as *Stell v. Savannah-Chatham County Board of Education* (1963).[20]

Intervenors carefully selected *Stell* as their test case to overturn *Brown* because observers considered the presiding judge, Frank M. Scarlett (U.S. District Court, Southern District of Georgia, Savannah Division), to be a staunch ally of segregationists (Tucker, 1994). Thus, it was no surprise Judge Scarlett granted the request for intervention. The intervenors recruited a number of "experts," most of whom were given grants by the Pioneer Fund, a foundation that promoted scientific racism (Tucker, 2002). The task was to put together a blue-ribbon panel of scientists to provide the "facts" about race, and thus expose the alleged faulty logic of *Brown* (Jackson, 2006).

In flagrant disregard for the *Brown* ruling, Judge Scarlett opined that the plaintiffs' claim asserting that segregation causes injury to Black children cannot be supported by any of the evidence presented before the court. As such, he concludes, "The court [his court] held that the decision in *Brown v. Board of Education of Topeka* was not binding on it."[21] Not unexpectedly, *Stell* attorneys appealed to the Fifth Circuit Court of Appeals.[22] In a stinging rebuke, the Fifth Circuit writes that the district court is bound by the U.S. Supreme Court in the *Brown* ruling, as the appellate court is. Furthermore, the appellate court notes that Judge Scarlett's ruling "was a clear abuse of its discretion for the trial court to deny appellants' motion for a preliminary injunction requiring" the school district to begin an expeditious desegregation of the local schools.[23] Finally, the appellate court required that the defendants submit a desegregation plan to the Fifth Circuit no later than July 1, 1963. Appellants appealed to the U.S. Supreme Court, but they were denied the writ of certiorari.[24]

As Newby (1967) comments, the *Stell* case represents the apex of scientific racism during the post-*Brown* era, and left the desegregationist movement in a state of interruption and indecision. A well-orchestrated legal effort to reverse *Brown* had failed. We must, however, keep the *Stell* case in proper perspective. It was an extraordinary victory for integrationists at the local level, but as a whole, school desegregation across the South moved at an imperceptible rate of progress right after *Brown* to 1964 (Vergon, 1988). Over this 10-year period, the number of Black students who enrolled in schools with their White counterparts rose, on the average, around 1% yearly. By AY 1964–1965, approximately 9 in 10 Black students in the 17 states of the southern and border areas attended completely segregated schools (Vergon). Other regions also remained very segregated. In the 32 states of the North and West, the majority (60%) of Black students were enrolled in chiefly schools of students of color (U.S. Commission on Civil Rights, 1975; cited in Vergon). School segregation also remained at fairly high levels for Mexican American students in the post-*Brown* era. In the five states of the Southwest (Arizona, California, Colorado, New Mexico, and Texas), where the vast majority of Mexican American students attend school, nearly 1 in 2 of these students in 1968 were enrolled in elementary and secondary schools in which they made up the predominant ethnic group (50%–100%). Furthermore, 1 in 5 Mexican American K-12 students attended schools in which they made up the near total enrollment (80%–100%) (U.S. Commission on Civil Rights, 1971).

Period of Meaningful School Desegregation

Some scholars view the period from 1968 to the middle and late 1970s as a time of "meaningful progress" in school desegregation efforts (e.g., Brown, 2004; Vergon, 1988). At the beginning of this era, legal action by the courts largely consisted of the issuance of orders to eliminate the various obstacles that school districts used to impede the enrollment of Black students in White schools (Vergon). One case in particular that helped to quicken the pace of the dilatory movement of school desegregation was *Green v. County School Board of New Kent County* (1968),[25] considered to be the most significant school desegregation case reaching the U.S. Supreme Court since *Brown* 14 years earlier. At the time, New Kent County—located in rural, Eastern Virginia—had a population of 4,500 people, split evenly between Whites and Blacks. There were close to 1,300 students enrolled, 740 Black and 550 White, in the two schools—one Black (Watkins School) and one White (New Kent School).[26] De jure segregation was maintained pursuant to the Virginia Constitution codes of 1950, in clear violation of the *Brown* ruling.[27] In order to stay eligible for federal funding, 5 months after *Green* was filed the school board adopted a "freedom of choice" plan,[28] which subsequently became the lightning rod in *Green*.

After 3 years of implementation of the plan, not 1 White student had enrolled in Watkins School and 115 Black pupils had opted to enroll in New Kent School. Yet, 85% of the Black students in the county continued to attend the all-Black Watkins School. In sum, the High Court concluded, "The school system remains a dual system."[29] In the *Green* opinion of 1968, the U.S. Supreme Court ruled that freedom-of-choice plans are not ends in themselves in desegregation strategies. If there are other reasonable means (e.g., modification of school attendance zones) to achieve effectively a school district that is unitary, then they must be used. Freedom-of-choice plans, employed solely as the mechanism to attain desegregation, are "unacceptable."[30] The most important development resultant of the *Green* ruling was that the Supreme Court operationalized what a dual school system is. The opinion underscores that the "racial identification" of the New Kent County schools "was complete." Such identification extended to segregation with respect to: (a) students, (b) faculty, (c) staff, (d) extracurricular activities, (e) transportation, and (f) facilities.[31] In later legal scholarship, these six aspects became known as the "*Green* factors" (e.g., Brown, 2004; Clark, 1995; Moore, 2002). Implicit in the *Green* decision was that in order to attain unitary status, a school district must remove racial identifiability along the six points.[32] In *Green*, the High Court vacated the judgment of the Fourth Circuit Court of Appeals, which had affirmed the District Court, and remanded the case to the latter court for additional proceedings that are consistent with the opinion of the *Green* court.[33]

The impact of the *Green* ruling on subsequent school desegregation outcomes and litigation was positive and far-reaching (e.g., Clotfelter, 2004; Irons, 2002). For example, the year following the *Green* decision, the National Association for the Advancement of Colored People took on one of the most anti-desegregationist states—Mississippi. The federal district courts there were quite hostile toward desegregation, but the Fifth Circuit overruled their decisions and rendered compliance orders pursuant to the mandate of *Green*. In the summer months of 1969, the Fifth Circuit ordered the desegregation of 33 school districts in Mississippi, commencing with school openings in the fall (Irons).

In regard to Mexican American students, they also benefitted during this era of meaningful school desegregation (Valencia, 2008, chapter 1). Prior to 1970s, Mexican Americans were legally considered "other White" for purposes of desegregation, and thus not protected under the Fourteenth Amendment—as Blacks were pursuant to the *Brown* ruling of 1954. As such, some school districts in Texas used a ploy: Arguing that Mexican Americans were "other White," these devious districts desegregated their schools by pairing Black and Mexican American students and, thus, claimed that the district was unitary. In *Cisneros v. Corpus Christi Independent School District* (1970),[34] based on the melding of testimony regarding racial discrimination and ethnic identifiability, attorneys for the plaintiffs contended that the Mexican American people are a readily identifiable ethnic group. Presiding Judge Woodrow Seals, Southern District of Texas (Houston), found not only that Mexican Americans have "been discriminated against as a class" but also that "because they are an identifiable ethnic minority they are more susceptible to discrimination."[35] His ruling, in effect, found that Mexican American students could protect themselves under the Equal Protection Clause, as Blacks had been doing since *Brown*.

The watershed *Cisneros* decision prompted a flurry of school desegregation cases involving Mexican Americans in Texas (see Valencia, 2008, p. 8, Table 1). In the landmark U.S. Supreme Court case, *Keyes v. School District No. 1 of Denver, Colorado* (1973)[36]—which was the first time in history that the High Court had an opportunity to rule on a desegregation case not confined to the South—the court found that "Hispanos constitute an identifiable class for purposes of the Fourteenth Amendment."[37] The issue of whether Mexican American students are an identifiable ethnic minority class sufficient to bring them under the protection of *Brown* had finally been settled—and by the nation's highest court.

The era of meaningful school desegregation came to an end via the commonplace events of jurisprudence—in this instance, political appointments of judges and the workings of their hearts and minds. In a 2004 article published in the *University of Illinois Law Review,* Judge Boyce F. Martin Jr. of the Sixth Circuit Court of Appeals notes that with the election of Richard Nixon as president in

1968, the demise of school desegregation began. It was well known that Nixon had strong opposition to the liberal Warren Court, which had the reputation of handing down decisions that expanded civil rights (e.g., *Brown,* 1954). During his campaign for president, Nixon spoke loudly about his disapproval of "judicial activism" and called for a High Court that would strictly interpret the Constitution.[38] After he was elected, President Nixon appointed four conservative justices from 1969 to 1971 to the U.S. Supreme Court—Warren E. Burger (chief justice), Harry Blackmun, Lewis F. Powell Jr., and William Rehnquist.[39] In his article, Judge Martin comments that the Burger Court severely undermined the ability of inner-city Black students to gain access to desegregated schools, which triggered the slowdown, if not erosion, of the movement to desegregate the nation's public schools. Subsequently, although school desegregation continued until around 1988, efforts to end racial isolation in schools lost favor in the courts and among the public, and the pace of desegregation dramatically declined.

Contemporary Status of School Desegregation

By the mid-2000s, school desegregation had not been earnestly pursued in the bulk of school districts for more than 2 decades (Ryan, 2007). In light of the deceleration of the school desegregation movement in the U.S., the goal of having children and youths of diverse racial/ethnic backgrounds attend school together has become even more elusive. Evidence of the current lethargy in desegregating K-12 public schools is also seen in the number of school districts still operating under a desegregation order in which the U.S. government is a party to the litigation. In 2005, the Civil Rights Division of the U.S. Department of Justice reported that there were 328 school districts under desegregation orders[40] in 16 states.[41] Another factor to consider in contemporary school desegregation pursuits is that only a small percentage of school districts take race into consideration in the assignment of students. In a 2004 U.S. Department of Education report, approximately 1,000 (6.3%) of almost 16,000 school districts in the country utilized race as a factor in assigning students (Ryan). Still yet another obstacle to current school desegregation is the issue I earlier discussed—the current prevalence of school segregation. The data in Table 4.1 speak loudly to how difficult it will be to desegregate the nation's schools when students of color overwhelmingly attend schools in which they are the majority group (i.e., 50%–100%, 90%–100%, or 99%–100%).

On top of these problems, another debilitating blow was struck to public elementary and secondary school desegregation efforts by the U.S. Supreme Court's 2007 decision in *Parents Involved in Community Schools v. Seattle School District No. 1.*[42] This case, hereafter referred to as *PICS,* had to do with *voluntary* desegregation plans in which "freedom of choice" was used. Around the time of *PICS,* only a handful of school districts in the nation (less than 30) had voluntary, freedom-of-choice desegregation plans (Ryan, 2007), but now even these strategies are in jeopardy and the opportunity for students of color and White students to attend desegregated schools has been, for the most part, highly compromised. On June 28, 2007, the Supreme Court—in a 5–4, 185-page decision—struck down voluntary desegregation plans in Seattle, Washington (which involved high schools), and in Louisville, Kentucky (involving elementary schools). In both districts, school officials used a student's race as *a* factor in school assignments. Furthermore, both the Seattle and Louisville school districts' plans had a freedom-of-choice component in which students, in their applications, could indicate a first- and second-choice school. Appellants in *PICS* were White students who were denied their first choice because the assignment would create racial imbalance at that particular school.[43] Seattle appellants, for example, claimed that the use of race for school assignments violated their rights under the Equal Protection Clause of the 14th Amendment, Title VI of the Civil Rights Act of 1964, and the State of Washington Civil Rights Act.[44]

The consolidated *PICS* cases before the U.S. Supreme Court were from the Ninth and Sixth Circuits, which affirmed that the desegregation plans served a compelling state interest and were narrowly tailored.[45] Chief Justice John C. Roberts, who wrote the majority opinion, comments, however, "The districts have also failed to show that they considered methods other than explicit racial classifications [i.e., race-neutral options] to achieve the stated goals."[46] He elaborates:

> Our established strict scrutiny test for racial classification, however, insists on "detailed examination, both as to ends as to means . . . " Simply because the school districts may seek a worthy goal does not mean they are free to discriminate on the basis of race to achieve it, or that their racial classifications should be subject to less exacting scrutiny.[47]

Justice Anthony M. Kennedy, who joined the majority (i.e., conservative justices Samuel A. Alioto, John C. Roberts, Antonin G. Scala, and Clarence Thomas), wrote a concurring opinion—which is in agreement with the majority opinion but applies "different emphasis, precedents, or logic to reach the same determination" (Hill & Hill, 1995, s.v. "concurring opinion"). Differing from his fellow justices in the majority, who did not acknowledge that the two school districts had identified a compelling interest in their arguments, Justice Kennedy notes that diversity is a compelling educational objective that a school district may strive for.[48] He also differs from his majority colleagues on the issue of race as a factor in desegregation efforts. He comments that sections of the majority opinion by Justice Roberts "imply an all-too-unyielding insistence that race cannot be a factor in instances when, in my view, it may be taken into account."[49] Continuing this point, Justice Kennedy comments, "The plurality opinion is too dismissive of the legitimate interest government has in ensuring all people have equal opportunity regardless of their race."[50] Finally, his concurring opinion offers some suggestions, other than systematic and individual race typing, for school desegregation. In the concluding section of this chapter, I will briefly discuss his recommendations.

As one might have expected, enmity filled the pages of the various opinions in the *PICS* ruling. Ryan (2007) aptly notes, "On a first read, one is struck by the dramatic rhetoric, heightened emotion, sharp disagreement, and accusations of bad faith coursing through this 185-page collection of opinions" (p. 134). For example, Justice Roberts comments that the dissent by Justice Stephen G. Breyer "selectively relies on inapplicable precedent and even dicta while dismissing contrary holdings, alters and misapplies our well-established legal framework for assessing equal protection challenges to express racial classifications, and greatly exaggerates the consequences of today's decision."[51] In his concurring opinion, Justice Thomas remarks that the school districts' justification in pursuing voluntary desegregation plans was "nothing [more] but an interest in classroom aesthetics and a hypersensitivity to elite sensibilities."[52]

In the dissenting opinion (joined by Justices Ruth Bader Ginsburg, David H. Souter, and John Paul Stevens), Justice Breyer denounces the majority opinion in his 68-page opinion, commenting that it undermined the promise of Brown—integrated education—and asserted that the decision "cannot be justified in the name of the Equal Protection Clause."[53] He also notes that the majority opinion is regressive: "The Court's decision today slows down and sets back the work of local school boards to bring about racially diverse schools."[54] In his conclusion, Justice Breyer states that the majority opinion denies parents' wishes for their children to attend schools with fellow children of diverse races/ethnicities. He expands:

> The plurality is wrong to do so. The last half-century has witnessed great strides toward racial equality, but we have not yet realized the promise of Brown. To invalidate the plans under review is to threaten the promise of Brown. The plurality's position, I fear, would break that promise. This is a decision that the Court and the nation will come to regret.[55]

To be sure, the *PICS* decision is not a simple one to comprehend. In their analysis of the case, Gutman and Dunleavy (2007) fittingly conclude that the High Court's ruling is "fractured," in that "no *five* judges agreed to exactly the same thing" [italics added]" (p. 42). That is, four of five members of the majority opinion asserted that neither prong of the strict scrutiny standard (compelling interest, narrow tailoring) was met. Regarding the dissenting opinion, four of four argued that both points of the strict scrutiny analysis were satisfied. As such, the majority opinion demonstrates the voices of four justices, not five. Thus, it was Justice Kennedy in his concurring opinion who really decided the case. Drawing from Gutman and Dunleavy, I believe that any deep understanding of the *PICS* ruling is best achieved by staking out what Justice Kennedy states in his concurring opinion regarding how race can be taken into account in school desegregation plans. In the next section, I return to Justice Kennedy's suggestions, along with other thoughts on how we might realize high-quality integrated schools.

Toward Systemic Transformations

After reading the foregoing, one might be inclined to throw his or her hands in the air and frustratingly exclaim, "My goodness, in light of all the obstacles facing school desegregation and given the reality that efforts to dismantle segregated schools have met with disfavor by the courts and the public, why even bother with attempts to desegregate and integrate our schools!" To be sure, there are some scholars and educators who share this sentiment. A notable example is the late, distinguished Derrick Bell (1930–2011), who supervised over 300 cases dealing with school segregation, was the first Black professor to earn tenure at Harvard Law School, and is considered a pioneer in the study of critical race theory (Root Staff, 2011). In his 2004 book, *Silent Covenants:* Brown v. Board of Education *and the Unfulfilled Hopes for Racial Reform*, Bell raises a provocative question about the *Brown* (1954) ruling. He composed a mock scenario demonstrating how the U.S. Supreme Court might have ruled in a very different manner. Bell (p. 21) begins by noting, "Today [May 17, 1954] we uphold our six decades-old decision in *Plessy v. Ferguson,* 163 U.S. 537 [1896]"). In this alternative opinion, Bell states that although the Supreme Court is sympathetic to the Negro petitioners and acknowledges the harm caused by school segregation, the "equal" notion in the "separate but equal" doctrine established in *Plessy* has not been stringently enforced. Therefore, Bell continues in his alternative version, the High Court has the authority to accord relief under the *Plessy* precedent. That is, three points of relief are required to be implemented for all students in segregated school districts across the country: (a) "equalization" (equalize, for example: teacher-pupil ratios, salary, teacher training and experiences); (b) "representation" (i.e., restructure school boards and other policymaking entities so they reflect the percentages of students by race in school districts); (c) "judicial oversight" (i.e., judges of federal district courts shall establish committees to monitor compliance of mandates "a" and "b"; school districts that fail to meet these mandates shall be held in noncompliance).

What would prompt Bell—a highly experienced litigator of school desegregation cases and seasoned voice of how to implement *Brown* (see Bell, 2004, chapter 10)—to abandon the integrationist approach (which he refers to as a "racial-balance" remedy; see Bell, chapter 11) and advocate a separate but equal approach to schooling for Black students (i.e., equally funded schools, equal representation on school boards, fully monitored compliance process)? He offers a number of explanations. First, although the *Brown* ruling was important in serving as a catalyst for the Black struggle for civil rights, in itself the decision served as a reinforcer of fiction—namely, that the Supreme Court's judgment, in which it rejected the harm and barriers of segregation, led to the false belief that the road to racial equality was now open. Second, the mandate of desegregation at "all deliberate speed" voiced in *Brown II* was ineffective, thus giving White southerners ample time to devise tactics to avoid school desegregation. Third, the position of petitioners in *Brown* that school segregation depicted Blacks as a "damaged race" can be viewed as a "scathing derogation" of Black children and adults (p. 137). Fourth, after school desegregation actually began, the outcomes for Black students were far from desirable—as seen, for example, in long, one-way bus rides to the receiving White schools, academic resegregation, irrelevant curriculum via-à-vis the Black experience, obstacles to Black parental engagement in the schools, and frequent racial animus by White students and teachers toward Blacks.

In sum, Bell (2004) notes, "Zealous faith in integration blinded us to the actual goal of equalizing educational opportunities for black children, and led us to pursue integration without regard to, and often despite, its ultimate impact on the well-being of students" (p. 113). Put in a similar way, Bell comments that civil rights lawyers' beliefs and commitments to integration eclipsed the educational priorities of their plaintiffs (also, see Ladson-Billings, 2007, 2013). To be sure, the perspective of Bell on the *Brown* ruling is controversial. Although his separate but equal position runs counter to that of most scholars who believe in school integration, his views are certainly worth thinking about. Bell forces us to ponder how to conceptualize "racial equality" in public education and the role of White privilege in maintaining the status quo. His reflections lead to the requirement that we reassess and replace "racial-equality ideology with specific programs leading to tangible goals" (p. 189).

There are others, however, who assert that school desegregation's time is not over and we need to continue such efforts, particularly school integration, with a renewed vigor (e.g., Frankenburg & Debray, 2011). I join my fellow colleagues in this commitment, but do so with a qualifying point. I am in favor of school integration, but concomitantly such schools must offer educational opportunity for all students (e.g., full funding, highly prepared teachers, multicultural curriculum). In this concluding section, I offer some thoughts on how we might work toward the goal of having students of color and their White peers together attend schools in which all students have an equal educational opportunity to learn.

Before going any further, I need to draw an important distinction between two terms: *desegregation* and *integration*. Unfortunately, these concepts have been used as though they are synonymous, but they are not. Desegregation, which can be mandated by the courts, has to do with the school reassignment of students (based on race) so the racial identifiability of the receiving school is eliminated (Hughes, Gordon, & Hillman, 1980). By contrast, integration is a much more complex undertaking. It is a social process that involves the actual mixing of students of color and their White counterparts in settings, particularly the classroom, that allow for close social contact. As discussed earlier in this chapter, the implementation of the contact hypothesis—the driver of intergroup contact theory—can lead to prejudice reduction, friendships, and the reciprocal acceptance and civility for others. As Hughes et al. (1980) remind us, integration cannot be made mandatory by the courts. Judges cannot force one person to like another person. As such, effective integration can come about only through collective and assiduous efforts by school board members, teachers, counselors, administrators, students, and members of the community. In the pursuit of school integration, we must be mindful that desegregation is just the beginning. Without true integration, students of color in the receiving or host school are very likely (especially in middle and high schools) to experience academic resegregation via tracking, which is just as invidious as segregation by race (e.g., Mickelson, 2001; Oakes, 1995; Valencia, 1996a, 1996b).[56] Furthermore, it is important to emphasize that integration does not work through some mysterious process of osmosis. "Simply sitting next to a white student does not guarantee better educational outcomes for students of color" (Orfield et al., 2012, p. 8). What is important for students of color in the process of integration is attaining access to the resources (e.g., high-quality teachers, substantial funding) that are typically found in middle- and high-SES White schools, and that lead to superior academic achievement outcomes.

As a preface to a number of proposals that may have utility in school desegregation endeavors, it would be prudent to return to the U.S. Supreme Court in *PICS*, particularly Justice Kennedy's concurring opinion, in which he offered some suggestions for school desegregation:

> School boards may pursue the goal of bringing together students of diverse backgrounds and races through other means [i.e., not systematic use of race], *including strategic site selection of new schools; drawing attendance zones with general recognition of the demographics of neighborhoods; allocating resources for special programs; recruiting students and faculty in a targeted fashion; and tracking enrollments, performance, and other statistics by race* [italics added]. These mechanisms are race conscious but do not lead to different treatment based on a classification that tells each student he or she is to be defined by race, so it is unlikely any of them would demand strict scrutiny to be found permissible.[57]

In the remainder of this section, I offer a number of ideas that can serve as possible ways to continue with the pursuit of school desegregation. In part, I draw from some of Justice Kennedy's suggestions. The following thoughts are not intended to be comprehensive proposals, but rather as points designed to foster discussion.

1. *Site selection of new schools.* This proposed strategy to promote school desegregation is attractive because it falls within the suggestions provided by Justice

Kennedy in his concurring opinion in *PICS*. According to a 2013 report by the National Clearinghouse for Educational facilities, in AY 2110–2011 there were 98,817 public elementary and secondary schools operating in the U.S. Furthermore, in the same AY, 1,665 new schools were opened and 1,929 closed; most of these new and closed schools were public.[58] Overall, however, there is a great need for the construction of new schools. It is projected that from 2010 to 2050, 30,000 new schools (750 per year over 4 decades) will need to be built in the U.S. (Stevenson, 2010). In regard to regional patterns, however, the need for new public schools varies. School closures have occurred in large numbers, for example, in Chicago and Detroit (Valencia, 2012). Yet, in other locations dramatic growth in student populations has prompted the necessity for new schools. In California, for example, in 2009 there was a need for new schools for 1 million additional students.[59] In Texas, local voters approved bonds of $1.5 billion in November 2011 for new school construction (Scott Nabers, 2012). As I discussed earlier in this chapter, California and Texas are among the top states in the racial isolation of Latino/Latina and Black students and their White peers. In biracial or multiracial communities in California and Texas, the strategic site selection of new schools could truly assist in efforts to achieve desegregation.

Clearly, due to the political nature of education, where new schools are built in a community is a difficult decision. There are school board members who are beholden to their constituents, and there are some White parents who will fight to keep their privilege by voicing the mantra of "NIMBY" (not in my backyard), the ubiquitous challenge to new constructions (e.g., schools, mental health clinics, big box chain stores, homeless shelters; see, e.g., Mensing, 2012). Yet, for the strategy of site selection of new schools to be successful, demographers, urban planners, and infrastructure experts must work closely with local leaders and community activists in this pursuit. Furthermore, state governments must take more proactive roles in imparting guidance to municipalities in the school site selection process. For example, in California's *School Site Selection and Approval Guide*, there are 12 criteria, in rank order of importance, to be considered. They are, in part, "safety," "location," "environment," "soils," "topography," and "size and shape."[60] Conspicuously absent is a criterion that speaks to the function of "helps promote racial integration."

2. *Drawing and adjustment of school attendance zones.* This strategy has some promise to bring about school desegregation, at least on paper. Also, this is one of the suggestions noted by Justice Kennedy in his concurring opinion in *PICS*. As of 2012, there were more than 14,000 public school districts operating in the U.S.[61] The number of school attendance zones (hereafter referred to as SAZs) varies considerably by the enrollment size of the district. For example, in the small Santa Barbara (California) Unified School District, 15,326 pre-K to grade 12 students were enrolled in 2012 (58% Latino/Latina; 34% White; 8% other). As of 2013, there were 13 elementary schools, with their respective SAZs.[62] In the moderate size Arlington (Texas) Independent School District, there were 63,493 pre-K to 12

students enrolled in 2013 (39% Latino/Latina; 30% White; 24% Black; 7% other). At the elementary level, 51 schools operated within 51 SAZs.[63]

The main points about SAZs are that they are omnipresent and manipulatable. Periodically, due to the need to build new schools, close some, or consolidate underenrolled schools, school districts are forced to make adjustments in their SAZs (Bhargava, Frankenburg, & Le, 2008). The situation in which changes in SAZs can have the most significant impact on school desegregation is new school site selection and the drafting of the new SAZ. As I note in the previous section on site selection of new schools, it is forecast that in light of the current and future growth of the K-12 public school population, there will be a need to build 750 schools every year for 40 consecutive years (2010 to 2050) (Stevenson, 2010). If strategic planning of the SAZs for these new schools is done with desegregation in mind, much can be accomplished in the pursuit of desegregated, and ideally, integrated education. It is very likely, however, that this strategy will be met with opposition by some parents who eschew the idea that their children will no longer have the comfort of attending their "neighborhood school." As such, school board members, educators, and community leaders will need to work in concert to convince reluctant parents of the value of SAZs that lead to desegregation.

3. *Implementation of magnet schools.* This strategy for school desegregation has considerable appeal. First, magnet schools have been in existence for some time now. Second, in his concurring opinion in *PICS,* among his suggestions to help promote desegregated schools Justice Kennedy did not explicitly mention magnet schools, but he did refer to "allocating resources for special programs."[64] Magnet schools have their origin in the 1960s, and their popularity soared in the middle of the 1970s as a method to merge school desegregation goals with greater parental choice (Siegel-Hawley & Frankenberg, 2012a). In 2000, the U.S. Department of Education estimated that over 50% of all sizable urban school districts were utilizing magnet schools for purposes of desegregation (Smrekar & Goldring, 2000; cited in Siegel-Hawley & Frankenberg, 2012a). In 2008–2009, the National Center for Education Statistics noted that more than 2.5 million public school students attended magnet schools, and currently such schools constitute the largest means of parental choice. Although the goal of magnet schools in reducing racial isolation has somewhat waned, school desegregation remains an integral aspect of such programs (Siegel-Hawley & Frankenberg, 2012a). In light of the limited school desegregation choices prompted by the *PICS* ruling, continued interest and funding in magnet schools by the federal government must be encouraged and local districts should renew their efforts in implementing magnet schools as a strategy to reduce racial isolation (Smrekar & Goldring, 2011).

4. *Implementation of two-way dual language programs.* This is another option that has appreciable promise for school desegregation, and it appears to fall within Justice Kennedy's suggestion in his *PICS* concurring opinion that has to do with

the allocation of resources for distinctive programs.[65] What is especially attractive about this strategy is that it involves students from different racial/ethnic and language backgrounds learning together in the same classroom, thus setting the stage for close contact and the process of integration. Given that language is a vehicle of culture, these programs are ideal in helping to promote cross-cultural learning, understanding, and appreciation—important goals of school integration. Furthermore, such programs, if structured correctly and taught by well-trained teachers, can lead to students' high academic performance, and therefore reduction in TAG.

Two-way dual language programs (hereafter referred to as two-way programs) are special curricular approaches within the rubric of bilingual education. These programs are enrichment strategies (i.e., not remedial) designed to develop biliteracy in students as well as the deliverance of high levels of academic subject matter via two languages. Students enrolled in two-way programs consist of English learners (ELs; e.g., Spanish speakers who are acquiring English skills) and native English speakers (e.g., White students). Both groups of students are presented with instruction in both languages in an integrated classroom setting (Izquierdo, 2011). Two-way programs have developed considerable popularity, and the number of them has dramatically increased. In 1962, the Dade County Public Schools (Miami, Florida) established the very first program, and subsequently two-way programs spread throughout the U.S., particularly in states such as California, New Mexico, New York, Washington, and Texas.[66] By the year 2000, the number of programs had grown to 260, and by 2011 the count swelled to 2,000 (Wilson, 2011), with Texas leading the country with about 700 elementary schools having such programs (Solís, 2012).

In regard to the academic advantages of two-way programs, research findings have shown much promise. For example, Izquierdo (2011) reports that prior to the adoption of a two-language program, the Ysleta Independent School District (El Paso, Texas) was one of the poorest performing districts in the state. After the program became established, by 2004 native English-speaking and EL students in the two-way program (grades 3–11) outperformed their peers who were not enrolled in the program; the criterion variable was the Texas Assessment of Academic Skills Reading/Language Arts tests. Similar results for students enrolled in two-way programs in the Houston Independent School District have also been reported (Thomas & Collier, 2003). With respect to the social context of two-way programs, there is some theoretical and empirical research that these curricular strategies can have positive outcomes. In their review of germane research from Canada and the U.S., Genese and Gándara (1999) conclude that two-way programs can and do lead to improved intercultural attitudes between ELs and native speakers, as well as enhanced self-esteem among students.

5. *The housing-school interconnection.* In chapter 3, "The 'Other' Gaps," I discussed gaps in income, housing, and health. Regarding housing gap reform (in the concluding section on "Toward Systemic Transformations" in chapter 3),

I underscored that housing segregation and school segregation are extremely difficult to disentangle. As such, I informed the reader that the most fitting place to discuss reform for the housing gap would be in this present chapter on school segregation. Allow me to summarize the main points I covered in chapter 3 concerning the housing gap. First, residential location is a great determinant of the price of housing. Second, such location is highly linked with the academic quality and reputation of the nearby schools. Third, the preponderance of the literature on segregation focuses on separate housing or separate schools—seldom the interrelation between the two types of isolation. Fourth, the most fruitful manner to examine the housing gap is via the concept of geography of opportunity. This notion can best be viewed as an opportunity process in which residential location serves as a channel to high-performing schools, which is a reality that low-SES students of color seldom experience because their parents are financially unable to afford the housing in neighborhoods where these highly preferred schools are located.

In principle, at least, the housing-school interconnection makes a great deal of sense in the pursuit of school desegregation. The attractiveness of such an approach rests in the reality of human proximity and its likely consequences. That is, families of diverse backgrounds (particularly along lines of race/ethnicity; SES) living relatively close together should be able to interact in the same neighborhoods, which can lead to mutual acceptance and respect. Children of these varied social circumstances can take the same bus to school, or walk to school together, and perhaps form friendships. And, most importantly, they can attend the same classes in the same schools—ideally high-performing ones. Most of the endeavors to promote a merging of the housing-school interconnection have been via governmental interventions. It is tempting to ask whether such programs have succeeded or failed, but the more important query is: What can we learn from the results of these approaches, particularly about how policies of assisted housing mobility can be made more effective (Turner & Briggs, 2008)?

The most notable governmental project to assist low-SES people of color with housing mobility is the Gautreaux program.[67] Not surprisingly, this ambitious undertaking in metropolitan Chicago was born of litigation (Polikoff, 2006).[68] In 1966, Dorothy Gautreaux (et al.), a resident of the Black-segregated housing projects in Chicago, a community organizer, and lead plaintiff in the Gautreaux legal case (Lewis, 2006), filed suit in 1966. The complaint in this housing discrimination lawsuit was that the Chicago Housing Authority (CHA) and the Department of Housing and Urban Development (HUD) had intentionally segregated Blacks by constructing over 10,000 public housing units in Black inner-city enclaves from 1954 to 1967, thus perpetuating racial segregation (Lewis). After considerable time, the U.S. District Court (Northern District, Illinois) finally found that the CHA and HUD had violated the 14th Amendment and federal statues (Polikoff). The Seventh Circuit Court of Appeals affirmed (*Gautreaux v. Chicago Housing Authority*, 1974), as did the U.S. Supreme

Court (*Hills v. Gautreaux*, 1976). Resultant of the ruling in *Hills,* the Gautreaux program was established to permit residents of public housing (overwhelmingly low-SES Black) to obtain Section 8 certificates in order to move away to private apartments either in the suburbs ("suburban movers"), where most of the residents were middle- or upper-SES Whites, or in the city of Chicago ("city movers"). In all, 7,000 families took part in the program between 1976 and 1998. The suburban movers relocated to 115 suburbs located in six counties in the Chicago area (Rosenbaum, DeLuca, & Tuck, 2005).

There have been a number of studies undertaken by an array of researchers who have investigated the outcomes of the Gautreaux program. An example is the work of Rosenbaum et al. (2005).[69] The authors report that suburban mover students, compared to their city mover peers, had higher rates of (a) graduating from high school, (b) matriculating to college, (c) attending 4-year colleges (in comparison to 2-year colleges), and (d) obtaining a job after college (and earning higher salaries). With respect to student interactions, suburban movers were more likely than the city movers to (a) spend time doing homework with White students, (b) engage in out-of-school activities with their White peers, and (c) visit White students in their homes. Concerning employment patterns of heads of household, suburban movers—compared to city movers—had higher rates of securing jobs. Rosenbaum et al. conclude that the relocation of suburban movers led to a substantial amount of "bridging" socially based interactions that cut across lines of race (p. 158). These positive research findings from the Gautreaux program, however, have been questioned by some investigators. For example, Duncan and Zuberi (2006) point out a methodological issue: The suburban and city mover participants were created by self-selection, and thus there was no control group. Duncan and Zuberi also note that later research on the Gautreaux program demonstrated no employment advantages for suburban movers over city movers.

Aside from critiques such as this, a number of scholars find that housing mobility programs such as Gautreaux have proven successful in improving the participants' physical and mental health, adolescent behavior (such as crime reduction), school success, and employment (e.g., Turner & Briggs, 2008). Such research findings should force us to ask key questions about how to create more effective housing mobility to benefit those in need. What social processes in mixed-SES neighborhoods operate that help to forge these life improvements? What societal attitudes lead to or thwart these gains? How can the structural obstacles in the larger society, especially in the economy, be reckoned with? On this latter concern, Turner and Briggs underscore, "A change of address alone will never compensate for the major structural barriers low-skilled people face in our economy" (p. 1).

In the final analysis, the school segregation of low-SES students of color is a principal mesolevel factor in understanding their school failure, as well as their school success. Historically, the segregation of these children and youths in separate and unequal schools has been the crucible in which school failure has originated and festered. Notwithstanding the many difficult and lengthy legal battles to desegregate the nation's public schools, students of color—particularly Latino/Latina and Black—currently face hypersegregation. These students deserve much more of our attention and energy to begin a renewed campaign so they can attend integrated schools in which equal educational opportunity for all is the norm.

Notes

1. For a comprehensive coverage of *Brown*, see: Jackson (2001); Klarman (2004); Kluger (2004); Ogletree (2004).
2. Brown v. Board of Education of Topeka, 347 U.S. 483, 495 (1954).
3. Also, see: Orfield (2009); Siegel-Hawley and Frankenberg (2012b).
4. Austin (city) QuickFacts from the U.S. Census Bureau. Retrieved June 14, 2013 from: quickfacts.census.gov/qfd/states/48/4805000.html.
5. Also, see: Valencia (2011, pp. 64–65).
6. This paragraph draws from, with revisions, Valencia, Menchaca, and Donato (2002, p. 73, 79–80, 90). Some remaining portions of this chapter build on, with revisions: Valencia (2005, pp. 411, 417); Valencia (2008, pp. 3–4, 14–15, 37, 52, 61–62, 67, 76–78, 335); Valencia (2010, pp. 24–28); Valencia (2011, pp. 51–52, 54); Donato, Menchaca, and Valencia (1991, p. 28).
7. The concept of ethnic imbalance/balance stems from the 1960s, when state education agencies (see, e.g., Cal. Admin. Code, Title V, §10421) and other governmental entities (e.g., U.S. Commission on Civil Rights, 1971) sought to ascertain the degree of segregation of Whites and students of color within the schools of a district. The arithmetical formula commonly used to calculate the ethnic imbalance/balance in a district was the "±15%" rule of thumb.
8. In my analysis of school segregation in the AISD, I did not include the district's charter schools, Alternative Education Campuses (designed for the administration of alternative disciplinary education), and the Ann Richard's School for Young Women Leaders (grade 6 through 12).
9. Researchers have also investigated the converse hypothesis: School desegregation is associated with improved academic achievement of students of color. This is a complex body of research (e.g., Ready & Silander, 2011), so I do not cover it here. The essential finding, however, is that there are, generally, positive academic consequences for students of color who attend desegregated schools (see, e.g., Cook, 1984; Linn & Welner, 2007; Mickelson, 2002).
10. I have previously conducted similar analyses in the AISD elementary schools and obtained the same results. For AY 1998–1999, see Valencia (2000, p. 450, Figure 1). For AY 2002–2003 and AY 2008–2009, see, respectively, Valencia (2008, p. 12, Figure 1.1) and Valencia (2011, p. 52, Figure 2.10).
11. Roberts v. City of Boston, 59 mass. 198 (1849).
12. *Id.* at 208–209.
13. Gong Lum v. Rice, 275 U.S. 78 (1927).
14. *Id.* at 81–82.
15. Rice v. Gong Lum, 139 Miss. 760 (1925).

16. *Id.* at 780.
17. For cases involving Blacks and their victories in segregating higher education, see, for example: *McLaurin v. Oklahoma State Regents (1950*; see Kluger, 2004, pp. 265–268) and *Sweatt v. Painter (1950*; see Goldstone 2006, chapter 1).
18. Mendez v. Westminister, 64 F. Supp. at 548 (S.D. Cal. 1946).
19. Brown v. Board of Education of Topeka, 349 U.S. 294 (1955).
20. For an expanded discussion of *Stell*, see Valencia (2010, pp. 24–28).
21. *Id.* at 667.
22. Stell v. Savannah-Chatham County Board of Education, 318 F.2d 425 (S.D. Ga. 1963).
23. *Id.* at 427.
24. Roberts v. Stell, 379 U.S. 933 (1964).
25. Green v. County School Board of New Kent County, 391 U.S. 430 (1968).
26. *Id.* at 432.
27. *Id.*
28. *Id.* at 433.
29. *Id.* at 441.
30. *Id.* at 440–441.
31. *Id.* at 435.
32. Green v. County School Board of New Kent County, 391 U.S. at 436 (1968).
33. *Id.* at 442.
34. Cisneros v. Corpus Christi Independent School District, 324 F. Supp. 599 (S.D. Tex, 1970).
35. *Id.* at 614.
36. Keyes v. School District No. 1 of Denver, Colorado, 413 U.S. 189 (1973).
37. *Id.* at 197.
38. *History of the Burger Court. The Supreme Court opinion writing database.* Retrieved August 7, 2013 from: http://supremecourtopinions.wustl.edu/?rt=index/history.
39. *Id.*
40. *Pending school districts operating under desegregation cases to which the United States is a party, 2005.* Washington, DC: U.S. Department of Justice, Civil Rights Division. Retrieved August, 21, 2013 from: http://198.173.245.213/pdfs/caselist2004.pdf.
41. *Id.* The 16 states are: Arizona, Arkansas, California, Connecticut, Florida, Georgia, Illinois, Indiana, Louisiana, Mississippi, North Carolina, South Carolina, Tennessee, Texas, Utah, and Virginia.
42. Parents Involved in Community Schools v. Seattle School District No. 1, 127 S.Ct. 2738 (2007).
43. See *id.* at 2748 for an example of one such White student who was denied his first choice school.
44. *Id.* at 2748.
45. *Id.* at 2749.
46. *Id.* at 2760.
47. *Id.* at 2765.
48. *Id.* at 2789.
49. *Id.* at 2791.
50. *Id.*
51. *Id.* at 2761.
52. *Id.* at 2770, note 3.

53. Parents Involved in Community Schools v. Seattle School District No. 1, 127 S.Ct. at 2801 (2007.
54. *Id.* at 2835.
55. *Id.* at 2837.
56. See Valencia et al. (2002, p. 95 and Table 3.6, p. 96) for a discussion of Valencia (1996a, 1996b).
57. Parents Involved in Community Schools v. Seattle School District No. 1, 127 S.Ct. at 2792 (2007).
58. *School building statistics.* Washington, DC: National Clearinghouse for Educational Facilities. Retrieved August 27, 2013 from: www.ncef.org/ds/statistics.cfm.
59. *Effects of population: education.* Alexandria, VA: Negative Population Growth. Retrieved August 27, 2013 from: www.npg.org/factssheets/education.pdf.
60. *School site selection and approval guide.* Sacramento, CA: School Facilities Planning Division, California State Department of Education. Retrieved August 27, 2013 from: www.cde.gov/ls/fa/sf/schoolsiteguide.asp.
61. *School districts: People and households.* Washington, DC: U.S. Department of Commerce, Bureau of the Census. Retrieved August 30, 2013 from: http://www.census.gov/did/www/schooldistricts/.
62. *Fast Facts: 2013.* Santa Barbara, CA: Santa Barbara Unified School District. Retrieved August 30, 2013 from: www.sbunified.org/.
63. *District statistics.* Arlington, TX: Arlington Independent School District. Retrieved August 30, 2013 from http://www.aisd.net/information/diststats.aspx.
64. Parents Involved in Community Schools v. Seattle School District No. 1, 125 S.Ct. at 2792 (2007).
65. *Id.*
66. *Dual language: Bilingual education.* Woodstock, IL: Woodstock Community School District 200, Department of Language & Cultural Education. Retrieved September 6, 2013 from: http://lang.woodstockschools.org/dual-language-program. Also, see Collier and Thomas (2004).
67. Another significant housing mobility is the Moving to Opportunity for Fair Housing Demonstration (MTO), which was inspired by the Gautreaux program. For more on the MTO, see, for example: Duncan and Zuberi (2006); Goering (2005); Goering and Feins (2003); Turner and Briggs (2008).
68. Alexander Polikoff served as lead attorney in the Gautreaux case. See his book, Polikoff (2006), for a history and outcome of the lawsuit.
69. See Rosenbaum et al. (2005) for the various studies they cite.

References

Allport, G. W. (1954). *The nature of prejudice.* Reading, MA: Addison Wesley.

Bell, D. (2004). *Silent covenants:* Brown v. Board of Education *and the unfulfilled hopes for racial reform.* New York: Oxford University Press.

Bhargava, A., Frankenberg, E., & Le, C. Q. (2008). *Still looking to the future: Voluntary K-12 school integration: A manual for parents, educators, and advocates.* New York: NAACP Legal Defense and Education Project, Inc. (LDF) and Civil Rights Project/Proyecto Derechos Civiles. Retrieved August 31, 2013, from: www.naacpidf.org/document/still-looking-future-voluntary-k-12-school-integration.

Bond, H. M. (1934). *The education of the Negro in the American social order.* New York: Prentice-Hall.

Brown, L. T. (2004). Brown v. Board of Education *and school desegregation: An analysis of selected litigation.* Unpublished doctoral dissertation, Virginia Polytechnic Institute and State University, Blacksburg.

Brown v. Board of Education of Topeka, 347 U.S. 483 (1954), *supp. op.*, 349 U.S. 294 (1955).

Cisneros v. Corpus Christi Independent School District, 324 F. Supp. 599 (S.D. Tex. 1970).

Clark, W.A.V. (1995). The expert witness in unitary hearings: The six *Green* factors and spatial-demographic change. *Urban Geography, 16,* 664–679.

Clotfelter, C. T. (2004). *After Brown: The rise and retreat of school desegregation.* Princeton, NJ: Princeton University Press.

Collier, V. P., & Thomas, W. P. (2004). The astounding effectiveness of dual language education for all. *NABE Journal of Research and Practice, 2,* 1–20.

Cook, T. D. (1984). What have black children gained academically from school integration? Examination of the meta-analysis evidence. In T. D. Cook, D. Armor, R. Crain, N. Miller, W. Stephan, H. Walberg, & P. Wortman (Eds.). *School desegregation and black achievement* (pp. 6–42). Washington, DC: National Institute of Education, U.S. Department of Education. (ERIC Document Reproduction Service No. ED 241 671) Retrieved February 17, 2013, from: www.eric.ed.gov:80/PDFS/ED241671.pdf.

Delgado v. Bastrop Independent School District of Bastrop County, Civil Action No. 388 (W.D. Tex. June 15, 1948).

Donato, R., Menchaca, M. and Valencia, R. R. (1991). Segregation, desegregation, and integration of Chicano students: Problems and prospects. In R. R. Valencia (Ed.), *Chicano school failure and success: Research and policy agendas for the 1990s* (pp. 27–63). Stanford Series on Education and Public Policy. London: Falmer Press.

Duncan, G. J., & Zuberi, A. (2006). Mobility lessons from Gautreaux and Moving to Opportunity. *Northwestern Journal of Law and Social* Policy, *1,* 109–126. Retrieved November 3, 2013, from: http://scholarlycommons.law.northwestern.edu/cgi/viewcontent.cgi?article=1007&context=njlsp&sei-redir=1.

Espinosa, R. W., & Ochoa, A. (1986). Concentration of California Hispanic students in schools with low achievement: A research note. *American Journal of Education, 95,* 77–95.

Frankenburg, E., & Debray, E. (Eds.). (2011). *Integrating schools in a changing society: New policies and legal options for a multiracial generation.* Chapel Hill: University of North Carolina Press.

Gautreaux v. Chicago Housing Authority, 503 F.2d 930 (7th Cir. 1974).

Genese, F., & Gándara, P. (1999). Bilingual education programs: A cross-national perspective. *Journal of Social Issues, 55,* 665–685.

Goering, J. (2005). Expanding housing choice and integrating neighborhoods: The MTO experiment. In X. de Souza Briggs (Ed.), *The geography of opportunity: Race and housing choice in metropolitan America* (pp. 127–149). Washington, DC: Brookings Institution Press.

Goering, J., & Feins, J. D. (Eds.). (2003). *Choosing a better life? Evaluating the Moving to Opportunity social experiment.* Washington, DC: Urban Institute Press.

Goldstone, D. (2006). *Integrating the 40 acres: The 50-year struggle for racial equality at the University of Texas.* Athens: University of Georgia Press.

Gong Lum v. Rice, 275 U.S. 78 (1927).

Gonzales, v. Sheely, 96 F. Supp. 1004 (D. Ariz. 1951).

Gutman, A., & Dunleavy, E. (2007). The Supreme Court ruling in *Parents v. Seattle School District.* Sending *Grutter* and *Gratz* back to school. *Industrial-Organizational Psychologist, 45,* 41–49.

Hill, G. N., & Hill, K. T. (1995). *Real life dictionary of the law: Taking the mystery out of legal language.* Los Angeles: General Publishing Group.

Hills v. Gautreaux, 425 U.S. 284 (1976).

Hughes, L. W., Gordon, W. M., & Hillman, L. W. (1980). *Desegregating America's schools.* New York: Longman.

Irons, P. (2002). *Jim Crow's children: The broken promise of the* Brown *decision.* New York: Penguin Books.

Izquierdo, E. (2011). Two way dual language education. In R. R. Valencia (Ed.), *Chicano school failure and success: Past, present, and future* (pp. 160–172). New York: Routledge.

Jackson, J. P., Jr. (2001). *Social scientists for social justice: Making the case against segregation.* Critical America Series. New York: New York University Press.

Jackson, T. (2006, March). The fight against integration: Segregation did not fall without a fight. *American Renaissance, 17.* Retrieved January 10, 2008, from: www.amren.com/mtnews/archives/2008/01/the_fight_again.php.

Jaeger, C. (1987). *Minority and low income high schools: Evidence of educational inequality in metro Los Angeles* (Working Paper No. 8). Chicago: Metropolitan Opportunity Project, University of Chicago.

Keyes v. School District No. 1 of Denver, Colorado, 413 U.S. 189 (1973).

Klarman, M. J. (2004). *From Jim Crow to civil rights: The Supreme Court and the struggle for racial equality.* New York: Oxford University Press.

Kluger, R. (2004). *Simple justice: The history of* Brown v. Board of Education *and black America's struggle for equality.* New York: Vintage Books.

Kucsera, J., & Flaxman, G. (2012). *The western states: Profound diversity but severe segregation for Latino students.* Los Angeles: Civil Rights Project/Proyecto Derechos Civiles at the University of California at Los Angeles. Retrieved September 15, 2012, from: civilrightsproject.ucla.edu/research/k-12-education/integration-and-diversity/mlk-national/the-western-states-profound-diverstiy-but-severe-segregation-for-latino-students.

Ladson-Billings, G. (2007). Can we at least have *Plessy*? The struggle for quality education. *North Carolina Law Review, 85,* 1279–1292.

Ladson-Billings, G. (2013). Foreword. In J. K. Donnor & A. D. Dixon (Eds.), *The resegregation of schools: Education and race in the twenty-first century* (pp. xiii–xxiii). New York: Routledge.

Lewis, T. (2006, February 23). *Gautreaux* housing case lawyer calls for end to black ghettos. *Leadership Conference.* Retrieved November 1, 2013, from: www.civilrights.org/fairhousing/laws/gautreaux-housing-case-lawyer-calls-for-end-to-black-ghettos.html.

Linn, R. L., & Welner, K. G. (Eds.). (2007). *Race-conscious policies for assigning students to schools: Social science research and the Supreme Court cases.* Washington, DC: National Academy of Education. Retrieved January 6, 2012, from: www.naeducation.org/Meridith_Report.pdf.

Martin, B. F., Jr. (2004). Fifty years later, it's time to mend *Brown's* broken promise. *University* of *Illinois Law Review, 2004,* 1203–1221.

McLaurin v. Oklahoma State Regents, 339 U.S. 637 U.S. (1950).

Mendez v. Westminister, 64 F. Supp. 544 (S.D. Cal. 1946), *aff'd sub nom* Westminister v. Mendez, 161 F.2d 774 (9th Cir. 1947).

Mensing, S. (2012, November 26). The final solution to the NIMBY question. *Rowan Free Press.* Retrieved December 29, 2013, from: rowanfreepress.com/2012/11/26/the-final-solution-to-the-nimby-question/.

Mickelson, R. A. (2001). Subverting *Swann*: First- and second-generation segregation in the Charlotte-Meckenburg schools. *American Educational Research Journal, 38,* 215–252.

Mickelson, R. A. (2002, August). *The academic consequences of desegregation and segregation: Evidence from the Charlotte-Mecklenburg schools.* Paper presented at the

Conference on the Resegregation of Southern Schools, University of North Carolina at Chapel Hill. Retrieved January 6, 2012, from: http://civilrightsproject.ucla.edu/research/k-12-education/integration-and-diversity/the-academic-consequences-of-desegregation-and-segregation-evidence-from-the-charlotte-mecklenburg-schools/mickelson-academic-consequences-desegregation.pdf.

Mitchell, R. E., & Mitchell, D. E. (2010, April). *Assessing multiethnic school segregation: Measurement and interpretation*. Paper presented at the meeting of the American Educational Research Association, Denver, CO. Retrieved June 12, 2013, from: bulldog2.relands.edu/fac/ross_mitchell/AERA_DistributionPaper.pdf.

Moore, M. L. (2002). Unclear standards create an unclear future: Developing a better definition of unitary status. *Yale Law Review, 112,* 311–351.

Newby, I. A. (1967). *Challenge to the court: Social scientists and the defense of segregation, 1954–1966*. Baton Rouge: Louisiana State University Press.

Oakes, J. (1995). Two cities' tracking and within-school segregation. *Teachers College Record, 96,* 681–690.

Ogletree, C. J., Jr. (2004). *All deliberate speed: Reflections on the first half of* Brown v. Board of Education. New York: W. W. Norton.

Orfield, G. (1988, July). *The growth and concentration of Hispanic enrollment and the future of American education*. Paper presented at the National Council of La Raza Conference, Albuquerque, NM.

Orfield, G. (2009). *Reviving the goal of an integrated society: A 21st century challenge.* Los Angeles: Civil Rights Project/Proyecto Derechos Civiles at the University of California at Los Angeles. Retrieved January 16, 2010, from: http://civilrightsproject.ucla.edu/research/k-12-education/integration-and-diversity/reviving-the-goal-of-an-integrated-society-a-21st-century-challenge/orfield-reviving-the-goal-mlk-2009.pdf.

Orfield, G., Kucsera, J., & Siegel-Hawley, G. (2012). *E pluribus … separation: Deepening double segregation for more students.* Los Angeles: Civil Rights Project/Proyecto Derechos Civiles at the University of California at Los Angeles. Retrieved September 15, 2012, from: civilrightsproject.ucla.edu/research/k-12-education/integration-and-diversity/mlk-national.

Pettigrew, T. F., & Tropp, L. R. (2006). A meta-analytic test of intergroup contact theory. *Journal of Personality and Social Psychology, 90,* 751–783.

Polikoff, A. (2006). *Waiting for Gautreaux: A story of segregation, housing, and the black ghetto.* Evanston, IL: Northwestern University Press.

Ready, D. D., & Silander, M. R. (2011). School racial and ethnic composition and young children's cognitive development: Isolating family, neighborhood, and school influences. In E. Frankenberg & E. Debray (Eds.), *Integrating schools in a changing society: New policies and legal options for a multiracial generation* (pp. 91–113). Chapel Hill: University of North Carolina Press.

Roberts v. City of Boston, 59 Mass. 198 (1849).

Romo v. Laird, Civil Action No. 21617 (Superior Court, Maricopa County, Arizona October 5, 1925). Unpublished *Romo* decision and case file documents available at the Organization of American Historians website: http://www.oah.org/publs/magazine/deseg/Muñoz.html. Retrieved February 1, 2012.

The Root Staff. (2011, October 6). Legal scholar Derrick Bell dead at 80. Retrieved October 27, 2013, from: www.theroot.com/buzz/legal-scholar-derrick-bell-jr-dies-80.

Rosenbaum, J., Deluca, S., & Tuck, T. (2005). New capabilities in new places: Low-income black families in suburbia. In X. de Souza Briggs (Ed.), *The geography of opportunity: Race and housing choice in metropolitan America* (pp. 150–175). Washington, DC: Brookings Institution Press.

Ryan, J. E. (2007). The Supreme Court and voluntary integration. *Harvard Law Review, 121,* 131–157.

Salomone, R. (1986). *Equal education under law: Legal rights and federal policy in the post-*Brown *era.* New York: St. Martin's Press.

Santamaria v. Dallas Independent School District, Civil Action No. 3:06-CV-692-L, 2006 U.S. Dist. LEXIS 83417 (N.D. Tex. November 16, 2006), *motion granted in part, and denied in part,* 2007 U.S. Dist. LEXIS 26821 (N.D. Tex. April 10, 2007).

Scott Nabers, M. (2012, January 13). Population increases drive school construction, tech upgrades. *Houston Business Journal.* Retrieved August 27, 2013, from: www.bizjournals.com/houston/print-edition/2012/01/13/population-increases-drive-school.html?page=all.

Siegel-Hawley, G., & Frankenberg, E. (2012a). *Reviving magnet schools: Strengthening a successful choice option: A research brief.* Los Angeles: Civil Rights Project/Proyecto Derechos Civiles at the University of California at Los Angeles. Retrieved August 31, 2013, from: civilrightsproject.ucla.edu/research/k-12-education/integration-and-diversity/reviving-magnet-schools-strengthening-a-successful-choice-option.

Siegel-Hawley, G., & Frankenberg, E. (2012b). *Southern slippage: Growing school segregation in the most desegregated region of the county.* Los Angeles: Civil Rights Project/Proyecto Derechos Civiles at the University of California at Los Angeles. Retrieved September 15, 2012, from: civilrightsproject.ucla.edu/research/k-12-education/integration-and-diversity/mlk-national/southern-slippage-growing-school-segregation-in-the-most-desegregated-region-of-the-century/Hawley-MLK-South-2012-2012.pdf.

Smrekar, C., & Goldring, E. (2000). *School choice in urban America: Magnet schools and the pursuit of equity.* New York: Teachers College Press.

Smrekar, C., & Goldring, E. (2011). Magnet schools, MSAP, and new opportunities to promote diversity. In E. Frankenberg & E. Debray (Eds.), *Integrating schools in a changing society: New policies and legal options for a multiracial generation* (pp. 232–240). Chapel Hill: North Carolina Press.

Solís, D. (2012, February 25). Dual-language programs in Dallas-area schools, across state. *Dallas News.* Retrieved September 6, 2013, from: www.dallasnews.com/news/education/headlines /20120225-dual-language-programs-growing-in-dallas-area-schools-across-state.ece.

Stell v. Savannah-Chatham County Board of Education, 222 F. Supp. 667 (S.D. Ga. 1963).

Stevenson, K. R. (2010). *Educational trends shaping school* planning*, design, construction, funding and operation.* Washington, DC: National Clearing House for Educational Facilities. Retrieved August 30, 2013, from: www.ncef.org/pubs//educationaltrends.pdf.

Sweatt v. Painter, 339 U.S. 629 (1950).

Texas Education Agency. (2013a). *Campus-level student enrollment reports, 2012–2013, Austin Independent School District.* Austin: Author. Retrieved August 8, 2013, from: http://ritter.tea.state.tx.us/adhoccrpt/adste.html.

Texas Education Agency. (2013b). *Student enrollment reports: Selected campus totals by district name—Austin ISD.* Analysis generated June 18, 2013, from the Texas Education Agency's online database, at http://ritter.tea.state.tx.us/adhocrpt/adste.html.

Thomas, W. P., & Collier, V. P. (2003). The multiple effects of dual language. *Educational Leadership, 61,* 61–64.

Tucker, W. H. (1994). *The science and politics of racial research.* Urbana: University of Illinois Press.

Tucker, W. H. (2002). *The funding of scientific racism: Wickliffe Draper and the Pioneer Fund.* Urbana: University of Illinois Press.

Turner, M. A., & Briggs, X. de Souza. (2008, March). *Assisted housing mobility and the success of low-income minority families: Lessons for policy, practice, and future research* (Brief No. 5). Washington, DC: Urban Institute, Metropolitan Housing and Communities Center. Retrieved November 1, 2013, from: www.urban.org/UploadedPDF/411638_assisted_housing.pdf.

U.S. Commission on Civil Rights. (1971). *Mexican American education study, report 1: Ethnic isolation of Mexican Americans in the public schools of the Southwest.* Washington, DC: Government Printing Office.

U.S. Commission on Civil Rights. (1975). *Twenty years after* Brown v. Board of Education. Washington, DC: Government Printing Office.

Valencia, R. R. (1984). *Understanding school closures: Discriminatory impact on Chicano and Black students* (Policy Monograph Series, No. 1). Stanford, CA: Stanford University, Stanford Center for Chicano Research.

Valencia, R. R. (1996a). *Course enrollments by race/ethnicity in a desegregated Southwestern high school.* Unpublished report.

Valencia, R. R. (1996b). *The Phoenix Union High School District desegregation plan and efforts: An analysis.* Report submitted to plaintiffs' counsel, Albert M. Flores. *United States of America v. Phoenix Union High School District #210, et al.* case number CIV 85 1249 PHX CAM, Consent Decree and Desegregation Order, United States District Court, District of Arizona, Phoenix, Arizona, May 15, 1985 for U.S. District Court of Arizona.

Valencia, R. R. (2000). Inequalities and the schooling of minority students in Texas: Historical and contemporary conditions. *Hispanic Journal of Behavioral Sciences, 22,* 445–459.

Valencia, R. R. (2005). The Mexican American struggle for equal educational opportunity in *Mendez v. Westminister:* Helping to pave the way for *Brown v. Board of Education. Teachers College Record, 107,* 389–423.

Valencia, R. R. (2008). *Chicano students and the courts: The Mexican American legal struggle for educational equality.* Critical America Series. New York: New York University Press.

Valencia, R. R. (2010). *Dismantling contemporary deficit thinking: Educational thought and practice.* Critical Educator Series. New York: Routledge.

Valencia, R. R. (2011). Segregation, desegregation, and integration of Chicano students. In R. R. Valencia (Ed.), *Chicano school failure and success: Past, present, and future* (3rd ed., pp. 42–75). New York: Routledge.

Valencia, R. R. (2012). Activist scholarship in action: The prevention of a Latino school closure. *Journal of Latinos and Education, 11,* 69–79.

Valencia, R. R., Menchaca, M., & Donato, R. (2002). Segregation, desegregation, and integration of Chicano students: Old and new realities. In R. R. Valencia (Ed.), *Chicano school failure and success: Past, present, and future* (2nd ed., pp. 70–113). London: RoutledgeFalmer.

Vasquez Heilig, J., & Holme, J. J. (2013). Nearly 50 years post-Jim Crow: Persisting and expansive school segregation for African American, Latina/o and ELL students in Texas. *Education and Urban Society, 45,* 609–632.

Vergon, C. B. (1988). The evolution of the school desegregation movement: Implications for equity and excellence. *Equity and Excellence, 24,* 26–35.

Wells, A. S., Holme, J. J., Revilla, A. T., & Atanda, A. K. (2004). How society failed school desegregation policy: Looking past the schools to understand them. *Review of Research in Education, 28,* 47–100.

Wilson, D. M. (2011). Dual language programs on the rise. *Harvard Education Letter, 27,* 1–2. Retrieved September 6, 2013, from: http://hepg.org/hel/article/496.

5

TEACHER QUALITY

This mesolevel factor, "Teacher Quality," is concerned with classroom teachers—the backbone of the very large public prekindergarten to grade 12 (pre-K to 12) educational sector. Indeed, this is a huge enterprise. The U.S. Department of Education projects that in the fall of 2015 there will be 3,403,000 full-time-equivalent (FTE) public elementary and secondary school teachers in the nation[1] teaching 50,773,000 public pre-K to12 students,[2] of which about half will be students of color.[3] Given that over 3 million FTE pre-K to 12 teachers are employed nationally in public education, there is bound to be variability among this workforce of teachers—for example, in their length of experiences, teaching in-field, certification status, and performance on certification tests. These variables are typically subsumed under ("teacher quality" characteristics; e.g., Rice, 2003).[4]

Furthermore, because these teachers are directly responsible for instructing a national pre-K to 12 student enrollment that is a smidgen over 50% students of color (see chapter 1, Table 1.12, present book), coupled with the extensive prevalence of school failure among many of these children and youths, a critical question arises: For those teachers who are poorly qualified, to what extent do their limitations contribute to the poor academic performance of students of color (particularly Mexican Americans, Puerto Ricans, other Latinos/Latinas, and Blacks)—and thus subsequently to TAG? To address this important question, the chapter is organized around these topics: (a) inequitable distribution of teacher quality characteristics, (b) the relation between teacher quality characteristics and student academic performance, and (c) systemic suggestions to improve the overall quality of teachers who aspire to teach students of color.

Inequitable Distribution of Teacher Quality Characteristics

Numerous research studies report that teacher quality characteristics (e.g., length of experience, teacher turnover) are inequitably distributed across race and SES in the nation's public schools, meaning that many low-SES students and pupils of color (which frequently covary) are shortchanged on teacher effectiveness. In this brief review of germane literature, my focus is on the *distribution* of those features of teachers that are assumed to be predictive of student academic achievement.[5] It is important to note that the study of teacher quality seldom uses direct measures. Rather, indirect indices (e.g., years of experience), which serve as proxies, are utilized to assess the effectiveness of teachers (cf. Clotfelter, Ladd, Vigdor, & Wheeler, 2007). In a later section, I cover the research that has investigated the *association* between teacher quality characteristics and student academic performance, with particular emphasis on students of color.

In this following literature review on the inequitable distribution of teacher quality characteristics, I organize it around three aspects of teacher effectiveness that are most frequently investigated in the extant research. Based on my sense of this corpus of studies, I cluster these characteristics under the following rubrics: (a) teaching experience, (b) teacher qualifications, and (c) teacher turnover. A number of studies examine more than one teacher quality characteristic, so some of the investigations I discuss under each factor are not mutually exclusive.

Before beginning this review of germane literature, it is important to discuss the common finding of covariation of race and SES (e.g., Betts, Rueben, & Danenberg, 2000; LaViest, 2005; Valencia & Suzuk, 2001, chapter 3; chapter 3, this volume). In the briefest sense, students of color (specifically Mexican Americans, some other Latino/Latina groups [e.g., Puerto Ricans], and Blacks) are more likely to come from low-SES backgrounds compared to their White peers. That is, there is considerable covariation (correlated variation) between a group's race and their SES. For example, Betts et al. (2000) report a correlation of .73 between lower-student SES and a higher percentage of students of color in California public schools. I raise this matter of the covariation between race and SES because in some of the studies that follow, the researcher does not investigate race, per se, but notes only that the student groups or schools under study are low SES. In these cases, we can assume—given the substantial association between race and SES—that the student groups attending such low-SES schools are predominantly students of color.

1. *Teaching experience.* Here, I discuss the inequities of less-experienced teachers being assigned to public schools in which students of color, many who do poorly on academic indices, are the predominant population. Novice teachers, especially first-year ones, face three frequent challenges: the struggle with classroom management, little guidance and resources for curriculum development, and working in environments with unsupportive teacher colleagues and administrators (Goodwin, 2012).[6] As such, inexperience in teachers' formative

years of employment often results in them being less effective compared to their peers who have more teaching experience. The implication is that schools with greater proportions of less-experienced teachers have a lesser-quality teaching personnel (Clotfelter et al., 2007).

My search for germane studies on the inequitable distribution of teachers by teaching experience resulted in 17 investigations.[7] Some of these studies use national databases (e.g., Barton, 2003), whereas others rely on data from multiple states (e.g., Illinois, Ohio, and Wisconsin; see Peske & Haycock, 2006) or single states (e.g., North Carolina; see Clotfelter, Ladd, & Vigdor, 2010). Even some investigations examine a single school district (e.g., School District of Philadelphia; see Neild, Useem, & Farley, 2005).

In regard to national data, Barton and Coley (2009)—drawing from the 2007 National Assessment of Educational Progress report—note that Black and Latino/Latina eighth graders were more likely to have teachers with 4 years or fewer of teaching experience (as an elementary or secondary school teacher). Specifically, 20% of White, 28% of Black, and 30% of Latino/Latina students had such inexperienced teachers (p. 13, Figure 5). These disparities reflect national statistics from about a decade earlier. Using data from the 1998 *Fast Response Survey System: Teacher Survey on Professional Development and Training*,[8] Mayer, Mullens, Moore, and Ralph (2000) report that students of color were more likely to have had teachers with 3 years or fewer of teaching experience. That is, 21% of teachers in high-enrollment schools of color had less teaching experience compared to 10% of teachers in low-enrollment schools of color; 13% of teachers in medium-enrollment of schools of color had 3 or fewer years of teaching experience (p. 13, Figure 2.3).

An example of a study that utilized state-level data is one by Sunderman and Kim (2005), who report California AY 2002–2003 information. The authors present data (p. 21, Figure 2) showing that 14% of teachers in schools with the highest 25% of students of color (89%–100% enrollment) had 1–2 years of teaching experience. By contrast, 10% of teachers in schools with the lowest 25% of students of color (0%–35%) had 1–2 years of experience. Similar data have been reported for Texas public schools. Hanushek, Kain, O'Brien, and Rivkin (2005), drawing from AY 1995–1996 to 2000–2001 statistics for Texas public schools, note that 12% of Latino/Latina and Black fourth- and eighth-grade students—compared to 7% of their White counterparts—were taught by first-year teachers. In a later Texas study, Education Trust (2008) reports data from AY 2005–2006 and notes that of the 50 largest school districts studied, 42 (84%) of them had higher percentages of teachers with fewer than 3 years of teaching experience in the district schools with the highest enrollment of students of color, compared to the schools with the lowest enrollment of such students (p. 10, Appendix A). For example, in the Austin ISD, the highest enrollment schools of color had 20.9% less-experienced teachers, compared to 8.2% of such teachers in the lowest enrollment schools of color in the district—a relative risk ratio of 2.6.

2. *Teacher qualifications.* In this section, I examine another aspect of teacher effectiveness, "teacher qualifications," that frequently appears as a subject of study in the literature on teacher quality characteristics. Under the rubric of teacher qualifications, researchers investigate such factors as: (a) whether teachers possess a major or minor, (b) they are assigned classes in- or out-of-field, (c) the competitive reputation of their undergraduate institution, (d) type of teaching licensure (e.g., emergency, provisional, regular), (e) licensure test scores, and (f) whether they have been certified by the National Board for Professional Teaching Standards. Later (in the section on "The Relation Between Teacher Quality Characteristics and Student Academic Achievement"), I will comment further on the importance of teacher qualifications. For now, however, it will suffice to note that such qualifications are key to successful teaching and learning. To ignore the considerable data pointing to the widespread, disproportionate assignment of teachers with poor qualifications to high-enrollment schools of color shows a shocking disregard for the education of Black, Mexican American, Puerto Rican, and other Latino/Latina, low-SES students of color.

My search for relevant investigations has led to a small, but rich, corpus of literature.[9] As are the studies on teaching experience, most of these on teacher qualifications are based on state-level data; few draw from national data. My focus is on the disproportionate percentage of teachers with poor qualifications who are assigned to schools in which students of color predominate the school enrollment. Let us begin this review by focusing on an investigation that uses national data; it is an older but informative study. Jerald (2002) reports 1999–2000 information from the U.S. Department of Education's Schools and Staffing Survey (SASS), a comprehensive survey of elementary and secondary public school education. The SASS, which uses a stratified probability sample design, covers a wide array of subjects (e.g., characteristics of teachers and principals, general school conditions).[10] Jerald reports a major finding most germane to this discussion.[11] Nationally, schools with high-enrollment of students of color (50% or more) were more likely to be assigned out-of-field teachers (29%), in comparison to schools with low-enrollment students of color (15% or less); 21% of assigned teachers in these schools were out-of-field (p. 4).[12] Such teaching is defined as: Teachers who are assigned to instruct in subjects that do not correspond to their education or training (Ingersoll, 2003a, p. 5).

In a more detailed analysis of the 1999–2000 SASS data, Ingersoll (2003a) reports out-of-field teaching by grades 7 to 12 teachers by core academic subjects. Nationally, teachers without a major or minor in the field were more likely to teach the following core subjects in high-poverty schools, compared to low-poverty schools:[13] English, mathematics, science, life science, physical science, social studies, and history (p. 15, Table 1). For example, in English classes, 41.7% of teachers instructing such courses in high-poverty schools had no major or minor in English. By contrast, 24% of teachers teaching English classes in low-poverty schools lacked a major or minor in English. Other research findings from Texas, for example, confirm the pattern that out-of-field teaching occurs more frequently in high-enrollment schools of color and low-SES schools (Education Trust, 2008; Fuller, 2010).

In an investigation of California public schools, Carroll et al. (2004) examine the inequities in the assignment of uncredentialed teachers (operationalized as 20% or more of the teachers in a school possess some type of emergency credential) in "high-risk" and "low-risk" schools (see note 27 for how these schools are defined). The authors report that high-risk schools were 12 times more likely than low-risk schools to have uncredentialed teachers (48% vs. 4%; p. 12, Figure 1).

In a related study, Lankford et al. (2002) report the inequitable distribution of teacher qualifications in New York State, drawing from data for AY 1999–2000. The authors examined core data from the Personnel Master File (PMF) of the Basic Education System of the New York State Education Department.[14] Table 5.1 presents some major findings from the analysis by Lankford et al. (2002). In New York State as a whole, students of color—compared to their White counterparts—are more likely to be taught by teachers who (a) are not certified in any subject taught, (b) failed the National Teacher Examination (General Knowledge Examination) or the New York State Teacher Certification Examinations (Liberal Arts and Science) on their first try, and (c) possess a Bachelor of Arts degree from a least-competitive college.[15] The results are quite striking, as noted by the respective relative risk ratios (calculated by the present author) shown in Table 5.1.[16] For example, students of color in the public schools of New York State are 2.5 times more likely to have a teacher not certified in any subject taught.

TABLE 5.1 Percentage of Teachers Not Certified in Any Subject, Having Failed General Knowledge or Liberal Arts and Science Examination, and Having a B.A. Degree from a Least-Competitive College: By Race of Student, New York State Public Schools, AY 1999–2000

	Teacher Qualification Attribute		
Student Race	*Not Certified in Any Subject Taught (%)*	*Failed General Knowledge or Liberal Arts and Science Examination (%)*	*B.A. Degree from a Least Competitive College (%)*
Of Color	16.6	21.2	21.4
White	6.7	7.1	10.2
Relative Risk Ratio	2.5	3.0	2.1

Source: Lankford, Loeb, and Wyckoff (2002, p. 47, Table 6). Adapted with permission of second author, S. Loeb.

3. *Teacher turnover.* There is "another" dropout problem affecting many of the nation's urban schools (Starkes, 2013). The concern over the premature exiting of teachers from K-12 public schools in the U.S. has prompted the National Commission on Teaching and America's Future (2007) in a policy brief to conclude that "America's teacher dropout problem is spiraling out of control" (p. 1). The report notes that teacher attrition has grown by 50% in a 15-year period (1992–2007), and the teacher turnover rate, nationally, was 16.8% in 2007. In some locations, the escalation of teacher turnover has captured the interest of state policymakers. A recent report to the North Carolina General Assembly (Educator Effectiveness Division, 2013) notes that of the total 95,028 K-12 teachers employed in the state during AY 2012–2013, 13,616 left their respective school districts—resulting in a 14.3% turnover rate, which was up from the 12.3% recorded in 2011–2012. Of the 13,616 teachers leaving in 2012–2013, nearly half (49.4%) had tenure.

Regarding *when* teachers leave schools, cumulative data reveal very high rates of attrition. In a study of New York City Public Schools (NYCPS), Marinell (2011) reports that for teachers who entered a middle school teaching job between 2002 and 2009, 27% left after 1 year, 55% after 3 years, and 66% after 5 years (p. 10, Table 1).[17] Other investigations report that about 50% of novice teachers depart within the first 5 years of commencing their jobs (e.g., Hafner & Owings, 1991; Ingersoll & Smith, 2003). Marinell also has informative data, as he shows that most middle school teachers in the NYCPS leave within 1 year of starting their employment, which supports other findings that first-year teachers have the highest departure rates (e.g., Boyd, Grossman, Lankford, Loeb, & Wyckoff, 2008; Donaldson & Johnson, 2010; Smith & Ingersoll, 2004).

Before commencing, it is important to note that some researchers think it is important to disaggregate the turnover rate by type of teacher attrition. Barnes, Crowe, and Schaefer (2007, pp. 11–12), in an attempt to provide clarity to the notion of teacher turnover, comment that three definitional aspects apply: First, there are "within-district movers"—teachers who leave their job at one school to take another teaching position in the following year in the *same* school district. Second, "cross-district movers" are teachers who leave their school and gain a job the next year in a *different* district. Third, "leavers" refer to teachers who end their employment at a school and do not gain employment in *any* school district. Some scholars combine the two mover categories and simply refer to them as "movers" (Smith & Ingersoll, 2004, p. 694, Figure 3). In sum, given that the turnover rate is an aggregate and confounded with movers and leavers, it is useful to utilize the distinctions Barnes et al. (2007) offer so researchers can obtain a more accurate quantitative understanding of teacher attrition.

The financial cost is a major concern of the teacher turnover issue. Strong agreement exists among researchers that the monetary costs of teacher turnover are enormous, particularly in school districts with chronic teacher attrition. Based on cost data from a 5-district study (Barnes et al., 2007)—which was commissioned by the National Commission on Teaching and America's Future (NCTAF)—plus information from the National Center for Education Statistics, the NCTAF report estimates that the national costs of teacher turnover in U.S. urban and non-urban public school districts is likely over $7.5 billion per year.[18] The NCTAF 2007 study also lists the annual estimated costs of teacher turnover in 24 select school districts (p. 5). For several of the nation's largest school districts, the expenditures are quite startling: New York City ($115.2 million), Los Angeles ($94.2 million), and Houston ($35.0 million). Such costs cover the continuous recruiting, hiring, and training of replacement teachers.[19]

Another issue of the teacher turnover concern has to do with a consistent finding in the literature: Schools with high enrollments of students of color from low-SES background face the most perilous consequences of teacher attrition. Study after study report that such schools have the highest rates of teacher turnover, and thus the students attending these schools are placed at further risk for school failure.[20] It is frequently mentioned that the "teaching quality gap" exacerbates the closing of TAG (National Commission on Teaching and America's Future, 2007, p. 2).

In regard to national data on teacher turnover, Barton (2003) presents data from the 2000 NAEP report. The percentages of fourth-grade students, by race/ethnicity, in public schools where teachers started the school year but did not return to work were: Black (43%), Latino/Latina (27%), and White (18%) (p. 13). This means that students of color, compared to their White peers, were much more likely to attend schools where the teacher turnover rate is higher. This pattern is confirmed 7 years later, when Barton and Coley (2009)—reporting NAEP data from 2007—show that 52% of Black, 44% of Latino/Latina, and 28% of White eighth-grade students in mathematics classes had teachers who departed from their jobs before the end of the school year. Also, a strong majority (67%) of students who were school lunch–eligible, in contrast to 41% who were school lunch–ineligible, were taught by a teacher who did not complete the school year (p. 14, Figure 7).

Considerable state-level data are available (e.g., Allensworth et al., 2009; Boyd et al., 2009; Clotfelter et al., 2007; see note 20, this chapter) that corroborate the national findings that low-performing schools, schools with high enrollments of low-SES students, and schools with high enrollments of students of color have the highest teacher turnover rates. For example, Carroll et al. (2004), in a study commissioned by the NCTAF,[21] find that California public school teachers working in "high-risk" schools in 2002 were 4 times more likely, compared to their fellow teachers employed in "low-risk" schools (43% to 11%), to report that the turnover of teachers is a "serious problem" in their respective schools.[22]

State information on teacher turnover by poverty status of schools is also available from North Carolina. Drawing from data at the North Carolina Education Research Center, Clotfelter et al. (2007) report that teacher turnover rates at the state level in 2004 were higher at high-poverty schools compared to low-poverty ones. For example, in the North Carolina elementary schools the turnover rate was 23.0% at high-poverty schools and 18.8% at low-poverty schools (p. 1365, Table 6). The same pattern is reported for the state's middle and high schools.

The Relation between Teacher Quality Characteristics and Student Academic Achievement

In the preceding section, I focused on the inequitable distribution of teacher quality characteristics. There is very strong evidence from the extant literature that low-SES students of color, as a group—when compared to White students of more advantageous SES background—are taught by less-experienced teachers, have instructors with less-favorable teacher qualifications, and attend schools with higher teacher turnover rates. The research findings discussed in the foregoing text are largely descriptive, pointing to a distinct pattern that teacher quality attributes are indeed distributed unfairly along variables of race and SES. The logical extension of this line of investigation is then to ask whether these teacher quality characteristics—experience, qualifications, and turnover—are associated with student academic performance and how students of color are affected. This is a crucial subject to explore as its inquiry can lead to evidence, as I shall present, attesting to the role of teacher quality attributes in the creation of TAG. Stated a bit differently, there are convincing data showing that the inequitable distribution of teacher quality characteristics translates into diminished academic achievement for students of color. My review of representative research is similarly organized as the preceding summary of studies on the inequitable distribution of teacher quality characteristics. That is, I discuss investigations that examine particular features of teacher effectiveness that have garnered attention in the literature—namely, teaching experience, teacher qualifications, and teacher turnover.

1. *Teaching experience.* Beginning teaching represents a number of difficult tasks for novices (e.g., Donaldson & Johnson, 2010; Goodwin, 2012). Managing student behavior, developing sound lesson plans, ensuring student academic growth, working with fellow colleagues and administrators, and meeting with parents are major challenges that new teachers must face and accomplish successfully. An assumption is that the average effectiveness of teachers (especially as measured by improvement in student achievement) comes about through time, as well as on-the-job development for junior teachers. Such growth is frequently labeled "returns to teacher experience" (Henry, Bastain, & Fortner, 2011). In light of this, it is not surprising that investigations of teacher effectiveness regularly find first-year teachers to have smaller student academic gains in comparison to such gains for students of more experienced teachers (e.g., Boyd, Grossman, Lankford, Loeb, & Wyckoff, 2006; Clotfelter et al., 2010; Henry et al., 2011).

For the research literature on the relation between teaching experience and student academic achievement, I was able to identify only a small number of studies—all state-level investigations, except for one of a specific school district.[23] In all studies, there is an undeviating pattern: Less experienced teachers instruct more often in high-enrollment schools of color or schools characterized as low-performing. In some of the investigations, the authors do not report data by race or SES, but rather by "low-performing" and "high-performing" schools. Given the strong, pervasive, and persistent association between race of students and academic achievement (see chapter 1, this volume), it is safe to assume that students of color are the predominant population served in low-performing schools in this corpus of research. For example, Peske and Haycock (2006) report that in Wisconsin public elementary schools, there are more novice teachers (24%) working in low-performing schools in which students do poorly in reading, compared to novice teachers (12%) in high-performing schools in which students do quite well in reading. Peske and Haycock also note almost identical percentages for beginner teachers in Wisconsin's low- and high-performing elementary schools in regard to mathematics achievement (p. 5, Figure 5).[24]

Drawing from Texas data, Fuller, Carpenter, and Fuller (2008) provide an informative study on teaching experience and its connection to academic achievement of students. The authors report statewide data on beginning teachers, years of teaching experience, and student performance (high school) on the Texas Assessment of Knowledge and Skills (TAKS) test, a state-mandated test covering four core subjects (English, mathematics, science, social studies). Table 5.2 presents the results of the analysis by Fuller et al. (2008). TAKS performance is shown by quintile 1 (lowest-performing students)) and quintile 5 (highest-performing students).[25] I also present the respective relative risk ratios, which I calculated. The data illustrate, as indicted by the relative risk ratios, that in the lowest-performing high schools (Q1), compared to the highest-performing ones (Q5), the students are more likely to be taught by beginning teachers in the various course subjects and by teachers with fewer years of teaching experience. This pattern holds across all 10 comparisons in Table 5.2. Fuller et al. (2008) also report data for Texas middle schools regarding percentages of beginning teachers and years of teaching experience by school TAKS performance (p. 60, Table A-6A) and find the same pattern as for the high schools.

2. *Teacher qualifications.* The connection between the qualifications a teacher possesses and the academic achievement of students is one of the most significant areas of research and policy setting in the field of public education. As a key component in affecting students' learning and achievement, the importance of teacher qualifications is acknowledged as a driving force in the federal NCLB Act of 2002. A paramount feature of the NCLB Act is the directive that a "qualified teacher" be placed in every classroom. The law defines a highly qualified teacher as having three basic requirements: (a) minimally, holding a bachelor's degree from an institution of higher education that is accredited; (b) having obtained a full state teaching certification; holding a provisional, temporary, or emergency certification or license does not meet the standard of being highly

TABLE 5.2 Percentage of Beginning Teachers, Years of Teaching Experience by High School Student Texas Assessment of Knowledge and Skills (TAKS) Performance: Texas, 2007

Teaching Quality Measure and Core Subjects	*School TAKS Performance*			
	By Quintile[a]		*Difference (Q5–Q1)*	*Relative Risk Ratio*
	Q1 (lowest)	*Q5 (highest)*		
Beginning Teachers				
Core Courses	10.8	4.3	–6.5**	2.5
English	10.4	4.0	–6.4**	2.6
Mathematics	9.9	4.0	–5.9**	2.5
Science	14.1	4.7	–9.4**	3.0
Social Studies	9.2	4.7	–4.5**	2.0
Years of Teaching Experience				
Zero	9.5	5.5	–4.1**	1.7
1–5	27.8	20.9	–6.8**	1.3
6–10	17.2	20.6	–3.3**	1.2
11–20	22.2	28.0	–5.8**	1.3
> 20	23.3	25.0	–1.8	1.1

Source: Adapted from Fuller, Carpenter, and Fuller (2008, p. 58, Table A-5A) with permission of the Association of Texas Professional Educators.

[a]School performance is based on percentage of all students passing all TAKS tests at all grade levels.
$^{*}p < .01$; $^{**}p < .001$.

qualified; and (c) demonstrating competency in the subject matter(s) he or she will teach (Learning Point Associates, 2007). The NCLB mandate of having qualified teachers was reenforced on March 13, 2010, when the Obama administration released "A Blueprint for Reform," which was to be used to frame the reauthorization of the Elementary and Secondary Education Act. The blueprint notes, in part, "The key to student success is providing an effective teacher in every classroom" (p. 3).[26]

Research findings on the relation between teacher qualifications and student academic achievement point to a rather uniformly lamentable conclusion: Low-SES, low-achieving students of color—in contrast to their higher-SES, higher-achieving White peers—are more likely to be taught by teachers with poorer teaching qualifications.[27] An example is the comprehensive investigation by Shields et al. (2001), who examined, in part, the maldistribution of California public school teachers. The authors note that in AY 2000–2001, 42,000 teachers in the state (14% of the teaching workforce) were deemed

"unprepared," which was operationalized as not having a preliminary or professional clear teaching credential. Shields et al. then examined the distribution of unprepared teachers across school-level Academic Performance Index (API) scores. The API, which measures performance on various academic subjects (e.g., English language arts, mathematics, science), is based on a growth model of student academic improvement, and is considered the keystone of California's Public Schools Accountability Act of 1999.[28] The authors report an appalling finding: Students attending California's lowest-achieving schools were 5 times more likely than their counterparts enrolled in the highest-achieving schools to have an unprepared teacher. Specifically, schools that performed at or below the lowest-achievement quartile on the API had 25% of the teachers who were unprepared, compared to 5% of unprepared teachers in schools that performed at or above the highest-achievement quartile on the API (p. 24, Figures 2–10).

In an investigation of New York City Schools, Lankford et al. (2002) present findings on the pervasive link between teacher qualifications and student academic achievement (based on the fourth-grade ELA examination).[29] The authors report the following average percentages of teachers with these attributes, by school achievement level (p. 48, Table 7):

A. Not certified in any assignment: lowest-achievement schools (22%); highest- achievement schools (3%).
B. Failing NTE General Knowledge or NYSTCE Liberal Arts exam:[30] lowest-achieving schools (35%); highest-achieving schools (9%).
C. Having a B.A. from a least competitive college: lowest-achieving schools (26%); highest achieving schools (10%).

In the final study I review here, I reexamine the earlier discussed Fuller et al. (2008) investigation of Texas public schools. The authors present statewide data on the relation between several aspects of teaching qualifications (i.e., percentages of high school teachers instructing out-of-field, not fully certified, and performance on teacher certification tests) and high school students' performance on the TAKS examination. Table 5.3 shows the results of the authors' analyses, along with relative risk ratios I have calculated. The findings reported by Fuller et al. confirm the consistent and robust pattern seen in other research studies that low-performing schools, compared to high-performing ones, are more likely to have higher proportions of teachers who are less qualified. The major finding in Table 5.3 is that in the 17 comparisons, 16 (94%) show a positive and statistically significant relation between teaching qualifications and TAKS performance. That is, high school teachers who have the more favorable teaching qualifications (i.e., teach less out-of-field; are fully certified; perform higher on certification tests) are more likely to work in the highest-performing schools as measured by TAKS scores.[31]

TABLE 5.3 Percentage of Out-of-Field Teachers, Teachers Not Fully Certified, and Teacher Certification Test Performance by High School Student Texas Assessment of Knowledge and Skills (TAKS) Performance: Texas, 2007

	School TAKS Performance			
Teaching Qualification Measure and Core Subjects	*By Quintile*[a]		*Difference (Q5–Q1)*	*Relative Risk Ratio*
	Q1 (lowest)	*Q5 (highest)*		
Out-of-Field				
Core Courses	26.2	13.4	−12.8**	2.0
English	23.2	11.7	−11.5**	2.0
Mathematics	18.9	7.8	−11.1**	2.4
Science	42.2	19.8	−22.4**	2.1
Social Studies	22.3	14.4	−7.9**	1.6
Not Fully Certified				
Core Courses	16.8	8.8	−8.0**	1.9
English	14.1	8.3	−5.8**	1.7
Mathematics	17.5	9.8	−7.8**	1.8
Science	21.5	8.9	−12.7**	2.4
Social Studies	14.6	7.5	−7.0**	2.0
Certification Test Performance				
% Failed Pedagogy	24.7	11.5	−13.2**	2.1
% Bottom Quintile Pedagogy	32.3	17.0	−15.3**	1.9
% Top Quintile Pedagogy	13.0	20.6	7.6**	1.6
% Failed English	24.6	13.4	−11.2**	1.8
% Failed Mathematics	38.0	21.8	−16.2**	1.7
% Failed Science	38.2	24.8	−13.4**	1.5
% Failed Social Studies	28.5	28.7	0.2	Na

Source: Adapted from Fuller, Carpenter, and Fuller (2008, p. 58, Table A-5A) with permission of the Association of Texas Professional Educators.

[a]School performance is based on percentage of all students passing all TAKS tests at all grades.
$^{**}p < .001$.

3. *Teacher turnover.* I discussed earlier that teacher attrition can lead to the disruption of the curriculum, particularly along lines of curricular planning, organization, and continuity (e.g., Donaldson & Johnson, 2010; Guin, 2004). For example, Guin sought to investigate the negative consequences of teacher turnover for school functioning. Her study site was a moderately large, racially segregated

urban school district (unnamed) enrolling about 47,000 students in 97 schools (70 elementary). Using a purposive sampling method of 15 elementary schools, Guin drew her data from the Staff Climate Survey, which the district administered (AYs 2000–2001 to 2002–2003). Only data from the Teacher Survey, a subset of questions, were analyzed. Guin also interviewed teachers and principals. In brief, Guin reports that in the high-teacher-turnover schools, in contrast to the low-turnover ones, (a) instructional programs were constantly being disrupted by the revolving door of the teaching staff; (b) professional development was frequently repeated, in a fragmented fashion, with the arrival of new teachers; and (c) teacher collaboration was compromised by having to deal with new teaching colleagues on a regular basis. This following quote by one of the interviewed teachers (a veteran) captures the sentiment of many of the other teachers: "We are constantly reinventing the wheel. And for those of us that stay, it drains our energy. You know you can't constantly be starting over. It leads to burnout" (p. 13). Guin also notes that schools serving low-SES pupils and students of color, which had the highest attrition rates, were the most harmed by the turbulence created by the teacher turnover.

A small, but instructive, body of research exists on the relation between teacher turnover and student academic performance. As a whole, these investigations find that rates of teacher attrition are higher in low-achieving schools, which are predominantly attended by low-SES students of color.[32] For instance, in the foregoing discussed study (Guin, 2004), the author reports that elementary schools with greater teacher turnover rates had a smaller percentage of students who met statewide standards in both reading ($r = -.31$, significant at .0001) and mathematics tests ($r = -.28$, significant at .0001).

In a study of 850,000 New York City fourth- and fifth-grade public school students over 8 years (AYs 2001–2002 and 2005–2010), Ronfeldt, Loeb, and Wyckoff (2013) find a negative effect of teacher attrition on students' achievement (ELA and mathematics), and the outcome was more pronounced in schools attended by low-achieving pupils and Black students. In a related investigation, Barnes et al. (2007) report teacher turnover and school-level student achievement data for Chicago Public Schools (CPS, Illinois) and Milwaukee Public Schools (MPS, Wisconsin) for AYs 2002–2003 and 2003–2004. The turnover rate in the low-performing schools (16th percentile or under, within the district) in the MPS was 2 times the turnover rate observed in the high-performing schools (defined as 84th percentile or above, within the school district). For the CPS comparison, there was a teacher attrition rate in the low-achieving schools 1.4 times the rate in the high-achieving schools.

In sum, the teacher turnover issue, as reviewed here in the context of teacher quality, is harmful for numerous low-SES students of color. This negative consequence for such students manifests in three ways. First, chronic teacher turnover, when viewed in the organizational setting of schools, often creates curricular discontinuity and undue strain among faculty. This eventually can lead to an unhealthy situation in schools with high enrollments of students of color—as such institutions are prone to school failure and do not need another stressor. Second, when teachers move from one school to another (intra- or interdistrict transfers) or leave the profession altogether, these instructors are typically replaced with novice teachers who are less experienced, and thus, as the literature finds, generally less effective. Third, teacher turnover is financially costly. This siphoning of much-needed money is improvident and could go to much more productive uses for the education of students of color—for example, hiring paraprofessional classroom aides, employing highly skilled tutors for one-on-one instruction, and purchasing computers for the classroom or a laboratory.

Toward Systemic Transformations

In light of the preceding review of literature on the inequitable distribution of teacher quality characteristics and the quantifiable relation between teacher quality and student academic performance, it becomes crystal clear that a highly qualified and effective teacher should be assigned to every classroom in those public schools in which students of color, many who experience school failure, make up the predominant population. It is this premise that guides the reform suggestions I discuss in this concluding section of the present chapter. In the literature I reviewed for this chapter, there is a small number of publications that provide recommendations as to how the quality of public school teachers can be improved (e.g., Barnes et al., 2007; Carroll et al., 2004; Fuller et al., 2008; Rice, 2003). In part, I cull from these works, others, and my own thoughts as springboards for eight suggestions designed to improve teacher quality. These structural, systemic guidelines are not intended to be formulaic in nature, but rather as narratives to generate much-needed discussion.

1. *Major shift in attitudes about teachers and teaching.* In some measure, K-12 public school teachers in the U.S. are the Rodney Dangerfields of the educational system—they get little to no respect.[33] Such failure to appreciate and value teachers and their profession has deep roots to a time in the latter 19th century when teaching was perceived as having an inferior stature and reputation, and over time became viewed as semiskilled work (Ingersoll, 2003a).[34] Historically, a disparaging attitude toward teachers was expressed in the old adage, "He who can, does. He who cannot, teaches." This disdainful statement about teachers and their occupation was written by Irish playwright George Bernard Shaw in his 1903 four-act drama, *Man and Superman.*[35] More recently, teachers and their unions have been demonized in the widely seen 2010 film *Waiting for Superman* (Chilcott & Guggenheim, 2010). Notwithstanding its wide audience appeal, awards, and financial success, the film has been heavily criticized for presenting distortions and partial truths (e.g., Ayers, 2010; Ginsberg, 2010; Weingarten, 2010). For example, Ayers comments that *Waiting for Superman* presents themes of "school failure as boiling down to bad teachers" and "unions are the boogeyman"

(p. 2). He also notes that the film is silent on the systemic problems of a troubled society—namely, that low-SES people have limited access to good jobs, decent wages, health care, and appropriate housing, all of which affect their children's education (see chapter 3, this volume).

Elevating the teaching profession to a position of high regard by demonstrating that a teaching career is a coveted path to follow is by no means an easy task to accomplish. With the appropriate monetary incentives, assertive recruitment, rigorous preservice training, and assiduous mentoring for beginning teachers (all to be discussed), teaching can be transformed into a profession of choice by aspiring teachers who desire to enter one of the most significant lines of employment in the country. The challenge before us is substantial: The improvement of teacher quality in the long run means that we need to start now to upgrade the quality of teachers (Ingersoll, 2003a). To begin, a profound shift is needed in how we perceive teachers and the teaching profession. Part of this sea change will necessitate moving away from what Ingersoll (2012b) calls a "deficit-teacher" perspective (p. 99), which blames teachers and their putative shortcomings (e.g., lack of effort, commitment, and ability) for school failure.

2. *Anti-deficit thinking curriculum in preservice teacher education.* This suggestion stems from much of the literature I have earlier explored in this chapter. First, it has been amply documented that teachers with less teaching experience and poorer teaching qualifications are more likely to work in low-SES, low-achieving schools that serve predominantly students of color. Second, research investigations consistently report that teacher turnover rates are higher in these types of schools. A third finding, one that I did not cover in my earlier reviews but that certainly is germane here, is that when teachers transfer (intra- or interdistrict) from a school with higher proportions of low-SES, low-achieving students of color, they often move to a school with lower percentages of such students. These students, mostly White, in the receiving schools tend to have higher achievement scores (e.g., Boyd et al., 2008; Goldhaber, Gross, & Player, 2009). For example, Boyd et al. (2008) report in a study of NYCPS elementary teachers that a substantial percentage of the more effective teachers transferred from lower-performing schools to higher-performing ones. This, the authors conclude, benefits the latter schools and exacerbates TAG as less-effective teachers are left behind.[36] These findings, as a whole, should raise some critical questions about teachers' perceptions of the educability of low-SES students of color: Does this transfer scenario suggest that teachers move because they do not prefer, tacitly or explicitly, to teach poor students of color? Do beginning teachers with more favorable teaching characteristics tend to gravitate toward schools with greater percentages of higher-SES, higher-achieving White students because these teachers perceive lower-SES, lower-performing students of color as hard to teach? Unfortunately, the literature I have reviewed for this chapter does not attempt to address these queries. As such, I have to turn to the available literature on deficit thinking in education.

In light of the frequent deficit thinking, low expectations, and stereotypes demonstrated by preservice teachers toward students (and people) of color, Marx (2006, pp. 128–134) developed an intervention program that seeks to confront and change her students' racism via seven discrete steps, as follows: (a) acknowledging one's own racism, (b) bringing attention to contradictions, (c) catching a glimpse of the shaky evidential base students relied on so they can attest to their faulty views, (d) challenging easy answers that might alleviate any racist beliefs that may affect the students' teaching, (e) drawing attention to the larger context of White racist effects on children of color, (f) recognizing and admitting their own racism and taking responsibility for their part in perpetuating it, and (g) moving past the guilt associated with White racism.

3. *Resolute recruitment and hiring of teachers of color.* This suggestion for improving the quality of teachers is partially related to the foregoing concern (no. 2) that some White teachers may eschew teaching in schools that are low-performing and mainly serve low-SES students of color. There are several justifications for increasing the number of K-12 public school teachers of color. First, there is an affirmative action issue—the large gap between the percentage of students of color and the percentage of teachers of color in the nation's schools, which is a long-standing and pervasive problem. For example, based on national data from nearly 45 years ago, Villegas and Lucas (2004, p. 76, Table 1) report that students of color in 1971 made up 22.2% of the total public school elementary and secondary school enrollment and teachers of color made up 11.7% of the total teaching force—an underrepresentation disparity of -47.3% (calculated by present author). More recent data confirm that these patterns of disparity persist unabatedly. Using national data, Ingersoll and May (2011) report that in AY 2008–2009 combined students of color made up 41% of the total elementary and secondary school enrollment and combined teachers of color made up 16.5% of all elementary and secondary teachers—which is a disparity of -59.8% teacher underrepresentation (calculated by present author).

A second rationale for an increase in the size of the teachers of color workforce has to do with racial/ethnic compatibility between student and teacher, which can result in favorable cognitive and affective outcomes for students of color. In their review of pertinent literature, Villegas and Lucas (2004) conclude that when students of color are taught by a same race/ethnicity teacher, increases occur in mathematics and reading achievement, dropout rates decrease, absences from school decline, school behavior improves, students are more frequently recommended by their teachers for honors classes, and teachers have high expectations that the students will go to college.[37] A case can be made that the theoretical underpinning of these findings of racial/ethnic suitability between teacher and student lies in the notion of the "presumption of shared identity," which has to do with there being a possible match between students and teachers along cultural, psychological, and physiological lines (Jackson, 1986, chapter 1). The cultural dimension is most apropos here.[38] Jackson (1986) speaks of a "common cultural heritage" (p. 22) that can exist between a student and teacher, with common elements, for example, of language, social class, cultural heroes, and familiar conventions and customs. To these, I suggest, one could add other shared background aspects, such as country of origin, community or geographical region where one grew up, family size, and educational attainment of parents, siblings, and relatives. The educational implication of Jackson's (1986) presumption of shared identity—if it indeed is met—is that teaching for the instructor becomes easier and more efficient, and we assume enhances the student's learning. Other scholars have developed similar lines of argument, such as Irvine's (1990) "cultural synchronization" and Villegas and Lucas's "cultural bridge to learning."

A third justification for having more teachers of color pertains to the issue of individuals of color having greater access to educational leadership roles, especially administrative positions of principals and superintendents. It is well known that principals are recruited from the ranks of teachers and superintendents from the ranks of principals. In light of the underrepresentation of teachers of color, this problem certainly has an adverse effect on the hiring of a greater number of principals of color—an unfortunate issue as principals, in particular, are highly valued leaders in helping to promote school success for students of color (McKenzie & Scheurich, 2007; Theoharis, 2007).

Given the foregoing justifications, a strong case can be made for arguing that an assiduous campaign needs to be mounted to identify and recruit more teachers of color to the profession. How can such an ambitious objective be realized? A conceptual beginning point is to view the shortage of teachers of color as a systemic problem requiring a systemic solution. A number of scholars use the metaphor of a "pipeline" to better understand the scarcity of teachers of color (e.g., Valencia & Aburto, 1991a; Villegas & Lucas, 2004). Along this pipeline, there are substantial leaks. For instance, in the case of Mexican Americans and other Latino/Latina students, there is a hemorrhage in the conduit at the high school level regarding dropouts (e.g., Rumberger & Rodríguez, 2011), and another major leak is seen in the matter of college matriculation of those students who do succeed in graduating from high school (Zarate, Sáenz, & Oseguera, 2011). As such, a systemic approach is needed to comprehend the shortage of teachers of color, and such a modus operandi requires proactions and interventions along the various junctures of the pipeline.

In regard to specific strategies to help seal the teacher workforce pipeline, or at least slow down the leaks, Villegas and Lucas (2004) discuss four types of programs:[39] (a) early recruitment of youths of color, focusing on pre–senior high school years; (b) articulation agreements between community colleges and 4-year colleges to ensure that transferring students of color take the correct course of study; this is a very important strategy, as Latino/Latina and Black students are more likely, than their White peers, to enroll in community colleges than in 4-year colleges (Provasnik & Planty, 2008); (c) career ladder opportunities for paraprofessionals (teacher aides); this is a prudent strategy given that paraprofessionals of color constitute an untapped and relatively plentiful source of future teachers (Villegas & Clewell, 1998); and (d) alternative pathways that lead to teacher certification (e.g., Teach for America; see Donaldson & Johnson, 2010).

In sum, teacher quality can be improved by hiring more teachers of color. It appears that other factors being equal, teachers of color are likely to have some advantage in teaching students of color and in fostering their learning, with whom they have shared identity. I do not mean to imply, however, that only teachers of color can teach, and should teach, students of color and that only White teachers can and should teach White students. Comprehensive knowledge of the subject matter, superior teaching skills, empathy for students, and a passion for teaching transcend the race/ethnicity of an excellent teacher.

4. *Monetary incentives for teacher recruitment, teacher retention, and the improvement of student achievement.* Some scholars have investigated a set of research questions about whether monetary incentives can be utilized to improve teacher quality. This certainly is a reasonable line of research given that employees at all levels in the world of work know that diligent and productive work often leads to financial gain (typically in the form of hourly, monthly, or yearly raises). Educational researchers of the teaching profession reverse this economic principle and ask whether providing monetary inducements can improve the quality of teaching. This set of investigatory queries appears to be framed around three questions: (a) Do financial incentives, as a recruitment tool, help attract high-quality aspirants to the teaching profession? (b) Do monetary bonuses reduce teacher turnover? and (c) Are teachers' salaries related to academic outcomes?[40] Surprisingly, given the importance of this line of research, there is only a handful of studies on these three issues. This could be related, in part, to the methodological problems surrounding this topic (see Loeb & Page, 2000).

The North Carolina Teaching Fellows Program (NCTFP) appears to be a quite successful strategy to utilize financial incentives to recruit high-quality teachers (Henry, Bastian, & Smith, 2012). In this state-funded merit-based program, high school seniors are recruited in light of their GPA (minimum 2.5), SAT scores (minimum 950), and a commitment to become teachers. Only about 20% of the applicants are accepted to the NCTFP, and the recruits receive a $26,000 forgivable scholarship ($6,500 per year for 4 years). At college, the Teaching Fellows enroll in the regular teacher education program, and they also receive special training unique to the NCTFP (e.g., classroom observations and one-on-one tutoring in the public schools, summer retreats). Upon certification, the teachers are required to teach for 4 years, and if the commitment is not met, the recipient is obliged to repay the scholarship with a 10% interest. Henry et al. (2012) undertook an exceptionally comprehensive evaluation of the NCTFP based on data from AYs 2005–2006 through 2009–2010; the sample included 1,306 recipients and a comparison group of 6,474 novice teachers. The major findings the authors report are as follows:

A. Teaching Fellows who taught at the elementary, middle, and high school levels—compared to the comparison group participants—had significantly stronger high school academic records (GPA; SAT scores; class rank).
B. Teaching Fellows, in comparison to the non-Teaching Fellows, had higher retention rates in their teaching jobs for 5 years or longer.
C. Teaching Fellows, in contrast to the non-Teaching Fellows, had students who showed higher gain scores in mathematics (grades 3–8).

Henry et al. (2012) find one downside of the NCTFP: Teaching Fellows are less likely, compared to the comparison group participants, to teach lower-performing and lower-SES students. To remedy this, the authors suggest that the NCTFP should consider increasing the amount of the scholarships for recipients who are willing to teach in schools that are low-achieving.

Another research question has to do with whether salaries of teachers are linked to student academic achievement. In their investigation of Texas teachers, Hanushek, Kain, and Rivkin (1999) examined data from specific school districts from the years 1993–1996. One of the authors' hypotheses was that if teachers' salaries were increased, then their students' academic achievement would increase. The basis of this conjecture is that a raise in salary would motivate teachers to work harder, and such effort would, in turn, manifest in gains in students' achievement, which was measured by fourth- and fifth-grade reading and mathematics scores on the Texas Assessment of Academic Skills test. The authors conclude that changes in teachers' starting salary have no significant effect on student achievement.

In a related study, Loeb and Page (2000) used a state-level panel set they created from the Public Use Microdata Samples (years 1960–1990). The authors' main dependent variable was the dropout rate, operationalized as the proportion of individuals, aged 16–19 years, residing in a state and not attending high school and not having a high school diploma. In their analysis, Loeb and Page first utilized the methodology employed in earlier research (e.g., Hanushek et al., 1999), and they replicated such results. Second, Loeb and Page adjusted for labor market factors (i.e., education and experience of teachers). By doing so, the authors found a positive effect of teacher wages on student achievement. That is, Loeb and Page estimate that increasing teachers' salaries by 10% decreases the high school dropout rate by 3% to 4%. The authors note that previous research investigations have failed to find significant links between teachers' salaries and student achievement outcomes because these studies have not controlled for non-pecuniary variation. Loeb and Page conclude that by raising teacher's wages, students' academic achievement can be improved.

In sum, although the evidence is scant, what is available points to the conclusion that monetary incentives for teachers can improve teacher quality by helping to recruit higher-quality teachers, reduce the teacher turnover rate, and increase student achievement. The extant literature, combined with economic justice and common sense, informs us that much more money needs to be spent so teacher quality can be enhanced. One can imagine, for example, all the positive incentive programs that school districts across the nation could develop with the billions and billions dollars wasted nationally dealing with the teacher turnover crisis (National Commission on Teaching and America's Future, 2007; see previous discussion, this chapter). Furthermore, it is well known that teaching is a lower-paying profession, and teachers suffer an earnings disadvantage, which Mishel, Allegretto, and Corcoran (2011) refer to as "the teaching penalty." Based on 2010 Census data, the authors report that in 2010 the mean weekly pay of K-12 teachers was almost 14% lower compared to workers who have similar educational attainment and experience.

In addition, teachers should not have to subsidize an underfunded educational system with their insufficient salaries. Ingersoll (2012b) estimates that in AY 2007–2008, teachers spent, on average, approximately $395 out of their pocket to pay for classroom supplies sans reimbursement. In 2014, the average expense was $500 (Shepard, 2014). In AY 2007–2008, Ingersoll (2012b) estimates that the total workforce of 4 million teachers, mostly women, made donations over $1.5 billion to pay for educational materials for their schools. It is clear that public school teachers need substantial raises. The implementation of this labor market incentive would, of course, require a major attitudinal transformation in how we perceive teachers and their world of work. Much is at stake for the good of U.S. public education. As Mishel et al. (2011) conclude, the overall improvement of teacher quality necessitates rectifying, in the labor market, the financial compensation disadvantage teacher face.

5. *Appropriate assignment of beginning teachers.* The findings in the comprehensive investigation of the Teach for America (TFA) recruits by Donaldson and Johnson (2010) provide a valuable lesson in how *not* to make teaching assignments for novice teachers. The TFA program, founded in 1989 as a nonprofit organization, is designed to recruit outstanding college students to teach for 2 years in public schools across the nation that primarily serve low-SES students.[41] The TFA is a fast-track certification program in which recruits receive 5 weeks of summer training (Korn, 2013). Once they begin their jobs, these new teachers earn compensations of $25,500 to $51,000 (salary and benefits), depending on the location of their work. Since the inception of TFA, 24,000 teachers have been placed in mostly large, urban schools that primarily serve low-SES, low-performing students of color (Tenney, 2013).

In their analysis, Donaldson and Johnson (2010) surveyed three cohorts of TFA teachers (years 2000, 2001, and 2002), who at the time of the online survey in 2007 had between 4 to 6 years of teaching experience. The authors report that elementary teachers who taught multiple grades, compared to their colleagues who taught single-grade classrooms, had higher risks of leaving their schools, particularly after the first year of teaching.[42] Regarding secondary teachers, those who taught multiple subjects, in comparison to peers who taught single-subject classes, had higher rates of resigning from teaching altogether. Finally, mathematics and science teachers who taught out-of-field had higher rates of resigning, compared to their counterparts who taught in-field. In their conclusion, Donaldson and Johnson suggest that administrators should be very cautious in putting beginning teachers at risk when making teaching appointments that are extremely challenging, especially for novices. Such misassignments, the authors say, come with a price—increased teacher turnover and diminished student achievement created by the turmoil of such turnover (see previous discussion, this chapter, of the effects of teacher turnover on student academic achievement).[43]

6. *Implementation of comprehensive mentoring support for beginning teachers in induction programs.* Historically, the word "mentor"—which has its roots in Greek mythology (Ragins & Kram, 2007)—has been used to describe an older, more experienced, and more established person in his or her profession who is responsible for the education and nurturance of a younger, less experienced, and newer person to the profession—that is, the protégée or novice. Furthermore, it has only been relatively recent (since the latter part of the 1970s) that the notion of mentoring has been discussed and investigated in the scholarly literature (Provident, 2005). In the field of education, mentoring is typically part of "induction" programs in which some school districts provide orientation, support, and guidance for new teachers as they make the transition to their job in teaching. These induction initiatives generally have a number of facets, such as teacher-teacher collaborations, informational seminars, instructional workshops—and the dominant element of teacher induction, personal guidance in the form of mentoring by a veteran teacher (Smith & Ingersoll, 2004). Given that school districts invest considerable time and effort in their induction programs, a good question to ask is whether these initiatives have positive effects on new teachers.[44]

One such study is by Smith and Ingersoll (2004), who drew their sample from a U.S. cohort comprising new teachers who began their employment in 1999–2000. The source of data was the Schools and Staffing Survey, and its supplementary measure, the Teacher Follow-up Survey. Using a complex stratified survey design, the nationally representative sample resulted in 3,235 teachers. Smith and Ingersoll's major finding most germane to the present discussion is that beginning teachers who were given a matched mentor (i.e., same field of teaching) and who took part in induction activities (e.g., collaboration with teacher colleagues) were less likely to transfer to other schools or to leave the teaching profession subsequent to their first year of employment. In sum, the *collective* elements of an induction program had a significant impact on reducing teacher turnover.

In another major study on the effects of mentoring and induction programs on teachers, Ingersoll and Strong (2011) undertook a comprehensive literature review of empirical evidence in which they examined teacher retention and other consequences (e.g., teachers' commitment to teaching, student achievement) of such programs for beginning teachers; this critical assessment involved 15 studies published since the 1980s. In this methodologically solid review, Ingersoll and Strong include only investigations in which (a) data were available for both induction program participants and non-participants, and (b) the results of significance tests were provided. Overall, the reviewed studies offer empirical support for the assertion that mentoring and induction programs for beginning teachers have positive effects. For example, these programs demonstrate that new teachers who participate are more likely to have higher rates of retention, to be more satisfied and committed in their work, and to have enhanced classroom instruction (e.g., maintaining behavioral management; keeping students task-oriented). Furthermore, and very importantly, nearly all the studies reviewed showed that these teachers had students who gained in academic achievement.

Given the positive and encouraging research findings on mentoring and teacher induction programs, it is unfortunate that school districts across the U.S. have not yet embraced such teacher support initiatives to the extent they should. In a comprehensive national review of state policies on teacher induction programs, Goldrick, Osta, Barlin, and Burn (2012) report that 27 (54%) of the 50 states have a requirement of *some type* of induction or mentoring support for beginning teachers. What is particularly lamentable is that only three (6%) of the states (Connecticut, Delaware, and Iowa) mandate that districts and schools provide comprehensive induction programs for new teachers (i.e., multiyear support, requirement that teachers complete an induction program in order to obtain a teaching license, provision of targeted program funding by the state). It is this type of high-quality, extensive induction program—with mentoring at the nexus—that results, for example, in better teacher retention rates and improved classroom practices of teachers. As Ingersoll (2012a) concludes, the data show that teacher induction is useful, but it depends on how much support one receives.

Two final points need to be made regarding mentoring and teacher induction. First, in discussing the positive impact of these initiatives, we must not lose sight of teachers and students of color. Research findings inform us that teachers of color, compared to their White colleagues, transfer more frequently to new schools or resign more often from teaching completely (Ingersoll & May, 2011). Thus, to improve their retention rates and classroom instruction, teachers of color should be prime targets to participate in mentoring and induction programs. In regard to students of color, their school success could be improved in light of the research literature that reports teachers who participate in mentoring and induction programs produce students who show, on average, gains in academic achievement. Second, a systemic implementation of comprehensive mentoring and induction initiatives will be financially costly. Are such programs good investments? The research on this query is quite meager in quantity. One cost-benefit analysis study, however, reports that a comprehensive mentoring program for beginning teachers in California showed a worthwhile investment

(Villar & Strong, 2007). Subsequent to 5 years, the return to the state was $1.66 for every $1.00 expended. The dividends showed in increased effectiveness of teachers and less teacher attrition (i.e., resulting in reductions of turnover rates and lower costs associated with teacher replacement costs due to turnover). Goldrick et al. (2012) note that the costs for comprehensive teacher induction programs can be "thousands of dollars" per new teacher (p. 22), and thus the price should be paid by local, state, and federal coffers. I dare say that these per-teacher costs mentioned by Goldrick et al. pale in comparison to those of some school districts that squander money on the teacher turnover crisis—for example, $15,325 spent on each teacher who leaves in the Milwaukee Public Schools (Barnes et al., 2007).

7. *Anti-deficit thinking and social justice curriculum in preprofessional training for principals.* The research literature informs us that school principals can be powerful and successful leaders (e.g., Brock & Grady, 2011; Hallinger & Heck, 1996; Wallace Foundation, 2013). Regarding the relation between leadership and student achievement, Waters, Marzano, and McNulty (2003) reviewed 70 studies based on 30 years of research. In their meta-analysis, the authors report that the average effect size is .25 (conveyed as a correlation coefficient). Expressed differently, this increase in the principals' leadership ability translates into a mean student achievement gain of 10 percentile points in the more successful school. Waters et al. (2003) note that 21 different leadership responsibilities (p. 4, Figure 3) serve as mechanisms to improve student academic performance—for example, "culture" (promotion of shared beliefs-cooperation); "curriculum, instruction, and assessment" (direct involvement in these facets); and "change agent" (willingness to challenge the status quo). Strong school principals have also been found to be influential in helping to reduce teacher turnover. For example, in their study of NYCPS, Boyd et al. (2009) find that the principal is an important element in decisions of teachers not to leave their schools. Teachers who perceived their principals more positively (e.g., encouraging, supportive) were more likely to stay.

Notwithstanding these research findings attesting to the leadership of school principals, there is another aspect of empirical investigations of these administrators—their inequitable distribution across schools—that raises serious concerns for the education of students of color. The empirical study by Loeb, Kalogrides, and Horng (2010) provides rich data on this issue via their investigation of the fourth largest school district in the U.S., the Miami-Dade County Public Schools (M-DCPS)—a racially/ethnically diverse district of White, Black, and Latino/Latina students, the latter being the majority at 57% in 2008. Loeb et al. (2010) used staff and student data from the administrative files of the M-DCPS for a 6-year period, AYs 2003–2004 through 2008–2009. The authors report that low-SES students, students of color, and low-achieving students are at a clear disadvantage in the district. Such pupils—in contrast to students characterized as higher SES, White, and higher achieving—are more likely to be enrolled in a school with a lower-quality principal, as expressed by several proxies of principal attributes. That is, these student groups placed at such an unfavorable situation are more likely to have a principal (a) who is a first-year administrator; (b) with less experience as a principal; (c) on an interim or temporary status; (d) without, at least, a master's degree; and (e) who earned a degree from a less-competitive college. These findings for the M-DCPS, the authors note, are mainly consistent with other studies that have examined the sorting of principals in a school district.[45]

As to how to explain the uneven distribution of principal characteristics across schools in the M-DCPS, Loeb et al. (2010) suggest that such sorting is jointly driven by the initial match when a principal is assigned a school *and* eventual principal transfers—which are shaped by principal preferences. To bring some clarity to this latter factor, the authors administered a survey to all district principals and asked them in what kinds of schools they would and would not like to work.[46] The principals consistently stated that they would prefer to work in schools deemed easier to administer (e.g., safe, appropriately resourced). Regarding the types of schools in which the principals prefer not to work, 27% said "a 'failing' school in need of reform." Furthermore, 12% of the principals said they did not want to work in a school with "many English-language learners," and 11% of the respondents stated that they prefer not to work in a school with "many students of poverty" (p. 222, Table 7). Loeb et al. (2010) conclude that the preferences given by some principals, as well as their actual behaviors (i.e., transfers to schools perceived as easier in which to work), "demonstrate an aversion" (p. 227) to leading those M-DCPS schools with high concentrations of low-SES, low-performing, EL pupils—and by proxy, students of color.

Considering the research findings in the study by Loeb et al. (2010) and in other investigations (e.g., Gates et al., 2005; Papa, Hamilton, & Wyckoff, 2002) that some principals have a disinclination to administer schools serving predominant enrollments of low-SES, low-achieving students of color, it makes sense to be proactive in the training of future principals. As noted by a number of scholars who advocate anti-deficit thinking, a well-instructed principal can be very effective in promoting and realizing school success for students of color (e.g., McKenzie & Scheurich, 2007; Reyes, 2005; Skrla, Scheurich, García, & Nolly, 2004). In order for future principals to learn how to effectively lead schools that are diverse along SES and racial/ethnic lines, they should have opportunities in their graduate training (best done in departments of educational administration) to become aware, confront, and transform any deficit thinking they may have of students of color. Because graduate students who are aspiring to become a principal are most likely on hiatus from teaching or are concurrently teaching and enrolled in graduate school, the curriculum on anti-deficit thinking I earlier propose in this chapter for White preservice teachers (e.g., Marx, 2006) should be applicable for these prospective principals. Once the future principal has proven successful in coming to grips with his or her deficit thinking, the aspirant should embark on preprofessional training designed to provide strategies that principals can utilize to assist teachers eliminate their own deficit thinking. A valuable curricular source on this is detailed in McKenzie and Scheurich (2004). The authors developed the construct of "equity traps," which they define as "ways of thinking or assumptions that prevent educators from believing students of color can be successful learners" (pp. 601–602).[47] The rationale underlying these strategies is to provide teachers, via the guidance of their principals, opportunities so they can transform their deficit thinking orientation to an assets-based perspective regarding communities of color, and the families and students residing there.

In my view, prospective principals should also have a well-grounded introduction to the theory and practice of social justice in their preprofessional training. Beginning around the late 1990s, the notions of leading and teaching for social justice have gained prominence in the field of education, as seen, for example, in a number of books on the topic (e.g., Ayers, Hunt, & Quinn, 1998; Darling-Hammond, French, & García-López, 2002; Gorski & Pothini, 2013). Although there are many conceptions of social justice, the one I find particularly lucid in capturing the field in a broad, systemic fashion is by Goldfarb and Grinberg (2002), who state that social justice focuses on transforming those institutional and organizational structures by vigorously engaging in the reclamation, appropriation, and advancement of rights concerned with equality. A good question to ask is: How does leadership for social justice differ from educational leadership? Theoharis (2007) brings needed insight to this query. First, the social justice area focuses not only on the characteristics of the educational leader (typically the school principal), but also very much on how to bring about institutional change. Second, the social justice domain, although emphasizing race and class concerns, is more inclusive, covering other marginalized groups (i.e., gender, disability, language, sexual orientation). Third, scholars make a number of distinctions between a "good leader" and a "social justice leader" (p. 252, Table 3). Theoharis comments, for example, that a good leader "works long and hard to make a great school," while a social justice leader "becomes intertwined with the life, community, and soul of the school" (p. 252). It is this ethos that a principal of social justice can communicate to his or her teachers to improve the quality of teaching and student learning.

8. *Rethinking teacher accountability*. How should we hold public school teachers accountable for their work? This is one of the most contentious issues in contemporary education. In the interest of space, I will only touch upon both sides of the debate. My focus will be on how to situate the controversy so we can better understand teacher evaluation within the context of a political and structural analysis. The contemporary standards-based movement in education—which has its origin in the "excellence" initiatives in the 1980s prompted by *A Nation at Risk: The Imperatives for Educational Reform* (National Commission on Excellence in Education, 1983) (see Valencia, 2010, chapter 4)—is framed by the mantra of "accountability" and is driven by high-stakes testing (Valencia & Pearl, 2010). Initially, such testing was primarily used to assess whether secondary students were meritorious enough to be awarded a high school diploma. Much

of the early research on high-stakes testing was concerned with the likely adverse impact on students of color (Valencia & Bernal, 2000). Later, a new dimension was added: High-stakes testing began to be used as a gatekeeper for the promotion of students to the next grade. Again, this application of high-stakes testing spurred researchers to investigate whether such assessments resulted in adverse impact on Latino/Latina and Black students (Valencia & Villarreal, 2005).

More recently, another use of high-stakes testing has materialized—the utilization of student achievement test scores to evaluate their teachers. This strategy, a statistical technique, gathers data on a student's academic improvement from one year to the another, and thus a gain score is obtained. The data are used, in turn, to ascertain a *teacher effect* on a student's learning (Doran & Fleischman, 2005). This procedure to measure teacher effectiveness is referred to as "value-added modeling" (Baker et al., 2010) or "value-added assessment" (Dorans & Fleischman). The notion of "value" in value-added modeling (VAM) means that an effective teacher is "adding value" (whatever that means) to the student, and the ineffective teacher is not (Saltman, 2010). The rationale behind VAM, which is becoming quite popular, is that it can be used to evaluate teachers for pay raises, one-time merit increases, tenure, or even termination (Baker et al.).

Some researchers comment that VAM has an important role in the evaluation of teachers, although it should not be used as the sole measure (Glazerman et al., 2010). Notwithstanding this positive support, VAM has been heavily criticized. For example, the Board of Testing of the National Research Council warns that proponents should not prematurely encourage the use of VAM to reward or penalize teachers (National Research Council, 2009). Furthermore, Henry Braun of the Educational Testing Service notes that the implementation and proposed use of VAMs bring up a number of concerns along lines of measurement, practice, and even philosophy (Braun, 2005). In a sustained critique, Baker et al. (2010) conclude that the use of student test scores to evaluate teachers is not adequately valid and reliable enough to be the basis of making high-stakes decisions about instructors. Furthermore, the authors note that VAM does not take into account a number of other factors that are associated with student learning and academic outcomes—namely, a student's earlier teachers, class size, school attendance, SES, language status, home intellectual environment, and social capital of parents. To these aspects, I would add: possible cultural loading and bias on tests, school segregation, school financing, curriculum differentiation (ability grouping and tracking), language suppression, cultural exclusion from the curriculum, and deficit thinking of teachers.

In order to further understand the controversy surrounding the issue of teacher accountability, I believe it is necessary to rethink the matter by positioning it in the context of a much broader debate: What is the primary source of the troubles afflicting the teaching profession with respect to teacher quality? Drawing from Ingersoll (2012b), there are two major views on how to address this query: the top-down accountability perspective and the very different viewpoint, the shared accountability and power perspective.[48] In regard to the former perspective, Ingersoll (2012b) states that this stance perceives schools as poorly managed, disorganized, and having low standards, and sees the cornerstone of the schools—teachers—doing what they wish in the privacy of their classrooms. As such, this assertion holds that low-quality teachers turn out students who perform poorly on academic measures. The remedy to fix the problem is to provide control from a centralized source in order to hold teachers more answerable for their students' learning. The primary tool to help fix this putative claim of teachers' lack of accountability is to connect student test scores to the evaluation of their respective teachers—that is, the use of VAM. Ingersoll (2012b) notes that the underlying assumption of the top-down accountability perspective is based on a "teacher deficit" point of view. This deficit thinking mindset asserts that the major source of the low quality of teachers exists in defects in teachers themselves. This endogenous explanation states that teachers lack commitment to their profession, do not have the requisite abilities to teach, and do not demonstrate the necessary engagement and effort to be high-quality instructors.

The primary problem with the top-down accountability perspective lies in the context in which it is embedded, the standards-based school reform movement. In Valencia and Pearl (2010, 2011), we argue that this movement is structurally misdirected because it tries to mend the symptoms of school failure (e.g., poor achievement), rather than the root causes (e.g., race- and class-based societal inequalities in income, housing, and health care; the ways schools are organized in impeding the optimal learning of students of color—e.g., inequities in school financing, and inequalities in gaining access to challenging, high-quality curriculum via tracking). Viewed in this manner, we consider the standards-based school reform movement to be riddled with deficit thinking because students of color and their teachers are blamed for school failure, and oppressive structural forces are held inculpable. An undeniable fact about high-stakes testing when it is used in schools as the final or near-exclusive arbiter to make important decisions is that it does not improve life chances for students of color and teachers any more than measuring the body's temperature reduces fever. In the haste to eliminate TAG, as well as to improve teacher quality, there has been no serious attempt to distinguish standards from obstacles.

The second perspective on what afflicts the teaching profession has to do with the lack of shared accountability and power. This position asserts that the major source of the difficulties related to teacher quality is not internally situated in teachers, but rather in how schools are organized around power arrangements. Ingersoll (2012b) discusses how teachers frequently have little control over their work. For example, they have little to no input in aspects such as: the establishment of the curriculum, curricular innovation, textbook choice, class size, the hiring of new teachers, and—very importantly in the case of the present discussion—the evaluation of their teaching. Based on his own research, Ingersoll (2012b) finds that schools in which teachers experience greater control over school structure and operations give rise to an environment that fosters more collegiality and cooperation among the teaching staff. This transformation, in turn, leads to teachers being more committed to their work, results in better teacher retention, and produces fewer student discipline problems. Considering these positive outcomes, Ingersoll (2012b)—drawing from the literature on organizational management and leadership—advocates a balanced and shared approach in the teacher's workplace, in which accountability and power must be present together. He asserts that by conceptualizing teacher quality as a school organizational issue in which power and control are central to daily operations, shared institutional arrangements need to be structured so the important work of teachers can be enhanced.

Given that the top-down accountability perspective—in which VAM is in the vanguard—is dubious because of its narrow, one-sided, and deficit thinking view in explaining teacher quality, the question remains: What might be a broader and assets-based approach to evaluate teachers? To best address this query, it is important to first lay down an important principle of assessment from the measurement community: "No major educational decision should ever be made on test sores alone" (Gronlund, 1985, p. 480). This dictum forms the basis of the *sine qua non* of educational assessment that multiple data sources should be used in assessing the various stakeholders in education—including teachers.

There is appreciable literature advocating the usage of multiple measures to evaluate teachers (e.g., Darling-Hammond, 2012; Hanover Research, 2012; Partee, 2012). A common thread that ties this corpus of scholarship is that integrating multiple data sources for teacher evaluation can increase the validity and reliability of the assessment due to the increased, diverse, and richer information that is obtained. The kinds of data sources that can be utilized are heterogeneous, including, for example: teacher self-assessments, classroom observations by the principal, parent surveys, student-achievement goal settings by teacher (Partee), student surveys (by older students), peer reviews, student portfolios (Hanover Research), teacher's lesson plans, teacher's instructional materials, videotapes of teaching, and teacher collaboration (Darling-Hammond, 2012).

Evidence of student learning can also be used, but given the drawbacks of VAM a modified approach should be employed. Darling-Hammond (2012) suggests, for instance, that a pre-/posttest measure of reading achievement (as assessed by a teacher-made test) be utilized, and the resultant information be integrated with the data from the other multiple measures that go into a teacher's evaluation. In addition to these preceding examples of multiple measures to evaluate a teacher's effectiveness, the study by Hallinan (2008) lends itself as something to consider for teacher evaluation. Her investigation's focus was on students' (6th, 8th, and 10th graders) attachment to school. She reports that students who perceive that their teachers praise and respect them, as well as care about them, are more likely to show a liking for school—compared to students who do not have such perceptions of their teachers. Hallinan also notes that students who demonstrated an attachment to school had improved academic achievement and enhanced social development (e.g., cooperative behaviors). In regard to the application of multiple means to evaluate teachers, perhaps a teacher's ability to exert an effect on whether pupils can develop an attachment to school can be part of the evaluative process.

The mesolevel factor of teacher quality is indeed a major dimension in the Three-M Systemic Model. Research study after study consistently report that the teacher quality characteristics of experience, qualifications, and turnover are inequitably distributed across schools by race and SES. Given that empirical evidence demonstrates that these teacher quality attributes are linked to pupil academic achievement, Mexican American, Puerto Rican, other Latino/Latina, and Black students—especially those from low-SES background—are shortchanged in opportunities to learn and achieve at optimal levels. We must refrain, however, from demonizing teachers, as so often happens. This deficit thinking mindset leads to unproductive and oppressive approaches in improving teacher quality. Rather, we must develop assets-based, equitable, and open-minded ways to help build the finest teacher workforce possible. Finally, we must be vigorous in our campaign to ensure that a highly qualified and effective teacher is placed in every classroom in all schools that primarily serve students of color.

Epilogue

About a month after I completed this chapter, a major legal decision was reached in early summer of 2014 that has bearing on the subject matter here—teacher quality. Several years ago, on May 14, 2012, *Vergara v. California* was filed in the Superior Court of the State of California, County of Los Angeles.[49] The plaintiffs in *Vergara* are 8 boys and girls, ranging in age from 7 to 15 years. The majority (n = 5, 63%) are Latino/Latina and attend schools in the Los Angeles Unified School District (LAUSD).[50] The defendants are many—for example, State of California, Governor Edmund G. Brown Jr., State Board of Education, and the LAUSD.[51] In very compressed form, the plaintiffs argue that California's "Permanent Employment Statute" for public school teachers (California Education Code section 44929.21, subdivision [b])[52] has no compelling interest as it eventually results in some teachers who are ineffective and creates disparate impact, particularly for "minority and economically disadvantaged students." Therefore, the statutes for granting teacher tenure violate the equal protection clauses of the California Constitution.[53]

In making their argument about the alleged unconstitutionality of the Permanent Employment Statute (PES), the plaintiffs' attorneys dwell on what they refer to as "grossly ineffective teachers." Although such teachers, the plaintiffs note, make up the "bottom five percent of all educators,"[54] the complaint is designed to zero in on this small sector of California teachers. The pages are riddled with the "grossly ineffective teachers" phrase, appearing on one page (no. 10) of the complaint 12 different times. In regard to the harmful effects of being taught by these teachers, the plaintiffs state in their complaint that one study finds "replacing a grossly ineffective teacher with even an *average* teacher—not an above-average or superior teacher—would increase students' cumulative lifetime income by a total of $1.4 million per classroom taught by that teacher."[55] The citation for this study and all references to research on teacher quality are not cited in the complaint. Thus, an independent confirmation of the veracity of this reported research cannot be done.

At the heart of the plaintiffs' complaint is the short amount of time it takes a teacher to be awarded tenure in California. The plaintiffs underscore that based on the PES, school districts are required to make a decision to grant, or not, permanent employment to new teachers subsequent to less than 18 months.[56] Sans citations, the complaint notes, "Several studies have shown that it is not possible to determine a teacher's long-term effectiveness during the first three years of teaching."[57] Furthermore, the plaintiffs make a point about the difficulty and financial costs associated with getting a teacher dismissed for poor classroom performance. Citing a *Los Angeles Weekly* article, it is stated in the complaint that from 2000 to 2010, the LAUSD had expenditures of $3.5 million in its attempt to dismiss seven teachers (of a workforce of 30,000); only four of the seven teachers were ultimately fired.[58] In sum, the plaintiffs argue that the PES and four related statutes are in violation of the equal protection provisions of California's Constitution, and therefore the plaintiffs sought a "permanent injunction enjoining the enforcement, application, or implementation" of the statutes.[59]

On June 10, 2014, Judge Rolf M. Treu handed down his decision in the *Vergara* case.[60] In short, he ruled that the plaintiffs successfully met their burden of proof on every issue brought forth. Based on testimony provided by plaintiffs' experts at trial, Judge Treu found the evidence on "grossly ineffective teachers" to be compelling to such an extent "it shocks the conscience."[61] He opined that the PES and related statutes "impose a real and appreciable impact on students' fundamental right to equality of education."[62] Furthermore, he concluded that this burden is unevenly placed on poor and racial/ethnic minority students, given that these students are taught in schools with a disproportionate percentage of teachers who are "underqualified, inexperienced, and out-of-field."[63] In sum, Judge Treu found the challenged statutes to be unconstitutional. He ordered an injunction, but he stayed it pending a review by the appellate court.

As expected, responses to Judge Treu's ruling were swift and widespread. The crux of the debate: Did the lawsuit truly have the goal of improving the education of students of color in California, or was it really motivated by a movement to privatize public schools in the state? The latter perspective appears to be more credible. A starting point is to examine who was behind the lawsuit. *Vergara* was brought forth and heavily funded by an organization called Students Matter, which was founded by Steven Welch—a millionaire Silicon Valley entrepreneur.[64] Columnist Dante Atkins (2014) writes that Welch has among his supporters Michelle Rhee,[65] founder and CEO of Students First, "a movement to transform public education."[66] Another Welch supporter is billionaire Eli Broad. The mission statement of the Broad Foundation is to transform "K-12 urban education through better governance, management, labor relations, and competition" (Derstine, 2013, p. 3). Atkins notes that Rhee and Broad are prominent figures in the "anti-union, pro-charter, school privatization movement" (p. 2).

The ruling by Judge Treu is troubling, and if affirmed at the appellate level, it will have draconian consequences for teachers. Although K-12 public school teachers do not have "tenure" as college professors often gain, teachers—once awarded permanent employment status—do have the right of due process in which they can challenge possible dismissal. This right will be lost if *Vergara* prevails (Miller & Mayhew, 2014). Another major problem with the *Vergara* lawsuit is that its backers view school reform via a myopic lens. Indeed, the inequitable distribution of teacher quality characteristics—as covered in the present chapter—is a significant issue apropos to low-SES students of color. Yet, there are a number of systemic ways, as I discuss, that we can consider to rectify the problem. The *Vergara* supporters, however, prefer to demonize the teaching force and use them as scapegoats for an education system that sorely needs structural transformations. Welch and his adherents fail to see that a number of factors contribute to the school failure of low-SES students of color—for example, inequities in school financing, curriculum differentiation, language suppression and cultural exclusion, and the "other gaps (e.g., in income and health care). In any event, let us be sanguine that justice will prevail in the appeal of the *Vergara* decision.

Notes

1. See Hussar and Bailey (2013, p. 55, Table 16).
2. *Id.*, p. 31, Table 1.
3. I extrapolated this number from data in Hussar and Bailey (2011, p. 5, Figure 3).
4. Also, see, for example, Fuller (2010); Kelly (2012); Valencia (2010, chapter 4).
5. Some remaining parts of this chapter build on, with revisions: Valencia (2010, pp. 119, 127–128, 136, 138–139, 152); Valencia (2011, p. 18); Valencia and Aburto (1991a, pp. 170–171); Valencia and Pearl (2011, p. 278).
6. Also, see, for example, Bartell (2004, chapter 1).
7. See Barton (2003); Barton and Coley (2009); Betts et al. (2000); Clotfelter Ladd, and Vigdor (2004, 2010); Clotfelter, Ladd, Vigdor, and Wheeler (2007); Education Trust (2008); Fuller (2010); Hanushek, Kain, O'Brian, and Rivkin (2005); Jackson (2009); Jerald (2002); Lankford, Loeb, and Wyckoff (2002); Mayer, Mullens, Moore, and Ralph (2000); Neild and Farley-Ripple (2008); Neild, Useem, and Farley (2005); Peske and Haycock (2006); Sunderman and Kim (2005).
8. The Fast Response Survey System was developed in 1975 by the U.S. Department of Education. The surveys are representative of the national level.
9. See Barton and Coley (2009); Betts et al. (2000); Carroll, Fulton, Abercrombie, and Yoon (2004); Clotfelter et al. (2004, 2007, 2010); Darling-Hammond (2004); Education Trust (2008); Fuller (2010); Ingersoll (2003a); Jackson (2009); Jerald (2002); Lankford

Loeb, and Wyckoff (2002); Neild and Farley-Ripple (2008); Peske and Haycock (2006); Shields et al. (2001); Sunderman and Kim (2005).

10. See *Schools and Staffing Survey (SASS)*. Washington, DC: National Center for Education Statistics, U.S. Department of Education. Retrieved January 25, 2014, from: http://nces.gov/surveys/sass/.
11. Richard M. Ingersoll is credited for doing the data analysis.
12. Jerald (2002) also reports data for 28 states in which comparative information is available. Based on my calculations, in 23 (82.1%) of these states, teachers taught secondary core academic subjects without at least a minor in the field more frequently in schools with high enrollments of students of color in comparison to schools with low enrollments of students of color (p. 8).
13. High-poverty schools are defined as schools in which more than 80% of the students received free or reduced-price lunches low-poverty schools are schools in which 15% or less of the students receive such prices (Ingersoll, 2003a, p. 15).
14. The PMF is administered annually to teachers and administrators in New York State public schools. Information obtained includes, for example, salary, sex, certification status, and degree status. See *Personnel Master File*, Albany: Information and Reporting Service, New York State Education Department, retrieved January 26, 2014, from: www.p12.nysed.gov/irs/pmf/.
15. To assess whether a teacher earned a B.A. degree from a least competitive college, Lankford et al. (2002) used Barron's College Admission Selector Rating. Barron's rating system, which is frequently used to measure college selectivity, classifies colleges into 10 competitive ratings. See Schmidt, Burroughs, Cogan, and Houang (2011) for a discussion of Barron's system.
16. For a refresher on the nature and utility of a relative risk ratio, see chapter 3, note 5, this volume.
17. Marinell (2011) also presents the very similar pattern for NYCPS elementary and high school levels.
18. See National Commission on Teaching and America's Future (2007, p. 11, Appendix) for a description of the methodology used to calculate the national cost of teacher turnover. Also, see the NCTAF Teacher Turnover Cost Calculator at: http://nctaf.org/teacher-turnover-cost-calculator/the-cost-of-teacher-turnover-study-and-cost-calculator/.
19. Barnes et al. (2007, pp. 13–14) provide a more comprehensive description of teacher turnover costs. The author's eight categories of costs are: (a) "recruiting and advertising," (b) "special incentives," (c) "administrative processing," (d) "training for new teachers," (e) "training for first-time teachers," (f) "training for all teachers," (g) learning curve," and (h) "transfer."
20. See Allensworth et al. (2009); Barnes, Crowe, and Schaefer (2007); Barton (2003); Barton and Coley (2009); Boyd, Grossman, et al. (2009); Carroll et al. (2004); Clotfelter et al. (2004, 2007); Donaldson and Johnson (2010); Education Trust (2008); Fuller, Carpenter, and Fuller (2008); Guin (2004); Hanushek et al. (2004, 2005); Ingersoll (2001); Jackson (2009); Neild et al. (2005); Scafidi, Sjoquist, and Stinebrickner (2007); Smith and Ingersoll (2004).
21. The data for the Carroll et al. (2004) investigation were collected by Louis Harris, who conducts yearly surveys of public school teachers.
22. Based on a school's percentage of students of color, pupils deemed English learners, and students who were receiving free or reduced-cost lunch, an "Index of Risk" was developed to classify schools.

23. See Betts et al. (2000); Clotfelter et al. (2004); Fuller et al. (2008); Hanushek et al. (2005); Lankford et al. (2002); Nye, Konstantopoulos, and Hedges (2004); Peske and Haycock (2006).
24. Peske and Haycock (2006, p. 5, Figure 5) note that schools deemed low-performing and high-performing in reading are 70.2% or lower and 96.2% or higher proficient, respectively; for mathematics, low-performing and high-performing schools are 57% or lower and 92.9% or higher proficient, respectively.
25. Fuller et al. (2008) also report quintiles 2, 3, and 4. For sake of brevity, I report only on quintiles 1 and 5.
26. *Elementary and Secondary Education Act reauthorization: A blueprint for reform* (March 13, 2010), retrieved February 2, 2014, from: www2.ed.gov/policy/elsec/leg/blueprint/index.html.
27. See Betts et al. (2000); Boyd et al. (2005, 2008); Clotfelter et al. (2004); Ferguson and Brown (2000); Fuller (2010); Fuller et al. (2008); Hanushek et al. (2005); Lankford et al. (2002); Nye et al. (2004); Peske and Haycock (2006); Shields et al. (2001).
28. *Academic Performance Index (API)*. Sacramento: California Department of Education. Retrieved February 7, 2014, from: www.cde.ca/gov/ta/ac/ap/.
29. See previous discussion of Lankford et al. (2002) for a description of how lowest- and highest-achievement schools were determined.
30. "NTE" is National Teacher Examination; "NYSTCE" stands for New York State Teacher's Certification Examination.
31. Fuller et al. (2008) also report an extremely similar pattern for middle school teachers in Texas (p. 60, Table A-6A).
32. See Barnes et al. (2007); Boyd et al. (2005, 2008); Fuller et al. (2008); Guin (2004); Hanushek et al. (2005); Rondfeldt, Loeb, and Wyckoff (2013).
33. Rodney Dangerfield (1921–2004), born Jacob Rodney Cohen, was a standup comedian and actor. He is best known for his catchphrase, "I don't get no respect," which he used as a theme in his monologues. See Wikipedia, *Rodney Dangerfield*. Retrieved February 16, 2014, from: http://en.wikipedia.org/wiki/Rodney_Dangerfield.
34. For this history, Ingersoll (2003a) draws from Etzioni (1969), Lortie (1975), and Tyack (1974).
35. Wikiquote. *Man and Superman*. Retrieved February 16, 2014, from: http://en.wikiquote.org/wiki/Man_and _Superman.
36. Horng (2009) offers a different perspective on why teachers transfer. In a study of California elementary schools, she finds that teachers mainly transfer, for example, for better working conditions and smaller class sizes and less so for characteristics of student bodies (e.g., race/ethnicity).
37. It should be noted, however, that other scholars conclude that the research on matching a student and teacher by race in regard to academic improvement of students of color is inconclusive (i.e., mixed; see Walsh & Tracy, 2004).
38. See Valencia and Aburto (1991a, pp. 170–172) for an extended discussion of shared identity.
39. For other sources regarding recruitment strategies for teachers of color, see, for example, Ayalon (2004); Bireda and Chait (2011); Kearney-Gissendaner (2005); Valencia and Aburto (1991b).
40. It is beyond the scope of this chapter to discuss the controversial subject of merit pay for teachers, which is given to them if students' achievement scores increase (e.g., see Clabaugh, 2009).

41. For more information on TFA, see its website at: www.teacherforamerica.org/.
42. In the literature, multiple-grade classrooms are also called multigrade, multiage, split-grade, and combination-grade classrooms.
43. Regarding whether student achievement is worse or better in multigrade classrooms, compared to single-grade classrooms, Mariano and Kirby (2009) find consistently negative (but small) effects on student achievement in the former type of classrooms.
44. See Smith and Ingersoll (2004) for a mention of a number of investigations that appear to offer support for the value of induction programs (e.g., job satisfaction of teacher; teacher efficacy; retention). Smith and Ingersoll note, however, that the existing studies have methodological problems. Also, for another, and much more comprehensive review of the impact of teacher induction programs, see Ingersoll and Strong (2011).
45. See citations in Loeb et al. (2010).
46. Loeb et al. (2010) also surveyed assistant principals, as they are likely to be next in the queue when a principalship opens in the district.
47. For a further discussion of equity traps, see Valencia (2010, pp. 135–138).
48. Also, see Ingersoll (2003b).
49. Complaint for Declaratory and Injunctive Relief, Vergara v. California, Civil Action No. BC48462, Superior Court, Los Angeles County, California, May 14, 2012. Retrieved June 21, 2014, from: studentsmatter.org/wp-content/uploads/2012/05/SM_First-Amended-Complaint_08.15.12.pdf.
50. *Id.* at 5–7.
51. *Id.* at 8.
52. *Id.* at 12.
53. *Id.* at 21.
54. *Id.* at 10.
55. *Id.*
56. *Id. at 12.*
57. *Id.*
58. *Id.* at 4.
59. *Id.* at 25.
60. Tentative Decision, Vergara v. California, Civil Action No. BC48462, Superior Court, Los Angeles County, California, June 10, 2014. Retrieved June 21, 2014, from: www.aalrreducationlaw.com/judge-rules-in-favor-of-students-in-vergara-v-california/.
61. *Id.* at 8.
62. *Id.*
63. *Id.* at 15.
64. To visit the website of Students Matter, go to: http://studentsmatter.org/.
65. Michelle Rhee had a prominent role in the anti-teacher union film, *Waiting for Superman.* For more on the film, see earlier discussion of the present chapter (section on "Toward Systemic Transformations").
66. See www.studentsfirst.org.

References

Allensworth, E., Ponisciak, S., & Mazzeo, C. (2009). *The schools teachers leave: Teacher mobility in Chicago Public Schools.* Chicago: Consortium on Chicago School Research, University of Chicago. Retrieved January 30, 2014, from: ccsr.uchicago.edu/publications/schools-teachers-leave-mobility-chicago-public-schools.

Atkins, D. (2014, March 16). *Vergara v. California*: The most dangerous lawsuit you probably haven't heard of. *Daily Kos.* Retrieved June 19, 2014, from: www.dailykos.com/story/2014/03/16/1284248/-Vergara-v-California-The-most-dangerous-lawsuit-you-probably-haven-t-heard-of#.

Ayalon, A. (2004). A model for recruitment and retention of minority students to teaching: Lessons from a school-university partnership. *Teacher Education Quarterly*, Summer, 7–23.

Ayers, R. (2010, September 17). An inconvenient Superman: David Guggenheim's new film hijacks school reform. *Huffington Post.* Retrieved February 16, 2014, from: www.huffingtonpost.com/rick-ayers-/incompetent-superman-_b_716420.html.

Ayers, W., Hunt, J. A., & Quinn, T. (Eds.). (1998). *Teaching for social justice: A democracy and education reader.* New York: New Press.

Baker, E. L., Barton, P. E., Darling-Hammond, L., Haertel, E., Ladd, H. F., Linn, R. L., Ravitch, D., Rothstein, R., Shavelson, R. J., & Shepard, L. A. (2010). *Problems with the use of student test scores to evaluate teachers* (Briefing Paper No. 278). Washington, DC: Economic Policy Institute.

Barnes, G., Crowe, E., & Schaefer, B. (2007). *The cost of teacher turnover in five schools districts: A pilot study.* Washington, DC: National Commission on Teaching and America's Future. Retrieved January 2, 2014, from: http://files.eric.ed.gov/fulltext/ED497176.pdf.

Bartell, C. A. (2004). *Cultivating high-quality teaching through induction and mentoring.* Thousand Oaks, CA: Corwin.

Barton, P. E. (2003). *Parsing the achievement gap: Baselines for tracking progress.* Princeton, NJ: Educational Testing Service. Retrieved January 3, 2014, from: www.ets.org/Media/Research/pdf/PICPARSING.pdf.

Barton, P. E., & Coley, R. J. (2009). *Parsing the achievement gap II.* Princeton, NJ: Educational Testing Service. Retrieved January 20, 2014, from: www.ets.org/Media/Research/pdf/PICPARSINGII.pdf.

Betts, J. R., Rueben, K. S., & Danenberg, A. (2000). *Equal resources, equal outcomes? The distribution of school resources and student achievement in California.* San Francisco: Public Policy Institute of California: Retrieved November 15, 2013, from: www.ppic.org/content/pubs/report/r_200jbr.pdf.

Bireda, S., & Chait, R. (2011). *Increasing teacher diversity: Strategies to improve the teacher workforce.* Washington, DC: Center for American Progress. Retrieved February 21, 2014, from: www.americanprogress.org/issues/2011//pdf/chait_diversity.pdf.

Boyd, D. J., Grossman, P., Ing, M., Lankford, H., Loeb, S., & Wyckoff, J. (2009). *The influence of school administrators on teacher retention decisions* (Working Paper No. 25). Washington, DC: National Center for Analysis of Longitudinal Data in Education Research. Retrieved January 1, 2014, from: www.urban.org/UploadedPDF/1001287_calderworkingpaper25.pdf.

Boyd, D., Grossman, P., Lankford, H., Loeb, S., & Wyckoff, J. (2006). How changes in entry requirements alter the teacher workforce and affect student achievement. *Education Finance and Policy, 1,* 176–216.

Boyd, D., Grossman, P., Lankford, H., Loeb, S., & Wyckoff, J. (2008). *Who leaves? Teacher attrition and student achievement* (Working Paper Series No. 14022). Cambridge, MA: National Bureau of Economic Research. Retrieved January 29, 2014, from: www.nber.org/papers/w/4022.

Boyd, D., Lankford, H., Loeb, S., & Wyckoff, J. (2005). Explaining the short careers of high-achieving teachers in schools with low-performing students. *American Economic Review, 95,* 166–171.

Braun, H. J. (2005). *Using student progress to evaluate teachers: A primer on value-added models.* Princeton, NJ: Educational Testing Service. Retrieved March 2, 2014, from: www.ets.org.Media/Research/pdf/PICVAM.pdf.

Brock, B. L., & Grady, M. L. (2011). *The daily practices of successful principals.* Thousand Oaks, CA: Corwin Press.

Carroll, T. G., Fulton, K., Abercrombie, K., & Yoon, I. (2004). *Fifty years after* Brown v. Board of Education: *A two-tiered education system.* Washington, DC: National Commission on Teaching and America's Future. Retrieved March 17, 2009, from: www.nctaf.org/resources/research_and_reports/nctaf_research_reports/rr_04_spe-cial_report.htm.

Chilcott, L. (Producer), & Guggenheim, D. (Director). (2010). *Waiting for Superman* (Film). (Available from www.amazon.com).

Clabaugh, G. K. (2009). Teachers merit pay: Is it a good idea? *Educational Horizons, 88,* 16–20.

Clotfelter, C. T., Ladd, H. F., & Vigdor, J. L. (2004). *Teacher quality and minority achievement gaps* (Working Paper Series No. San04–04). Durham, NC: Sanford Institute of Public Policy, Duke University. Retrieved November 17, 2013, from: research.sanford.duke.edu/papers/SAN04–04.pdf.

Clotfelter, C. T., Ladd, H. F., & Vigdor, J. L. (2010). Teacher credentials and student achievement in high school: A cross-subject analysis with student fixed effects. *Journal of Human Resources, 45,* 655–681.

Clotfelter, C. T., Ladd, H. F., Vigdor, J. L., & Wheeler, J. L. (2007). High-poverty schools and the distribution of teachers and principals. *North Carolina Law Review, 85,* 1345–1379.

Darling-Hammond, L. (2004). Inequality and the right to learn: Access to qualified teachers in California's public schools. *Teachers College Record, 106,* 1936–1966.

Darling-Hammond, L. (2012). *Creating a comprehensive system for evaluating and supporting effective teachers.* Stanford, CA: Stanford Center for Opportunity Policy in Education. Retrieved March 6, 2014, from: http://edpolicy/stanford.edu/sites/default/files/publications/creating-comprehensive-system-evaluating-and-supporting-effective-teaching.pdf.

Darling-Hammond, L., French, J., & García-López, S. P. (Eds.). (2002). *Learning to teach for social justice.* New York: Teachers College Press.

Derstine, K. (2013, February 24). Who is Eli Broad and why is he trying to destroy public education? *Defend Public Education.* Retrieved June 22, 2014, from: www.defendpubliceducation.net/.

Donaldson, M. L., & Johnson, S. M. (2010). The price of misassignment: The role of teaching assignments in Teach for America teachers' exit from low-income schools and the teaching profession. *Educational Evaluation and Policy Analysis, 32,* 299–323.

Doran, H. C., & Fleischman, S. (2005). Research matters: Challenges of value-added assessment. *Educational Leadership, 63,* 85–87. Retrieved March 2, 2014, from: www.ascd.org/publications/educational_leadership/nov05/vol63/num03/Challenges_of_Value-Added_Assessment.aspx.

Education Trust. (2008). *Their fair share: How Texas-sized gaps in teacher quality shortchange low-income and minority students.* Washington, DC: Author. Retrieved January 10, 2013, from: www.edtrust.org/files/publications/TXTheirFairShare.pdf.

Educator Effectiveness Division. (2013, December). *Report to the North Carolina General Assembly: 2012–2013 annual report on teachers leaving the profession* (No. G.S. 115C-12 [22]). Retrieved January 27, 2014, from: http://s3.amazonaws.com/cjtv-video-Attach-TeacherTurnoverReport_uploaded110113.pdf.

Etzioni, A. (Ed.). (1969). *The semi-professions and their organizations: Teachers, nurses, and social workers.* New York: Free Press.

Ferguson, R. F., & Brown, J. (2000). Certification test scores, teacher quality, and student achievement. In D. W. Grissmer & J. M. Ross (Eds.), *Analytic issues in the assessment of student achievement* (pp. 133–156). Washington, DC: National Center for Education Statistics.

Fuller, E. J. (2010). *Study on the distribution of teacher quality in Texas schools.* Austin: Association of Texas Professional Educators. Retrieved January 10, 2014, from: www.atpe/advocacy/issues/10_TeacherQuality_for_web.pdf.

Fuller, E. J., Carpenter, B., & Fuller, G. (2008). *Teacher quality & school improvement in Texas secondary schools.* Austin: Association of Texas Professional Educators. Retrieved March 17, 2009, from: www.atpe.org/Advocacy/Issues/teacherqualitystudy.asp.

Gates, S. M., Ringel, J. S., Santibañez, L., Guarino, C., Ghosh-Dastidar, B., & Brown, A. (2005). Mobility and turnover among school principals. *Economics of Education Review, 25,* 289–302.

Ginsberg, A. E. (2010). Waiting for Superman: He's "adequate" and near proficient! *Journal of Educational Controversy, 5,* 1–6. Retrieved February 16, 2014, from: www.wce.wwu.edu/Resources/CEP/ejournal/v005n002/a008.shtml.

Glazerman, S., Goldhaber, D., Loeb, S., Raudenbush, S., Staiger, D. O., & Whitehurst, G. J. (2010). *Evaluating teachers: The important role of value-added.* Washington, DC: Brown Center on Education Policy, Brookings Institution.

Goldfarb, K. P., & Grinberg, J. (2002). Leadership for social justice: Authentic participation in the case of a community center in Caracas, Venezuela. *Journal of School Leadership, 12,* 157–173.

Goldhaber, D., Gross, B., & Player, D. (2009). *Teacher career paths, teacher quality, and persistence in the classroom: Are schools keeping the best?* (Working Paper No. 29). Washington, DC: National Center for Analysis of Longitudinal Data in Education Research. Retrieved February 16, 2014, from: www.urban.org/uploadedpdf/1001432-teacher-career-paths-pdf.

Goldrick, L., Osta, D., Barlin, D., & Burn, J. (2012). *Review of state policies on teacher induction* (Policy Paper). Santa Cruz, CA: New Teacher Center. Retrieved February 23, 2014, from: www.newteachercenter.org/sites/default/files/ntc/main/resources/brf-ntc-policy-state-teacher-induction.pdf.

Goodwin, B. (2012). Research says: New teachers face three common challenges. *Educational Leadership, 69,* 84–85. Retrieved January 17, 2014, from: www.ascd.org/publications/educational-leadership/may12/vol69/num08/New-Teachers-Face-Three-Common-Challenges.aspx.

Gorski, P. C., & Pothini, S. G. (2013). *Case studies on diversity and social justice education.* New York: Routledge.

Gronlund, N. E. (1985). *Measurement and evaluation in teaching* (5th ed.). New York: Macmillan.

Guin, K. (2004). Chronic teacher turnover in urban elementary schools. *Education Policy Analysis Archives, 12*(42). Retrieved January 30, 2014, from: http://epaa.asu.edu/epaa/v12n42/.

Hafner, A., & Owings, J. (1991). *Careers in teaching: Following members of the high school class of 1972 in and out of teaching* (NCES Report No. 91–470). Washington, DC: National Center for Education Statistics, Institute of Education Sciences, U.S. Department of Education. Retrieved January 29, 2014, from: http://eric.ed.gov/?id=ED336386.

Hallinan, M. T. (2008). Teacher influences on students' attachment to school. *Sociology of Education, 81,* 271–283.

Hallinger, P., & Heck, R. H. (1996). Reassessing the principal's role in school effectiveness: A review of empirical research, 1980–1995. *Educational Administrative Quarterly, 32,* 5–44.

Hanover Research. (2012). *Best practices for including multiple measures in teacher evaluations.* Washington, DC: Author. Retrieved March 6, 2014, from: www.hanoverresearch.com/wp-content/uploads/2012/05/Best-Practices-for-Including-Multiple-Measures-in-Teacher-Evaluations-Membership.pdf.

Hanushek, E. A., Kain, J. F., O'Brian, D. M., & Rivkin, S. G. (2005). *The market for teacher quality* (Working Paper No. 11154). Cambridge, MA: National Bureau of Economic Research. Retrieved September 1, 2013, from: www.nber.org/papers/w11154.pdf?news_window=1.

Hanushek, E. A., Kain, J. F., & Rivin, S. G. (1999). *Do higher salaries buy better teachers?* (Working Paper No. 7082). Cambridge, MA: National Bureau of Economics Research. Retrieved February 23, 2014, from: www.amherst.edu/~sgrivkin/papers/salpap.pdf.

Hanushek, E. A., Kain, J. F., & Rivin, S. G. (2004). Why public schools lose teachers? *Journal of Human Resources, 39,* 326–354.

Henry, G. T., Bastain, K. C., & Fortner, C. K. (2011). Stayers and leavers: Early-career teacher effectiveness and attrition. *Educational Researcher, 40,* 271–280.

Henry, G. T., Bastain, K. C., & Smith, A. A. (2012). Scholarships to recruit the "best and brightest" into teaching: Who is recruited, where do they teach, how effective are they, and how long do they stay? *Educational Researcher, 41,* 83–92.

Horng, E. L. (2009). Teacher tradeoffs: Disentangling teachers' preferences for working conditions and student demographics. *American Educational Research Journal, 46,* 690–717.

Hussar, W. J., & Bailey, T. M. (2011). *Projection of education statistics to 2019* (38th ed., NCES 2011–017). Washington, DC: National Center for Education Statistics, Institute of Education Sciences, U.S. Department of Education. Retrieved November 5, 2013, from: nces.ed.gov/pubs2011/2011017.pdf.

Hussar, W. J., & Bailey, T. M. (2013). *Projections of education statistics to 2021* (40th ed., NCES 2013–008). Washington, DC: National Center for Education Statistics, Institute of Education Sciences, U.S. Department of Education. Retrieved November 5, 2013, from: nces.ed.gov/pubsearch/pubsinfo.asp?pubid=2013008.

Ingersoll, R. M. (2001). Teacher turnover and teacher shortages: An organizational analysis. *American Educational Research Journal, 38,* 499–534.

Ingersoll, R. M. (2003a). *Out-of-field teaching and the limits of teacher policy* (Document No. R-03–5). Seattle: Center for the Study of Teaching and Policy, University of Washington. Retrieved February 14, 2014, from: https://depts.washington.edu/ctpmail/PDFs/LimitsPolicy-R1–09–2003.pdf.

Ingersoll, R. M. (2003b). *Who controls teachers' work? Power and accountability in America's schools.* Cambridge, MA: Harvard University Press.

Ingersoll, R. M. (2012a). Beginning teacher induction: What the data tell us. *Phi Delta Kappan, 93,* 47–51.

Ingersoll, R. M. (2012b). Power, accountability, and the teacher quality problem. In S. Kelly (Ed.), *Assessing teacher quality: Understanding teacher effects on instruction and achievement* (pp. 87–109). New York: Teachers College Press.

Ingersoll, R. M., & May, H. (2011). The minority teacher shortage: Fact or fable? *Phi Delta Kappan, 93,* 62–65. Retrieved February 19, 2014, from: www.gse.upenn.edu/pdf/rmi/Fact_or_Fable.pdf.

Ingersoll, R. M., & Smith, T. (2003). The wrong solution to the teacher shortage. *Educational Leadership, 60,* 30–33.

Ingersoll, R. M., & Strong, M. (2011). The impact of induction and mentoring programs for beginning teachers: A critical review of the research. *Review of Educational Research, 81,* 201–233.

Irvine, J. J. (1990). *Black students school failure: Policies, practices, and prescriptions.* Westport, CT: Praeger.

Jackson, C. K. (2009). Student demographics, teacher sorting, and teacher quality: Evidence from the end of school desegregation. *Journal of Labor Economics, 27,* 213–256.

Jackson, P. W. (1986). *The practice of teaching.* New York: Teachers College Press.

Jerald, C. D. (2002). *All talk, no action, Putting an end to out-of-field teaching.* Washington, DC: Education Trust. Retrieved March 17, 2009, from: www2.edtrust.org/NR/rdonlyres/8DE64524–592E-4C83-A13A-6B1DF1CF8D3E/AllTalk.pdf.

Kearney-Gissendaner, J. (2005). *Minority teacher recruitment and retention strategies.* New York: Routledge.

Kelly, S. (Ed.). (2012). *Assessing teacher quality: Understanding teacher effects on instruction and achievement.* New York: Teachers College Press.

Korn, S. (2013, October 23). Why I said no to Teach for America, and why you should too. *Huffington Post.* Retrieved February 24, 2014, from: www.huffingtonpost.com/sandra-korn/why-i-said-no-to-teach-for-america_b_4151764.html.

Lankford, H., Loeb, S., & Wyckoff, J. (2002). Teacher sorting and the plight of urban schools: A descriptive analysis. *Educational Evaluation and Policy Analysis, 24,* 37–62.

LaViest, T. A. (2005). Disentangling race and socioeconomic status: A key to understanding health inequalities. *Journal of Urban Health, 82,* 26–34.

Learning Point Associates. (2007). *Understanding the No Child Left Behind Act: Teacher quality* (Quick Key 6). Nashville, ILL: Author. Retrieved December 8, 2013, from: www.learningpt.org/pdfs/qky6.pdf.

Loeb, S., Kalogrides, D., & Horng, E. L. (2010). Principal preferences and the uneven distribution across schools. *Education Evaluation and Policy Analysis, 32,* 205–229. Retrieved February 26, 2014, from: http://epa.sagepub.com/content/32/2/205.

Loeb, S., & Page, M. E. (2000). Examining the link between teacher wages and student outcomes: The importance of alternative labor market opportunities and non-pecuniary variation. *Review of Economics and Statistics, 82,* 393–408.

Lortie, D. (1975). *School teacher: A sociological study.* Chicago: University of Chicago Press.

Mariano, L. T., & Kirby, S. N. (2009). *Achievement of students in multigrade classrooms: Evidence from the Los Angeles Unified School District* (Working Paper No. WR-685-IES). Pittsburgh, PA: Rand Education. Retrieved February 24, 2014, from: www.rand.org/content/dam/rand/pubs/working_paper/2009/RAND_WR685.pdf.

Marinell, W. H. (2011). *The middle school teacher project: A descriptive analysis of teacher turnover in New York City middle schools.* New York: Research Alliance for New York City Schools. Retrieved January 26, 2014, from: http://media.ranycs.org/2011/002.

Marx, S. (2006). *Revealing the invisible: Confronting passive racism in teacher education.* New York: Routledge.

Mayer, D. P., Mullens, J. E., Moore, M. T., & Ralph, J. (2000). *Monitoring school quality: An indicators report* (NCES No. 2001–030). Washington, DC: National Center for Education Statistics, Institute of Education Sciences, U.S. Department of Education. Retrieved January 20, 2014, from: http://nces.ed.gov/pubs2001/2001030.pdf.

McKenzie, K. B., & Scheurich, J. J. (2004). Equity traps: A useful construct for preparing principals to lead schools that are successful with racially diverse students. *Educational Administration Quarterly, 40,* 601–632.

McKenzie, K. B., & Scheurich, J. J. (2007). King elementary: A new principal plans how to transform a diverse urban school. *Journal of Cases in Educational Leadership, 10,* 19–27.

Miller, J., & Mayhew, K. (2014, June 16). What's wrong with the *Vergara* decision for teachers. *San Diego Free Press.* Retrieved June 21, 2014, from: http://sandiegofreepress.org/2014/06/whats-wrong-with-the-vergara-decision-for-teachers/.

Mishel, L., Allegretto, S. A., & Corcoran, S. P. (2011). *The teaching penalty: An update through 2010* (Issue Brief No. 298). Washington, DC: Economic Policy Institute. Retrieved February 23, 2014, from: http://s1.epi.org/files/page/-/issuebriefs/IssueBrief298.pdf.

National Commission on Excellence in Education. (1983). *A nation at risk: The imperative for educational reform.* Washington, DC: U.S. Government Printing Office.

National Commission on Teaching and America's Future. (2007). *The high cost of teacher turnover* (Policy Brief). Washington, DC: Author. Retrieved January 27, 2014, from: http://files.eric.ed.gov/fulltext/ED498001.pdf.

National Research Council. (2009). *Letter report to the U.S. Department of Education on the Race to the Top Fund.* Washington, DC: National Academy Press. Retrieved March 2, 2014, from: www.nap.edu/catalog.php?record_id=12780.

Neild, R. C., & Farley-Ripple, E. (2008). Within-school variation in teacher quality: The case of ninth grade. *American Journal of Education, 114,* 271–305.

Neild, R. C., Useem, E., & Farley, E. (2005). *The quest for quality: Recruiting and retaining teachers in Philadelphia.* Philadelphia: Research for Action. Retrieved September 1, 2013, from: files.eric.gov/fulltext/ED485308.pdf.

Nye, B., Konstantopoulos, S., & Hedges, L. V. (2004). How large are teacher effects? *Educational Research and Policy Analysis, 26,* 237–257.

Papa, F. C., Hamilton, L, & Wyckoff, J. (2002). *The attributes and career paths of principals: Implications for improving policy.* Stanford: CA: Center for Education Policy Analysis, Stanford University. Retrieved February 28, 2014, from: http://cepa/stanford.edu/sites/default/files/Career_Paths_of_Principals.pdf.

Partee, G. L. (2012). *Using multiple evaluation measures to improve teacher effectiveness: State strategies from round 2 of No Child Left Behind Act waivers.* Washington, DC: Center for American Progress. Retrieved March 6, 2014, from: www.americanprogress.org/wp-content/uploads/2012/12/MultipleMeasures-2-INTRO.pdf.

Peske, H. G., & Haycock, K. (2006). *Teaching equality: How poor and minority students are shortchanged on teacher quality.* Washington, DC: Education Trust. Retrieved March 17, 2009, from: http://eric.ed.gov/ERICWebPortal/recordDetail?accno=ED494820.

Provasnik, S., & Planty, M. (2008). *Community colleges: Special supplement to The Condition of Education* (NCES 2008–033). Washington, DC: National Center for Education Statistics, Institute of Education Sciences, U.S. Department of Education. Retrieved February 21, 2014, from: nces.ed.gov/pubs2008/2008033.pdf.

Provident, I. M. (2005). Mentoring: A role to facilitate academic change. *Internet Journal of Allied Health Sciences and Practice, 3,* 1–7. Retrieved February 24, 2014, from: ijahsp.nova.edu/articles/vol3num2/Provident%20–%20Print%20Version.pdf.

Ragins, B. R., & Kram, K. E. (2007). The roots and meaning of mentoring. In B. R. Ragins & K. E. Kram (Eds.), *The handbook of mentoring at work: Theory, research, and practice* (pp. 3–15). Thousand Oaks, CA: SAGE.

Reyes, A. (2005). Recruiting principals as leaders for cultural and linguistic diversity. In K. Téllez & H. C. Waxman (Eds.), *Preparing quality educators for English language learners: Research, policy, and practice* (pp. 145–165). Mahwah, NJ: Lawrence Erlbaum.

Rice, J. K. (2003). *Teacher quality: Understanding the effectiveness of teacher attributes.* Washington, DC: Economy Policy Institute.

Ronfeldt, M., Loeb, S., & Wyckoff, J. (2013). How teacher turnover harms student achievement. *American Educational Research Journal, 50,* 4–36.

Rumberger, R. W., & Rodríguez, G. M. (2011). Chicano dropouts. In R. R. Valencia (Ed.), *Chicano school failure and success: Past, present, and future* (3rd ed., pp. 76–98). New York: Routledge.

Saltman, K. J. (2010, September 15). "Value-added" assessment: Tool for improvement or educational "nuclear option"? *Truthout.* Retrieved March 2, 2014, from: www.truth-out.org/archive/item/91775:valueadded-assessment-tool-for-improvement-or-educational-nuclear-option.

Scafidi, B., Sjoquist, D. L., & Stinebrickner, T. R. (2007). Race, poverty, and teacher mobility. *Economics of Education Review, 26,* 145–149. Retrieved January 31, 2014, from: www.psc.isr.umich.edu/pubs/abs/4660.

Schmidt, W., Burroughs, N., Cogan, L., & Houang, R. (2011). Are college rankings an indicator of quality education? *Forum on Public Policy: A Journal of the Oxford Roundtable, 3,* 1–14. Retrieved January 25, 2014, from: forumonpublicpolicy.com/vol2011no3/archive/schmidt.pdf.

Shepard, N. (2014, May 8). Teachers spending out of pocket for supplies, projects and field trips. *National Deseret News.* Retrieved September 7, 2014, from: national-deseretnews.com/article/1440/Teachers-spending-out-of-pocket-for-supplies-projects-and-field-trips.html.

Shields, P. M., Humphrey, D. C., Wechsler, M. E., Riehl, L. M., Tiffany-Morales, J., Woodworth, K., Young, V. M., & Price, T. (2001). *The status of the teaching profession 2001.* Santa Cruz, CA: Center for the Future of Teaching and Learning. Retrieved January 24, 2014, from: www.cftl.org/documents/2001reports/completereport.pdf.

Skrla, L., Scheurich, J. J., García, J., & Nolly, G. (2004). Equity audits: A practical leadership tool for developing equitable and excellent schools. *Educational Administration Quarterly, 40,* 133–161.

Smith, T. M., & Ingersoll, R. M. (2004). What are the effects of induction and mentoring on beginning teacher turnover? *American Educational Research Journal, 41,* 681–714.

Starkes, T. (2013, September 23). The other dropout problem in urban schools. *American Thinker.* Retrieved January 27, 2014, from: www.americanthinker.com/2013/09/the_other_dropout_problem_in_urban_schools.html.

Sunderman, G. L., & Kim, J. (2005). *Teacher quality: Equalizing educational opportunities and outcomes.* Cambridge, MA: Civil Rights Project at Harvard University. Retrieved November 2, 2013, from: files.eric.ed.gov/fulltext/ED489184.pdf.

Tenney, G. (2013, January 10). Obama pal Bill Ayers calls Teach for America "a fraud." *FoxNews.com.* Retrieved February 24, 2014, from: www.foxnews.com/us/2013/01/bill-ayers-chicago-union-boss-rip-teach-for-america/print.

Theoharis, G. (2007). Social justice educational leaders and resistance: Toward a theory of social justice leadership. *Educational Administration Quarterly, 43,* 222–258.

Tyack, D. B. (1974). *The one best system: A history of American urban education.* Cambridge, MA: Harvard University Press.

Valencia, R. R. (2010). *Dismantling contemporary deficit thinking: Educational thought and practice.* Critical Educator Series. New York: Routledge.

Valencia, R. R. (2011). The plight of Chicano students: An overview of schooling conditions and outcomes. In R. R. Valencia (Ed.), *Chicano school failure and success: Past, present, and future* (3rd ed., pp. 3–41). New York: Routledge.

Valencia, R. R., & Aburto, S. (1991a). Competency testing and Latino student access to the teaching profession: An overview of issues. In G. D. Keller, J. Deneen, & R.

Magallán (Eds.). *Assessment and access: Hispanics in higher education* (pp. 169–96). Albany: State University of New York Press.

Valencia, R. R., & Aburto, S. (1991b). Research directions and practical strategies in teacher testing and assessment: Implications for improving Latino access to teaching. In G. D. Keller, J. Deneen, & R. Magallán (Eds.), *Assessment and access: Hispanics in higher education* (pp. 197–234). Albany: State University of New York Press.

Valencia, R. R., & Bernal, E. M. (Eds.). (2000). The Texas Assessment of Academic Skills (TAAS) case: Perspectives of plaintiffs' experts [Special issue]. *Hispanic Journal of Behavioral Sciences, 22*(4).

Valencia, R. R., & Pearl, A. (2010). Conclusion: (A) The bankruptcy of the standard-based school reform movement; (B) Toward the construction of meaningful school reform: Democratic education. In R. R. Valencia, *Dismantling contemporary deficit thinking: Educational thought and practice* (pp. 148–158). Critical Educator Series. New York: Routledge.

Valencia, R. R., & Pearl, A. (2011). Conclusion: Toward school reform. In R. R. Valencia (Ed.), *Chicano school failure and success: Past, present, and future* (3rd ed., pp. 273–286). New York: Routledge.

Valencia, R. R., & Suzuki, L. A. (2001). *Intelligence testing and minority students: Foundations, performance factors, and assessment issues.* Series on Racial and Ethnic Minority Psychology. Thousand Oaks, CA: Sage.

Valencia, R. R., & Villarreal, B. J. (2005). Texas' second wave of high-stakes testing: Anti-social promotion legislation, grade retention, and adverse impact on minorities. In A. Valenzuela (Ed.), *Leaving children behind: How "Texas style" accountability fails Latino youth* (pp. 113–152). Albany: State University of New York Press.

Villar, A., & Strong, M. (2007). Is mentoring worth the money? A benefit-cost analysis and five-year rate of return of a comprehensive mentoring program for beginning teachers. *ERS Spectrum, 25,* 1–17.

Villegas, A. M., & Clewell, B. C. (1998). Increasing teacher diversity by tapping the paraprofessional pool. *Theory into Practice, 37,* 121–130.

Villegas, A. M., & Lucas, T. (2004). Diversifying the teacher workforce: A retrospective and prospective analysis. *Yearbook of the National Society for the Study of Education, 103,* 70–104.

The Wallace Foundation. (2013). *The school principal as leader: Guiding schools to better teaching and learning.* New York: Author. Retrieved February 27, 2014, from: www.wallacefoundation.org/knowledge-center/schoolleadership-effectiveprincipalleadership/The-School-Principal-as-Leader-Guiding-Schools-to-Better-Teaching-and-Learning-2nd-Ed.pdf.

Walsh, K., & Tracy, C. O. (2004). *Increasing the odds: How good policies can yield better teachers.* Washington, DC: National Council on Teacher Quality. Retrieved January 10, 2014, from: www.nctq.org/nctq/images/nctq-io.pdf.

Waters, T., Marzano, R. J., & McNulty, B. (2003). *Balanced leadership: What 30 years of research tells us about the effect of leadership on student achievement.* Denver, CO: Mid-Continent Research for Education and Learning. Retrieved February 27, 2014, from: www.ctc.ca.gov/educator-prep/ASC/5031RR_BalancedLeadership.pdf.

Weingarten, R. (2010). Five foundations for school success. In K. Weber (Ed.), *Waiting for Superman: How we can save America's failing public schools* (pp. 143–161). New York: PublicAffairs.

Zarate, M. E., Sáenz, V. B., & Oseguera, L. (2011). Supporting the participation and success of Chicanos in higher education. In R. R. Valencia (Ed.), *Chicano school failure and success: Past, present, and future* (3rd ed., pp. 120–140). New York: Routledge.

6

LANGUAGE SUPPRESSION AND CULTURAL EXCLUSION

Considering that language is a vehicle of culture, these two constructions of humankind are inextricably linked. In the context of the education of students of color, language suppression vis-à-vis English learners (ELs)—especially Mexican American and other Latino/Latina students—has been quite oppressive, historically, and even in contemporary times. In regard to cultural exclusion in the school curriculum, students of color have also experienced consistent injustice by acts of omission (e.g., exclusion of the role of women in a group's struggle for equality) and commission (e.g., negative stereotypes) when it comes to the history, plight, and achievements of their respective racial/ethnic groups. In the text that follows, the guiding question is: How do language suppression and cultural exclusion (another mesolevel factor in the Three-M Systemic Model) exacerbate the achievement gulf between students of color and their White peers? I also focus on the converse of this issue—namely, how bilingual education and the curricular infusion of multicultural knowledge can improve the academic achievement of students of color.

The present chapter is organized around the following topics: (a) the value of bilingualism and multicultural education; (b) students of color and the school curriculum: acts of omission and commission; (c) early language suppression and cultural exclusion: Mexican American students as a case in point; (d) the legal struggle for bilingual education; (e) the politics of demagogic anti-bilingualism and the campaign to eradicate bilingual education; (f) racism and cultural hegemony in Arizona public schools: the case of House Bill 2281; and (g) systemic transformations.

The Value of Bilingualism and Multicultural Education

Prior to the 1960s, many researchers and educators held a common misconception that bilingualism had negative consequences on cognitive development.[1] The literature that supported this fallacy can be traced to the turn of the century, when social concerns arose in the U.S. about the intellectual abilities of the "new" immigrants who were bilingual or were developing bilingually (Hakuta, 1986, 1990).[2]

About 3 decades ago, in his review of germane empirical studies, Hakuta (1986, 1987) notes that findings of over 30 investigations in different cultural settings confirmed the cognitive superiority of bilingual participants. More recent empirical studies and literature reviews report that bilinguals, compared to monolinguals, demonstrate advantages in various areas of cognition, including executive control, memory, metalinguistic awareness, creativity, visual-spatial skills, and intellectual performance (e.g., Bialystok, 2001, 2011; Gathercole et al., 2010; Marian & Shook, 2012).

In regard to multicultural education, a voluminous body of publications exists (e.g., Au, 2009; Banks & Banks, 2010; Grant & Chapman, 2008; Ramsey, 2004). Typically, these works cover the purposes, nature, misconceptions, and benefits of multicultural education. One of the most widely utilized models of conceptualizing multicultural education is presented by Banks (1993). His five dimensions are coined as follows: (a) content integration, (b) the knowledge construction process, (c) prejudice reduction, (d) an equity pedagogy, and (e) empowering school culture and social structure.[3]

In her review of pertinent literature, Zirkel (2008) seeks to address a question that is particularly applicable to the present chapter: In the context of Banks's (1993) model, are multicultural educational practices effective in improving the academic achievement of students of color and enhancing intergroup relations in the school setting? Regarding academic outcomes (to which I confine my discussion), Zirkel concludes—based on a small number of studies—that multicultural educational practices can improve the learning and engagement, and hence achievement, of students of color. She also reports an unanticipated finding: Improved academic performance was found to have considerable external validity—that is, across SES, achievement level, and race/ethnicity. The question remains, however, what might be a plausible hypothesis to explain why multicultural educational strategies assist in promoting academic improvement of students of color. Zirkel suggests that the answer may be found in the literature on the racial/ethnic identity development of students of color. These studies, she notes, consistently find that students of color who have solid and positive identities as racial/ethnic beings tend to have higher levels of academic achievement, educational aspirations, academic self-assurance, and engagement in school work.[4] To this hypothesis, I would add that a fruitful area to explore is confluent education, which refers to the blending of affective and cognitive components and their fused role in learning (Brown, 1971).

Students of Color and Cultural Knowledge in the School Curriculum: Acts of Omission and Commission

Given that multicultural educational strategies have been demonstrated to improve the academic achievement of students of color, as well as enhance intergroup relationships (see review by Zirkel, 2008), it is ironic that such practices are given only tokenistic attention in U.S. public schools (Banks, 2010). In the context of CRT, this is not at all surprising when viewed through the lens of power, the nature of knowledge, and White privilege. Scholars such as Michael Apple (1990, 1993a, 1993b) remind us that curricular knowledge (especially of a cultural nature) is a heavily contested arena. Knowledge, he notes, never enters the curriculum as a neutral collection of information to be dispersed to students. Rather, knowledge comes about via a "selective tradition," reflecting the values, experiences, tensions, and politics of those in power. In this fashion, the dominant group's knowledge becomes legitimized as the "official knowledge," while the knowledge of marginalized peoples is deemed unimportant, although such groups have made valuable contributions.

For example, Carter G. Woodson, considered the "Father of Black History" (Banks, 1996), wrote at length of the exclusion (except for negative stereotypes) of Blacks from the school curriculum. In his 1933 classic book, *The Mis-Education of the Negro,* he notes that one could study status quo history as presented in elementary school through college, and never would learn anything about Africa—except in a negative context. Woodson further comments that one would never become aware that "Africans first domesticated the sheep, goat, and cow, developed the idea of trial by jury, produced the first stringed instruments, and gave the world its greatest boon in the discovery of iron" (p. 21). He continues, making a piercing point about the oppressive impact that curricular knowledge can have: "If you can control a man's thinking you do not have to worry about his action. When you determine what a man shall think you do not have to concern yourself about what he will do" (p. 84).

Historically, individuals and advocacy organizations of color did not stand idly by while these curricular acts of omission and commission were being perpetrated. Contemporary multicultural education can be traced to the protests of these individuals and groups who vigorously complained about the treatment of people of color in the school curriculum. In his treatise of the subject, Zimmerman (2004) traces this agitation for "intergroup education," as it was called then, from the late 1920s to the late 1960s.[5] One highlight he discusses is what transpired in June 1944 in New York City. African American leaders met with public school officials to share their concern of how Blacks were being treated in history and other textbooks. Zimmerman (2004) notes that in music books, Blacks were referred to as "darkeys"; books of literature called them "coons" and "Sambo"; even geography textbooks underscored the "barbarity" of Africa. He also notes that the superintendent of New York City Schools, John E. Wade, had written a textbook extolling the Ku Klux Klan.

Concerns continue unabatedly about the omission and commission of cultural knowledge applicable to students of color. A recent example of a study is a textual analysis by Vasquez Heilig, Brown, and Brown (2012). The authors examine the 11th-grade U.S. history social studies standards as set by the 2010 revision of the Texas Essential Knowledge and Skills (TEKS), a blueprint designed to guide teachers on what to teach, and what knowledge pupils should have.[6] Drawing from CRT, Vasquez Heilig et al. (2012) explore how the standards address concerns regarding groups of color and the subjects of race and racism. Specifically, the authors coded each of the 165 standards based on whether it dealt with the variables of racial conflict, racial identity, and race. Key among the findings are: (a) there is a very limited handling of the participation and roles of people of color—especially American Indians and Asian Americans—in the historical narrative of the U.S.; (b) although race and racism are recognized in the history of the U.S., they are masked and distorted; and (c) the actual terms of "race" and "racism" were used sparsely. Vasquez Heilig et al. conclude that although the U.S. history social studies standards of TEKS have the appearance of satisfactorily addressing race, the standards concomitantly marginalize people of color. As such, these nuances lead to an "illusion of inclusion," which is the main title of the article by Vasquez Heilig et al.

Early Language Suppression and Cultural Exclusion: Mexican American Students as a Case in Point

At this juncture, I would like to cover how language was regularly suppressed in the schools and how cultural knowledge was routinely excluded in the curriculum. As a case in point, I frame these issues around Mexican American students in the Southwest. This narrative must begin by discussing an event that played a major role in shaping the future of Mexican Americans—the Mexican American War of 1846–1848. A key actor in the war was U.S. president James Knox Polk, who fervently believed in Manifest Destiny, the ideology that it was God's plan to dominate people of color and to expand westward by using any tactics necessary (Greenberg, 2012). Part of this bellicose expansionism was a U.S. plan to invade Mexico. Greenberg notes that Polk's conception of justice was undoubtedly molded by his background as a slave master. Also, she writes that Polk's attitude toward Mexico reeked of racism and imperialistic aggression: "Mexico, inferior in both race and power, must necessarily bend to the will of its neighbor" (p. 95).

On February 2, 1848, the Treaty of Guadalupe Hidalgo was signed and brought about an end to the Mexican American War and the annexation, by conquest, of over 500,000 square miles of territory by the U.S.[7] The eventual seizure of half of Mexico included present-day California, Nevada, and Utah, as well as sections of Arizona, Colorado, Kansas, New Mexico, Oklahoma, and Texas (Greenberg, 2012). In the field of Mexican American Studies, 1848 has become a far-reaching point of demarcation, as Mexicans who chose to stay in the U.S. became a conquered people. The treaty signaled the beginning of persistent racial prejudice and discrimination.[8] In the ensuing decades, Mexican Americans faced early segregation in, or exclusion from, for example, movie theaters, public accommodations (e.g., swimming pools), and restaurants (Acuña,

2007; Martínez, 1994), as well as housing (Ramos, 2001), juries (García, 2009), the labor market (Foley, 1997), and schools (Valencia, 2008). For many Mexican Americans, segregation spanned from the "cradle to the grave." There was forced segregation in maternity wards[9] and separate cemeteries for Mexican Americans and Whites (Carroll, 2003).

Historically, school officials forced Mexican American monolingual Spanish-speaking children to face the ubiquitous situation of "sink or swim": Learn English to survive, and if you do not, you will fail in school. Educators perceived the Mexican American Spanish-speaker as a "problem" to be fixed (González, 1990; Manuel, 1930). Hence, the exclusive teaching of English was the prevailing medium of instruction for beginners. This deficit thinking orientation of school officials and teachers affected a substantial proportion of the Mexican American student population. For example, Manuel estimates that about 90% of Tejano children who entered public schools for the first time in the 1920s did not have receptive and expressive skills in English.

Exclusion of the Spanish language in Southwestern schools persisted well into the 1960s. Not only did the schools eliminate Spanish as a means of instruction, but some officials in the Southwest also institutionalized "No Spanish" rules regarding conversational use of Spanish between students in classes and on school grounds (U.S. Commission on Civil Rights, 1972). Violations of the "No Spanish" rule often resulted in punishment of the transgressors. One form of penalty for violating the "No Spanish" rule was mandated "Spanish detention" classes (see Valencia, 2008, pp. 157–158).

In regard to cultural exclusion, many Mexican American students in the Southwest commonly endured Americanization programs and the omission of Mexican culture as an area of curricular study (González, 1990; San Miguel & Valencia, 1998). In the early part of the 20th century, the curriculum remained culturally subtractive due to the continuing assimilationist ideology and nativism. Instructional materials and school textbooks, for the most part, proceeded to either omit or distort the Mexican cultural heritage. School officials intended these oppressive policies to ensure the hegemony of Anglo culture. Such exclusion of curricular cultural knowledge of Mexican Americans continued for decades (U.S. Commission on Civil Rights, 1972).

In sum, Mexican American students have long experienced the oppressive practices of language suppression and cultural exclusion. In regard to the latter, contemporary studies show that Mexican American pupils still endure acts of omission and commission vis-à-vis their culture (e.g., Mintz, 2009; Ndura, 2004). With respect to language suppression, a later section of this chapter will discuss the systematic campaign to eradicate bilingual education. Yet, we should also be mindful that *individual* acts of language suppression still occur. One case involves the Turner Unified School District (TUSD) No. 202, located in Kansas City, Kansas. The TUSD, which states on its website that it "is a district that celebrates diversity,"[10] is racially/ethnically heterogeneous. In AY 2010–2011, the

K-12 enrollment of 4,094 was made up of 33.8% Latino/Latina, 10.5% Black, and 55.7% White and other students (Bent, 2012, p. 345). Included in the nine schools of the TUSD is Endeavor Alternative School (hereafter Endeavor), which is designed to help students earn their high school diploma via "non-traditional pathways."[11] On November 28, 2005, a Mexican American pupil at Endeavor, which had a rule that Spanish was not to be spoken on the school premises, was admonished to refrain from speaking Spanish during the lunch break. During the school period that followed, a teacher told the same student to stop speaking Spanish in the hallway. The student was sent to the office of the principal, who, in turn, suspended the youngster for violating the no-Spanish rule. Allegedly, the Endeavor principal told the boy, "If you want to speak Spanish, go back to Mexico" (Bent, p. 346). Subsequently, the boy's father, Lornzo E. Rubio, sued several teachers, the principal, school board members, and other parties.[12] The plaintiffs' claims were based on 14th Amendment and Title VI violations.[13] The federal court judge ruled for the defendants, opining that the teachers and principal had "decision-making" but *not* "policymaking" authority. Thus, the school district could not be held legally responsible. In sum, the judge ruled that the teachers and principal were exercising their discretion, and thus had qualified immunity (Bent).

Another example of recent language suppression is what transpired in Helpstead Independent School District, located about 50 miles northeast of Houston, Texas. This small district, which has a slight majority of Mexican American and other Latino/Latina students, has one middle school. On November 12, 2013, Hempstead Middle School principal Amy Lacey announced, over the school intercom, that students were prohibited from speaking Spanish, effective forthwith, on the campus. First placed on administrative leave in December 2013 for her actions, the school board decided on March 17, 2014, that her contract would not be renewed at the end of AY 2013–2014 (Gray, 2014).

The Legal Struggle for Bilingual Education

A number of catalysts fueled the campaign for bilingual education (e.g., the seminal Coral Way bilingual education experience in Dade County, Florida, in 1963; the emerging Chicano/Chicana movement of the late 1960s) (San Miguel, 2004; Valencia, 2008, chapter 4). These and other events eventually led to Congress passing the Bilingual Education Act (BEA) in 1967 and President Lyndon B. Johnson signing it into law in January 1968.[14] Notwithstanding this monumental political victory by bilingual education advocates in getting the BEA passed, the law suffered from a number of debilitating features—namely, being underfunded, categorical in nature and compensatory in intent, open-ended, ambiguous, and voluntary (San Miguel, 2004).[15] This last concern, the voluntary nature of programmatic participation, proved to be a key factor in triggering litigation during the early years of the 1968 BEA.

Considering that participation in the nascent federally sponsored bilingual education programs was voluntary, coupled with the paucity of such curricula in public schools, it was not unexpected that stakeholders would initiate lawsuits for the right to have bilingual education. The early legal struggle for bilingual education was a multiethnic undertaking. Chinese Americans initiated the landmark *Lau v. Nichols* (1974) case, and Puerto Ricans filed *Aspira of New York v. Board of Education of the City of New York* (1974) and *Rios v. Read* (1978).[16] In sheer quantity of lawsuits, however, Mexican Americans have been the torch-bearers in bilingual education litigation. In Valencia (2008, chapter 4), I discuss eight cases that Mexican American plaintiffs brought forth from 1972 to 1989 in their attempt to gain and maintain access to bilingual education.[17] Regarding legal strategies, the counsel for plaintiffs in each of the lawsuits typically based their complaint on violations of (a) due process and equal protection rights guaranteed by the 14th Amendment and (b) statutory rights under Title VI of the 1964 Civil Rights Act.[18]

The high-water mark of this corpus of lawsuits is *Castañeda v. Pickard* (1981), filed by Mexican Americans in 1978 in Raymondville, Texas, located in the lower Rio Grande Valley. In *Castañeda,* plaintiffs based their complaint, in part, on the Equal Educational Opportunity Act (EEOA) of 1974 (20 U.S.C. §1703[f]), in which the failure of school districts "to take *appropriate action* [italics added] to overcome language barriers" is considered an unlawful educational practice. The problem with the "appropriate action" requirement of the EEOA is that Congress did not specify what constitutes the phrase's mandate. As such, the courts differed, on a case-by-case basis, in their understanding of what is meant by "appropriate action" (Malakoff & Hakuta, 1990). To bring clarity to the issue, the Fifth Circuit in *Castañeda* then proceeded to devise a set of criteria that a federal court should consider if a school district's language-remediation program is challenged under §1703(f) of the EEOA. The threefold set of responsibilities—commonly referred to as the "*Castañeda* standard"—can be compressed as follows: the school district's language-remediation program (a) must be based on sound educational theory, recognized by experts; (b) must be effectively implemented with the necessary practices, resources, and personnel; and (c) must demonstrate, after a sufficient time for implementation, an effective reduction of language barriers. To sum, the *Castañeda* standard has become the most notable legal expression for the language rights of Mexican American ELs and other EL students.

The Politics of Anti-Bilingualism and the Demagogic Campaign to Eradicate Bilingual Education

Redolent of the nativistic assaults on language minorities and immigrants in the 1920s, particularly those who spoke Spanish, a backlash occurred in the late 1970s and early 1980s against the passage of the 1968 BEA (Wiley & Wright, 2004). One major development that helped fuel anti-bilingualism transpired on August 13,

1982, when Senator Samuel I. Hayakawa (R-CA) introduced an amendment to the U.S. Constitution in an attempt to make English recognized as the "official language" of the country. In his floor speech to the Senate, speaking in favor of his bill, he said, "Language is a unifying instrument which binds people together. When people speak one language they become as one, they become a society."[19] Upon leaving the Senate in 1983, Hayakawa joined with John Tanton to establish U.S. English, an organization that is devoted to "preserving the unifying role of the English language in the United States."[20] According to the Southern Poverty Law Center, which tracks the activities of hate groups and is dedicated to social justice,[21] Tanton has been linked to White nationalism, restrictive immigration policies, and eugenics (Beirich, 2009). Although U.S. English was not successful in getting a constitutional amendment to make English the official language of the nation, the movement prevailed at the state level. By the late 1990s, 23 states had passed laws requiring English as the recognized language (Crawford, 2000).

The English-only movement gained momentum in the 1980s and through the 1990s, and its increasing antipathy toward bilingualism set its eyes on a new target—bilingual education. Notwithstanding the grueling litigative and legislative victories Chinese Americans, Mexican Americans, and Puerto Ricans have made in their quest for bilingual education, several states experienced grave setbacks. On June 2, 1998, California voters passed Proposition 227 ("English for the Children" initiative) with a margin of 61% "yes" to 39% "no," and 30 years of bilingual education came to an end in the state (Cline, Nechochea, & Rios, 2004; Johnson & Martínez, 2000). Ironically, Proposition 227—which was a direct attempt to eradicate bilingual education—passed on the sesquicentennial of the Treaty of Guadalupe Hidalgo.

On the heels of the approval of Proposition 227, practically identical but somewhat stricter referenda to end bilingual education were passed in Arizona (Proposition 203) and Massachusetts (Question 2) by very similar margins (García, Wiese, & Cuéllar, 2011).[22] The intent of these restrictive language laws was to forbid the use of the mother tongue in the teaching of ELs. Prescribed instruction for these students would be Structured English Immersion (SEI) programs (Gándara et al., 2010). The leader behind these three successful plebiscites was a wealthy man named Ron Unz, who was trained as a theoretical physicist, ran unsuccessfully for California governor in 1994, and was publisher of *The American Conservative*.[23] Critics of this trinity of restrictive language policies assert that they erroneously blame ineffective bilingual education programs for the limited school success of ELs, ignore the research on how ELs acquire a second language, and incorrectly argue that bilingual education is opposed to the learning of English (Wiley & Wright, 2004). CRT can also inform us of a motive behind these restrictive language referenda. Some fault-finders of the initiatives maintain they are racially discriminatory. In regard to Proposition 227, for example, legal scholars Kevin R. Johnson and George A. Martínez claim that there is a "core racial motivation behind the law's enactment" (p. 1230).

The question most germane to this chapter and to the present book on students of color and TAG is: What have been the consequences of Proposition 227, Proposition 203, and Question 2 for the academic achievement of ELs? Fortunately, there are some data to address this most important query, which are comprehensively presented in the various chapters in Gándara and Hopkins's (2010) edited volume. In the interest of space, I only briefly note the key findings of these investigations:

1. *California.* Following the implementation of Proposition 227, Wentworth, Pelligrin, Thompson, and Hakuta (2010) compared achievement data (California Standards Test) from 2003 to 2007 for ELs and their English-only (EO) peers. The authors' primary conclusion is that present and former ELs are not performing at the same achievement levels in comparison to their counterparts who started school already knowing the English language.

2. *Arizona.* In a novel approach in studying the impact question, researchers Mahoney, MacSwan, Haladyna, and García (2010) contextualize their investigation by asking whether Proposition 203 met the "third prong" of the *Castaneda* standard—the requirement that a language-remediation program must demonstrate an effective reduction in language barriers for ELs. Mahoney et al. (2010) examined the SAT-9 scores of ELs who eventually were transitioned from SEI to mainstream EO instruction, and the authors report that the exited ELs suffer an unceasing and strong gap in achievement when compared to their EO peers. Thus, Mahoney et al. conclude that Proposition 203 fails to meet the effectiveness tine of the *Castaneda* standard.

3. *Massachusetts.* In their study, investigators Uriarte, Tung, Lavan, and Diez (2010) focused on Boston Public Schools. The authors used achievement data (Massachusetts Comprehensive Assessment Systems) from 2003 to 2006 for ELs and native English speakers. Uriarte et al. (2010) find that achievement gaps widened between the two groups of students, with the native English speakers performing at higher levels.

To sum, the findings across three states are strikingly similar, and thus lead to a major conclusion: The draconian trinity of Proposition 227, Proposition 203, and Question 2 has had negative consequences for the academic achievement of ELs. This is not surprising considering that these restrictive language policies are based on demagoguery rather than scientific research.

Racism and Cultural Hegemony in Arizona Public Schools: The Case of House Bill 2281

What transpired in January 2010 in Tucson, Arizona, constitutes Exhibit A in contemporary cultural hegemony and flagrant oppression against Mexican American students. To understand this ordeal, it is useful to go back to 2002. At the time, Augustine Romero—current director of Multicultural Student Services of the Tucson Unified School District (TUSD)—was appointed by the district's deputy superintendent, Becky Montano, to serve as director of Mexican American Studies (MAS). The program, which was open to all students, largely focused on literature, art, and history through the experiences of Mexican Americans, alongside state-mandated curricula.[24] The method of instruction incorporated, for example, an asset-based perspective of students (i.e., a rejection of deficit thinking), the promotion of higher-order thinking, Socratic dialogue, and the real-world experiences of Mexican Americans.[25]

On April 3, 2006, a development occurred that would begin to place the MAS program under a politically primed, focused scrutiny. It was the conclusion of Cesar Chávez week, which was sponsored by the Southern Arizona Cesar Chávez Holiday Coalition. On the last day of the event, the MAS program had the honor of serving as host for one of the guest speakers, Dolores Huerta, who is a labor leader, civil rights activist, and cofounder (with Chávez) of the United Farm Workers. Shortly into her speech at an assembly at Tucson High Magnet School (THMS), Huerta said, "Republicans hate Latinos" (Romero, 2011–2012). Her claim for the assertion, she noted, was based on the number of anti-Latino/Latina or anti-immigrant bills Republicans had sponsored (Sagara, 2006). In the audience at the high school was one student, head of the Teenage Republicans Club, who stated she was offended by the "hate speak" (Sagara). Huerta's words swiftly garnered the attention of the national media, and very importantly, the ear of the state superintendent of public instruction, Tom Horne, a Republican (Nevarez, 2010). On May 12, 2006, Horne dispatched his deputy superintendent, Margaret García-Dugan, to THMS, where she gave a damage control speech to an assembly of students. She said, in part, "I, a Republican Latina, definitely do not hate Latinos. To do so would make me hate myself, my family, and many of my friends. That is absurd."[26] Many students at the assembly, frustrated because they were not permitted to ask García-Dugan questions, rose to their feet in unison, and with taped mouths, more than 200 pupils walked out of the auditorium (Herreras, 2011).

The walkout by the students at García-Dugan's May 12, 2006, presentation triggered, in part, the beginning of Horne's nearly 4-year crusade to ban MAS at THMS. On June 11, 2007, he managed to get published "An Open Letter to the Citizens of Tucson" in a Tucson newspaper.[27] The letter, typed on his official State of Arizona Department of Education (ADE) letterhead, is directed to citizens of "all mainstream political ideologies" (Horne, 2007, p. 1). In the very first line of the missive, without restraint, Horne asserts, "The TUSD Ethnic Studies Program Should Be Terminated" (p. 1). He claims that the MAS program "teaches a kind of destructive ethnic chauvinism" (p. 2) that the local citizens should no longer permit.

In 2008, Horne attempted, unsuccessfully, to try to get ethnic studies banned via Senate Bill (SB) 1108. In 2009, he tried again with SB 1069, but the bill died on the legislative floor (Ginwright & Cammarota, 2011). Finally, in 2010 Horne assembled House Bill (HB) 2281, a third attempt to get a law that banned ethnic studies. It needs to be underscored, however, that although the three proposals were framed in terms of race neutrality, the efforts by Horne were clearly design to target the MAS program at THMS—given that the TUSD was the *sole* district in Arizona that housed an ethnic studies program (Power & Williams, 2012; Romero, 2011–2012). Horne's long campaign to ban the MAS program at THMS finally succeeded in 2010 when HB passed on April 28, was signed into law by Governor Jan Brewer on May 11, and became effective on December 31.[28] The most controversial part of the four-page bill is Arizona Revised Statute (A.R.S.) §15–112 (A), which reads as follows:

> A. A SCHOOL DISTRICT OR CHARTER SCHOOL IN THIS STATE SHALL NOT INCLUDE IN ITS PROGRAM OF INSTRUCTION ANY COURSES OR CLASSES THAT INCLUDE ANY OF THE FOLLOWING:
> 1. PROMOTE THE OVERTHROW OF THE UNITED STATES GOVERNMENT.
> 2. PROMOTE RESENTMENT TOWARD A RACE OR CLASS OF PEOPLE.
> 3. ARE DESIGNED PRIMARILY FOR PUPILS OF A PARTICULAR ETHNIC GROUP.
> 4. ADVOCATE ETHNIC SOLIDARITY OF THE TREATMENT OF PUPILS INSTEAD OF PUPILS AS INDIVIDUALS. (Arizona State Legislature, 2010, p. 1)

On December 30, 2010—one day before HB 2281 was set to go into effect, and one day before he was scheduled to begin his new job as Arizona attorney general—Horne found the MAS courses in the TUSD were violative of A.R.S §15–112(A) and gave the district 60 days to remove the course, or 10% of its budgetary allotment would be withheld.[29] John Huppenthal, the new state superintendent of public instruction, assumed his office on January 4, 2011, and soon after released a press statement noting that he supports Horne's finding of the violation. Huppenthal, however, did not enforce the ruling. Rather, he retained an independent consultant corporation, Cambrium Learning, for a fee of $110,000 to undertake an audit of the TUSD MAS programs.[30] The firm's task was threefold: (a) determine whether MAS was in compliance with A.R.S. §15–112(A), (b) consider whether the classes and curriculum of MAS were adequately aligned with the standards adopted by the State Board of Education, and (c) evaluate whether the design of the MAS programs helped to improve student achievement.[31]

The findings by Cambrium Learning (2011) were, overall, very positive regarding the MAS Department. With respect to whether MAS complies with the four prongs of A.R.S. §15–112(A), the report concludes it does indeed. That is, MAS does *not* (a) promote the overthrow of the U.S. government, (b) engender resentment toward a particular race or class of people, (c) have a curriculum primarily for students of a particular ethnicity, or (d) advocate ethnic solidarity over students as individuals. Moreover, the report at times speaks in glowing terms of the MAS. For example, "No observable evidence exists that instruction within the Mexican American Studies Department promotes resentment towards a race or class of people. *The auditors observed the opposite* [italics added], as students are taught to be accepting of multiple ethnicities of people" (p. 55). Regarding the question of whether MAS helps in promoting achievement among MAS students, the audit reports that these students, in comparison to a group of students not enrolled in the MAS, had higher passing rates in the state-mandated reading, writing, and mathematics tests—and higher rates of graduating from high school (Cambrium Learning, Appendix).[32] One would think that after such a favorable audit for MAS, this folly would come to an end. Such turn of events, however, was not to be the case. Huppenthal—who during his 2010 campaign for state superintendent of public instruction ran ads claiming he would "stop La Raza" (Avakian, 2012)—rejected the findings of the Cambrium Learning report. He stated that the auditors failed to visit an ample number of MAS classes and evaluate a sufficient amount of curricular materials.[33]

Subsequently, Huppenthal and some of his staff of the ADE reviewed parts of the same information Cambrium Learning evaluated, sans classroom observations and interviews, and came to a very different conclusion—the MAS program did *not* comply with A.R.S. §15–112(A). As such, on June 15, 2011, Huppenthal released a three-page notice concluding that *all* the MAS courses of the TUSD violated A.R.S. §15–112(A), and he gave the district 60 days to comply. Clearly under pressure not to lose up to $15 million of its budget, the Governing Board voted 4 to 1 on January 10, 2012, to end MAS (Planas, 2012; Rodríguez, 2012). Shortly after, a number of books used in the MAS program were banned from further usage. While students were in class, these proscribed books were placed in boxes and sequestered in storage (Bigelow, 2012).[34] Some of the banned books—e.g., *Occupied America: A History of Chicanos* by Rodolfo Acuña (2004); *Pedagogy of the Oppressed* by Paulo Freire (2000); and *Critical Race Theory: An Introduction* by Richard Delgado and Jean Stefancic (2001)—are considered classics.

With so much at danger of being lost, it was not unexpected that the various stakeholders of the TUSD MAS program would initiate a lawsuit. The plaintiffs—who include two TUSD students and 11 elementary, middle, and high school teachers who provide instruction in the TUSD MAS program—filed their motion for a preliminary injunction on November 14, 2011.[35] Plaintiffs in *Acosta v. Huppenthal* assert that HB 2281 violates their rights under the Due Process and Equal Protection Clauses of the 14th Amendment, 1st Amendment (free speech), Title VI, and the EEOA.

On March 8, 2013, Judge A. Wallace Tashima, a Ninth Circuit judge sitting by designation, ruled on *Acosta v. Huppenthal* in the U.S. District Court for the District of Arizona.[36] In his ruling, Judge Tashima notes that although the actions of the defendants may be seen by some as revealing a misconception of the goals and importance of ethnic studies, as well as showing little concern for the plight of minority communities, these issues "do not meet the high threshold needed to establish a constitutional violation" (p. 2). In regard to the alleged violation of the First Amendment, he opines that HB 2281 does not prohibit students' rights to speak openly in the classroom; rather the statute "is directed to school curricula" (p. 8). With respect to the issue of racial discrimination, he holds that the actions of the defendants do not constitute discriminatory intent. In logic that I find obfuscatory, Judge Tashima comments that although some parts of the record may be perceived as "spark[ing] suspicion that the Latino population has been improperly targeted, on the whole, the evidence indicates that Defendants targeted the MAS program, not Latino students, teachers, or community members who supported or participated in the program" (p. 27). This line of reasoning is puzzling. How can the study of a people via a curriculum be separated from the people themselves? One can argue that the intellectual study of an ethnic group and the group itself form an inextricable organic bond. Targeting the MAS via a legislative proscription is no different than crusading to "stop la raza," as Huppenthal voiced in his election campaign when he ran for Arizona state superintendent of public instruction. In any event, the final outcome of the lawsuit brought forth by the plaintiffs is pending. Appellants filed their brief in *Arce v. Huppenthal* to the Ninth Circuit on November 18, 2013.[37]

To sum, the Three-M Systemic Model informs us that language suppression and cultural exclusion are critical dimensions in understanding the school failure of students of color. Conversely, the inclusion of bilingual education and multicultural education has been shown, empirically, to improve the academic achievement of these youngsters. Language and culture are inseparable. Together, they shape the essence of what it means to be a member of an ethnic group. For anti-bilingual ideologues and monoculturalists to exhort the eradication of a group's language and culture in public schools is not only cruel but also counterproductive to the school success of students of color (Nieto, 1996).

Toward Systemic Transformations

It is important to keep in mind that the culture wars in public schools have been, and continue to be, fiercely contested political, moral, and pedagogical issues (Ovando & McLaren, 2000; Zimmerman, 2002). Thus, the quest for justice has to be set in the sphere of political struggle. Power is a highly guarded commodity and never given away. Marginalized, oppressed groups must take power away from those who control it. It is this fundamental reality that guides the systemic suggestions that follow.

1. *Multicultural education curriculum in preservice teacher education.* In light of the frequent acts of omission and commission of curricular cultural knowledge pertinent to students of color, the individual classroom teacher could be a significant change agent in promoting reform. But a major problem exists. Although K-12 public education in the U.S. serves a multiethnic/multiracial student population, with a gradually shrinking White proportion, teachers have very little training in

multicultural education (see, e.g., Celik & Amac, 2012; Levine, 2006; Menchaca, 1996). The national study by Levine is telling. Based on survey responses from over 5,000 alumni from numerous teacher education programs in the U.S., 52% of the respondents said that their programs addressed the "needs of students from diverse backgrounds" in a "moderately well" or "very well" fashion" (p. 32, Table 5). If we are to assume this question is a fairly reliable proxy for having received *some* training in multicultural education, then about one in two teachers are ill-prepared. Levine also reports that only 27% of the alumni state that their teacher education programs provided training in meeting the "needs of English proficient students" (p. 32, Table 5). Menchaca (1996) surveyed 107 master's students enrolled in an educational sociology graduate course—most of whom were aspiring to become teachers—and 81% of the respondents said they received extremely limited or no training in multicultural education while in their teacher education programs.

In sum, the available evidence informs us that multicultural education training must be greatly enhanced in teacher education programs. Such training should not be in the form of brief add-on units in existing courses, as is so often seen (e.g., Gollnick, 1995; Menchaca, 1996). Ideally, preservice teachers should be given the opportunity to become trained in a program in which there is a self-standing foundational course that comprehensively addresses the philosophy, goals, and curricular approaches of multicultural education. Furthermore, as Gollnick notes, such training should also be infused in the overall teacher training program and school reform should be viewed through the lens of cultural diversity and equity.

In addition to the dearth of multicultural education preparation preservice teachers receive, a related concern is the nature of the training prospective teachers are provided. A study by Colón-Muñiz, Brady, and SooHoo (2010) is informative here. Based on their survey and interviews of elementary teachers (who were the authors' former teacher education students), Colón-Muñiz et al. (2010) report that the respondents, in their multicultural education teaching, primarily focused on "heroes and holidays" (p. 98). This confirms findings by Banks (2010). He has identified four approaches for how teachers can integrate multicultural content in the curriculum: (a) "contributions"—level 1; (b) "additive"—level 2; (c) "transformation"—level 3; and (d) "social action"—level 4. In the contributions approach, the teacher makes curricular inserts of specific ethnic heroes/heroines (e.g., Booker T. Washington), holidays (Cinco de Mayo), and distinct cultural elements (e.g., Indian fry bread). By far, this approach is used the most often because it is the easiest to do, and is the safest (e.g., Pocahontas is more likely to be selected for study than Geronimo, the Chiricahua Apache leader who, in part, fought against the U.S. Army). A major limitation of the contributions approach is that it does not allow students to see the comprehensive roles peoples of color have played, and do play, in U.S. society. Rather, their accomplishments are viewed as appendages to the mainstream. As such, people of color and their contributions become trivialized, and this approach has the danger of reinforcing stereotypes. Ideally, in a foundations of multicultural education course in preservice teacher education, the study of Banks's (2010) four approaches for integration of multicultural content would be a centerpiece.

2. *Exploitation of the Castañeda standard.* To review for a moment, this guideline emanates from the landmark bilingual education lawsuit *Castañeda v. Pickard* (1981) in Texas. The Fifth Circuit formulated a set of criteria the federal courts could use to determine if a school district's language-remediation program met the "appropriate action" clause of the EEOA of 1974 (20 U.S.C §1703[f]). Namely, is a school district taking the necessary action to surmount the language barriers of limited-English proficient students? In brief, the three-pronged *Castañeda* standard calls for a language-remediation program to (a) be based on sound theory and research—prong 1; (b) be well implemented—prong 2; and (c) be able to demonstrate a reduction in language barriers—prong 3. The *Castañeda* standard has become so important in the area of ELs' rights that in 1997 the Office of Civil Rights unequivocally adopted the three-prong test to guide the office in its enforcement of Title VI (Losen, 2010).[38]

In light of the significance of the *Castañeda* standard in protecting the language rights of ELs—coupled with the development that studies of student achievement data are now emerging in regard to the impact of restrictive language policies in California, Arizona, and Massachusetts—vigorous challenges to these oppressive laws appear propitious, particularly concerning prong 3. There certainly is a precedent for drawing upon the *Castañeda* standard for questioning the legality of restrictive language laws. One day after California voters passed Proposition 227 in 1998, student plaintiffs and a number of civil rights advocacy groups filed a lawsuit in the U.S. District Court for the Northern District of California, San Francisco Division (*Valeria G. v. Wilson,* 1998). The plaintiffs, who sought a preliminary injunction against the implementation of the proposition, rested their claims, in part, on Title VI and 14th Amendment violations. The main thrust of the plaintiffs' case, however, was that Proposition 227 failed to meet the three-prong test of the *Castañeda* standard. Presiding judge Charles A. Legge ruled against the plaintiffs, determining that a major argument by the defendants was credible—that is, the claims of the plaintiffs are not yet "ripe" for a judge to render a decision. The ripeness requirement focuses on the lawsuit's timing, meaning that it has to be developed enough, and with specificity, so a judicial resolution can be handed down. In regard to the *Castañeda* standard, Judge Legge drew from the ripeness stipulation. Although he said Proposition 227 was based on *a* sound theory (SEI) (prong 1), he could not rule for an injunction because the language-remediation was not yet implemented (prong 2), and therefore no data were available to determine if the SEI program was effective in overcoming language barriers (prong 3). The plaintiffs appealed to the Ninth Circuit, and a three-member panel affirmed the district court's ruling (*Valeria v. Davis,* 2002). Appellants petitioned for a rehearing en banc, but the court denied it (*Valeria v. Davis,* 2003).

Given that Proposition 227 in California, Proposition 203 in Arizona, and Question 2 in Massachusetts have now been implemented for 13 to 17 years, the judicial issue of ripeness should be irrelevant if a new lawsuit is brought forth under the *Castañeda* standard. In a hypothetical case (let us use California), plaintiffs would probably argue, in part, the following: In regard to prong 1 (theory), a 1-year program in which ELs are immersed in English is not based on a sound educational theory. It takes an EL about 5–7 years in a second language learning environment to learn academic language proficiency (Hakuta, 2011). Such abilities, involve, for example, analogical thinking, comprehension-knowledge, vocabulary, and numerical calculation—some of the kinds of skills measured on most state-mandated achievement tests. With respect to effective implementation of the language-remediation program (prong 2), a problem exists regarding the necessary personnel. In AY 2010–2011, ELs in California disproportionately had interns as their teachers, rather than fully qualified instructors (Cody, 2013). This follows the pattern Hakuta (2002) reported a decade earlier. In California schools attended by 40% or more ELs, there were more than 6 times the percentage of non-fully credentialed teachers compared to schools that enrolled fewer than 7.5% ELs. Finally, concerning academic achievement results (prong 3), there are data from California that ELs who were in a SEI program and then transitioned to a mainstream class performed lower on the state-mandated achievement tests in comparison to their non-EL peers (Wentworth et al., 2010). Thus, a skilled civil rights attorney could argue: The *Castañeda* standard criterion that a language-remediation program must demonstrate an effective reduction of language barriers has not been met. To sum, enough time has passed to mount an assertive EEOA challenge to Proposition 227, with the *Castañeda* standard heading the offensive.[39]

3. *Initiation of compliance reviews*. One way to address the issue of curricular acts of omission and commission regarding cultural knowledge that is germane to students of color is to file a formal complaint. A case in point is the request for a compliance review jointly submitted on December 19, 2010, by Gary Bledsoe, president of the Texas National Association of Colored People (NAACP), and Joey D. Cárdenas Jr., Texas state director of the League of United Latin American Citizens (LULAC) (Bledsoe & Cárdenas, 2010). The authors directed their request for a compliance review (hereafter referred to as complaint) to the U.S. Department of Education, Office for Civil Rights, and claimed that the State of Texas, the Texas Education Agency, and the State Board of Education (SBOE) have violated, or will violate, Title VI and the 13th and 14th Amendments. Bledsoe and Cárdenas filed the complaint on behalf of African American and Latino/Latina K-12 public school students in Texas, and the NAACP and LULAC (p. 2). The complaint covers a number of concerns (e.g., curricular changes in textbooks; disparate discipline for students of color; underrepresentation of African American and Latino/Latina students in gifted and talented programs). Here, I confine my discussion to the SBOE's changes in social studies and history textbooks.

In order to understand what prompted the complaint by Bledsoe and Cárdenas (2010), we need to examine the nature of the Texas SBOE, an elected body that, in part, sets curricular standards. In 2010, the SBOE was highly politicized. The 15 members consisted of 10 Republicans and 5 Democrats, and, as such, voting was usually along party lines. Of the 10 Republicans, 7 were considered a "conservative bloc," with 1 of the remaining 3 Republicans joining them on pivotal votes (McKinley, 2010). Voting was also racialized, as the five Democrats were people of color (Bledsoe & Cárdenas, p. 4). Numerous references to racial bias apropos of curricular acts of omission and commission fill the complaint. For example, SBOE minutes (May 20–21, 2010) show that there was a vote of 9–6 against including Dolores Huerta and Henry Cisneros as significant historical individuals to study (p. 16).[40] Another example is that not one "abolitionist" made the "historical figures" list (p. 21). Furthermore, there is no mention in the standards concerning the important role of slavery in the development of the Republic of Texas, and the civil rights movement is provided no context regarding, for instance, lynchings of Tejanos and Blacks, Jim Crow laws, and voter rights violations (p. 22). The SBOE also wanted to have textbook modifications that would rename "slave trade" to "Atlantic triangular trade," which the board eventually dropped as a proposal (Editorial, 2010). On a more general note, the SBOE proposed changing "imperialism" to "expansionism" and "capitalism" to "free enterprise"—thus reflecting the highly politicized views of the majority of the SBOE (Paulson, 2010).

On May 21, 2010, the SBOE voted along party lines (9 to 5) to adopt the new textbook changes for curricular standards for social studies and history. The new guidelines established the foundation for textbooks that millions of Texas schoolchildren will study and material on which they will be tested for years to come. Also, the Texas standards could have national ramifications, as publishers nationally often adapt their books to those used in Texas, one of the largest buyers of textbooks in the nation (Stutz, 2010). SBOE member Mary Helen Berlanga (D-Corpus Christi), said, "I don't think any teacher would accept work like this. They would throw it in the trash. We've done an injustice to the children of this state." Cynthia Dunbar (R-Richmond)—a staunch conservative SBOE member and author of *One Nation Under God: How the Left Is Trying to Erase What Made Us Great* (2008)—commented, "I believe that no one can read the history of our country without realizing that the Good Book and the spirit of the Savior have from the beginning been our guiding geniuses" (Stutz, pp. 1–2). In their complaint, Bledsoe and Cárdenas (2010) sought relief by asking the Office for Civil Rights to undertake an expedient review, and that any resolution to the concerns or litigation that may arise should involve an injunction of the SBOE curricular changes that are deemed racially offensive and historically incorrect. Unfortunately, the OCR replied that school textbooks are not within its jurisdiction, and forwarded the complaint to the OCR office in Dallas for its review, which also determined that textbooks are outside the jurisdiction of the OCR (G. Bledsoe, personal communication, April 7, 2014). This is a puzzling decision by the OCR, given that part of its charge is to investigate civil rights discriminatory violations under Title VI. Does not a teacher calling a Mexican American student, for example, a racial epithet (which has prompted OCR investigations) have the same consequence of omitting and distorting the Mexican American experience from the curriculum? One can argue that they are both acts of racial discrimination.

In closing, the mesolevel factor of language suppression and cultural exclusion of the Three-M Systemic Model has been, and continues to be, a major concern for students of color. The siege on bilingual education, which began in 1998 in California and at the federal level in 2002 (San Miguel, 2004), has taken its toll on myriad ELs—mostly Mexican Americans and Puerto Rican children. What is next? The website of ProEnglish—which promotes itself as "The Nation's Leading English Language Advocates"—shows a list of 11 states, most of which have bilingual education programs.[41] Might some of these states be the next targets for restrictive language policies and meet the same outcome experienced by California, Arizona, and Massachusetts? It would be prudent in these 11 states for a broad spectrum of advocates and stakeholders of bilingual education to mount proactive campaigns to protect their interests.

And the culture wars continue. What transpired in Arizona with HB 2281 and in Texas with the SBOE's politicization of history and social studies textbooks reflects the ascendancy of ultraconservatism into the school curriculum. For those who champion educational equality and anti-racist curriculum for students of color, the political resolve for rights and justice must be stronger than ever. A recent example of such a commitment is what transpired in Texas. A broad coalition of advocacy groups and individual activists have been supporting a stand-alone elective high school course on Mexican American Studies (MAS) in a state where Mexican American and other Latino/Latina students made up the slight majority (51.8%) of the public school enrollment in AY 2013–2014.[42] There are over 200 elective courses in the Texas curriculum (e.g., Web gaming, floral design), but none on ethnic studies (Ahmed, 2014). On April 9, 2014, the Texas SBOE—in a bipartisan vote of 11–3—did *not* approve a stand alone MAS course, but it did allow individual districts to decide themselves whether to provide such a course—as well as elective classes in African American, Asian American, and Native American Studies (Ahmed). Although this is considered a victory by proponents, some critics argue that the SBOE dodged the issue of a stand alone MAS course, and thus school districts may not have an incentive to develop such an MAS course, or as other ethnic studies offerings (Editorial, 2014).

Notes

1. This paragraph builds on, with revisions, Valencia (2008, p. 159). Some remaining parts of the present chapter draw, with revisions, from: Valencia (2008, pp. 155–159, 165, 168, 176, 189–190, 194–195, 361 [note 11], 312 and 363); Valencia (2011, pp. 9–10); San Miguel and Valencia (1998, p. 366).

2. The U.S. experienced its greatest period of immigration from 1830 to 1930. Historians typically divide this century-long era into two periods: the "old" immigration (1830–1882) and the "new" immigration (1882–1930). See Chorover (1979).
3. See Banks (1993) for an explication of the five dimensions.
4. See Zirkel (2008, pp. 1151–1152) for the citations of these studies.
5. For an extended coverage of the curricular culture war dealing with race, religion, and sex education, see Zimmerman (2002). See Brown, Heilig, and Brown (2013) for a discussion of the curricular revision struggle germane to African Americans.
6. See *Texas Essential Knowledge and Skills* (www.tea.state.tx.us/index2.aspx?id=6148).
7. See Griswold del Castillo. *Wars' End: Treaty of Guadalupe Hidalgo.* PBS. Retrieved March 17, 2014, from: www.pbs.org/kera/usmexicanwar/war/wars_end_guadalupe.html.
8. See Acuña (2007); Griswold del Castillo (1990); Menchaca (2001); Perea (2003); Rendón (1971).
9. See *Cisneros v. Corpus Christi Independent School District*, 324 F. Supp. at 613 (S.D. Tex. 1970).
10. See *Welcome to Turner.* Retrieved March 19, 2014, from: www.turnerusd202.org/ .
11. See *About Endeavor High School.* Retrieved March 19, 2014, from: www.turnerusd202.org/page.cfm?p=3443.
12. *Rubio v. Turner Unified School District* No. 202, 453 F. Supp. 2d 1295 (D. Kan. 2006).
13. Congress passed Amendment XIV to the U.S. Constitution on June 13, 1868, and ratified it on July 9, 1868. The Equal Protection Clause is mentioned in Section 1 of the 14th Amendment: "Nor shall any state deprive any person of life, liberty, or property without due process of law; nor deny to any person within its jurisdiction the equal protection of the law." Title VI of the 1964 Civil Rights Act (Public Law 88–352) requires the following: No person in the United States shall, on the ground of race, color, or national origin, be excluded from participation in, be denied the benefits of, or be subjected to discrimination under any program or activity receiving federal financial assistance (42 U.S.C. §2000d).
14. Technically, the BEA emerged as Title VII-Bilingual Education Programs (Public Law 90–247) of the Elementary and Secondary Education Act. For Public Law 9–247, see www.gpo.gov/fdsys/pkg/STATUTE-81/pdf/STATUTE-81-Pg783.pdf.
15. See Valencia (2008, pp. 165–166) for a synopsis of these five concerns.
16. See Valencia (2008, pp. 362–363 [note 29] and pp. 365–366 [note 44]) for a discussion of *Lau,* and Valencia (2008, pp. 362–363 [note 29]) for a discussion of *Aspira* and *Rios.*
17. See Valencia (2008, p. 166, Table 4.1) for a list of the cases.
18. See note 13, this chapter, for an explanation of the rights guaranteed under the 14th Amendment and Title VI.
19. See "Legislation: Sen. Hayakawa." U.S. English. Retrieved March 21, 2014, from: www.us-english.org/view/26.
20. See website for U.S. English Foundation, Inc. at: http://usefoundation.org/.
21. See website for the Southern Poverty Law Center at: splcenter.org/.
22. For other discussions of Proposition 227, Proposition 203, and Question 2, see García et al. (2011); Ryan (2002); Wiley and Wright (2004).
23. See "Summary Biography of Ron Unz." Retrieved March 22, 2014, from: www.ronunz.org/summary-biography/.
24. Plaintiff's Motion for Preliminary Injunction, Acosta v. Huppenthal, Civil Action No. 10–623 at 7 (D. Ariz. November 14, 2011). Retrieved March 24, 2014, from: images.huffingtonpost.com/2011–11–15-EthnicStudiesmotion.pdf.

25. Brief of Appellants, Arce v. Huppenthal, Nos. 13–15657–13–15760 at 7 (9th Cir. November 18, 2013). Retrieved March 24, 2014, from: digitalcommons.law.seattleu.edu/cgi/viewcontent/cgi?article=1000.
26. See "Full Text of Dugan's Speech." *Arizona Daily Star,* May 12, 2006. Retrieved March 24, 2014, from: http://azstarnet.com/news/full-text-of-dugan-s-speech/article_e7b06f08-d7eb-593a-9aea-c2d69ba6f757.html.
27. Hector Tobar (2011), reporter for the *Los Angeles Times,* notes that the letter was published in a Tucson newspaper, but he does not mention it by name—neither could I locate it.
28. See *supra* note 25 at 12–13, this chapter.
29. *Id.* at 13.
30. *Id.* at 14.
31. *Id.*
32. A later, independent study by Cabrera, Milem, and Marx (2012) confirms the Cambrium Learning (2011) findings. Cabrera et al. (2012) report that students in the TUSD MAS program—compared to non-MAS students—had higher academic achievement test scores and graduation rates from high school.
33. See *supra* note 25 at 16, this chapter.
34. *Id.* at 19 (list of seven books banned by TUSD Governing Board).
35. See *supra* note 24, this chapter.
36. Memorandum of Order, Acosta v. Huppenthal, Civil Action No 10–623 (D. Ariz. March 8, 2013). Retrieved March 28, 2014, from: http://018c8b.netso/host.com/Daily/wp-content/uploads/2013/03/Tashima-ruling.pdf.
37. See *supra* note 25, this chapter.
38. See U.S. Commission on Civil Rights (1997) for details.
39. Also, see Losen (2010) and Myhill (2004).
40. Henry Cisneros was the first Latino mayor of a major city (elected in 1981, San Antonio). In 1993, President Clinton appointed him as Secretary of Housing and Urban Development. See "Hispanic Heritage." Cengage Learning. Retrieved March 25, 2014, from: www.gale.cengage.com/free_resources/chh/bio/ cisneros_h.htm.
41. See ProEnglish website at: www.proenglish.org/projects/bilingual-education.html.
42. Texas Education Agency (2014).

References

Acuña, R. F. (2004). *Occupied America: A history of Chicanos* (5th ed.). New York: Longman.

Acuña, R. F. (2007). *Occupied America: A history of Chicanos* (6th ed.). New York: Longman.

Ahmed, A. (2014, April 9). SBOE opts for compromise on Mexican-American Studies. *Texas Tribune.* Retrieved April 16, 2014, from: www.texastribune.org/2014/04/08/activists-support-mexican-american-studies-class-a/.

Apple, M. W. (1990). *Ideology and curriculum* (2nd ed.). New York: Routledge.

Apple, M. W. (1993a). *Official knowledge: Democratic education in a conservative age.* New York: Routledge.

Apple, M. W. (1993b). The politics of official knowledge: Does a national curriculum make sense? *Teachers College Record, 95,* 222–241.

Arizona State Legislature. (2010). *Text of House Bill 2281.* Phoenix, AZ: Author. Retrieved March 23, 2014, from: www.azleg.gov/legtext/49leg/2r/bills/hb2281s.pdf.

Aspira of New York v. Board of Education of the City of New York, Civil Action No. 72–4002 (S.D.N.Y. August 29, 1974), 423 F. Supp. 647 (S.D.N.Y. 1976).

Au, W. (Ed.). (2009). *Rethinking multicultural education: Teaching for racial and cultural justice.* Milwaukee, WI: Rethinking Schools.

Avakian, B. (2012, February 26). Battleground Tucson: The fight for ethnic studies. *Revolution.* Retrieved March 26, 2014, from: www.revcom.us/a/261/tucson_fight_for_ethnic_studies-en.html.

Banks, J. A. (1993). Multicultural education: Historical development, dimensions, and practice. *Review of Research in Education, 19,* 3–49.

Banks, J. A. (2010). Approaches to multicultural curriculum reform. In J. A. Banks & C.A.M. Banks (Eds.), *Multicultural education: Issues and perspectives* (7th ed., pp. 233–256). New York: Wiley.

Banks, J. A., & Banks, C.A.M. (Eds.). (2010). *Multicultural education: Issues and perspectives* (7th ed.). New York: Wiley.

Banks, S. L. (1996). Carter Godwin Woodson. In F. C. Jones-Wilson, C. A. Asbury, M. Okazawa-Rey, D. K. Anderson, S. M. Jacobs, & M. Fultz (Eds.), *Encyclopedia of African-American education* (pp. 523–525). Westport, CT: Greenwood Press.

Beirich, H. (2009, February). *John Tanton and the nativist movement.* Southern Poverty Law Center. Retrieved March 21, 2014, from: www.splcenter.org/publications/the-nativist-lobby-three-faces-of-intolerance/john-tanton-and-the-nativist-movement.

Bent, S. J. (2012). "If you want to speak Spanish, go back to Mexico"?: A First Amendment analysis of English only rules in public schools. *Ohio State Law Journal, 73,* 343–394. Retrieved March 19, 2014, from: moritzlaw.osu.edu/students/groups/oslj/files/2012/05/73.2.Bent_.pdf.

Bialystok, E. (2001). *Bilingualism in development: Language, literacy, and cognition.* New York: Cambridge University Press.

Bialystok, E. (2011). Reshaping the mind: The benefits of bilingualism. *Canadian Journal of Experimental Psychology, 65,* 229–235.

Bigelow, B. (2012, summer). From Johannesburg to Tucson. *Rethinking Schools, 26,* 1–4. Retrieved March 23, 2014, from: www.rethinkingschools.org/archive/26_04/26_04_bigelow.shtml.

Bledsoe, G., & Cárdenas, J. D., Jr. (2010). *Texas state conference of the National Association for the Advancement of Colored People and Texas League of United Latin American Citizens request for compliance review.* Submitted to U.S. Department of Education, Office for Civil Rights. Retrieved April 1, 2014, from: www2.mysanantonio.com/PDFs/ComplianceReview.pdf.

Brown, A. L., Vasquez Heilig, J., & Brown, K. (2013). From segregated, to integrated, to narrowed knowledge. In J. K. Donnor & A. D. Dixson (Eds.), *The resegregation of schools: Education and race in the twenty-first century* (pp. 27–43). New York: Routledge.

Brown, G. I. (1971). *Human teaching for human learning: An introduction to confluent education.* New York: Viking.

Cabrera, N. L., Milem, J. F., & Marx, R. W. (2012). *An empirical analysis of the effects of Mexican American Studies participation on student achievement within Tucson Unified School District.* Tucson: AZ. Report submitted to Special Master Dr. Willis D. Hawley on the Tucson Unified School District Desegregation Case. Retrieved March 27, 2014, from: big.assets.huffingtonpost.com/Mexican-American-Studies_11.14.12.pdf.

Cambrium Learning. (2011). *Curriculum audit of the Mexican American Studies Department, Tucson Unified School District, Tucson, Arizona.* Miami Lakes, FL: Author. Retrieved March

25, 2014, from: www.tucsonweekly.com/images.blogimages/2011/06/16/1308282079-az_masd_audit_final_ 1_pdf.

Carroll, P. (2003). *Felix Longoria's wake: Bereavement, racism, and the rise of Mexican American activism.* Austin: University of Texas Press.

Castañeda v. Pickard, 648 F.2d 989 (5th Cir. 1981), *aff'd,* 781 F.2d 456 (5th Cir. 1986).

Celik, S., & Amac, Z. (2012). Are teacher education programs failing the nation's urban schools? A closer look at pre-service teachers' beliefs about working with inner-city students. *Journal of Multiculturalism in Education, 8,* 1–22. Retrieved March 29, 2014, from: https://www.wtamu.edu/webres/File/journals/MCJ/Volume%208%20Number%201/Celik%20%20Are%20Teacher%20Education%20 Programs%20Failing%20the.

Chorover, S. L. (1979). *From genius to genocide: The meaning of human nature and the power of behavioral control.* Cambridge, MA: MIT Press.

Cline, Z., Necochea, J., & Rios, F. (2004). The tyranny of democracy: Deconstructing the passage of racist propositions. *Journal of Latinos and Education, 3,* 67–85.

Cody, A. (2013, April 12). TFA faces a California showdown over qualifications to teach English learners. *Education Week Teacher.* Retrieved April 1, 2014, from: http://blogs.edweek.org/teachers/living-in-dialogue/2013/04/tfa_faces_a_ california_showdow.html.

Colón-Muñiz, A., Brady, J., & SooHoo, S. (2010). What do graduates have to say about multicultural teacher education. *Issues in Teacher Education,* Spring, 85–108. Retrieved March 29, 2014, from: www1.chapman.edu/ITE/public_html/ITESpringIO/12colonetal.pdf.

Crawford, J. (2000). Anatomy of the English-only movement. In J. Crawford (Ed.), *At war with diversity: U.S. language policy in an age of anxiety* (pp. 4–30). Clevedon, UK: Multilingual Matters.

Delgado, R., & Stefancic, J. (2001). *Critical race theory: An introduction.* New York: New York University Press.

Dunbar, C. (2008). *One nation under God: How the left is trying to erase what made us great.* Oviedo, FL: HigherLife.

Editorial. (2010, May 25). Politicized curriculum in Texas. *New York Times.* Retrieved April 2, 2014, from: www.nytimes.com/2010/05/26/opinion/26wed4.html?_r=0.

Editorial. (2014, April 14). A trumped up controversy. *San Antonio Express-News.* Retrieved April 16, 2014, from: www.mysanantonio.com/default/article/A-trumped-up-controversy-5401783.php.

Equal Educational Opportunity Act, Pub. L. No. (93–380), 88 Stat. 515 (1974).

Foley, N. (1997). *The white scourge: Mexicans, blacks, and poor whites in Texas cotton culture.* Berkeley: University of California Press.

Freire, P. (2000). *Pedagogy of the oppressed.* New York: Continuum.

Gándara, P., & Hopkins, M. (Eds.). (2010). *Forbidden language: English learners and restrictive language policies.* New York: Teachers College Press.

Gándara, P., Losen, D., August, D., Uriarte, M., Gómez, M. C., & Hopkins, M. (2010). Forbidden language: A brief history of U.S. language policy. In P. Gándara & M. Hopkins (Eds.), *Forbidden language: English learners and restrictive language policies* (pp. 20–33). New York: Teachers College Press.

García, E. E., Wiese, A., & Cuéllar, D. (2011). Language, public policy, and schooling: A focus on Chicano English language learners. In R. R. Valencia (Ed.), *Chicano school failure and success: Past, present, and future* (3rd ed., pp. 143–159). New York: Routledge.

García, I. M. (2009). *White but not equal: Mexican Americans, jury discrimination, and the Supreme Court.* Tucson: University of Arizona Press.

Gathercole, V.C.M., Thomas, E. M., Jones, L., Gausch, N. V., Young, N., & Huges, K. (2010). Cognitive effects of bilingualism: Digging deeper for the contributions of language dominance, linguistic knowledge, socio-economic status, and cognitive abilities. *International Journal of Bilingual Education and Bilingualism, 13,* 617–664. Retrieved March 13, 2014, from: http://eric/ed/gov/?id=EJ895097.

Ginwright, S., & Cammarota, J. (2011). Youth organizing in the Wild West: Mobilizing for educational justice in Arizona! *Voices in Urban Education, 30,* 13–21.

Gollnick, D. M. (1995). *National and state initiatives for multicultural education.* (ERIC Document Reproduction Service No. ED 382 698)

González, G. G. (1990). *Chicano education in the era of segregation.* Philadelphia: Balch Institute Press.

Grant, C. A., & Chapman, T. K. (Eds.). (2008). *History of multicultural education* (Vol. 2). New York: Routledge.

Gray, L. (2014, March 18). Principal who told kids not to speak Spanish will lose job. *Houston Chronicle.* Retrieved March 20, 2014, from: www.chron.com/news/houston-texas/article/Principal-who-told-kids-not-to-speak-Spanish-will-5327528.php.

Greenberg, A. S. (2012). *A wicked war: Polk, Clay, Lincoln, and the 1846 U.S. invasion of Mexico.* New York: Alfred A. Knopf.

Griswold del Castillo, R. (1990). *The Treaty of Guadalupe Hidalgo: A legacy of conflict.* Norman: University of Oklahoma Press.

Hakuta, K. (1986). *Mirror of language: The debate on bilingualism.* New York: Basic Books.

Hakuta, K. (1987). Degree of bilingualism and cognitive ability in mainland Puerto Rican children. *Child Development, 58,* 1372–1388.

Hakuta, K. (1990). Language and cognition in bilingual children. In A. M. Padillar, H. F. Fairchild, & C. M. Valadez (Eds.), *Bilingual education: Issues and strategies* (pp. 47–59). Newbury Park, CA: Sage.

Hakuta, K. (2002). *English language learner access to basic educational necessities in California: An analysis of inequities.* Expert report offered in *Williams v. State of California.* Retrieved April 1, 2014, from: www.decentschools.com/expert_reports/hakuta_report.pdf.

Hakuta, K. (2011). Educating language minority students and affirming their equal rights: Research and practical perspectives. *Educational Researcher, 40,* 163–174.

Herreras, M. (2011, November 17). Ethnic studies myths. *Tucson Weekly.* Retrieved March 24, 2014, from: www.tucsonweekly.com/tucson/ethnic-studies-myths/Content?oid=3180662.

Horne, T. (2007, June 11). *An open letter to the citizens of Tucson.* Phoenix: State of Arizona Department of Education. Retrieved March 24, 2014, from: nau.edu/uploadedFiles/Academic/CAL/Philosophy/Forms/An%20Open%20Letter%20to%20Citizens%20of%20Tucson.pdf.

Johnson, K. R., & Martínez, G. A. (2000). Discrimination by proxy: The case of Proposition 227 and the ban on bilingual education. *U.C. Davis Law Review, 33,* 1227–1276.

Lau v. Nichols, 483 F.2d 791 (9th Cir. 1973), *cert. granted,* 412 U.S. 938 (1973), *rev'd,* 414 U.S. 563 (1974).

Levine, A. (2006). *Educating school teachers.* Washington, DC: Education Schools Project. Retrieved March 29, 2014, from: www.edschools.org/pdf/Educating_Teachers_Report.pdf.

Losen, D. (2010). Challenging limitations: The growing potential for overturning restrictive language policies and ensuring equal educational opportunity. In P. Gándara &

M. Hopkins (Eds.), *Forbidden language: English learners and restrictive language policies* (pp. 195–215). New York: Teachers College Press.

Mahoney, K., MacSwan, J., Haladyna, T., & García, D. (2010). *Castañeda's* third prong: Evaluating the achievement of Arizona's English learners under restrictive language policy. In P. Gándara & M. Hopkins (Eds.), *Forbidden language: English learners and restrictive language policies* (pp. 50–64). New York: Teachers College Press.

Malakoff, M., & Hakuta, K. (1990). History of language minority education in the United States. In A. M. Padilla, H. F. Fairchild, & C. M. Valadez (Eds.), *Bilingual education: Issues and strategies* (pp. 27–43). Newbury Park, CA: Sage.

Manuel, H. T. (1930). *The education of Mexican and Spanish-speaking children in Texas.* Austin: Fund for Research in the Social Sciences, University of Texas at Austin.

Marian, V., & Shook, A. (2012). The cognitive benefits of being bilingual. *Cerebrum, 13,* 1–7. Retrieved March 13, 2014, from: www.ncbi.nim.nih.gov/pmc/articles/PMC3583091.

Martínez, G. A. (1994). Legal indeterminacy, judicial discretion and the Mexican-American litigation experience: 1930–1980. *U.C. Davis Law Review, 27,* 555–618.

McKinley, J. C., Jr. (2010, March 12). Texas conservatives win curriculum change. *New York Times.* Retrieved April 2, 2014, from: www.nytimes.com/2010/03/13/education/13texas.html?_r=0.

Menchaca, M. (2001). *Recovering history, constructing race: The Indian, Black, and White roots of Mexican Americans.* Austin: University of Texas Press.

Menchaca, V. D. (1996). Multicultural education: The missing link in teacher education programs. *Journal of Educational Issues of Language Minority Students, 17,* 1–9. Retrieved March 29, 2014, from: www.ncela.us/files/rcd/BE020 692/Multicultural_Education.pdf.

Mintz, S. (Ed.). (2009). *Mexican American voices: A documentary reader* (2nd ed.). Chichester, UK: Wiley-Blackwell.

Myhill, W. M. (2004). The state of public education and the needs of English language learners in the era of "No Child Left Behind." *Journal of Gender, Race & Justice, 8,* 393–447.

Ndura, E. (2004). ESL and cultural bias: An analysis of elementary through high school textbooks in the Western United States of America. *Language, Culture, and Curriculum, 17,* 142–154.

Nevarez, A. (2010, May 17). The AZ ethnic studies ban: HB 2281. *Daily Kos.* Retrieved March 24, 2014, from: www.dailykos.com/story/2010/05/17/867162/-The-AZ-Ethnics-Studies-Ban-HB2281#.

Nieto, S. (1996). *Affirming diversity: The sociopolitical context of multicultural education* (2nd ed.). White Plains, NY: Longman.

Ovando, C. J., & McLaren, P. (Eds.). (2000). *The politics of multiculturalism and bilingual education: Students and teachers caught in the crossfire.* Boston: McGraw-Hill.

Paulson, A. (2010, May 19). Texas textbook war: "Slavery" or "Atlantic triangular trade"? *Christian Science Monitor.* Retrieved April 2, 2014, from: www.csmonitor.com/USA/Education/2010/0519/Texas-textbook-war-Slavery-or-Atlantic-triangular-trade.

Perea, J. F. (2003). A brief history of race and the U.S. Mexican border: Tracing the trajectories of conquest. *UCLA Law Review, 51,* 283–312.

Planas, R. (2012, April 19). Neither banned nor allowed: Mexican American Studies in limbo in Arizona. *Fox New Latino.* Retrieved March 26, 2014, from: http://latino.foxnews.com/latino/news/2012/04/19/neither-banned-nor-allowed-mexican-american-studies-in-limbo-in-arizona/.

Powers, J. M., & Williams, T. R. (2012). State of outrage: Immigrant-related legislation and education in Arizona. *Journal of the Association of Mexican-American Educators, 6,* 13–21. Retrieved March 23, 2014, from: https://amaejournal.asu.edu/index.php/amae/article/download/87/70.

Ramos, C. (2001). The educational legacy of racially restrictive housing covenants: Their long term impact on Mexican Americans. *Scholar: St. Mary's Law Review on Minority Issues, 4,* 149–184.

Ramsey, P. G. (2004). *Teaching and learning in a diverse world: Multicultural education for young children* (3rd ed.). New York: Teachers College Press.

Rendón, A. (1971). *Chicano manifesto.* New York: Macmillan.

Rios v. Read, 480 F. Supp. 14 (E.D.N.Y. 1978).

Rodríguez, R. (2012, January 3). Arizona's apartheid war against Mexican American Studies. *Common Dreams.* Retrieved March 27, 2014, from: www.commondreams.org/view/2012/01/03–5.

Romero, A. F. (2011–2012). The hypocrisy of racism: Arizona's movement towards state-sanctioned apartheid. *Journal of Educational Controversy, 6,* 1–6. Retrieved March 25, 2014, from: www.wce.wwu.edu/Resources/CEP/eJournal/v006n001/a013.shtml.

Ryan, W. (2002). The Unz initiatives and the abolition of bilingual education. *Boston College Law Review, 43,* 487–519. Retrieved March 22, 2014, from: http://lawdigitalcommons.bc.edu/bclr/vol43/iss2/4.

Sagara, E. (2006, April 13). "Hate-speak" at school draws scrutiny. *Tucson Weekly.* Retrieved March 24, 2014, from: http://tucsoncitizen.com/morgue/2006/04/13/9256-hate-speak-at-school-draws-scrutiny/.

San Miguel, G., Jr. (2004). *Contested policy: The rise and fall of federal bilingual education in the United States, 1960–2001.* Denton: University of North Texas Press.

San Miguel, G., Jr., & Valencia, R. R. (1998). From the Treaty of Guadalupe Hidalgo to *Hopwood.* The educational plight and struggle of Mexican Americans in the Southwest. *Harvard Educational Review, 68,* 353–412.

Stutz, T. (2010, May 22). Texas State Board of Education approves new curriculum standards. *Dallas Morning News.* Retrieved April 3, 2014, from: www.dallasnews.com/news/education/headlines/20100521-Texas-State-Board-of-Education-approves-9206.ece.

Texas Education Agency. (2014). *2013–2014 student enrollment: Statewide totals.* Austin, TX. Retrieved May 21, 2014, from: http://ritter.tea.state.tx.us/adhocrpt/index.html.

Tobar, H. (2011, January 14). Cal State Northridge professor caught in Arizona controversy. *Los Angeles Times.* Retrieved March 25, 2014, from: http://articles.latimes.com/2011/jan/14/ local/la-me-0114-tobar-20110114.

Uriarte, M., Tung, R., Lavan, N., & Diez, V. (2010). Impact of restrictive language policies on engagement and academic achievement of English learners in Boston Public Schools. In P. Gándara & M. Hopkins (Eds.), *Forbidden language: English learners and restrictive language policies* (pp. 65–85). New York: Teachers College Press.

U.S. Commission on Civil Rights. (1972). *Mexican American education study, report 3: The excluded student: Educational practices affecting Mexican Americans in the Southwest.* Washington, DC: Government Priority Office.

U.S. Commission on Civil Rights. (1997). *Equal educational opportunity and nondiscrimination for students with limited English proficiency: Federal enforcement of Title VI and Lau v. Nichols.* Equal Educational Opportunity Series. (Vol. 3). Washington, DC: Author.

Valencia, R. R. (2008). *Chicano students and the courts: The Mexican American legal struggle for educational equality*. Critical America Series. New York: New York University Press.

Valencia, R. R. (2011). The plight of Chicano students: An overview of schooling conditions. In R. R. Valencia (Ed.), *Chicano school failure and success: Past, present, and future* (3rd ed., pp. 3–41). New York: Routledge.

Valeria G. v. Wilson, 12 F. Supp.2d 1007 (N.D. Cal. 1998), *aff'd sub nom* Valeria v. Davis, 307 F.3d 1036 (9th Cir. 2002), *pet. for reh'g en banc denied*, 320 F.3d 1014 (9th Cir. 2003).

Vasquez Heilig, J., Brown, K. D., & Brown, A. L. (2012). The illusion of inclusion: Race theory textual analysis of race and standards. *Harvard Educational Review, 82*, 403–424.

Wentworth, L., Pellegrin, N., Thompson, K., & Hakuta, K. (2010). Proposition 227 in California: A long-term appraisal of its impact on English learner student achievement. In P. Gándara & M. Hopkins (Eds.), *Forbidden language: English learners and restrictive language policies* (pp. 37–49). New York: Teachers College Press.

Wiley, T. G., & Wright, W. E. (2004). Against the undertow: Language-minority education policy and politics in the "age of accountability." *Educational Policy, 18*, 142–168.

Woodson, C. G. (1933). *The mis-education of the Negro*. Washington, DC: Associated.

Zimmerman, J. (2002). *Whose America? Culture wars in the public schools*. Cambridge, MA: Harvard University Press.

Zimmerman, J. (2004). *Brown*-ing the American textbook: History, psychology, and the origins of modern multiculturalism. *History of Education Quarterly, 44*, 46–49.

Zirkel, S. (2008). The influence of multicultural educational practices on student outcomes and intergroup relations. *Teachers College Record, 110*, 1147–1181.

7

CURRICULUM DIFFERENTIATION

I broadly define curriculum differentiation (hereafter referred to as CD)[1] as the sorting of students into instructional groups based on perceived and/or measured educability.[2] Such sorting is typically done by teachers at the elementary school level. At the middle and high school levels, instructional sorting is informed in combination by academic counselors, parental guidance, and student choice. Slavin (2003) presents a useful framework for describing contemporary CD. "Within-class ability grouping" refers to groupings (e.g., in reading) of students of similar ability levels in elementary school classes. "Between-class ability groupings" is in reference to student sorting by ability in separate classes in middle schools. Finally, "tracking" historically refers to types of curricular assignments, or programs of study (e.g., college preparatory, general), in high school. In contemporary times, however, tracking is not thought of as rigid programs of study, but is more appropriately seen as variations (different course taking) on a subject-by-subject basis (e.g., English, mathematics; see Loveless, 2013; Oakes, 2005).

CD is ubiquitous in the U.S. and abroad (e.g., Argentina, Belgium, New Zealand, Scotland) (Schofield, 2010). A problem arises, however, when strong links are found between race and/or SES of students and CD. These racialized and class-based patterns are commonplace and signal grave concerns of inequities in the stratification of knowledge and the exacerbation of TAG (e.g., Gamoran & Mare, 1989; Oakes, 2005). As we shall see, CD for students of color, especially of low-SES background, is associated with lower academic achievement performance, diminished self-esteem, lower rates of college matriculation, and less probability of gaining employment in a credentialed society. To address this significant mesolevel factor of the Three-M Systemic Model, I cover the following topics: (a) a brief history of CD, (b) pervasiveness of CD and sorting by race and class, (c) CD and unequal educational opportunities for students of color, and (d) systemic transformations.

A Brief History of CD

CD first came into widespread practice in the 1920s with the advent of mass intelligence and achievement testing (see, e.g., Chapman, 1988; Valencia, 1997). The historical justification for CD was grounded in the belief that too many differences in ability among students in the same classroom created ineffectual climates for teaching and learning. The argument went as follows: The presence of "slow learners'" and "fast learners" being instructed together results in frustration for the former and boredom for the latter. As such, CD advocates asserted that having classes with an excessive variability in mental ability made for a pedagogical disadvantage. The solution? CD. The sorting tools? Intelligence and achievement tests. The anticipated results? Efficiency (Valencia, 1997).

Regarding early CD practices and students of color, let us take Mexican Americans as an illustration. These students were typically taught in one of three schooling situations: (a) a segregated "Mexican" school, which was the most common arrangement; (b) self-contained and separate classrooms in racially/ethnically mixed schools; or (c) mixed classrooms in mixed schools. In these contexts, particularly the first two, Mexican American students were presented with an inferior, unequal education that led to the implicit tradition of a differentiated curriculum in which these children and youths underwent sorting into slow learner and vocational classes—a practice that eventually became institutionalized throughout the Southwest (González, 1990). This CD was partially shaped by omnipresent beliefs that Mexican American students were not cut out for "book study" or "seat work" (cf. Stanley, 1920, p. 715), and thus they should be trained for "hand and eye education" (Young, 1922, p. 70). Such dead end CD for Mexican American pupils and other students of color was prompted, in part, by prominent scholars' deficit thinking views toward these students. For example, Terman (1916)—in one of the most infamous statements ever made about the putative cognitive deficits of students of color—maintained that because their [Spanish-Indian, Mexican, and Negro] "dullness seems to be racial, or at least inherent in the family stocks from which they come [these children] . . . should be segregated in special classes." Terman continues by saying these children should be provided "instruction which is concrete and practical. They cannot master abstractions, but they can often be made efficient workers, able to look out for themselves" (pp. 91–92).[3]

By the mid-1920s, U.S. public schools used group-administered intelligence and achievement tests with great frequency, and bureaucracies arose to handle the mass testing and use of results. The U.S. Department of the Interior, Bureau of Education (1926; cited in Chapman, 1988) published a survey that sought to report the use of homogeneous grouping via group intelligence tests results.

Based on data from 292 cities with populations ranging from 10,000 to more than 100,000, the percentages of municipalities reporting homogeneous ability grouping for the various school levels were: elementary (85%), junior high (70%), and high school (49%). The same report notes that 250 (85%) of the 293 cities surveyed used group intelligence tests in student classification. Thus, since the publication of the National Intelligence Test in 1920—the first group-administered test used in schools—U.S. public schools were highly differentiated in curriculum by the mid-1920s, and group intelligence and achievement tests served as the main sorting mechanisms. By 1932, 75% of 150 large cities had school districts that made curricular assignments of students using such instruments (Tyack, 1974). CD had become entrenched in the nation's public schools.

Pervasiveness of CD and the Sorting by Race and Class

Continuing into the 1940s and 1950s, group intelligence testing had taken on a life of its own—and such assessments continued to have a major role in CD. Writing at the beginning of the fall semester in 1949, Benjamin Fine, columnist for the *New York Times Magazine,* notes that from September to June 20,000,000 children in U.S. public schools would be compelled to take a test to measure their intelligence. He further comments that the sheer number of students to be tested underscores

> the position of influence to which IQ . . . tests have risen in little more than a generation in American school systems. In nearly all, they are used in greater or lesser degree to determine when a child should begin to read, whether another should go to college, and if a third is likely to grow up to be a dolt or an Einstein—that is, whether he is "worth worrying about" or "simply beyond help." (p. 7)

Although Fine's remarks may be interpreted as a bit on the hyperbolic side regarding the sway of intelligences testing on students' futures, they still speak to the strong marriage between intelligence testing and CD.

Based on a Southwestern study of 45 years ago (AY 1970–1971), the U.S. Commission on Civil Rights (1974) provides definitive data confirming that CD traversed the portal from history to contemporary times with respect to harmful effects on students of color. The Commission reports two major findings. First, of about 1,100 public schools surveyed in the five states of the Southwest, 63.4% of the elementary schools and 79.3% of the secondary schools carried out some type of heterogeneous instructional grouping. Second, these practices showed racialized patterns of CD. Although the majority of Mexican American students (52.7%) and White students (59.1%) were enrolled in medium-ability classes at comparable proportions, Mexican American students were overrepresented in low-ability classes more than twofold and underrepresented in high-ability classes by about twofold. The Commission notes that assignments to these varied ability-level classes were based on the results of intelligence and achievement tests, as well as teacher and counselor recommendations. All of these bases of sorting Mexican American students have shortcomings—possible linguistic and cultural loading in the assessment instruments (Valencia, 2008, chapter 3; Valencia & Suzuki, 2001, chapter 5), and deficit thinking views of the students' educability by teachers and counselors (Valencia, 2010, chapter 5).

Interest in CD generated further and considerable attention after the 1985 publication of *Keeping Track: How Schools Structure Inequality*, by Jeannie Oakes, especially along lines of race and class stratification in public schools. Subsequently, numerous studies and treatises on CD have appeared,[4] and even some criticism of the opponents of differentiated curriculum (e.g., Loveless, 1999a). One such investigation of curricular sorting by race/ethnicity is by Braddock and Dawkins (1993), who analyzed data from the base year and follow-up of the National Educational Longitudinal Study of 1988 (National Center for Education Statistics, 1992); the authors focused on eighth graders. Table 7.1 presents enrollment data for the distribution of African American, Latino/Latina, and White students across four types of ability-grouped English and mathematics classes.[5] The findings by Braddock and Dawkins indicate that students, as designated by race/ethnicity, are not randomly distributed across high- and low-ability classes, but rather that the patterns for these two types of ability groupings are racialized—as many other studies before and after report.

TABLE 7.1 Percentage Distribution of African American, Latino/Latina, and White Eighth-Grade Students in Four Ability Group Levels by Subject: National, 1988

Subject, Race/Ethnicity and Sample Size	*Ability Group Level*			*Mixed*
	Low	*Middle*	*High*	
English				
African American (n=1,029)	34	38	15	13
Latino/Latina (n=649)	29	42	18	12
White (n=684)	14	40	32	15
Mathematics				
African American (n=1,051)	35	35	15	16
Latino/Latina (n=698)	25	41	18	15
White (n=986)	15	40	35	10

Source: Adapted from Braddock and Dawkins (1993, p. 327, Table 1) with permission of first author, J. H. Braddock II.

Table 7.1 shows that African American and Latino/Latina eighth-grade students are far from parity in English high-ability classes,[6] and are overrepresented, compared to their White peers, in low-ability English classes. The same types of patterns are seen in Table 7.1 for the distribution of students in mathematics.

There is some evidence that CD begins very early in the in the schooling of children.[7] Condron (2007) draws on partial data from the Early Childhood Longitudinal Study–Kindergarten Cohort (ECLS-K), which is a nationally representative sample containing more than 21,000 children who started kindergarten in the fall of 1998 (U.S. Department of Education, 2001). Condron measured "skill group placement" (a rank) based on two questions teachers were asked pertaining to (a) the number of reading groups he/she had, and (b) which reading group a particular student was assigned to. To gather data on how teachers evaluated a student's skills in literacy and language, Condron tapped into questions teachers responded to regarding whether a child was considered "as not yet, beginning, in progress, intermediate or proficient" in various skill areas (e.g., letter recognition, reading books that are simple). He also gathered data on how teachers evaluated a student's social and behavioral skills. Condron's analyses of the data show stark disparities in reading group placement. In regard to SES, he reports that students ascribed to be in the four lower-SES quintiles are assigned to the lower-ranked reading groups more frequently than were students in the high-SES quintile (all statistically significant at p less than .01). With respect to race/ethnicity, the author finds that African American and Latino/Latina children, compared to their White counterparts, are placed more often in the lower-ranked reading groups (significant at p less than .001). Another finding by Condron is worth noting. He reports that about 70% to 75% of the first-grade teachers who participated in the ECLS-K study engage in placing their students into instructional groups for reading. The fact that the overwhelming majority of U.S. children are and will be sorted into reading groups as they begin their schooling career certainly raises serious questions about equal educational opportunity for young low-SES pupils and students of color who are disproportionately placed in the lower-instructional groups.

Notwithstanding the ubiquity of CD practices and their sorting effects, an important question remains: How can we best explain the mechanisms that drive such stratification along dimensions of race and class? Building somewhat upon Condron (2007), I think the debate can be framed around three explanations: One perspective, which I coin the *pedagogical* argument, is that teachers sort young students into instructional groups because teachers believe it is easier to teach them (see Oakes, 2005, chapter 1; Terman, 1922). A second view, the *cultural capital* argument, is that CD operates through the allocation of more favorable grouping placements to students who are evaluated higher by teachers regarding academic, social, and behavioral skills (Condron; Lareau, 1987, 2000). A third perspective, the *deficit thinking* argument, asserts that teachers sort young low-SES pupils and students of color into lower-ability groups because teachers have class

and racial animus toward these students, as well as holding unfavorable views of their educability (see Valencia, 2010, chapters 4 and 5). In the remainder of this section, I briefly touch on these assertions.

The pedagogical argument for CD, as we have discussed, has its roots in the early 1920s during the rise of the intelligence/achievement testing movement, when students were regularly evaluated for instructional grouping. Terman, a prominent advocate of CD, proffers this major principle: "A reasonable homogeneity in the mental ability of pupils who are instructed together is a *sine qua non* of school efficiency" (1922, p. 7). Over time, this educational tenet became lodged in U.S. classrooms. Many teachers believe that CD makes it much easier to teach small groups of students with similar ability and skill levels. Conversely, heterogeneous, or mixed-ability groups, is a difficult challenge for teachers and takes valuable time away from his or her daily instruction. There is some recent empirical evidence from teachers that supports the rationale of efficiency underlying the pedagogical perspective. In a phone survey of a nationally representative sample of 1,000 elementary and secondary school teachers, Markow and Cooper (2008) asked participants if they "agree" or "disagree" with this statement: "My classes have become so mixed in terms of students' learning abilities that I can't teach them effectively." Of the respondents, 43% said they "agree" (p. 62, Figure 2.26). Such surveys results may partially help to explain the resurgence in the use of ability groups by teachers. Drawing from NAEP data, Loveless (2013) reports that the proportion of students assigned to ability groups (grade 4 reading) mushroomed from 28% in 1998 to 71% in 2009—a 154% increase (p. 16, Table 2.1). In all, the pedagogical position for CD has some attraction for many teachers because homogeneous grouping of students makes instruction easier. The issue remains, however, about the consequences (Oakes, 2005, chapter 1). That is, does the end (differentiated, unequal access to knowledge) justify the means (CD)?

The cultural capital view is a somewhat more complex explanation of a mechanism for CD. A starting point for understanding this interpretation is to see how cultural capital is conceptualized. In their attempt to untangle the notion, Lamont and Lareau (1988) define it as having "widely shared . . . cultural signals [consisting of] attitudes, preferences, formal knowledge, behaviors, goods and credentials [that are] used for social and cultural *exclusion*" [italics added] (p. 156). Social exclusion includes certain occupations and resources, and cultural exclusion involves being denied access to high-status groups. Applying the cultural capital perspective to CD, aspects of students' cultural capital (academic, behavioral, and social skills) are evaluated against standards established by the teacher, who is an agent of the institution that shares a wide set of cultural signals—namely, certain expectations regarding student skills in the spheres of academic work (e.g., reading comprehension), classroom behaviors (e.g., attention span), and social interactions (e.g., interpersonal relationships) (Condron, 2007). In a test of the cultural capital view of CD, Condron reports that first-grade teachers rated students of color, lower-SES pupils, boys, and children from single-parent families lower in cultural capital in comparison to White, high-SES pupils, girls, and children from homes with both parents. These ratings by academic skills and ascribed/background characteristics led to, in part, students' placements in instructional reading groups, in which low-SES and students of color, for instance, were assigned by teachers to low-ability reading groups. In sum, students who teachers perceived as having greater cultural capital were rewarded with access to higher-status groups (i.e., higher-ranked reading placement). Within the context of CRT, the cultural capital perspective as an explanation of CD is a valuable contribution to the social stratification literature because it demonstrates that schools are not neutral, value-free institutions. Rather, they are agencies in which curricular sorting by teachers is greatly shaped by knowledge of a student's race and class, other ascriptive and background features, and teachers' evaluations of students' academic skills.

The deficit thinking perspective of CD also offers insights as to why teachers sort students into instructional groups. As I discussed in some detail in chapter 2, deficit thinking is an endogenous theory that "blames the victim." In regard to education, deficit thinkers believe that pupils (primarily low-SES students of color) who experience academic achievement difficulties do so because of deficits or deficiencies in themselves, their cultures, and families. These putative deficits are expressed, deficit thinkers assert, in students' cognitive shortcomings and an absence of achievement motivation, dysfunctional cultures, and parents who fail to value the importance of education. As such, some teachers hold views that students of color have limited educability and should be placed in low-ability instructional groups. There is, however, little evidence on teachers' *actual* CD practices across race and class in the same classroom, so we have to examine the indirect information, which follows.

1. *Preservice teachers' beliefs about the educability of students of color.* In chapter 5, I introduced the work of Marx (2006), who discusses the prevalence of deficit thinking in colleges of education where preservice teacher education students learn stereotypes of low-SES pupils and students of color. These aspiring teachers express such deficit thinking in four ways involving: (a) culture, (b) language, (c) families, and (d) self-esteem and intelligence. It is likely that these deficit thinking attitudes acquired in preservice training solidify over time and eventually influence how teachers form ability groups based on their educability perceptions of students of color, particularly of low-SES background.

2. *Inservice teachers' beliefs about the educability of students of color.* Williams's (2008) study of 12 White, female elementary school teachers working in a predominantly Black school (68%; 92% students of color; 100% Title 1 pupils) in the Northwest is informative. Based on the results of focus group discussions with the participants, Williams reports that the "theme of deficit thinking was pervasive throughout the data" (p. 106) with respect to the students and their parents. On achievement motivation, one teacher stated, "I have the students

who it's so painful to see that in the third grade, they already, they don't care. They're unbelievably unmotivated and there's not a punishment or reward or consequence that you can give them" (p. 106). On educability perceptions, another participant commented,

> Intellectual ability; there's some biological stuff there and if there's not much to work with. If you have somebody with a below average IQ, you're going to have a problem with the child learning. There's just not a lot of IQ to work with and you get two sub IQs having a baby and that baby is going to have hard time. (p. 109)

With such deficit thinking perceptions of the students' work behaviors and alleged educability, it would not be surprising that the teachers routinely provided non-academically challenging, minimally engaging instruction.

A related investigation of teachers' beliefs about students and grouping practices is by Solomon, Battistich, and Hom (1996). The participants included 476 K-6 teachers (78% White) in 24 suburban and urban schools in six U.S. school districts located in the Northeast, Southeast, South Central, and West Coast. Based on the percentage of students enrolled in the subsidized lunch program, the authors divided the schools into three poverty categories: low, medium, and high. As expected, race/ethnicity correlated with poverty level—for example, Black students were overrepresented and underrepresented in the high-poverty and low-poverty groups, respectively. Solomon et al. assessed teachers' beliefs and classroom practices via a questionnaire and classroom observations. Among the numerous findings, the authors report that the students in the high-poverty schools had less engaging instruction (e.g., cooperative learning) and had less of their schoolwork displayed in the classroom. Particularly noteworthy was that teachers in the high-poverty schools showed greater skepticism toward students' learning abilities. This finding was even maintained when student achievement was controlled, thus leading Solomon et al. to conclude that such expectations exerted a powerful effect on teachers' attitudes.

To sum, the pedagogical, cultural capital, and deficit thinking perspectives all offer understandable, but not acceptable, explanations of why teachers practice CD. For the sake of analysis, I have discussed them separately. They are, however, not mutually exclusive. For example, take the case of a first-grade teacher who works in a crowded public school predominantly serving Mexican American and White students. Her principal is forced to get a waiver approval to increase her class size to 26 students, above the maximum number of 22. Therefore, to make her work easier, she forms instructional groups for reading. This CD rationale, combined with her perceptions (false) of the limited educability of the Mexican American children, results in these students being disproportionately placed in the low-ability groups.

Although teachers likely utilize some combination of the three views for their grouping practices, a legitimate question to raise is: Which of the three perspectives has the most sway in explaining the mechanism of CD? Drawing from CRT, I lean toward the deficit thinking argument. I believe that because deficit thinking is so pervasive in educational thought apropos of low-SES students of color (Valencia, 1997, 2010; Williams, 2008), such a mindset serves as the underlying reservoir from which biased teachers draw to make CD decisions. Furthermore, the strength of deficit thinking is quite robust as a shaper of teachers' educability perceptions and actual grouping placements of students of color. Some empirical research shows that race- and SES-based inequalities in CD placement endure even after controlling for students' academic achievement (e.g., Lucas & Berends, 2002; Solomon et al., 1996).

CD and Unequal Educational Opportunities for Students of Color

The primary concern about the effects of CD is that access to equal educational opportunities is enhanced for middle- and high-SES White students and thwarted for working-class and low-SES students of color. A reality of curricular sorting is that it leads to the stratification of knowledge—meaning that some students, who are already privileged, will gain access to a richer, more engaging, and higher-quality instruction and knowledge that will eventually assist them in earning entry to the credentialed society. Other students, mostly low-SES children and youths of color, will be sorted into instruction that is far less rigorous and less valuable for their future in the world of work. Viewed in this manner, CD exacerbates TAG. In this section, I briefly cover three ways in which CD leads to unequal educational opportunities: (a) instructional inequalities, (b) teacher-student interactional inequalities, and (c) knowledge status inequalities. My focus is primarily on what transpires during the teaching and learning process.

1. *Instructional inequalities.* In a review of scholarly literature of reading instruction provided to young "good" and "poor" readers, Allington (1983) presents an expansion of the intuitive and logical premise that "students are more likely to learn what they are taught than what they are not taught" (p. 548). Although he does not discuss ability grouping by race and SES, his conclusions, nonetheless, are informative in the context of the present chapter. The key findings are as follows.

A. *Allocation of time for reading.* On average, teachers allot about the same amount of instructional time for groups of good and poor readers. Considering that the extant literature finds greater instructional time leads to better readers with higher achievement, Allington (1983) notes that one can contend that equivalence in this case is not equitable. That is, poor readers should have *more* time for instruction so they can improve their skills.

B. *Engaged time for reading instruction.* Good readers, compared to poor readers, have been found to exhibit greater engaged instructional time. Specifically, good readers show more on-task behaviors as demonstrated by being highly motivated, less distractible, and mature. Allington (1983) comments that many teachers believe poor readers lack these favorable characteristics because the students have inherent flaws. This deficit thinking perspective does not hold teachers accountable—namely, their failure to construct learning environments that will allow struggling readers to become engaged in their instruction.

C. *Emphases for reading instruction.* In their reading instruction, Allington (1983) reports that teachers emphasize a more meaningful discussion of book stories for good readers and less so for poor readers. Such instructional emphases focus on contextual reading, comprehension questions asked by the teacher, and less attention to the fundamentals of reading, such as decoding of words.

D. *Quantity and mode of reading assignments by teacher.* Allington (1983) notes that although time allocation for reading is quite important for reading instruction, a more appropriate measure is the number of words read by a student. Based on his own research, he finds that good readers, compared to poor readers, read approximately 3 times more words in their reading groups. Furthermore, around 70% of such reading by good readers is done silently, whereas the poor reader groups do it orally. These differences in quantity and mode of words read have serious implications because the amount of silent reading has been found to be a robust predictor of reading achievement (e.g., Rasinski, Samuels, Hiebert, Petscher, & Feller, 2011; Rosseau, 2012).

E. *Teacher interruption during reading instruction.* All young readers make errors, or miscues, during reading. Research findings show that during reading instruction, teachers interrupt proportionately more frequently poor reader groups following students' errors. Allington (1983) comments that such repeated interruptions of errors of poor readers may send them an encouragement to rely on external monitoring, rather than self-correction. This is an important point, as a student's self-correction of errors is a strong predictor of reading progress.

Later research findings confirm some of the conclusions Allington (1983) draws. For example, Gamoran (1986) investigated the ability grouping practices for reading instruction in 12 Chicago first-grade classrooms. Based on observations recorded 12 times over the course of a year, he finds that the higher-ranked groups, in comparison to the lower-ranked ones, learned more words and phonics skills. He concludes that the main reason for the differences in learning rate is that teachers actually taught more words and phonic skills to the higher-ability groups. Gamoran reports no SES effects on instructional groupings.

In a related study, researchers Pallas, Entwisle, Alexander, and Stluka (1994) investigated ability-group effects on mathematics and reading achievement (first grade) based on data collected in 19 Baltimore elementary schools. The authors report that students placed in the higher-ability reading groups, in comparison to their peers in the lower-ability groups, were exposed to instruction of higher quality and performed higher in achievement. The authors point out, however, that the correlation between higher grouping and higher achievement is a distance from being perfect. That is, some students with similar achievement performance were placed in groups for reading that ranked from anywhere next to the top or bottom in the class. Pallas et al. find no grouping effects by race or SES, because of restricted variability on these ascribed variables.

The foregoing studies provide strong evidence that CD is associated with instructional inequalities. Although the literature review by Allington (1983) does not examine race and SES effects, nor does Gamoran (1986) or Pallas et al. (1994) find such effects, this body of research is still important because it is underscores the harmful instructional consequences of ability grouping for students who are experiencing academic difficulties. Thus, this literature raises important implications regarding equal learning opportunities for low-SES students of color, who tend to be overrepresented in low-ability groups.

2. *Teacher-student interactional inequalities.* The transmission of formal knowledge from teacher to student is central to the enterprise of schooling. As a considerable amount of literature informs us, the allocation of instruction is often provided in ability groups marked by race and SES, in which low-SES students of color are placed, on the average, in the lower groups. We must be mindful, however, that the heart of the schooling process is the varying interactions between teachers and students (e.g., teachers praising students; teachers encouraging students) and that these interactions are highly significant in promoting student learning (Liberante, 2012; U.S. Commission on Civil Rights, 1973). Teacher-student interactions are ubiquitous, but when they become racialized and/or SES-based, we need to be concerned. I have decided to discuss this issue in the present chapter on CD because such interactions occur in the curricular context and can affect a student's learning and achievement. The brief review that follows covers teacher-student interaction patterns *and* teachers' expectations of students. For ease of communication, I cluster both under "interactions."

In Rist's (1970) classic study he examined teachers' interactions with and expectations of young elementary schoolchildren. The investigation took place in St. Louis, Missouri, at a school in which *all* students, teachers, staff, and administrators were Black; 55% of the pupils had families receiving Aid to Dependent Children (ADC). For his methodology, Rist utilized a microethnography in which he observed a kindergarten class twice a week for 1.5 hours over the period of a year.[8] At the beginning of the AY, the kindergarten teacher, Mrs. Caplow (pseudonym), had early social information for each of the students—for example, whether the child had preschool experience, whether the family was receiving ADC, parents' educational attainment, family size, child's medical background, and information from a behavioral questionnaire. Based on this knowledge plus about a week of observing the children, Mrs. Caplow, *sans any academic achievement data*, made permanent seating assignments on the eighth day of school—and they were not randomly done. At table 1, which was the closest to her, the students had parents, by far, with the highest levels of income, employment, and educational attainment. At tables 2 and 3, the students had parents with the lowest levels on these SES indices. Rist also reports that the students at table 1, compared to those at tables 2 and 3, wore nicer and cleaner clothes, were lighter in skin color, and had a better command of Standard English.

What emerged from these stark contrasts in seating arrangements were dramatic differences in how Mrs. Caplow interacted with the students. Rist (1970) notes that the teacher consistently called on table 1 students for "show and tell," to lead the class in the Pledge of Allegiance, and to be class leaders in other situations (e.g., on class projects, visits to the library, school tours). Mrs. Caplow also had far more verbal interactions with table 1 students, and vice versa. Furthermore, she had table 1 students serve as exemplars for speaking Standard English. She also demonstrated different perceptions of the children's educability, telling Rist that the table 1 students were her "fast learners" and the table 2 and 3 children were her "slow learners." The latter children, whom she expected to fail, "had no idea of what was going on in the classroom" (pp. 414, 422). In his explanation of Mrs. Caplow's different expectations and interactions with the students, Rist suggests that she was using her own background—having a college-educated mother and siblings, middle-SES—as the normative reference group. Although Rist does not discuss it by name, he is referring to Mrs. Caplow's use of cultural capital as the primary mechanism for her differential interactions with the students. Finally, we learn from Rist's study that shared identity between teacher and student (discussed in chapter 5, this volume) can backfire on occasions in which some students benefit, but at the expense of other pupils.

The most comprehensive and frequently cited study to date of teacher-student interactions involving Mexican American students is by the U.S. Commission on Civil Rights (1973).[9] The investigation included 429 racially/ethnically mixed classrooms (grades 4, 8, 10 and 12) in California, New Mexico, and Texas—which at the time enrolled 60% of all Mexican American students in the U.S. and 90% of the total in the Southwest region. Of the 422 participating teachers, 91% were White and 9% Mexican American. Staff members of the Commission were thoroughly trained to use a modified version of the Flanders Interaction Analysis System, which is designed to assess three types of classroom behavior: (a) teacher (e.g., praising or encouraging students, acceptance of student ideas), (b) student (e.g., student talk—initiation), and (c) composite (e.g., positive teacher response). The Commission observers report that Mexican American students, compared to their White counterparts, received significantly less praise and encouragement from their teachers. Furthermore, teachers were found to spend significantly less time in asking questions of Mexican American students, and they provided more non-criticizing talk to White pupils than to Mexican Americans. The Commission concludes that the findings indicate a picture in which teachers are failing to include Mexican American students in the process of teaching to the comparable extent as White students. One explanation the Commission offers for the interactional disparities, especially for the lower grade, is homogeneous seating patterns by ability. It is suggested that the physical detachment of Mexican American and White students prompted teachers to use perceived educability of students as a mechanism for her/his interaction patterns. A particularly interesting finding is that Mexican American teachers, compared to their White peers, gave more praise or encouragement to White students. This pattern should be treated with great caution because the very small sample size of Mexican American teachers compromises the statistical power for making inferential comparisons.

A small but informative corpus of later empirical studies supports the findings of the landmark U.S. Commission on Civil Rights (1973) report that teachers interact less favorably with Mexican American students compared to their White peers (e.g., Buriel, 1983; Losen, 1995, 1997; Pizarro, 2005). For example, Buriel's study of teacher-student interactions involved 40 Mexican American and 59 White fourth- and fifth-grade students in five classrooms randomly selected from three public elementary schools in a Southern California suburb. To gather interactional data, he used the Brophy-Good Dyadic Interaction Observation System, which consists of 14 variables (e.g., product questions, process questions, teacher affirmation following correct answer by student). The unit of analysis was the interaction between the teacher and the individual student, the preferred method.[10] SES, student achievement level, and English proficiency—possible confounding variables—were controlled. Buriel reports that even with these controls, he found one racial/ethnic difference, significantly so, occurring uniformly across the five classrooms: The Mexican American students, compared to their White peers, received less teacher affirmation subsequent to a correct response by a student. Although this is a sole finding, it has serious implications given that a teacher's positive reinforcement via vocal praise is likely the principal factor in increasing student learning. Buriel notes that considering his control for confounding variables, teachers may have been using student race/ethnicity as a cue in their differences in affirmation following correct answers—thus, racial prejudice may have been implicated.

Subsequent investigations provide some confirmation of the earlier research that teachers interact less favorably with students of color. Dusek and Joseph (1983) utilized a meta-analysis to examine the bases of teacher expectancies. In regard to race/ethnicity of students, one of the variables studied,[11] the authors identified 24 investigations that met their criteria for selection; the authors included only Black and White student comparisons in their analysis. Dusek and Joseph report that of the 24 studies examined, 11 (46%) showed teacher expectancies in which White students were favored, and the other 13 (54%) investigations resulted in a finding of no expectancy effect for race/ethnicity.[12] In another meta-analysis of teacher expectancies across race/ethnicity, the results of Baron, Tom, and Cooper (1985) also find that teachers held higher expectations for White students compared to Black pupils. As to a possible explanation for such teacher expectancies, it is suggested that teachers may be relying on racially prejudicial stereotypes that Black students are expected to do not as well in school as their White counterparts (Dusek & Joseph). This deficit thinking perspective would be in line with some of the literature on teachers' educability perceptions of students of color that we have covered thus far.

3. *Knowledge status inequalities.* In her comprehensive study of tracking in 25 U.S. junior and senior high schools, Oakes (1985) and her research staff observed 224 classes: 75 high-track, 85 average-track, and 64 low-track classes—approximately divided between English and mathematics. Regarding English, she reports appreciable differences between the types of knowledge students are exposed to in the high-track and low-track classes. High-track students, who are disproportionately White, study, for example, classic and modern literature, features of various literary genres (e.g., poetry, the novel), and literary elements (e.g., irony, the use of metaphors). These students are also expected to produce expository writing and research reports. In high-track mathematics classes, topics of study tend to focus, for instance, on numeration systems, statistics, probability theory, and mathematical models. Oakes (1985) refers to the types of knowledge transmitted in the high-track English and mathematics classes as "high-status" knowledge, which is a prerequisite for matriculation to and success in colleges and universities.

In the low-track English classes, students, who are disproportionately of color, primarily read young adult fiction (e.g., romance, gangs) written at levels of basic literacy. Teachers concentrate on instructing reading skills, via workbooks. Students' written assignments mainly focus on short, fundamental paragraphs, and on skill development that has real-world application post–high school—namely, filling out job applications. In regard to low-track mathematics classes, Oakes (1985) notes that students' academic work emphasizes basics, such as skills in computation and arithmetical facts. Not surprisingly, teachers focus on consumer mathematical skills (e.g., how to figure simple and compound interest). To sum, the CD Oakes (1985) observed in her study clearly demonstrates knowledge status inequalities. Students in high-track classes are being taught high-status knowledge, which is highly valued types of knowledge for preparation and matriculation to higher education, and eventual entry to the credentialed society. By sharp contrast, students in the lower-track classes are being exposed to types of knowledge that help prepare them for passage into the non-credentialed workforce.

The classic tracking study by Oakes (1985) served as an incentive for subsequent research on knowledge status inequalities. Swail, Cabrera, and Lee (2004), for instance, drew from the National Educational Longitudinal Study (NELS), which tracked eighth graders from 1988 to 2000. The authors report that 63.3% of African American and 58.6% of Latino/Latina students—compared to 40.5% of White students—were not qualified to attend postsecondary education. At the other end of the qualifications range, about twice the percentage of White students (41.8%) were accomplished enough for matriculation to higher education compared to African Americans (22.1%) and Latinos/Latinas (25.3%).[13] A likely factor explaining these racial/ethnic differences in qualification, Swail et el. note, is the highest level of high school mathematics completed—which is the principal gatekeeper for matriculation to higher education. For Latino/Latina students, as a case in point, the NELS data show that they are less likely to have taken the higher -mathematics courses, in comparison to the NELS cohort as a whole. For example, Latinos/Latinas completed high school calculus at half the rate of all NELS students.

Toward Systemic Transformations

Considering that CD has such a long tradition in U.S. K-12 public education, any systemic reform will certainly be challenging. The pedagogical rationale for CD is deeply entrenched among teachers because they believe sorting students by ability for instruction makes their work considerably easier. This is hard to argue against. Nonetheless, teachers need to be asked whether the end justifies the means. The cultural capital perspective on CD carries powerful influences among teachers (e.g., shared cultural cues as to which students to include and exclude). The valued shared identity that eventually develops between the teacher and some of her students leads to their enhanced learning, but to denial of equal educational opportunity for others pupils—a zero-sum outcome. The deficit thinking perspective also helps to explain why teachers use CD. Certainly, it remains a difficult task to change the mindsets of teachers who rely on irrational, prejudicial assumptions to sort students into instructional groups in which some children will receive higher-quality knowledge and instruction, while others will not. Notwithstanding these serious obstacles to providing an equal education for students of color, many scholars have called for comprehensive reform. In this section, I present several suggestions for discussion that have some promise for tackling the inequalities created by CD.

1. *Rethinking the notion of meritocracy.* James Truslow Adams, renowned historian, is given credit for conceiving the phrase "American Dream." In his 1931 book, *The Epic of America*, he notes:

> The *American Dream* [is] that dream of a land in which life should be better and richer and fuller for every man, with opportunity for each according to *ability and achievement* [italics added]. . . . It is not a dream of motor cars and high wages merely, but a dream of social order in which each man and woman shall be able to attain to the fullest stature of which they are innately capable, and be recognized by others for what they are, *regardless of the fortuitous circumstances of birth and position* [italics added]. (p. 404)

Fueling the heart of the American Dream is the ideology of "meritocracy," coined by Michael Young in his 1958 book, *The Rise of the Meritocracy*. All societies have ideologies about rewarding individuals. Such systems—in both beliefs and practices—contain standards for deeming who is meritorious as well as the nature of the rewards. In the U.S. and other capitalist countries, current meritocracy is predicated on the belief that true individuals exist, detached from racial/ethnic and SES identifications (Valencia, Menchaca, & Valenzuela, 1993). The meritocratic perspective finds expression in the following formula: Merit = ability + effort (Allen, 2011). Meritocracy, as a belief system, is ingrained in the psyche of people living in the U.S. Recently, a World Values Survey found that the majority (60%) of U.S. citizens believe that poor people, if they tried sufficiently, could become wealthy (Friedman, 2012).

There is a major problem with the notion of meritocracy: *It is an illusion.* In their 2004 book, *The Meritocracy Myth*, Stephan McNamee and Robert Miller point out that there is a chasm between how people think the U.S. opportunity system functions and how, in reality, it does work. McNamee and Miller call this gap "the meritocracy myth," arguing that there are a number of nonmerit obstacles to upward mobility—which they refer to as "social gravity," or forces (e.g., low educational attainment, racial discrimination) that have a tendency to keep people in niches they already inhabit. Conversely, some of these nonmerit factors that help promote mobility include inheritance (financial and cultural capital), advantaged standards of living, excellent medical care, financial safety nets, geographical opportunities (e.g., residing near high-performing schools), and parental educational attainment. The myth of meritocracy, as outlined by McNamee and Miller, can be empirically documented. In the foregoing quote by Adams (1931), progenitor of the American Dream notion, he notes that a person can attain his or her aspirations regardless of birth and social origins. If this were true, then each person has an "equal chance of becoming unequal in a society" where one's race/ethnicity and SES have no influence on mobility (Nicholas, 1999). Yet, these factors, which highly covary, do have predictive import. Racialized patterns abound in the U.S. In chapter 3, I discuss the ubiquitous racialized patterns in regard to inequalities in income, housing, and health care.

Meritocracy is a seductive belief system. Given that K-12 public schools are reward-oriented and sorting institutions, it is no surprise that the educational system has embraced meritocracy. Accordingly, the business of schools is to sort students—the more meritorious from the less. Those students who are deemed the most deserving—which is typically determined by one's performance on achievement and cognitive tests, academic products, and individual effort—will reap the rewards. These benefits include, for example, being placed in the high-ability instructional groups in elementary school, gaining access to the high-status knowledge classes in secondary school, matriculating to the more prestigious colleges, obtaining the best jobs, and earning the higher salaries (Valencia et al., 1993). There are two problems with this analysis of how meritocracy functions in the educational system. First, it dismisses how race and class inform the sorting process. Meritocracy, as a color-blind and class-blind perspective of success, overlooks the historical, social, and economic conditions that favor the ascendancy of middle- and upper-SES White students and disfavor low-SES students of color. Second, meritocracy is framed around deficit thinking. Given that the point of departure is the individual, failure in academic production and/or work habits are typically deduced by the teacher as being caused by a student's incompetence and/or poor motivation. Exogenous factors (e.g., being taught by a poorly qualified teacher, lack of a home computer) are seldom considered.

I believe it is critical for preservice teacher education students to have a healthy curricular dose in which they confront the meritocratic narrative.[14] The rationale underlying a didactic approach is that in order for teachers to create a more equitable education for students of color, teachers need to first examine themselves regarding their socialized beliefs about meritocracy (Alvarado, 2010). In a stand alone module or a comprehensive section in a specific course (e.g., Social Foundations of Education), students might be exposed to the following: (a) discussion of the history of meritocracy; (b) personal and familial experiences/beliefs about meritocracy; (c) discussion of cultural capital and other nonmerit factors of mobility; (d) coverage of race- and class-based patterns of income, housing, medical care, and academic achievement indices; (e) their own conflicting views, if any, regarding meritocracy; and (f) their personal action plan apropos of the inequitable consequences of instructional sorting when they become teachers.

2. *Detracking for equal educational opportunity*. The term "detracking" of schools is something of a misnomer, because it conjures up the narrow image of untracking *high schools*. A more accurate depiction is a comprehensive shift from homogeneous to heterogeneous groupings across the spectrum of K-12 schooling. However, given that the moniker "detracking" is widely used in the literature, I utilize it here—and broadly construe it to include elementary, middle, and high school levels of public education.

Advocates of detracking certainly agree that it is a daunting undertaking. Oakes (1992) comments that based on successful examples of detracked schools, we can draw from three lessons. First, detracking involves far more than merely mixing pupils into diverse classrooms. Close attention needs to be paid to, for example, the interrelationships between grades, curricular content changes, how student assessments will be done, special needs of some students, teacher training in cooperative learning and other instructional techniques, and teacher support. The major lesson to be learned is that a "culture of detracking" is more important to develop than any specific change in school/classroom arrangements. Second, the status quo must be challenged. The rigid norms that support CD—such as reification of the concept of intelligence, the notion of meritocracy, and deficit thinking views of low-SES students of color—need to be vigorously contested and replaced with norms, for instance, of high expectations of all students, rigorous instruction, and promotion of student agency. Third, advocates of detracking need to be aware that it is a sociopolitical process in which some parents, mostly White and of middle- and upper-SES background, will protest. Such parents will assert that their children will be deprived of access to the coveted high-ability groups/classes. To win these parents over, informed administrators, teachers, and community leaders must persuade the parents—via research evidence from detracking studies, democratic principles, and good will—that their children will not suffer academically, and will only be enriched by sharing the same teaching/learning space with children of diverse backgrounds.

With respect to the overall timeline of CD, the detracking movement is a relatively recent development. Research findings in the 1980s (e.g., Gamoran, 1986; Oakes, 1985) and the 1990s (e.g., Gamoran, 1992; Hallinan, 1992; Pallas et al., 1994) report that students placed in low-ability groups/classes, compared to their counterparts assigned to high-ability groups/classes, performed not as well on achievement tests. This key finding, coupled with the growing evidence that low-SES students of color were disproportionately taught in low-ability groups/classes, created a backlash against CD (Hallinan, 2004). In the 1990s, the incipient movement to reform CD began to yield results. Initially, these detracking initiatives (e.g., Accelerated Schools Project, the Padeia Proposal) did not explicitly propose detracking, but they drew from its principles (Wheelock, 1992).

The major challenge detracking advocates must confront is related to the two concerns that Tom Loveless, a proponent of tracking, raises (see, e.g., Loveless, 1999a, 1999b).[15] He underscores that researchers need to demonstrate empirically that detracking leads to two benefits (Loveless, 1999b). First, heterogeneous instructional grouping must reduce TAG. Second, such grouping practices cannot adversely affect high-achieving students. An exemplar of research that has attempted to examine these two concerns has occurred in Rockville Centre School District (RCSD), one of the most studied detracked districts in the U.S. (Burris & Garrity, 2008; Burris & Welner, 2005; Burris, Wiley, Welner, & Murphy, 2008; Garrity, 2004). The RCSD is located in Rockville, New York, a largely wealthy suburban community (Burris & Garrity).[16] Based on recent data, the RCSD's seven elementary schools, one middle school, and one high school enroll 3,540 students (80.2% White; 10.3% Latino/Latina; 6.4% Black; 3.0% Asian/Pacific Islander); 11.7% of the district's students are deemed economically disadvantaged.[17]

The RCSD detracking account begins in 1987 when newly appointed Superintendent William H. Johnson noticed that tracking was a major contributing factor in creating and maintaining TAG in his district. Thus, in 1989 he slowly embarked on a multiyear process of untracking—starting with the elementary school gifted program, and then moving through the middle school and high school.[18] In 1993, he set a goal: By the year 2000, 75% of students in South Side High School (SSHS) would earn the prestigious Regents diploma. At the time, 58% of SSHS students graduated with a Regents' diploma (Burris & Garrity, 2008). To earn this highly regarded diploma, a student must pass at least eight end-of-course Regents examinations—two each in laboratory sciences, social studies, and mathematics and one each in foreign language and English language arts (Burris & Welner, 2005). This specified curriculum is commonly considered a pathway lined with college preparatory courses (Burris & Garrity).

Results of the detracking initiative in the RCSD have proven quite successful, based on the two criteria presented by Loveless (1999b)—namely, there is a reduction in TAG, and high-achieving students do not lose academic ground. For example, between 1995 and 1997, just 23% of Black and Latino/Latina passed the Regents algebra examination before entering SSHS. Subsequent to detracking, the rate tripled to 75%. For White and Asian American students the pass rate went from 54% to 98% (Burris & Welner, 2005). The outcomes for students earning a Regents diploma were particularly remarkable. For students who entered SSHS in 1996, and graduated in 2000, 32% of Blacks and Latino/Latina students and 88% of Whites and Asian American were awarded a Regents diploma. For the 1999 cohort (SSHS graduating class of 2003), TAG had been sharply cut: 82% of Black and Latino/Latina and 97% of White and Asian American students earned a Regents diploma. These rates for Black and Latino/Latina SSHS students eclipsed the New York state rate for *White and Asian American* students (Burris & Welner). It appears that the academic excellence established at the detracked RCSD continues unabatedly. Based on 2014 "best high school rankings" by *U.S. News and World Report* (determined by the criteria of students/teacher ratio, college readiness, and scores on mathematics and English proficiency tests), the RCSD ranked 23 in the state of New York.[19] This is quite an accomplishment, considering that in AY 2011–2012 there were 1,105 public high schools in the entire state.[20] The excellent academic outcomes demonstrated by the RCSD are not isolated, as there are a number of instances of successful detracking programs.[21]

3. *Multiple pathways to student success.* Multiple Pathways (hereafter referred to as MP) is a creative and comprehensive approach designed to radically transform the rigidity of high school tracking. The idea for a MP approach first appears in a 1997 article written by Robert J. Monson, superintendent of Independent School District 197 in Mendota Heights, Minnesota.[22] Monson's district was one of nine that received funding for a demonstration project to implement MP at the high school level. Then, MP was designed to provide a number of pathways, or curricular options, so students could show the same proficiency level to graduate from high school. These MPs included, for example, a postsecondary options program, a customized program, and an interactive technology program. Monson asserts that MP has much less of the stigma associated with student sorting and promotes a more egalitarian approach to learning than the conventional high school model. More recently, the notion of MP as a school reform has been given visibility by Oakes and Saunders (2008b) in their edited volume *Beyond Tracking: Multiple Pathways to College, Career, and Civic Participation.*

As Oakes and Saunders (2008c) discuss, the debate over reforming the high school, which waxes and wanes according to economic and social plights, typically revolves around two positions: (a) Schools need a strong college preparatory curriculum available for all students; and (b) schools need to increase their vocational education curriculum, particularly for those students who do not aspire to go to college. The MP approach, however, does not view school reform as an either/or proposition. Upon graduation, all students will have a broad spectrum of postsecondary options for success in both college *and* professional careers. Oakes and Saunders (2008a) conceptualize MP as a replacement for the comprehensive high school. A number of small-scale high schools and programs, "pathways" within these units, offer students the foundations for academic growth and experiences in the real world, as well as planning for civic participation. MP may be different in their themes, organization of course work, time spent on and off the individual campus, associations with community colleges and 4-year colleges, and relationships with local businesses.

Of course, the main question one should ask of MP advocates is: Does it improve the academic achievement of students, particularly low-SES youths of color? One affirmative response to this important query is provided by Oakes and Saunders (2008a), who discuss the success of the Kearney High Educational Complex (KHEC), located in San Diego, California. The KHEC enrolls grade 9 to 12 students, the majority being Latino/Latina, and contains four independent magnet schools: School of International Business; Stanley E. Foster Construction Technology Academy; School of Digital Media and Design; and School of Science, Connections, and Technology. All enrolled students are provided a challenging curriculum that prepares them for college, and each student chooses a theme that corresponds to his or her interests. The Stanley E. Foster Construction Technology Academy (CTA), for example, has a remarkable academic track record. For the 2007 graduating class, 81% of the students were accepted for college admission; 36% were selected by 4-year universities. Furthermore, graduates of the CTA have priority to enroll in the College of Construction Management and Engineering at San Diego State University—with the assurance of a full scholarship. Finally, and quite an extraordinary accomplishment, is that the CTA has a graduation rate of 99%.

In all, MP has great potential to reform CD and its negative consequences for low-SES students of color. Research finds that MP demonstrates promise in the following areas: enhancing student engagement, increasing learning, improving high school graduation and college matriculation rates, improving the learning needs of ELs, and promoting civic participation and leadership (Oakes & Saunders, 2008c).[23]

While MP is an attractive approach to consider for high school reform and is gaining considerable attention, caution must be used in structuring the program. A case in point is what transpired in the state of Texas. Largely spurred by interests in the business sector, the Texas Legislature approved HB 5 on May 27, 2013, and Governor Rick Perry signed it on June 10, 2013.[24] HB 5, which went into effect at the beginning of AY 2014–2015, requires that each incoming ninth-grade student select one of five "endorsements" as a pathway of study: Science, Technology, Engineering, and Mathematics; Business and Industry; Public Service; Arts and Humanities; Multidisciplinary Studies (Intercultural

Development Research Association, 2013). Another aspect of HB 5 is that the conventional and rigorous "4X4" requirement of 16 core courses has been diluted to 4 courses in English, and 3 each in science, mathematics, and social studies (Weldon, 2013). Furthermore, Algebra II, which is generally deemed a gateway course for collegiate success, was dropped as a graduation requirement. HB 5 certainly has its critics. For example, Raymund Paredes, Texas Higher Education Commissioner, says that HB 5 will lead to a decrease in the number of students ready for college (McKenzie, 2013). This concern is particularly germane for low-SES students of color, who as a group, have lower rates of being prepared for higher education. Another criticism is that the HB 5 endorsements will create a new scheme of tracking and adversely affect low-SES students of color (Intercultural Development Research Association).

Of the four mesolevel factors covered in part III, CD is one of the most egregious in creating and maintaining TAG. This elitist practice—which is based on the assumption that some students are more deserving than others—leads to three types of inequalities for many low-SES students of color—namely, in instruction, teacher-student interactions, and knowledge status. CD has been, and continues to be, shaped by powerful norms and belief systems associated with pedagogical justifications, cultural capital, and deficit thinking. Yet, the structure and organization of the classroom need not be in the stranglehold of this undemocratic instructional approach to teaching and learning. The detracking and MP narratives are certainly not panaceas, nor should they be viewed as such given the deep levels of structural inequality in society and schools, but they should at least be given an opportunity to demonstrate, on larger scales, their promise as tools of reform.

Notes

1 Grammatically, "curricular" should be used when it serves as an adjective. The use of "curriculum differentiation," however, is so entrenched in the literature that I utilize it here, instead of "curricular differentiation."

2 This introduction, and other parts of this chapter, build on (with revisions), Valencia (2011, pp. 14, 31), Valencia and Suzuki (2001, pp. 21, 27), and Valencia, Menchaca, and Valenzuela (1993, pp. 10–11).

3 For the larger context and expanded interpretation of this Terman (1916) quote, see Valencia (2010, pp. 14–16).

4 See, for example, Dauber, Alexander, and Entwisle (1996); Lucas (1999); Lucas and Gamoran (2002); Oakes (2005); Wheelock (1992).

5 Braddock and Dawkins (1993) also provide ability grouping data for American Indians and Asian Americans (p. 327, Table 1).

6 In Table 1 (p. 327), Braddock and Dawkins calculate parity indices. For the sake of space, I do not list them in my Table 7.1.

7 For the quintessential investigation, see the classic study by Rist (1970).

8 Rist (1970) also followed the students into grades 1 and 2. Here, I confine my discussion to his observations of the kindergarten class.

9 This paragraph builds on, with revisions, Valencia (2002, p. 24).
10 Buriel (1983) points out that the U.S. Commission on Civil Rights (1973) used the class level as the basis for coding and the classroom means of White and Mexican American students as the unit of analysis. He comments that this procedure presents a threat to reliability of the findings.
11 Dusek and Joseph (1983) also examine, for example, student variables of social class, attractiveness, gender, and conduct.
12 See Dusek and Joseph (1983) for the citations of these 24 studies.
13 The "qualified" and "not qualified" percentages for each racial/ethnic group do not sum to 100% because the NELS data also has a "minimally qualified" category, which I do not include in this discussion.
14 My suggestions here slightly build on Alvardo (2010), whose focus is on higher education admissions staff.
15 For a critique of Loveless (1999a), see Welner and Mickelson (2000).
16 The RCSD has undergone a name change. On its website (http://rvcschools.org/pages/Rockville_Centre_UFSD) it is referred to as the Rockville Centre Unified Free School District.
17 See www.neighborhoodscout.com/ny/rockville-centre/schools.
18 For a detailed chronology of how the RCSD was detracked, see Burris and Garrity (2008).
19 See www.usnews.com/education/best-high-schools/new-york/rankings.
20 See http://nces.ed.gov/programs/digest/d13/tables/dt13_216.70.asp.
21 See, for example, Álvarez and Mehan (2006); Boaler (2006); Cooper (1996); Horn (2006); Oakes (2008); Pool and Page (1995); Wheelock (1992).
22 For a brief overview of the evolution of MP, see Oakes and Saunders (2008a).
23 Stern and Stearns (2008) note, however, that these findings need to be interpreted with caution due to unmeasured differences among students enrolled in MP.
24 See *Texas Legislature Online, History* (www.legis.state.tx.us/BillLookup/History.aspx?LegSess=83R&Bill=HB5).

References

Adams, J. T. (1931). *The epic of America.* Boston: Little, Brown.

Allen, A. (2011). Michael Young's *The rise of the meritocracy:* A philosophical critique. *British Journal of Educational Studies, 59,* 367–382. Retrieved April 28, 2014, from: www.shef. ac.uk/polopoly_fs/1.155163!/file/philosophicalcritique.pdf.

Allington, R. L. (1983). The reading instruction provided readers of differing reading abilities. *Elementary School Journal, 83,* 548–559.

Alvardo, L. A. (2010). Dispelling the meritocracy myth: Lessons for higher education and student affairs education. *Vermont Connection, 31,* 10–20. Retrieved April 26, 2014, from: www.uvm.edu/-vtconn/v31/Alvardo.pdf.

Álvarez, D., & Mehan, H. (2006). Whole-school detracking: A strategy for equity and excellence. *Theory into Practice, 45,* 82–89.

Baron, R., Tom, D.Y.H., & Cooper, H. M. (1985). Social class, race and teacher expectations. In J. B. Dusek (Ed.), *Teacher expectancies* (pp. 251–269). Hillsdale, NJ: Lawrence Erlbaum.

Boaler, J. (2006). How a detracked mathematics approach promoted respect, responsibility and high achievement. *Theory into Practice, 45,* 40–46.

Braddock, J. H., II, & Dawkins, M. P. (1993). Ability grouping, aspirations, and attainments: Evidence from the National Educational Longitudinal Study of 1988. *Journal of Negro Education, 62,* 324–336.

Buriel, R. (1983). Teacher-student interactions and their relationship to student achievement: A comparison of Mexican-American and Anglo-American children. *Journal of Educational Psychology, 75,* 889–897.

Burris, C. C., & Garrity, D. T. (2008). *Detracking for excellence and equity.* Alexandria, VA: Association for Supervision and Curriculum Development.

Burris, C. C., & Welner, K. G. (2005). Closing the achievement gap by detracking. *Phi Delta Kappan, 86,* 594–598.

Burris, C. C., Wiley, E., Welner, K. G., & Murphy, J. (2008). Accountability, rigor, and detracking: Achievement effects of embracing a challenging curriculum as a universal good for all students. *Teachers College Record, 110,* 571–608.

Chapman, P. D. (1988). *Schools as sorters: Lewis M. Terman, applied psychology, and the intelligence testing movement, 1890–1930.* New York: New York University Press.

Condron, D. J. (2007). Stratification and educational sorting: Explaining ascriptive inequalities in early childhood reading group placement. *Social Problems, 54,* 139–160.

Cooper, R. (1996). Detracking reform in an urban California high school: Improving the schooling experiences of African American students. *Journal of Negro Education, 65,* 190–208.

Dauber, S. L., Alexander, K. L., & Entwisle, D. R. (1996). Tracking and transitions through the middle grades: Channeling educational trajectories. *Sociology of Education, 69,* 290–307.

Dusek, J. B., & Joseph, G. (1983). The bases of teacher expectancies: A meta-analysis. *Journal of Educational Psychology, 75,* 327–346.

Fine, B. (1949, September 18). More and more, the IQ idea is questioned. *New York Times Magazine,* pp. 7, 72–74.

Friedman, H. S. (2012, July 24). America's incomplete thoughts about inequality and meritocracy. *Huffington Post.* Retrieved April 26, 2014, from: www.huff ingtopost.com/howard-steven-friedman/americas-incomplete-thoug_b_1696282.html.

Gamoran, A. (1986). Instructional and institutional effects of ability grouping. *Sociology of Education, 59,* 185–198.

Gamoran, A. (1992). Synthesis of research: Is ability grouping equitable? *Educational Leadership, 50,* 11–17.

Gamoran, A., & Mare, R. D. (1989). Secondary school tracking and educational equality: Compensation, reinforcement, or neutrality? *American Journal of Sociology, 94,* 1146–1183.

Garrity, D. (2004). Detracking with vigilance. *School Administrator,* August, 1–7.

González, G. G. (1990). *Chicano education in the era of segregation.* Philadelphia: Balch Institute Press.

Hallinan, M. T. (1992). The organization of students for instruction in the middle school. *Sociology of Education, 65,* 114–127.

Hallinan, M. T. (2004). The detracking movement: Why children are still grouped by ability. *Education Next, 4,* 1–4. Retrieved April 29, 2014, from: http://educationnext.org/the-detracking-movement/.

Horn, I. S. (2006). Lessons learned from detracked mathematics departments. *Theory into Practice, 45,* 72–81.

Intercultural Development Research Association. (2013, October). *Tracking, endorsements and differentiated diplomas—When "different" really is less—A post session update* (IDRA Policy Note). San Antonio, TX: Author.

Lamont, M., & Lareau, A. (1988). Cultural capital: Allusions, gaps and glissandos in recent theoretical developments. *Sociological Theory, 6,* 153–168.

Lareau, A. (1987). Social class differences in family-school relationships: The importance of cultural capital. *Sociology of Education, 60,* 73–85.

Lareau, A. (2000). *Home advantage: Social class and parental intervention in elementary education.* Lanham, MD: Rowman & Littlefield.

Liberante, L. (2012). The importance of teacher-student relationships, as explored through the lens of the NSW Quality Teaching Model. *Journal of Student Engagement: Education Matters, 2,* 2–9.

Losen, K. M. (1995). Mexican American students and classroom interaction: An overview and critique. *Review of Educational Research, 65,* 283–318.

Losen, K. M. (1997). *Listen to the silences: Mexican American interaction in the composition classroom and community.* Norwood, NJ: Ablex.

Loveless, S. R. (1999a). *The tracking wars: State reform meets school policy.* Washington, DC: Brookings Institution Press.

Loveless, T. (1999b). Will tracking reform promote social equity? *Educational Leadership, 56,* 28–32.

Loveless, T. (2013). *How well are American students learning? The resurgence of ability grouping and persistence of tracking* (Vol. 2). Washington, DC: Brown Center on Education Policy, Brookings Institution.

Lucas, S. R. (1999). *Tracking inequality: Stratification and mobility in American high schools.* New York: Teachers College Press.

Lucas, S. R., & Berends, M. (2002). Sociodemographic diversity, correlated achievement, and de facto tracking. *Sociology of Education, 75,* 328–348.

Lucas, S. R., & Gamoran, A. (2002). Tracking and the achievement gap. In J. E. Chubb & T. Loveless (Eds.), *Bridging the achievement gap* (pp. 171–198). Washington, DC: Brookings Institution Press.

Markow, D., & Cooper, M. (2008). *Metlife survey of the American teacher: Past, present, and future.* New York: Metlife. Retrieved April 10, 2014, from: http://files.eric.ed.gov/full text/ED504457.pdf.

Marx, S. (2006). *Revealing the invisible: Confronting passive racism in teacher education.* New York: Routledge.

McKenzie, B. (2013, March 21). Why Texas legislators are about to make a big mistake. *Dallas Morning News,* pp. 1–2. Retrieved May 17, 2014, from: http://educationblog.dallasnews.com/2013/03/raymund-paredes-warns-about-austins-proposed-changes-for-high-school-graduation-plans.html/.

McNamee, S. J., & Miller, R. K., Jr. (2004). *The meritocracy myth.* Lanham, MD: Rowman & Littlefield.

Monson, R. J. (1997). Redefining the comprehensive high school: The multiple pathways model. *NAASP Bulletin, 81,* 19–27.

National Center for Education Statistics. (1992). *First follow-up: Student component data file user's manual.* Washington, DC: Author.

Nicholas, T. (1999). *The myth of meritocracy: An inquiry into the social origins of Britain's business leaders since 1850* (Working Paper No. 53/99). London: Department of Economic History, London School of Economics. Retrieved April 25, 2014, from: www.lse.ac.uk/economicHistory/pdf/wp5399.pdf.

Oakes, J. (1985). *Keeping track: How schools structure inequality.* New Haven, CT: Yale University Press.

Oakes, J. (1992). Foreword. In A. Wheelock, *Crossing the tracks: How "untracking" can save American's schools* (pp. ix–xv). New York: New Press.

Oakes, J. (2005). *Keeping track: How schools structure inequality* (2nd ed.). New Haven, CT: Yale University Press.

Oakes, J. (2008). Keeping track: Structuring equality and inequality in an era of accountability. *Teachers College Record, 110,* 700–712.

Oakes, J., & Saunders, M. (2008a). Introduction. In J. Oakes & M. Saunders (Eds.), *Beyond tracking: Multiple Pathways to college, career, and civic participation* (pp. 1–16). Cambridge, MA: Harvard Education Press.

Oakes, J., & Saunders, M. (Eds.). (2008b). *Beyond tracking: Multiple Pathways to college, career, and civic participation.* Cambridge, MA: Harvard Education Press.

Oakes, J., & Saunders, M. (2008c). Beyond tracking: Multiple Pathways of possibility and challenge. In J. Oakes & M. Saunders (Eds.), *Beyond tracking: Multiple Pathways to college, career, and civic participation* (pp. 251–267). Cambridge, MA: Harvard Education Press.

Pallas, A. M., Entwisle, D. R., Alexander, K. L., & Stluka, M. F. (1994). Ability-group effects: Instructional, social, or institutional? *Sociology of Education, 67,* 27–46.

Pizarro, M. (2005). *Chicanas and Chicanos in school: Racial profiling, identity battles, and empowerment.* Austin: University of Texas Press.

Pool, H., & Page, J. A. (1995). *Beyond tracking: Finding success in inclusive schools.* Bloomington, IN: Phi Delta Kappan Educational Foundation.

Rasinski, T., Samuels, S. J., Hiebert, E., Petscher, Y., & Feller, K. (2011). The relationship between a silent reading fluency instructional protocol on students' reading comprehension and achievement in an urban school setting. *Reading Psychology, 32,* 75–97.

Rist, R. C. (1970). Student social class and teacher expectations: The self-fulfilling prophecy in ghetto education. *Harvard Educational Review, 40,* 411–451.

Rosseau, A. S. (2012). *Effects of silent reading on intermediate students' reading growth.* Unpublished master's thesis, Northern Michigan University, Marquette.

Schofield, J. W. (2010). International evidence on ability grouping with curriculum differentiation and the achievement gap in secondary schools. *Teachers College Record, 112,* 1492–1528.

Slavin, R. E. (2003). *Educational psychology: Theory and practice* (7th ed.). Boston: Allyn and Bacon.

Solomon, D., Battistich, V., & Hom, A. (1996). Teacher beliefs and practices in schools serving communities that differ in socioeconomic level. *Journal of Experimental Education, 64,* 327–347.

Stanley, G. C. (1920). Special schools for Mexicans. *Survey, 44,* 714–715.

Stern, D., & Stearns, R. (2008). Evidence and challenges: Will Multiple Pathways improve students' outcomes? In J. Oakes & M. Saunders (Eds.), *Beyond tracking: Multiple Pathways to college, career, and civic participation* (pp. 37–54). Cambridge, MA: Harvard Education Press.

Swail, W. S., Cabrera, A. F., & Lee, C. (2004). *Latino youth and the pathway to college.* Washington, DC: Pew Hispanic Center. Retrieved April 23, 2014, from: pewhispanic.org/files/reports/31.pdf.

Terman, L. M. (1916). *The measurement of intelligence: An explanation of and a complete guide for the use of the Stanford revision and extension of the Binet-Simon scales.* Boston: Houghton Mifflin.

Terman, L. M. (1922). *Intelligence tests and school reorganization.* Yonkers-on-the-Hudson, NY: World Book.

Tyack, D. (1974). *The one best system: A history of American urban education.* Cambridge, MA: Harvard University Press.

U.S. Commission on Civil Rights. (1973). *Mexican American education study, report 5: Teachers and students.* Washington, DC: Government Printing Office.

U.S. Commission on Civil Rights. (1974). *Mexican American education study, report 6: Toward quality education for Mexican Americans.* Washington, DC: Government Printing Office.

U.S. Department of Education. (2001). *User's manual for the ECLS-K base-year public-use data files and electronic codebook* (NCES 2001–029). National Center for Education Statistics. Washington, DC: U.S. Government Printing Office.

U.S. Department of the Interior, Bureau of Education. (1926). *Cities reporting the use of homogenous grouping and of the Winnetka technique and the Dalton plan* (City School Leaflet No. 22). Washington, DC: Government Printing Office.

Valencia, R. R. (1997). Genetic pathology model of deficit thinking. In R. R. Valencia (Ed.), *The evolution of deficit thinking: Educational thought and practice* (pp. 41–112). Stanford Series on Education and Public Policy. London: Falmer.

Valencia, R. R. (2002). The plight of Chicano students: An overview of schooling conditions and outcomes. In R. R. Valencia (Ed.), *Chicano school failure and success: Past, present, and future* (2nd ed., pp. 3–51). London: RoutledgeFalmer.

Valencia, R. R. (2008). *Chicano students and the courts: The Mexican American legal struggle for educational equality.* Critical America Series. New York: New York University Press.

Valencia, R. R. (2010). *Dismantling contemporary deficit thinking: Educational thought and practice.* Critical Educator Series. New York: Routledge.

Valencia, R. R. (2011). The plight of Chicano students: An overview of schooling conditions and outcomes. In R. R. Valencia (Ed.), *Chicano school failure and success: Past, present, and future* (3rd ed., pp. 3–41). New York: Routledge.

Valencia, R. R., Menchaca, M., & Valenzuela, A. (1993). The educational future of Chicanos: A call for affirmative diversity. *Journal of the Association of Mexican American Educators,* 5–13.

Valencia, R. R., & Suzuki, L. A. (2001). *Intelligence testing and minority students: Foundations, performance factors, and assessment issues.* Series on Racial and Ethnic Minority Psychology. Thousand Oaks, CA: SAGE.

Weldon, K. (2013, November 27). Law modifies graduation requirements. *Community Impact Newspaper.* pp. 1–3. Retrieved May 17, 2014, from: http://impactnews.com/austin-metro/southwest-austin/law-modifies-graduation-requirements/.

Welner, K. G., & Mickelson, R. (2000). School reform, politics, and tracking: Should we pursue virtue? *Educational Researcher, 29,* 22–26.

Wheelock, A. (1992). *Crossing the tracks: How "untracking" can save America's schools.* New York: New Press.

Williams, J. K. (2008). *Unspoken realities: White, female teachers discuss race, students, and achievement in the context of teaching in a majority Black elementary school.* Unpublished doctoral dissertation, Oregon State University, Corvallis.

Young, K. (1922). *Mental differences in certain immigrant groups: Psychological tests of South Europeans in typical California schools with bearing on the educational policy and on the problems of racial contacts in this country* (Vol. 1, No. 11). Eugene: University of Oregon Press.

Young, M. (1958). *The rise of the meritocracy, 1870–2033: An essay on education and society.* London: Thames and Hudson.

PART IV

Microlevel Factors

8

PARENTAL ENGAGEMENT AND EMPOWERMENT

All parents, across different racial/ethnic and SES groups, have aspirations that their children will succeed in school.[1] A copious body of quantitative and qualitative research evidence shows that a major predictor of elementary and secondary students' school success is the degree of their parents' involvement in schooling. A *sine qua non* in educational discourse is that the more parents get involved in their children's schooling, the more successful their offspring will be—particularly in the improvement of academic achievement and the fostering of favorable attitudes toward learning. In the U.S., parental involvement in education has a long history, beginning with the Pilgrims, who believed strongly in the primacy of such participation (Jeynes, 2011, chapter 1).

In this chapter, several key questions guide my analysis. How does the literature on parental involvement apply to low-SES parents of color and the reduction of TAG? Given that many parents of color do not have equal opportunity to partake in school activities germane to their children, how can these barriers be dismantled? How can parents of color become further empowered so they can become agents of change?

Five sections frame this chapter: (a) discussion of the conventional manner in which parental involvement is conceptualized by researchers; (b) summary of the literature on the value of parental involvement; (c) examination and critique of the myth that low-SES parents of color do not value education; (d) summary of the research findings that demonstrate parents of color do indeed value education and do participate, in various ways, in the education of their children; and (e) discussion of a number of suggestions of how we can work toward systemic reform in the area of parental engagement and empowerment in education.

The Conventional Conceptualization of Parental Involvement

An important starting point to ask is: What constitutes parental involvement? Lareau (2000) notes that researchers typically conceptualize such involvement to include parents preparing their children for school (e.g., reading to children, teaching the alphabet and simple counting), attending events at school (e.g., parent-teacher conferences), and following through on teacher requests (e.g., playing word games at home with the child). Some researchers, Lareau (2000) adds, include the parental activity of providing a location so the child can do his or her homework, as well as ensuring that the homework is completed. To all these activities, one could add, for instance, parental participation in school activities (e.g., serving as a classroom volunteer or field trip supervisor), and parents purchasing supplementary learning aids and materials (e.g., books, calculators, and home computers).

A major problem with this "list-of-involvement-activities-good-parents-do" approach to conceptualizing parental involvement is that it is derived from a deficit thinking perspective (Barton, Drake, Pérez, St. Louis, & George, 2004; Moreno & Valencia, 2011) and therefore has limited applicability to low-SES families of color. This conventional understanding of parental involvement views such parents as manipulatable subjects having no or little power, and thus they have to be taught how to become responsible, nurturing parents. Any parental failure to attend an event deemed important by the school (e.g., Parent-Teacher Association meeting) or to participate in other involvement activities (e.g., monitoring of homework) means the child is doomed to suffer academically. In the concluding section of this chapter, "Toward Systemic Transformations," I discuss the need for a paradigmatic shift regarding a reconceptualization of parental involvement in ways that bridge the complex interconnections between "what" low-SES parents of color do and "how" they are able to do what they do. This revised narrative provides an important distinction between parental *involvement*, an "accommodationist" perspective, and parental *engagement*, a "transformational" perspective (Olivos, Ochoa, & Jiménez-Castellanos, 2011).

Why Parents Get Involved in the Education of Their Children and Why Involvement Is Important

One major criticism of the research on parental involvement is that it is somewhat disjointed and lacks clarity (e.g., some inconsistent findings, lack of operational definitions). This is largely due to the field not having a strong theoretical framework to guide it (Fan & Chen, 2001). To rectify this matter, Hoover-Dempsey and associates have developed a comprehensive model of parental involvement in their children's education (e.g., Hoover-Dempsey & Sandler, 1995, 1997; Hoover-Dempsey et al., 2005). In one of their earlier publications, Hoover-Dempsey and

Sandler (1995) frame their model by asking the following three key questions: For what reasons do parents become involved in their children's education? How do they select specific forms of involvement? How does such involvement lead to positive schooling outcomes for their children? For the purposes of this chapter, the model discussed in Hoover-Dempsey and Sandler (1995) provides the most value. First, it offers sound theoretical guidance for the field. Second, it has solid applicability for providing further understanding of the involvement of low-SES parents of color—my target population.

Figure 8.1 presents an adaptation of the Hoover-Dempsey and Sandler (1995) model of parental educational involvement. The theoretical framework begins at *Level I: Parental Involvement Decision,* and such a choice to become involved is "'influenced" (i.e., shaped) by the (a) parent's construction of his or her role, and (b) parent's sense of efficacy in helping his or her children do well in school. These two influences are shaped, in turn, by the parent's own direct and vicarious experiences in school, verbal persuasion by others (e.g., relatives and friends) of the value of parental involvement, and the parent's emotional concerns about helping his or her children. A third influence has to do with general opportunities parents have for involvement. Level I of the model has relevance for understanding the complexities of involvement of some parents of color. For example, given that many low-SES parents of color have limited educational attainment (see chapter 1, Table 1.5, this volume), they may have doubts about their efficacy in helping their children do certain aspects of homework (e.g., calculating square root). As such, they often resort to alternative involvement options to help their children succeed (discussed in next paragraph).

As seen in Figure 8.1, *Level II: Parent's Choice of Involvement Forms* is influenced by three factors: (a) types of parent's skills and knowledge, (b) mix of demands of total time and energy (from family and employment demands), and (c) invitations and demands for involvement (from children and teachers). Once again, the Hoover-Dempsey and Sandler (1995) model has utility in understanding the nature of educational involvement of low-SES parents of color. For instance, in regard to what parents know and can do, there is the "funds of knowledge" notion of Latino/Latina households (González, Moll, & Amanti, 2005) in which children learn about, for example, auto mechanics, carpentry, religion, medicine, healing, and academic literacy (Villenas & Foley, 2011). Other types of funds of knowledge activities might include farming, ranching, mining, roofing, cooking, and childcare (Moll, Amanti, Neff, & González, 1992).

Valdés's (1996) ethnographic account of 10 Mexican-origin families is also informative regarding cultural variations in the nature of parental skills and knowledge. She reports that mothers socialize their children for academic competence via *consejos* (advice-giving narratives) and close supervision. Furthermore, mothers provide character-building so their children can be *bien educado* (well mannered) and have *respecto* (respect) and a strong work ethic. These values and

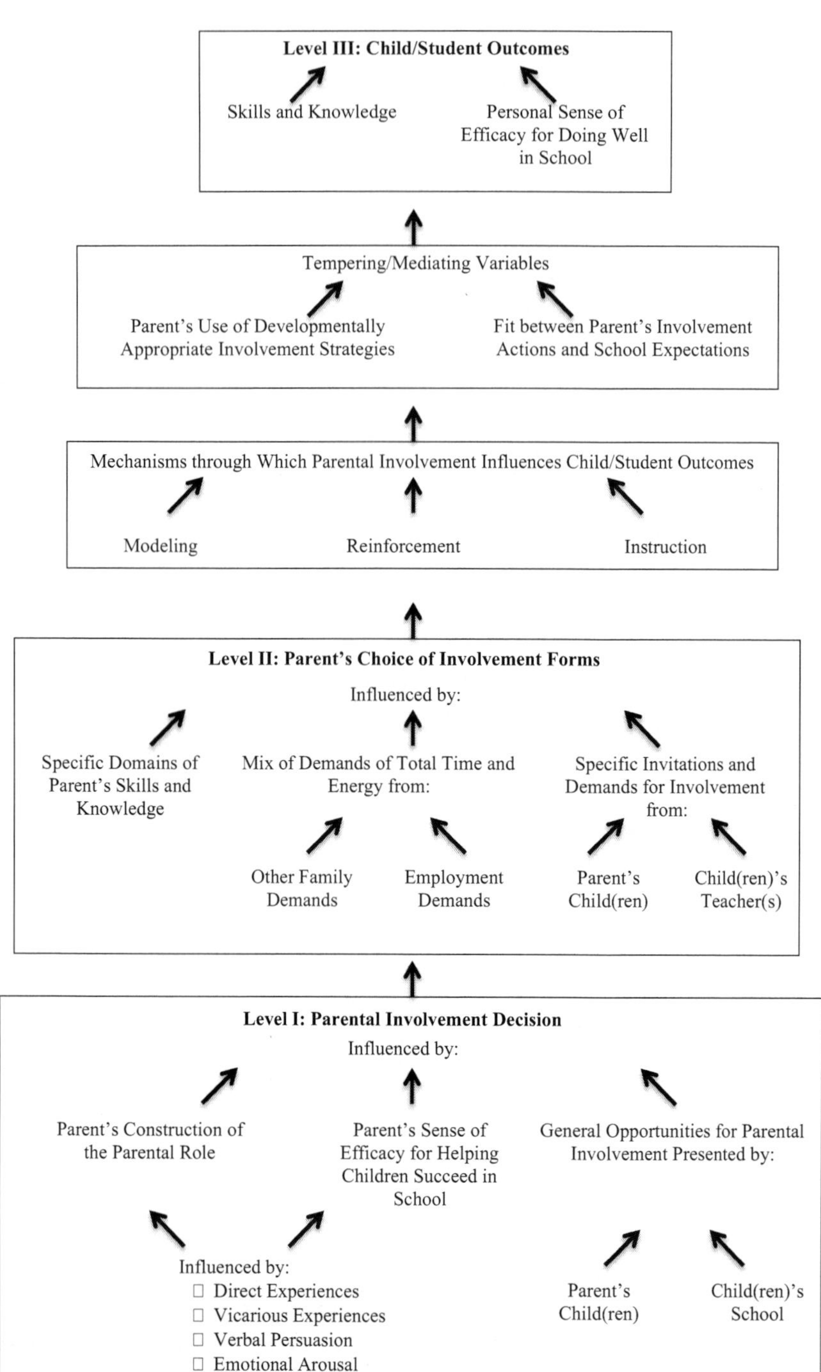

FIGURE 8.1 Causal and Specific Model of Parental Involvement

Source: Adapted from Hoover-Dempsey and Sandler (1995, pp. 11–12, Figure 2) with permission of K. Hoover-Dempsey and H. M. Sandler.

personal qualities instilled through *consejos* are commonly described as homilies, but the cultural nuance is lost in this characterization. *Consejos* encompass the communication of familial expectations through emotional empathy and compassion—and often an intimate narrative (Delgado-Gaitán, 1994, 2004; Valdés, 1996; Villenas & Foley). Here is an example of a *consejo* in which a Latino immigrant father from the Texas Rio Grande Valley uses work (hard physical labor) as a vehicle to convey to his children the importance and opportunities their education affords:

> *Pues y les ensenado lo que es el trabajo y lo duro ques es. O sea, ellos saben que si no se enfocan en los estudios, eso va a ser el trabajo que les va tocar. Yo les he abierto los ojo a esa realidad.* [Well, I have shown them what work is and how hard it is. So they know if they don't focus in their studies, that is the type of work they'll end up doing. I've opened their eyes to that reality.] (López, 2001, p. 427)

Viewed in the context of CRT, *consejos* speak loudly to the importance of experiential knowledge of oppressed people in their quest for improved education and lives.

The mix of employment demands (see Level II in Figure 8.1) is also instructive in understanding the educational involvement of low-SES parents of color. For example, a Latina parent notes, "Most of us work all day, and we're docked pay if we leave work to go talk to the teachers. That's why we do it only in emergencies" (Delgado-Gaitán, 2004, p. 5). This lack of visibility is misconstrued by some educators to mean that Latino/Latina parents do not care about their children's academic progress. Moreover, it can indicate a lack of understanding by educators of the practical constraints of many working-class parents of color (Moreno & Valencia, 2011). In regard to parental perceptions of the welcoming climate of schools (i.e., invitations and demands for involvement; see Level II in Figure 8.1), some research finds that Latino/Latina parents view schools as cold and indifferent to their needs. Furthermore, schools are often unprepared to accommodate non-English-speaking Latino/Latina parents who are unfamiliar with school policies and procedures (López, 1977; Nieto, 1985; Valdés, 1996).

The pinnacle of the Hoover-Dempsey and Sandler (1995) model of parental involvement is *Level III: Child/Student Outcomes* (see Figure 8.1), which is influenced by tempering/mediating variables—and shaped, in turn, by parental modeling, reinforcement, and instruction. One outcome, skills and knowledge, covers a wide range of parental teaching/child learning activities, such as preliteracy and prenumerosity skills development in younger children, and parental assistance in science projects in older children. The second outcome, a child's sense of efficacy for doing well in school, is also highly valued. Parents can help promote a strong sense of efficacy in the child via a number of ways—for example, monitoring the accuracy of homework assignment completions, giving praise, modeling appropriate behavior (e.g., turn-taking), and using *consejos* to encourage excellent academic work.

The Myth That Parents of Color Do Not Value Education

An abundant corpus of literature documents the positive relation between the degree of parents' participation in their children's education (e.g., monitoring homework) and their offspring's educational achievement, particularly in regard to academic performance on tests, high school graduation, and positive attitudes toward the learning process.[2] Although researchers find this association between parental educational involvement and their children's academic achievement to exist across varying SES and racial/ethnic groups, a myth lingers—notwithstanding counterevidence—that low-SES parents of color typically do not value the importance of education, fail to inculcate this value in their children via academic socialization, and seldom participate in parental involvement activities. This pathologization of parents of color stems from three bases: (a) the culture of poverty and "at-risk" variants of the deficit thinking model, (b) the erroneous equation of behavior and values, and (c) the power of teacher ideology.

1. *The culture of poverty and "at-risk" discourses.* The first basis of the myth that low-SES parents do not value education springs from the deficit thinking model, largely from the culture of poverty version, as well as the "at-risk" student/family variant (see chapter 2, this volume). The pseudoscientific reasoning of the argument goes as follows: Mexican American, Puerto Rican, and Black parents—for instance—do not hold education high in their value hierarchy, and this leads to inadequate familial socialization for academic competence, which in turn contributes to the school failure of their children.

The fallacy of these parents' of color indifference to the value of education has a long history in the academic literature. In a 1926 master's thesis, for example, Taylor sought to investigate the possible reasons for "pedagogical retardation" (being overage for grade level) among young school-age Mexican American children in Albuquerque, New Mexico. Although the author did acknowledge some exogenous factors for being behind in school (e.g., excessive school transfers), he honed in on the "indifference of [the] family toward [the] value of education" (p. 173). Taylor comments, "The difficulty lies in the home . . . The large percentage of illiterate parents, found especially among the Mexican population, *fails to understand the full value of the opportunity offered by the public schools*" [italics added] (pp. 176–177). In another master's thesis, conducted in Southern California, Gould (1932) comments, "*As a general rule, the* [Mexican] *parents lack any desire for education*" [italics added] (p. 20). These early deficit thinking researchers failed to understand the obstacles Mexican American parents faced that blocked their efforts to express fully their appreciation for and value of education—for example, not being welcome at school because of racial animus, language barriers, and the need for parents and older children to work. This latter issue, economic demands, was particularly salient. Pratt (1938), in a study of Mexican American agricultural workers in Delta, Colorado, notes that their children had school attendance problems because they had "no shoes to wear, no clothes to wear, too sick, [and] had to work" [most frequent response] (p. 96).

The myth that parents of color do not value education gained considerable momentum in the scholarly literature on "cultural deprivation" of the 1960s, an extension of the culture of poverty model (see chapter 2, this volume). The deficit thinking social constructions of the "culturally deprived" child—along with similar monikers of the "culturally disadvantaged" and "socially disadvantaged" child—had all too familiar target populations: "Whites, Negroes, Puerto Ricans, Mexicans, and all others of the poverty group who basically share a common design for living" (Marans & Lourie, 1967, p. 20).[3] It was not uncommon to read comments from scholars such as, "The socially disadvantaged child lacks. . . . Two parents who: read a good deal; read to him; *show him they believe in the value of education* [italics added]; reward him for good school achievement" (Havighurst, 1966, p. 18). Another example of mythmaking during the era of "cultural deprivation" is seen in Dougherty (1966), who, sans a single empirically based study, asserts, "*Parental indifference to the value of education is transmitted to the child* [italics added] where school careers are naturally characterized by poor attention, low achievement, and early leaving" (p. 389).

Contemporary writings on the culture of poverty have also helped to perpetuate the myth that low-SES parents (disproportionately of color) do not value education. A leading voice in this discourse is Ruby Payne (see chapter 2, this volume), self-proclaimed "leading expert on the *mindsets* [italics added]" of the poor, middle class, and affluent (Payne, 2005, front cover). She asserts that for poor people, education "is revered as abstract but not as *reality*" (Payne, 2005, p.42). In another of her self-publications, she contends, "For many parents in generational poverty, school is not given a high priority. It is often feared and resented" (Payne, 2006, p. 6). It needs to be underscored that these claims made by Payne are empirically baseless. She fails to discuss the substantial body of scholarly research that finds low-SES parents of color think highly of the value of education and do become involved, concretely and not abstractly, in their children's schooling (to be discussed later). Drawing heavily from the culture of poverty literature, Payne's deficit thinking demonizes low-SES parents of color, and it is couched in a perspective that has no scientific support (Valencia, 2010, chapter 3).

The literature on the "at-risk" student/family variant of the deficit thinking model also has helped to maintain the myth of low-SES parents' of color insouciance toward their children's education. The "at-risk" student framework, which I introduced in chapter 2, is a pupil-centered perspective, which uses an inventory of characteristics thought to predispose a student to school failure (e.g., being retained a grade; see, e.g., Frymier & Gansneder, 1989). The "at-risk" student approach of understanding achievement problems is a type of deficit thinking because it ignores any assets and capabilities of the student, while focusing on the putative personal and familial deficiencies of the individual student (Swadener & Lubeck, 1995; Valencia, 2010, chapter 4). In her book on "at-risk" students, Swanson (1991) remarks that numerous students deemed "at-risk" are from families "that do not have the same reverence for our institutions and desire for an education. Their parents do not have the same respect for teachers, and they don't demand excellence in the schools or from their children" (p. 74). Swanson continues her deep dive into deficit thinking, commenting that "They [low-SES parents] don't communicate to their children that educational achievement will pay big dividends in their lives. They don't want to hassle their children about schoolwork and leave motivation to the schools" (p. 74). In some of the literature on "at-risk" students, *mothers* are targeted as the source of children's academic problems (Lubeck, 1995). She points to a statewide (North Carolina) survey of school principals and superintendents, in which respondents associated "at-risk" status with maternal employment, poverty, single parenting, and racial/ethnic minority status. Administrators made reference to the roots of these "problems" mainly through innuendo: "*We have large numbers of children who come from homes with no emphasis on education*" [italics added] (Lubeck & Garrett, 1990, p. 336).

One of the most recent examples seen in the scholarly literature about the alleged non-involvement of low-SES parents of color in their children's education is noted in the late Herman Badillo's 2006 book, *One Nation, One Standard*. Badillo, born in Puerto Rico, is the first Puerto Rican in U.S. history to be elected to the House of Representatives. Voted into office in 1970, the former Congressman (D-New York), a "lifelong liberal" (p. 6), switched to the Republican Party in 1998. In his book, he devotes considerable time to a policy analysis of the shortcomings of the educational system that negatively affect Latino/Latina and Black students (e.g., curricular tracking, elitism of gifted programs). Notwithstanding his acknowledgment of these oppressive educational practices vis-à-vis students of color, Badillo places the burden of academic improvement of Latino/Latina students on the shoulders of their parents. Sans empirical evidence and in a deficit thinking manner, he claims:

> Hispanics have simply failed to recognize the overriding importance of education . . . (p. 30)
>
> To be blunt, educating Hispanic children is not the duty of the governmental school system. This is *their* duty, as parents, family members, neighbors, and citizens. Whenever a child is left behind, it is not the fault of the teachers, or the principals, or the school chancellor, or the mayor, or the president. It is

> *their* fault. Hispanics have no one to blame but themselves for the disastrous high-school [sic] dropout rates of the younger members of the community. (p. 51)

At the book's end, Badillo is more specific in his deficit thinking directed toward Latino/Latina parents. He asserts, "Hispanic parents rarely get involved with their children's schools. They seldom attend parent-teacher conferences, ensure that children do their homework, or inspire their children to dream of attending college" (p. 196).

The communication of the myth of low-SES parents' of color indifference to the importance of education is not confined to scholarly outlets. The fallacy also has been expressed through prominent individuals making such pronouncements in some forum that subsequently capture the attention of the media (especially newspapers and television). A case in point is Lauro Cavazos, Mexican American, and first Latino to hold a cabinet position (U.S. Secretary of Education in President George H. Bush's administration). In April 1990, he made comments that set off a storm of disputation. At a press conference in San Antonio, Texas, which was designed to inform the public of the beginning of a series of regional hearings on Latino/Latina educational concerns, Cavazos stated, "*Hispanics have always valued education . . . but somewhere along the line we've lost that. I really believe that, today, there is not that emphasis*" [italics added] (Snider, 1990, p. 1). Predictably, his remarks met with condemnation—quickly and widely. For example, Dr. José A. Cárdenas, the executive director of the Intercultural Development Research Association in San Antonio at the time, and lifelong educational activist, countered, "It's [Cavazos's assertions] a simple case of the victim being blamed for the crime" (Snider, p. 1).

Secretary Cavazo's unfounded and insulting statements about Latino/Latina parents' alleged attitude toward education certainly provoked outcries. This resultant uproar paled, however, in comparison to the commotion generated by similar comments Professor Lino Graglia made at a news conference on September 10, 1997, at the University of Texas at Austin. At that time, Graglia, constitutional law professor, was chosen as honorary cochairman of the newly established group, Students for Equal Opportunity—a coterie who was "tired of hearing only from supporters of affirmative action" (Roser, 1997, p. B1). At the campus press conference, where the new student group made its debut, Graglia made the following remarks regarding affirmative action, race, and academic performance at the University of Texas School of Law:

> The central problem is that Blacks and Mexican Americans are not academically competitive [with Whites] . . . Various studies seem to show that Blacks [and] Mexican Americans spend less time in school. *They have a culture that seems not to encourage achievement* [italics added] . . . failure is not looked upon with disgrace.[4]

In an *NBC Today* interview on September 12, 1997, reporter Matt Lauer asked Graglia if he had any statistical backing for his cultural statements about students of color and educational achievement:

GRAGLIA: I'm not an expert on educational matters.

LAUER: But you do agree with the statement that came out of yours that says they [Blacks and Mexican Americans] have a culture that seems not to encourage achievement?

GRAGLIA: Well, I meant to say that there are some cultures, like some Asian cultures that insist more highly on the students going to school and achieving in school . . .

The egregious pronouncements from Graglia, who has a long history of speaking out against affirmative action and using busing for school desegregation (Roser & Tanamachi, 1997), drew national and international media coverage, and swift denunciations.[5] Among the public condemnations were replies by the UT Austin School of Law dean, UT Austin interim president, UT system chancellor, student organizations, professors, civil rights organizations, and lawmakers of color (Martin, 1997; Roser & Tanamachi). Senator Gregory Luna, head of the State Hispanic Caucus, stated, "It seems we're in an era where the Ku Klux Klan does not come in white robes but in the robes of academe" (Martin, p. 1). UT Austin students of color were also very involved in the protest against Graglia. They staged a sit-in at the School of Law, and helped organize a political rally in which Reverend Jesse Jackson, in front of 5,000 people, lambasted Graglia (Roser & Tanamachi).

The perpetuation of the myth that low-SES parents of color do not value education, as seen in the scholarly literature and the Cavazos and Graglia incidents, serves as a reminder that irresponsible assertions made about families of color—in which such remarks are shaped by deficit thinking, ahistoricism, ignorance of the scholarly evidence, and bigotry—have no benefit in understanding TAG.

2. *The erroneous equation of behavior and values.* A second way in which parents of color are pathologized regarding their putative indifference to the value of education has to do with how some scholars wrongly equate behavior and values. To illustrate this issue, I use Mexican Americans as a case in point. The myth of Mexican American's indifference to the worth of education can be more fully understood when viewed as part of a historical tradition in which they are described under the "Mexican American cultural model (stereotype)" in which their alleged value orientations are presented as the root cause of their social problems (Hernández, 1970). Such stereotyping was unmasked in a landmark 1968 article by cultural anthropologist Octavio I. Romano-V. In his review essay, Romano discusses the scholarly flaws of a number of anthropologists and sociologists who conducted research on Mexican Americans from the 1940s to the 1960s and concluded that the value orientations of Mexican Americans lead to dysfunctional behaviors.[6] Some of these value orientations Romano identifies

are ahistoricism, fatalism, laziness, politically apathetic, acceptance of segregation, prone to criminality, and lack of achievement motivation.[7]

The Mexican American stereotype model is grounded in the long-standing fallacy that behavior is equated with values. There are two major problems with this line of reasoning (Allen, 1970). First, the behavior = values equation is a nonequivalence. The fact that an individual behaves in a specific way does not suggest he/she wants to do so due to his or her values or beliefs. Usually, behavior can be explained by exogenous factors (e.g., a Puerto Rican mother does not attend a parent-teacher conference at school because she does not have transportation). Second, the notion that values can be inferred from specific behaviors and used to explain such behaviors is tautological. To have utility for the explanation of behavior, values must be measured independently of the behaviors one is trying to explain.

A good example of how some scholars wrongly equate behavior with values is seen in the work of economist Thomas Sowell. In his 1981 book, *Ethnic America: A History*, he has a chapter on "The Mexicans." Sowell states, "*The goals and values of Mexican Americans have never centered on education*" [italics added] (p. 266). How does Sowell, who has written a history of ethnic groups in the U.S., support this sweeping generalization? What specific evidence does he marshal to defend such a brazen assertion? Sowell does so by noting comparative high school completion rates across race/ethnicity: "As of 1960, 13 percent of Hispanics in the Southwest completed high school, compared to only 17 percent for Blacks in the same region, 28 percent among non-Hispanic Whites, and 39 percent among Japanese Americans" (p. 266). It appears that Sowell is making this argument: *Because Mexican Americans have the lowest high school graduation rate of the groups he compares, Mexican Americans do not value education.* Explicit in his reasoning is that Mexican Americans are the makers of their own educational problems because achievement motivation is very low on their hierarchy of values.

A significant shortcoming with Sowell's (1981) claim that Mexican Americans in the Southwest do not value education is that he fails to discuss the far different interpretations of TAG proffered by the authors who presented the original data from which Sowell draws. Grebler, Moore, and Guzmán (1970, p. 143, Table 7.1) attribute the differences in high school completion rates, in part, to intragroup (i.e., White and Mexican American) variations in immigrant status, rural-urban locale, poverty, and some home environment aspects (e.g., language). Grebler et al. also present a structural inequality explanation to account for the differences in high school graduation rates:

> The extreme disparities in different locales suggest also a hypothesis concerning a strategic determinant in a larger society: the extent to which local social systems and, through these, the school systems have held the Mexican American population in a subordinate position. (p. 170)

Sowell's claim that Mexican American's goals and values have never focused on education stands out as one of the most reckless and unfounded statements ever made about Mexican Americans and their schooling. Not only is his assertion inaccurate, but also he presents it in a book about ethnic groups in the U.S.—a type of source that should be committed to the highest level of scholarship, not mythmaking.

3. *The power of teacher ideology.* A third means in which the fallacy that low-SES parents of color do not value education is maintained comes from the belief system of some teachers. Examples of such attitudes are seen in Williams (2008; introduced in chapter 7, this volume), who studied deficit thinking beliefs of White, female teachers in a predominantly Black elementary school. Based on focus group results, Williams reports these exemplars: "I see my kids as complete victims of their families, to be brutally honest" (p. 110). Another teacher added, "I sense a lot of chaos; just a kind of dysfunctional chaos" (p. 110). One teacher, who recalled the time a parent failed to show up for a conference, stated, "I suspect she was napping" (p. 110). Another teacher, when asked what she would tell parents, answered, "If you want . . . to be a successful adult you need to take some parenting classes" (p. 111). On the topic of respect, a teacher said, "It's really hard to even respect them at all as human beings" (p. 112). With an eye closer to the subject of parental involvement, a number of teachers agreed that, "There's just a lack of parental participation or involvement" (p. 114). One teacher added, "I think there's a lack of parent support; it's a huge thing" (p. 114).

The White teacher bias toward Black parents Williams (2008) reports can best be explained by, and rooted in, what Cooper (2003) calls the "power of teacher ideology" (p. 103). That is, teachers who adhere to the view that society is meritocratic are inclined to believe (mistakenly) that the schools are also.[8] Cooper notes that such teachers are not apt to see schools as agencies of social reproduction that restrict the opportunities of students from families who possess few economic advantages to acquire the necessary skills, knowledge, and cultural capital—as defined by the mainstream and powerful school culture—to move upward to the SES levels of their more privileged peers (Laureau, 2000). In light of this meritocratic perspective, Cooper continues, some teachers draw from their ideological beliefs and display deficit thinking toward low-SES parents (especially of color) and their children. In her case study of 14 Black mothers who had children attending Los Angeles, California, schools, Cooper finds that all of the parents had strong, positive beliefs about the value of education. Namely, the participants believed that a good education would improve life chances for their children, lead to financial security, and provide the necessary tools to combat racism against them. Notwithstanding these favorable attitudes toward education, the parents said that teachers failed to understand their frantic work schedules, struggles to make a living, and the responsibilities of being a single parent. Teachers, the parents stated, misinterpreted their sometimes lack of visibility in parental involvement activities as not caring about their children's education. Cooper notes that such misconceptions stoked the teachers' bias and were detrimental to establishing a solid parent-teacher relationship.

Parents of Color Involvement in Their Children's Education: The Empirical Evidence

For over 20 years, I have taught an undergraduate course, "Chicano Educational Struggles," at The University of Texas at Austin. The course is a testimony to the long-standing historical and contemporary campaign by the Mexican American community (broadly defined) for educational equality. In the course, I cover five themes in which these struggles have been expressed: (1) litigation, (2) advocacy organizations, (3) individual activists, (4) political demonstrations, and (5) legislation.[9] I believe that this five-prong approach to examining the quest for equal educational opportunity by Mexican Americans can be adapted for other marginalized ethnic groups, such as Puerto Ricans and African Americans. These indefatigable commitments by people of color speak emphatically as counternarratives to the fallacy of indifference to education. In addition to this thematic five-prong approach to understand how people of color value education, there is also a substantial corpus of scientific evidence, both qualitative and quantitative, that documents that low-SES parents of color care deeply about the education of their children and do participate in a number of ways. This body of studies can be divided into three clusters of targeted groups: (a) exclusively or predominantly Black parents,[10] (b) exclusively or predominantly Latino/Latina parents,[11] and (c) racially/ethnically diverse groups of parents.[12] In light of the volume of this literature, I confine the following review to representative studies of these three groupings.

1. *Black parents.* In this first-of-its-type study, Barnard (2004) employed a longitudinal design to investigate whether early parental involvement led to later academic success of children. The participants included families receiving services in the Child-Parent Centers (CPC) offered by the Chicago Public Schools. The 1,165 children and their parents (90% of whom were mothers) of the CPCs served as participants in the Chicago Longitudinal Study. Of the total participants, 95% were Black and the children attended Title I schools. The CPCs, an early intervention program, offered, for instance, language-based activities, preschool education, and extended support services while the child was in elementary school. Furthermore, the CPCs had some parental empowerment activities (e.g., opportunities to serve on the School Advisory Council, to obtain the GED, and to assist in designing educational activities). Based on parental involvement data (obtained from parents' and teachers' reports) and student academic records in high school, Barnard reports that early parental educational involvement (e.g., frequency of reading to child, conferencing with the teacher) was associated years later with positive student academic outcomes—namely, reduced rates of dropping out from high school, higher rates of on-time school completion, and

increased grade completion. The main implication Barnard draws for practice is that early parental involvement in children's education is cost -effective and can lead to favorable, lasting benefits for parents and children.

In the investigation by Jackson and Remillard (2005), the authors sought to understand how low-income Black mothers serve as educational resources for their children (mostly third graders) attending a public school in an urban area. Specifically, Jackson and Remillard wanted to investigate how the mothers constructed their roles regarding the mathematics education of their children. The families participated in the Educational Scholarship Program (a pseudonym), which offered full scholarships for college if the children successfully finished high school. The primary source of data was from interviews of mothers (N = 10) conducted during home observations.[13] One major finding the authors report is that all the parents communicated that they valued education and were involved in their children's schooling, as demonstrated, for instance, in monitoring school progress, assisting with homework, and navigating how to help their children with the new mathematics program. Particularly salient was the finding that the parents provided learning opportunities in mathematics in out-of-school settings—for example, teaching their children about measurement and time when doing the laundry, assisting with the calculation of the monthly bills, and doing conceptual groupings and calculations when putting away Christmas tree ornaments. Principal conclusions Jackson and Remillard draw from their study is that (a) the parents are very much involved in the education of their children and (b) the parents engage in mathematics education via ways that are likely invisible to the teachers. As such, we need to rethink the nature of Black parents' educational involvement, especially the creative, informal approaches to teaching outside the school environment.

The study by McWayne et al. (2004) included a sample of 307 kindergarten children (95% Black) and their parents. The authors recruited the children (overwhelmingly low-income) from seven public elementary schools in a sizable district in the Northeast. Participating parents filled out several instruments, including the Parent Involvement in Children's Education Scale (PICES) and the parent version of the Social Skills Rating System (SSRS). The PICES, which contains 40 items, measures a number of parental involvement activities—for example, "I ask my child about his/her day," "I help my child practice what he/she learns at school," and "I talk with the teacher about how my child is doing." As to the parent form of the SSRS, it assesses prosocial behaviors of the children (e.g., cooperation, self-control). The teacher version of the SSRS also has a Competence subscale, and measures children's skills in mathematics, reading, classroom behavior, and motivation. McWayne et al. report that, overall, parents who were involved provided very positive learning environments. Furthermore, parents who were more involved have children with greater prosocial skills, higher academic achievement, and motivation to achieve. One significant conclusion the authors present is that families and schools need to co-construct—via collaborative discourse—a manageable understanding of what constitutes "parent involvement," meaning that teachers should avoid an approach to involvement in which strategies are dictated to the parents.

2. *Latino/Latina parents.* In their study, Keith and Lichtman (1994) draw from the National Education Longitudinal Study (NELS) of 1988. Of the 24,000 eighth-grade students who participated, the authors investigated solely the subsample of students who self-identified as being Mexican American (n = 1,714). The slight majority (51%) of the students attended schools (overwhelmingly public) in the West. In this nationally representative investigation, the majority (57%) of the Mexican American parents did not complete high school or have a high school diploma/GED.[14] The student participants of the NELS survey were asked to complete a Parent Involvement questionnaire, which includes a number of activities (e.g., parent-student discussion about plans in high school, parent's support of home learning, parent's educational aspirations for child). For the dependent variable of academic achievement, Keith and Lichtman developed a composite index based on each student's test scores in mathematics, reading, social studies, and science. As predicted, Parent Involvement scores showed a moderate effect on the composite academic achievement measure. As well, the independent variable had significant effects on all four achievement scores. In light of TAG, the authors underscore that Mexican American parental involvement in their middle school children's education appears to be very important.

Considering the underrepresentation of Mexican Americans in higher education (i.e., 4-year institutions; see Zarate, Sáenz, & Oseguera, 2011), it is important to examine the role of Mexican American parent involvement in instilling college aspirations in their children. In his study, Ceja (2004) sought, in part, to address this subject. His participants were 20 female Mexican American high school seniors attending an inner-city school in greater Los Angeles. All of the participants, who were first-generation college-bound students, had goals to attend institutions in the systems of the University of California (n = 7), California State University (n = 7), and California community college (n = 6). The parents of the participants had low educational attainment levels, and many did not have English fluency. Based on extensive interviews, Ceja's major finding was that the parents had a pronounced value about the importance of their daughters going to college and receiving a degree. The parents communicated these messages in a number of ways: for example, telling their daughters a college education will lead to a successful career, pointing out their own lived experiences about not having enough schooling, and informing their daughters that they need to avoid the hardships of constantly working in low-paying jobs. Furthermore, many of the participants noted that their parents expressed, very early, the importance of going to college. One student recalled that even while she was in elementary school, her parents would say, "You have to get good grades if you're going to go to college" (p. 351). Ceja concludes that Mexican American parents, notwithstanding their very limited experience in the U.S. educational system, are able to help develop a "culture of possibility"[15] in the family setting, as well as resiliency in their daughters.

Still yet another study that debunks the myth that Mexican American parents do not value education (Valencia & Black, 2002) is the transgenerational parental involvement case study by Black (1996). Participants were 10 Mexican American adults (4 grandparents and 6 parents) from 6 families living in Austin, Texas. All participants were bilingual or spoke English and had resided in Texas from two to five generations. Based on interview data, Black reports that the participants demonstrated involvement in their grandchildren's and children's education in external and internal ways. For example, regarding the former, one grandmother was a life member of the PTA, and one parent—who had been forced to drop out of high school when she became pregnant as a teenager—later served as PTA president of her child's school. One mother noted that when her daughter was in elementary school, she called the teacher every Friday to find out about homework due on Monday. With respect to internal types of involvement, one father said, "We help our kids with homework around the kitchen table every night" (Valencia & Black, p. 97). One grandmother, with only 2 years of schooling, explained, "I couldn't help them [my children], but my husband always did" (Valencia & Black, p. 97). In other instances, the participants' *consejos* were all too familiar. A father said, "We talk to our kids about their ambitions. Anyone can flip a burger. You're not gonna do that. You're gonna need more education" (Valencia & Black, p. 98). A grandmother told of scolding her daughter, who did not want to go to school one day: "Do you want to be like me," she asked, "and know nothing? The only job I could get is in the laundry or the kitchen. No money. Do you want that?" (Valencia & Black, p. 98). In sum, the power of Black's study is that the grandparents' and parents' testimonies provide evidence that the value of education is transmitted transgenerationally in Mexican American families.

3. Racially/ethnically diverse groups of parents. Jeynes (2005) undertook a meta-analysis of 41 studies involving the relation between parental involvement and children's academic achievement. His general question was whether parental involvement improves academic outcomes of children. Although he sought to examine four queries, I confine this discussion to the question of whether the predicted positive association between involvement and achievement holds across race/ethnicity. The participants in the 41 investigations were urban K-6 children (more than 20,000) and their parents. Of the total studies, Jeynes (2005) notes that eight of them had participants who were, for instance, "very diverse," "mostly minority," and "one-fourth minority" (see Table 1, pp. 248–249). By perusing most of these eight investigations, I was able to ascertain that the participants included, in varying mixes for the most part, White, Black, Latino/Latina, and Asian American children. Jeynes (2005) reports statistically significant relations between a number of parental involvement activities (e.g., monitoring of homework; regularly reading with children; holding high expectations of children's success, attending and participating in school functions) and several measures of student academic achievement (e.g., GPA, scores on standardized achievement tests). He notes that the broad relation between involvement and achievement held across race/ethnicity for the entire meta-analysis. His finding corroborates the meta-analysis conducted by Fan and Chen (2001) of 25 studies in which the participants included parents and children of racially/ethnically diverse families. A major conclusion of Jeynes (2005) is that involvement of parents of color in their children's education appears to be one way in which TAG can be reduced.

In their investigation, researchers Stevenson, Chen, and Uttal (1990) selected a representative sample of 1,161 first, third, and fifth graders from schools (overwhelmingly public) from the metropolitan area of Chicago. Participant students included Whites (59.2%), Blacks (20.7%), Latinos/Latinas (15.0%), and "other" (.5%). In regard to the children's parents, the SES levels (i.e., educational attainment, income) were, as expected, higher for Whites. Furthermore, Spanish was the spoken home language for 84% of the Latino/Latina families. The focus of reporting by Stevenson et al. is on intergroup differences in parental beliefs about their children's academic achievement. Some germane findings are: (a) both Black and White mothers, compared to Latina mothers, had higher educational expectations for their children to go to college; (b) Black and Latina mothers, in comparison to the White mothers, expressed greater enthusiasm for their children's positive attitudes toward school; and (c) all mothers agreed that parents need to work closely with their children on homework assignments, but Black and Latina mothers agreed more strongly; the Latina mothers, however, felt less capable of helping with reading and mathematics. A major point one can take from this study is that the findings of such strong beliefs of the mothers of color about academic achievement defy the myth of lack of parental involvement. Also, the authors note that when they controlled for SES, the achievement levels of the children from the three groups are quite similar. Furthermore, Stevenson et al. comment that the beliefs of these mothers "are similar to those associated with higher, not lower, levels of [children's] achievement" (p. 521). One explanation the authors proffer for the subsequent school failure of many students of color is that CD in middle and high school, coupled with lower expectations of teachers, may diminish the high achievement motivation established in elementary school.

Toward Systemic Transformations

The preceding discussion and review of germane literature leave us with two incontrovertible conclusions. First, parental involvement in children's education, as a broad principle, is a key factor in promoting achievement motivation and academic success for one's offspring. Second, low-SES parents of color care deeply about the value of education and do get involved in a myriad of ways. Yet, notwithstanding these two points, why is it that the educational involvement dimension of parents of color has not received the full attention it warrants in any discussion of school reform? I believe that the major explanation reduces to *barriers*—specifically, obstacles along the lines of (a) how the literature, in general, conceptualizes parental involvement, (b) how educators erroneously view (i.e., via a deficit thinking lens) the parental involvement of parents of color, and (c) how schools, via their top-down, school-centric approach to parental involvement, fail to see the value of jointly establishing a bottom-up, community-centric strategy for parental involvement. The following systemic suggestions, which are not mutually exclusive and thus have some overlapping features, are intended to stimulate needed discourse on how parents of color can become more fully empowered in their profound roles of advocates for the academic success of their children.

1. *Reconceptualizing the notion of "parental involvement."* Although parents have been involved in their children's education in some form or other since the inception of public schooling, the 1960s sparked a particular interest in parental involvement patterns. A major perspective from this period was oriented toward "parent education," which held that low-SES parents, especially of color, lacked parenting skills and a basic understanding of their role as their child's first teacher. It was these skills, or the lack thereof, that was at the root of school failure of low-SES students of color (Moreno & Valencia, 2011). The theory that framed this orientation was based on the earlier cultural and environmental deficit thinking models, particularly the putative inadequate academic socialization of children by their parents (Pearl, 1997). Parental involvement was therefore based on providing parents with the "correct" values, attitudes, beliefs, and behaviors to interact with their children (Valentine & Stark, 1979). Contemporary literature and discourse on parental involvement have been chiefly formulated in regard to what parents "do" and how these behaviors are consonant with the child's needs or the school's goals (Barton et al., 2004). This manner of comprehending parental involvement, especially among low-SES parents of color, relies on, some scholars assert, deficit thinking because it focuses on presumed deficiencies rather than strengths in these families (e.g., Barton et al.; Olivos, 2006; Olivos et al., 2011). In sum, though the deficit thinking view of low-SES parents of color and their educational involvement is more subtle than in decades past, these parents continue to be largely perceived as manipulatable and powerless beings (Barton et al.).

In light of these concerns, a number of scholars in recent years have been calling for a paradigm shift in the ways we view educational involvement among low-SES parents of color (e.g., Barton et al., 2004; Olivos, 2006; Olivos et al., 2011). For example, Olivos et al. comment that educational researchers, school officials, and teachers often subscribe to a narrow spectrum of behaviors that fall under the rubric of legitimate types of parental involvement (e.g., Epstein et al., 2002). As such, low-SES parents of color are required to change in attitudes and behaviors to meet the expectations of the schools, rather than the schools working as partners with parents. Thus, status quo discourse on parental involvement has limited utility in understanding the educational involvement of parents of color.

This issue, coupled with a deficit thinking approach by the schools in viewing parents of color, has led some scholars to argue for a systemic change in how we conceptualize the notion of parental involvement. Given that the prevailing view of educational involvement of low-SES parents revolves around an "accommodationist" perspective, what is sorely needed is an approach that focuses on a more "transformational" outlook via parental *engagement* (Olivos et al., p. 11).

What is the difference between the meaning of parental "involvement" and parental "engagement"? To start with, a dictionary definition is useful. One meaning for involvement is "the act of taking part in an activity, event, or situation." A definition for engagement is "the feeling of being involved in a particular activity."[16] At first glance, the two meanings appear extremely similar. Further analysis, however, reveals a nuance. The word "feeling" in engagement is telling, carrying connotations of affect, ownership, and agency—while involvement suggests a static and linear act of participation. Though helpful for understanding the distinction between involvement and engagement, we need to go beyond semantics—and examine deeper levels of conceptualization.

Let us continue with this unpacking of the two notions, using education as the context. Ferlazzo (2011) comments that when schools aim for parental involvement, they frequently lead with their "mouths"—establishing needs and objectives and then telling parents how they can be instrumental. By contrast, schools that have parental engagement as their mission frequently lead with their "ears," listening to the aspirations, thoughts, and concerns of parents. As such, the objective of parental engagement is not to assist clients but rather to attain partners (p. 12). Barton et al. (2004) also offer helpful insights into the parental involvement vs. parental engagement difference. Involvement focuses largely on "what" parents do in regard to their children's schooling (e.g., attend a parent-teacher conference), and engagement is about the "hows" and "whys" of a parent's participation (p. 3). The engagement process, Barton et al. assert, is interactive and dynamic, and in this process parents call on their varied lived experiences, as well as resourcefulness, to designate their interfacings with the schools. Viewed in this manner, and in the context of the experiential knowledge tenet of CRT, engagement can lead to parental empowerment (to be discussed later).

2. *Fostering parent–preservice teacher relationships.* Notwithstanding the reality that teachers have some sort of contact with the parents of their students, the overwhelming percentage of classroom teachers are poorly trained in the working knowledge of parental and community involvement (Katz & Bauch, 1999). Furthermore, considering the deficit thinking views held of families of color by some preservice teachers (e.g., Marx, 2006; Young, 2007) and by inservice teachers (McKenzie & Scheurich, 2004; Williams, 2008), it would be prudent to mount a proactive, concerted curricular campaign to reach students in teacher education programs before they enter the teaching profession.

An example of a curricular intervention is reported by Sutterby, Rubin, and Abrego (2007), professors of education at the University of Texas at Brownsville (a Hispanic-serving institution [HSI] located on the Texas-Mexico border).[17] The authors undertook an investigation with 160 preservice teachers (86% Latina, mostly Mexican American) who participated in an afternoon reading tutoring program with pre-K through first-grade pupils attending a local elementary school (100% Latino/Latina; 99% low-SES; 55% ELs). A component of the tutoring program required that the preservice teachers communicate with the parents before and after the tutoring period. At the onset of the program, the preservice teachers demonstrated, at times, condescending demeanors toward the families (Abrego, Rubin, & Sutterby, 2006). Sutterby et al. (2007) collected data on the preservice teachers, including open-ended questions, pre- and post-surveys, weekly journal reflections, and end-of-course reflections. The researchers also gathered data from the parents via focus groups, conducted mainly in Spanish. The authors report that the preservice teachers viewed the parents as possessing a number of strengths in supporting their children, including *esfuerzo* (effort) in wanting to help their children in any way they could. The parents also demonstrated *orgullo* (pride) in the accomplishments of their children and held high expectations for the youngsters.

In a companion article that supplements Sutterby et al. (2007), Abrego et al. (2006) report that based on the preservice teachers' reflections, these aspiring teachers commented that they were able to build valuable communication skills, confidence, and sound expectations for their future work with parents. Second, the preservice teachers noted that they gained insights into the importance of establishing positive, friendly relationships (*amistades;* see Sutterby et al.) with parents as valued partners. Third, these future teachers remarked that they were able to work with the parents in developing literacy skills, an empowering process in itself. One preservice teacher reflected that it is the role of the teacher to serve as a facilitator. She continued by noting that teachers need to take the responsibility "to provide parents methods and tips that can help parents get involved in reading to their child. There are many things that parents can do during reading time with them even if they don't know how to read" (p. 8).

A similar curricular effort that corroborates the work of Abrego et al. (2006) and Sutterby et al. (2007) is reported by Munter (2004). The participants ($N = 45$) included, in part, students enrolled in the teacher education program at the University of Texas at El Paso, an HSI located adjacent to the Texas-Mexico border. Though not mentioned, I assume the preservice teachers were primarily Mexican American. The initiative described is Project *Podemos* ("We can do it" in Spanish). A major component of the project is a parental engagement unit, designed for future teachers who aspire to teach in bilingual-multicultural communities. The principal objective of Project *Podemos* is to build reciprocal trust between the preservice teacher and the parents, who are overwhelmingly immigrant. These future teachers receive training via course work, school-based activities, and engagement with parents. A veteran teacher accompanied each preservice teacher during home visits in order to help him/her reflect on the experience. A highlight of the project is Parent Power Night, which are meetings designed to promote open dialogue, enable parents to acquire skills, and focus on the varied assets and knowledge the parents possess. Based on a pre-postmeasure survey, Munter reports that for each of the six questions asked, there were gain scores (see Table 1, p. 25). For example, "I feel that I am prepared to develop a parent involvement plan for my classroom" (premeasure, 82% agreement; postmeasure, 94% agreement). Overall, Project *Podemos* appears to be quite successful. Underscoring the importance of a teacher-parent partnership, one preservice teacher concluded, "What I know now is that I am only one part of the equation. I feel that I can make a difference as a teacher, but ultimately, I will need parental help and guidance" (p. 27).

In the final analysis, we can draw three key conclusions from the preceding research. First, the studies just reviewed (Abrego et al., 2006; Munter, 2004; Sutterby et al., 2007), plus other related investigations (e.g., Hiatt-Michael, 2001; Katz & Bauch, 1999; Morris & Taylor, 1998), provide convincing evidence that preservice teachers who receive training in parental involvement report that they develop confidence and the necessary skills to effectively work with parents once they enter the teaching profession. Second, successful curricular interventions directed to parental engagement training in teacher education programs appear to be adaptable for widespread implementation. Of course, colleges of education will need to provide the necessary commitment via financial resources and personnel to do the training. Third, aspiring teachers of color—in this case, Mexican Americans—are not immune from harboring deficit thinking views of low-SES parents of color (Abrego et al.). Mexican American preservice teachers may share an ethnic identity with Mexican American parents, but this does not necessarily translate into a shared identity of lived experiences involving SES, culture, and location of where one is raised (Sutterby et al.). As such, we must be mindful that deficit thinking toward parents of color can transcend race/ethnicity of educators, and therefore these condescending attitudes must be vigorously identified, confronted, and rectified.

3. *Advocating a community-centric over a school-centric approach to parental engagement.* As I have underscored earlier, the preponderance of the parental involvement research focuses on activities defined and deemed most important by the schools (e.g., monitoring homework). Although this school-centric perspective emphasizes involvement tasks that are indeed beneficial for the academic development of children, parents typically lack power in decision making in schools and are delegated to supporting school-defined objectives regarding what is best for their children (Lawson, 2003). By sharp contrast, there is a counternarrative—the community-centric approach to parental engagement. In this view, schools are conceptualized as institutions that should serve the community, provide greater opportunities and services that the parents consider important, and build communication with and respect for parents, especially their opinions (Lawson). In another model for understanding the distinctions between the school-centric

and community-centric approaches, the former emphasizes, for example, specific activities and parents as individual beings, and parents are expected to follow the school's program. A community-centric perspective focuses on relationships and parents as constituents of a collective, and parents are given opportunities to lead and set agendas (Warren, Hong, Rubin, & Uy, 2009).

One of the appealing features of a community-centric strategy to foster the educational engagement of low-SES parents of color is that this approach is quite adaptable in meeting local needs. For example, before it was unfairly closed in 2011, Park Oaks Elementary School (79.6% low-SES Latino/Latina students)—which is located in the predominantly White middle- to high-SES Conejo Valley Unified School District in Southern California—had an exemplary parental engagement program (Valencia, 2012). Some of these aspects included: (a) evening parent education and English language classes, (b) classroom volunteering opportunities, (c) a group (*Padres Haciendo La Diferencia* [Parents Making a Difference]) designed to promote community-school unity, (d) a Spanish-speaking clerk in the office, (e) a PTA president who was bilingual, and (f) a bilingual outreach coordinator.

A more comprehensive community-centric approach is described by Warren et al. (2009), who report what transpired in three case studies: the Quitman Street Community School in Newark, New Jersey (largely Black and low-SES), Camino Nuevo Charter Academy in Los Angeles, California, and the Logan Square Neighborhood Association in Chicago, Illinois (both predominantly Latino/Latina and low-SES). In each of these community-based organizations (CBOs), the stakeholders developed a relational approach to establish parental engagement. For example, at Camino Nuevo Charter School there are culturally germane classes and programs on Latino music and dance, school doors are open to 6 p.m., parents organize regular meeting among themselves and the executive director to discuss concerns and programs, and the school has a full-time parent coordinator of engagement. Furthermore, 50% of the school's paraprofessionals, teachers, and administrators are Spanish-English bilingual. Teachers there are trained and committed to teach a social justice curriculum, and they work closely with parents in community development (e.g., neighborhood cleanups, health fairs). Overall, this CBO appears to be successful in helping parents get empowered via engagement. As well, the students showed significant increases in academic achievement based on state-mandated tests. In sum, the parents at Camino Nuevo Charter Academy School have expressed a sense of belonging, which is in dramatic contrast to the alienation many experienced in the Los Angeles public schools. One parent remarked, "Here at this school we can easily talk to the principals and teachers. [The] community is very open and very easy to access" (p. 2225).

The most comprehensive community-centric approach to parental engagement is the full-service community school (FSCS), which is a public school open seven days a week, year-round, and is available to families before, during, and after school (Dryfoos, 2002). The idea behind the FSCS is to create an active hub of education and provide valuable services for parents and their children, mainly in low-SES sectors. Examples of these services include: housing and employment services; care for dental, medical, and mental health needs; recreational and after-school events; literacy programs for parents; computer use; tutoring; and, very importantly, parental engagement opportunities. The FSCS is a partnership in regards to financial costs. The local school system covers the cost of education, and the other services are paid by a combination of external funding (e.g., foundations, federal government) (Dryfoos). What is quite surprising about FSCSs is that they are seldom cited in school reform discussions. This is unfortunate, as the FSCS has considerable potential for successfully transforming education for low-SES students of color. Based on a number of program evaluations—though they vary in design rigor—the results are encouraging. Improvements have been seen in parental involvement, student academic achievement, school attendance, and access to health care (Dryfoos).

4. *Empowering parents as change agents.* The term "empower" is frequently used in discussions of marginalized groups. Before I go further in sharing some ideas about how to understand the empowerment of low-SES parents of color as active agents of change in advocating for their children's school success, it would be useful to describe the essential features of this significant and complex concept. A good starting point is to understand that empowerment means there has to be a transformation in power relationships, at the location of both *agency* and *structure* (Pettit, 2012). Agency refers to the capacity of an individual and a collective to think and take action on their own concerns and interests, and structure pertains to the institutions, normative beliefs, and rules that allow and restrict thinking and behavior. Discourse on well-grounded practices of empowerment and participation (e.g., Barton et al., 2004), as well as the development of empowerment theory (e.g., Alsop, Bertelsen, & Holland, 2006), very much considers agency and structure together, and their interaction (Pettit). For example, a campaign to transform state laws that discriminate in school financing of high-enrollment schools of color (structure) needs to include, for example, raising public awareness, gaining the support of teacher unions, and filing a lawsuit (agency).

A second important characteristic of the notion of empowerment is that the structure of power runs deep and, as such, is more difficult to see and challenge than agency. Thus, power constantly must be contested. As an example, let us draw from Barton et al. (2004), who describe, in part, the experience of Miranda. She is a Black working-class mother of two who is raising children on her own. Miranda reports she is very engaged in her children's education. She is able at times to observe her children in school, as well as their teachers. She recalls one day during an observation:

> I had to put one teacher in check . . . what made me so mad at him is he told the whole class, "I only have one smart child in this classroom."

> That burned me up cause if you only got one smart child in this classroom, you calling the rest of them stupid. And I was like, oh, no wonder we can't get this math done because you're dumb. Let's go. I went straight to him with no hesitation. I went straight to him and asked him you only got one smart child in your classroom? . . . you calling my baby dumb in her face, you know . . . I haven't heard one complaint about him saying things like that and she's getting the work done. But it took Mama to go up there and check him. (p. 7)

Miranda, exercising agency, dared to contest the embedded deficit thinking views of her child's teacher and the structural underpinnings of the school culture that allow such beliefs. Miranda's desire for her child to do well in mathematics prompted her need to "check" the teacher, notwithstanding that her action challenged the tradition of the school and annoyed the teacher.

There are a number of parental engagement models particularly pertinent to low-SES parents of color—for example, the Transformational Parental Engagement Model (Ochoa, Olivos, & Jiménez-Castellanos, 2011), the Democratic Schooling Model (Pearl, 2011), the Ecologies of Parental Engagement Model (Barton et al., 2004), and the Parent Advocate's Model (Johnson, 2011). I confine my discussion to the Parent Advocate's Model (PAM), as it appears to have most relevance to practice, and it was developed by parents of color themselves. The PAM derives from the work of Project U-Turn (PUT), a nonprofit organization founded in 1999. The group, which has about 200 parents, serves working-class parents and a diverse group of parents of color whose children attend public schools in communities of South Los Angeles County. PUT takes pride in transforming itself from a group of "school spectators to active education participants" (Johnson, p. 149). The organization eschews attempts by schools to instruct them in "parenting skills" and "how to work with our children" in the home setting (p. 147). Rather, PUT parents consider themselves engaged participants of action research and advocates for their children. The parents are proactive in asking demanding questions about the quality of teaching (e.g., asking to see lesson plans of the teacher) and adequacy of school resources. Over time, the parents of PUT have, through assiduousness, acquired agency and voice by shifting from the conventional approach of parental involvement to increased participatory roles and advocacy.

Johnson (2011) notes that the development of the PAM was triggered by the organization's reaction to Epstein's (2001) model of parental involvement, which is considered by many to be the definitive framework. Johnson comments that Epstein's model is not appropriate for the needs of PUT. This approach relies on parental accommodation to the schools and it fails to see the potential of parents as leaders and advocates. The model, Johnson asserts, disempowers parents of color. As such, PAM recasts the Epstein model to meet the needs of its constituents. PAM contains seven kinds of action-based strategies that parents direct:

> Type I: Access to Information and Data Collection
> Type II: Parents in Decision Making Roles
> Type III: Parents as Student Advocates
> Type IV: Parents as Leaders at Home and in the School Community
> Type V: Effective Two-Way Communication
> Type VI: Acquiring District Level Support
> Type VII: Creating a Friendly School Atmosphere. (pp. 151–155)

To be sure, parental engagement as a vehicle to help reduce TAG is a force to be reckoned with. But we must be realistic regarding the politics of education. Public schools are far from being neutral institutions, and, in many instances, they are not responsive to low-SES parents of color. By their use of particular linguistic structures, embedded cultural capital, curriculum, governance, and assumptions of the home environments, schools "invite" certain segments of the community and discourage others to participate. This selectivity on the part of schools, and the resultant alienation many parents of color experience, has forced a number of working-class Latino/Latina and Black parents, in particular, to mount effective campaigns of parental engagement. These initiatives have led to empowerment in which parents of color have challenged the hegemony of schools through action research, participatory democracy, and child advocacy. We must applaud such efforts and wholeheartedly support these proud parents of color as they continue their struggle for school reform.

Notes

1. The first paragraph of this chapter builds on, with revisions, Moreno and Valencia (2002, p. 239). Other parts of this chapter draw from, with revisions, Moreno and Valencia (2011, pp. 197–199, 203–204), Valencia (2010, p. 131), Valencia and Black (2002, pp. 84–91), and Valencia and Solórzano (1997, p. 192).
2. See, for example, Barnard (2004); Englund, Luckner, Whaley, and Egeland (2004); Fan (2001); Fan and Chen (2001); Hampton, Fantuzzo, Cohen, and Sekino (2004); Hawkes and Plourde (2005); Henderson and Berla (1994); Hong and Ho (2005); Jeynes (2003, 2005); Patall, Cooper, and Robinson (2008); Sheldon (2003).
3. For a discussion of the "cultural deprivation" era, see Pearl (1997).
4. This quote by Graglia is taken from a news clip of the September 10, 1997, news conference at UT Austin shown on *NBC Today*, September 12, 1997 (Lauer, 1997).
5. It appears that Graglia's views on affirmative action have hurt him. According to Martin (1997), reporter of the UT Austin *Daily Texan*, "Former President Ronald Reagan [in 1986] pulled away from appointing Graglia to the 5th U.S. Circuit Court of Appeals after complaints about his remarks regarding affirmative action" (p. 2).
6. See, for example, Edmonson (1957); Heller (1968); Kluckhohn and Strodbeck (1961); Madsen (1964); Tuck (1946).

7. For critiques of these Mexican American stereotypes, see Hernández (1970); Menchaca (2000); Romano-V (1968).
8. See chapter 7, this volume, for a discussion on the myth of meritocracy.
9. See Moreno and Valencia (2011, pp. 200–201) for further discussion.
10. See, for example, Barnard (2004); Cooper (2003); Gutman and McLoyd (2000); Hill et al. (2004); Jackson and Remillard (2005); McWayne, Hampton, Fantuzzo, Cohen, and Sekino (2004); Samaras and Wilson (1999); West-Olatunji, Sanders, Mehta, and Behar-Horenstein (2010). For the most recent research on Black families, see Jeynes (2011, chapter 5).
11. See, for example, Black (1996); Ceja (2004); Delgado-Gaitán (1992); Espinoza-Herold (2007); Hossain and Shipman (2009); Keith and Lichtman (1994); Martínez, DeGarno, and Eddy (2004); Moreno (2002); Valdés (1996); Waterman (2008). Overwhelmingly, the parental involvement research on Latinos/Latinas is with Mexican Americans. For the most recent research on Latino/Latina families, see Jeynes (2011, chapter 5).
12. See, for example, Fan (2001); Fan and Chen (2001); Hong and Ho (2005); Jeynes (2005, 2011, chapter 5); Lee and Bowen (2006); Stevenson, Chen, and Uttal (1990).
13. Of the 10 interviewees, 2 were grandmothers.
14. See Keith and Lichtman (1994, Table 1, p. 260) for full demographic information of the participants.
15. See Gándara (1995).
16. Online MacMillan Dictionary. Retrieved June 13, 2014, from: www.macmillandictionary.com/us/dictionary/american/invovlement.
17. An HSI enrolls 25% or more Hispanic full-time undergraduates (see Zarate et al., 2011, p. 135, note 16 for further explanation).

References

Abrego, M. H., Rubin, R., & Sutterby, J. A. (2006). They call me *maestra*: Preservice teachers' interactions with parents in a reading tutoring program. *Action in Teacher Education, 28,* 3–12.

Allen, V. I. (1970). The psychology of poverty: Problems and prospects. In V. I. Allen (Ed.), *Psychological factors in poverty* (pp. 367–383). Chicago: Markham Press.

Alsop, R., Bertelsen, M., & Holland, J. (2006). *Empowerment in practice: From analysis to implementation.* Washington, DC: World Bank.

Badillo, H. (2006). *One nation, one standard: An ex-liberal on how Hispanics can succeed just like other immigrant groups.* New York: Sentinel.

Barnard, W. M. (2004). Parent involvement in elementary school and educational attainment. *Children and Youth Services Review, 26,* 39–62.

Barton, A. C., Drake, C., Pérez, J. G., St. Louis, K., & George, M. (2004). Ecologies of parental engagement in urban education. *Educational Researcher, 33,* 3–12.

Black, M. S. (1996). *Historical factors affecting Mexican American parental involvement and educational outcomes: The Texas environment from 1910–1996.* Unpublished doctoral dissertation, Harvard University, Cambridge, MA.

Ceja, M. (2004). Chicana college aspirations and the role of parents: Developing educational resiliency. *Journal of Hispanic Higher Education, 3,* 338–362.

Cooper, C. W. (2003). The detrimental impact of teacher bias: Lessons learned from the standpoint of African American mothers. *Teacher Education Quarterly, 30,* 101–116.

Delgado-Gaitán, C. (1992). School matters in the Mexican-American home: Socializing children to education. *American Educational Research Journal, 29,* 495–513.

Delgado-Gaitán, C. (1994). *Consejos:* The power of cultural narratives. *Anthropology and Education Quarterly, 25,* 298–316.

Delgado-Gaitán, C. (2004). *Involving Latino families in schools: Raising student achievement through home-school partnerships.* Thousand Oaks, CA: Corwin Press.

Dougherty, L. G. (1996). Working with disadvantaged parents. In J. F. Frost & G. R. Hawkes (Eds.), *The disadvantaged child: Issues and innovations* (pp. 389–394). New York: Houghton-Mifflin.

Dryfoos, J. (2002). Full-service community schools: Creating new institutions. *Phi Delta Kappan, 83,* 393–399.

Edmonson, M. S. (1957). *Los manitos: A study of institutional values.* New Orleans, LA: Middle America Research Institute, Tulane University.

Englund, M. M., Luckner, A. E., Whaley, G.J.L., & Egeland, B. (2004). Children's achievement in early elementary school: Longitudinal effects of parental involvement, expectations, and quality of assistance. *Journal of Educational Psychology, 96,* 723–730.

Epstein, J. L. (2001). *School, family, and community partnerships: Preparing educators and improving schools.* Boulder, CO: Westview Press.

Epstein, J. L., Sanders, M. G., Simon, B. S., Salinas, K. C., Jansorn, N. R., & VanVoorhis, F. L. (2002). *School, family, and community partnerships* (2nd ed.). Thousand Oaks, CA: Corwin Press.

Espinoza-Herold, M. (2007). Stepping beyond *si se puede: Dichos* as a cultural resource in mother-daughter interaction in a Latino family. *Anthropology and Education Quarterly, 38,* 260–277.

Fan, X. T. (2001). Parental involvement and students' academic achievement: A growth modeling analysis. *Journal of Experimental Education, 70,* 27–61.

Fan, X. T., & Chen, M. (2001). Parental involvement and students' academic achievement: A meta-analysis. *Educational Psychology Review, 13,* 1–22.

Ferlazzo, L. (2011). Involvement or engagement? *Educational Leadership, 68,* 10–14.

Frynier, J., & Gansneder, B. (1989). The Phi Delta Kappan Study of Students at Risk. *Phi Delta Kappan, 71,* 142–146.

Gándara, P. (1995). *Over the ivy walls: The educational mobility of low-income Chicanas.* Albany: State University of New York Press.

González, N., Moll, L. C., & Amanti, C. (Eds.). (2005). *Funds of knowledge: Theorizing practices in households and classrooms.* Mahwah, NJ: Lawrence Erlbaum.

Gould, B. (1932). *Methods of teaching Mexicans.* Unpublished master's thesis. University of Southern California, Los Angeles.

Grebler, L., Moore, J. W., & Guzmán, R. C. (1970). *The Mexican-American people: The nation's second largest minority.* New York: Free Press.

Gutman, L. M., & McLoyd, V. C. (2000). Parents' management of their children's education within the home, at school, and in the community: An examination of African-American families living in poverty. *Urban Review, 32,* 1–24.

Hampton, V., Fantuzzo, J., Cohen, H. L., & Sekino, Y. (2004). A multivariate examination of parental involvement and the social and academic competencies of urban kindergarten children. *Psychology in the Schools, 41,* 363–377.

Havighurst, R. J. (1966). Who are the socially disadvantaged? In J. F. Frost & G. R. Hawkes (Eds.), *The disadvantaged child: Issues and innovations* (pp. 15–23). New York: Houghton Mifflin.

Hawkes, C. A., & Plourde, L. A. (2005). Parental involvement and its influence on the reading achievement of 6th grade students. *Reading Improvement, 42,* 47–57.

Heller, C. S. (1968). *Mexican-American youth: Forgotten youth at the crossroads.* New York: Random House.

Henderson, A., & Berla, N. (Eds.). (1994). *A new generation of evidence: The family is critical to student achievement.* Columbia, MD: National Committee for Citizens in Education.

Hernández, D. (1970). *Mexican American challenge to a sacred cow* (Monograph No. 1). Los Angeles: Mexican American Cultural Center, University of California.

Hiatt-Michael, D. B. (2001). *Preparing teachers to work with parents.* Washington, DC: Eric Clearinghouse on Teaching and Teacher Education. (ERIC Document Reproduction Service No. ED 460 123)

Hill, N. E., Castellino, D. R., Lansford, J. E., Nowlin, P., Dodge, K. A., Bates, J. E., & Petit, G. S. (2004). Parent academic involvement as related to school behavior, achievement, and aspiration: Demographic variations across adolescence. *Child Development, 75,* 1491–1509.

Hong, S., & Ho, L-Z. (2005). Direct and indirect longitudinal effects of parental involvement on student achievement: Second-order latent growth modeling across ethnic groups. *Journal of Educational Psychology, 97,* 32–42.

Hoover-Dempsey, K. V., & Sandler, H. M. (1995). Parental involvement in children's education: Why does it make a difference? *Teachers College Record, 97,* 310–331.

Hoover-Dempsey, K. V., & Sandler, H. M. (1997). Why do parents become involved in their children's education? *Review of Educational Research, 67,* 3–42.

Hoover-Dempsey, K. V., Walker, J.M.T., Sandler, H. M., Whetsel, D., Green, C. L., Wilkins, A. S., & Clossen, K. E. (2005). Why do parents become involved? Research findings and implications. *Elementary School Journal, 106,* 105–130.

Hossain, Z., & Shipman, V. (2009). Mexican immigrant fathers' and mothers' engagement with school-age children. *Hispanic Journal of Behavioral Sciences, 31,* 468–491.

Jackson, K., & Remillard, J. (2005). Rethinking parent involvement: African American mothers construct their roles in the mathematics education of their children. *School Community Journal, 15,* 51–73

Jeynes, W. H. (2003). A meta-analysis—The effects of parental involvement on minority children's academic achievement. *Education and Urban Society, 35,* 202–218.

Jeynes, W. H. (2005). A meta-analysis of the relation of parental involvement to urban elementary school achievement. *Urban Education, 40,* 237–269.

Jeynes, W. H. (2011). *Parental involvement and academic success.* New York: Routledge.

Johnson, M. (2011). A parent advocate's vision of a 21st-century model for bicultural parent engagement. In E. M. Olivos, O. Jiménez-Castellanos, & A. M. Ochoa (Eds.), *Bicultural parent engagement: Advocacy and empowerment* (pp. 145–158). New York: Teachers College Press.

Katz, L., & Bauch, J. P. (1999). The Peabody Family Involvement Initiative: Preparing preservice teachers for family/school collaboration. *School Community Journal, 9,* 49–68.

Keith, P. B., & Lichtman, M. V. (1994). Does parental involvement influence the academic achievement of Mexican-American eighth graders? Results from the National Education Longitudinal Study. *School Psychology Quarterly, 9,* 256–272.

Kluckhohn, F. R., & Strodbeck, F. L. (1961). *Variations in value orientations.* New York: Row, Petersen.

Lareau, A. (2000). *Home advantage: Social class and parental intervention in elementary education.* Lanham, MD: Rowman & Littlefield.

Lauer, M. (1997, September 12). *Today.* New York: National Broadcasting.

Lawson, M. A. (2003). School-family relations in context: Parent and teacher perceptions of parent involvement. *Urban Education, 38,* 77–133.

Lee, J-S., & Bowen, N. K. (2006). Parent involvement, cultural capital, and the achievement gap among elementary children. *American Educational Research Journal, 43,* 193–218.

López, O. (1977). Parent participation in education: Three levels—one model. *Journal of Instructional Psychology, 3,* 45–49.

López, R. G. (2001). The value of hard work: Lessons on parental involvement from an (im)migrant household. *Harvard Educational Review, 71,* 416–437.

Lubeck, S. (1995). Mothers at risk. In B. B. Swadener & S. Lubeck (Eds.), *Children and families "at promise": Deconstructing the discourse of risk* (pp. 50–75). Albany: State University of New York.

Lubeck, S., & Garrett, P. (1990). The social construction of the "at-risk" child. *British Journal of Sociology of Education, 11,* 327–340.

Madsen, W. (1964). *Mexican-Americans of South Texas.* Case studies in Cultural Anthropology Series. New York: Holt, Rinehart, and Winston.

Marans, A. E., & Lourie, R. (1967). Hypotheses regarding the effects of child-rearing patterns on the disadvantaged child. In J. Hellmuth (Ed.), *Disadvantaged child* (Vol. 1, pp. 17–41). New York: Brunner/Mazel.

Martin, D. H. (1997, September 12). Remarks raise lawmakers' ire. *Daily Texan,* pp. 1–2.

Martínez, C. R., Jr., DeGarmo, D. S., & Eddy, J. M. (2004). Promoting academic success among Latino youths. *Hispanic Journal of Behavioral Sciences, 26,* 128–151.

Marx, S. (2006). *Revealing the invisible: Confronting passive racism in teacher education.* New York: Routledge.

McKenzie, K. B., & Scheurich, J. J. (2004). Equity traps: A useful construct for preparing principals to lead schools that are successful with racially diverse students. *Educational Administration Quarterly, 40,* 601–632.

McWayne, C., Hampton, V., Fantuzzo, J., Cohen, H. L., & Sekino, Y. (2004). A multivariate examination of parent involvement and the social and academic competencies of urban kindergarten children. *Psychology in the Schools, 41,* 363–377.

Menchaca, M. (2000). History and anthropology: Conducting Chicano research. In R. Rochín & D. Valdés (Eds.), *Toward a new Chicano history* (pp. 167–181). East Lansing: Michigan State University Press.

Moll, L. C., Amanti, C., Neff, D., & González, N. (1992). Funds of knowledge for teaching: Using a qualitative approach to connect homes and classrooms. *Theory into Practice, 31,* 132–141.

Moreno, R. P. (2002). Teaching the alphabet: An exploratory look at maternal instruction in Mexican American families. *Hispanic Journal of Behavioral Sciences, 24,* 191–205.

Moreno, R. P., & Valencia, R. R. (2002). Chicano families and schools: Myths, knowledge, and future directions for understanding. In R. R. Valencia (Ed.), *Chicano school failure and success: Past, present and future* (2nd ed., pp. 227–249). New York: RoutledgeFalmer.

Moreno, R. P., & Valencia, R. R. (2011). Chicano families and schools: Challenges for strengthening family-school relationships. In R. R. Valencia (Ed.), *Chicano school failure and success: Past, present, and future* (3rd ed., pp. 197–210). New York: Routledge.

Morris, V. G., & Taylor, S. I. (1998). Alleviating barriers to family involvement in education: The role of teacher education. *Teaching and Teacher Education, 14,* 219–231.

Munter, J. H. (2004). Tomorrow's teachers re-envisioning the roles of parents in schools: Lessons learned in the U.S./Mexico border. *Thresholds in Education, 30,* 19–29.

Nieto, S. (1985). Who's afraid of bilingual parents? *Bilingual Review, 12,* 179–189.

Ochoa, A. M., Olivos, E. M., & Jiménez-Castellanos, O. (2011). The struggle for democratic and transformative parent engagement. In E. M. Olivos, O. Jiménez-Castellanos, & A.

M. Ochoa (Eds.), *Bicultural parent engagement: Advocacy and empowerment* (pp. 206–227). New York: Teachers College Press.

Olivos, E. M. (2006). *The power of parents: A critical perspective of bicultural parent involvement in public schools.* New York: Peter Lang.

Olivos, E. M., Ochoa, A. M., & Jiménez-Castellanos, O. (2011). Critical voices in bicultural parent engagement: A framework for transformation. In. E. M. Olivos, O. Jiménez-Castellanos, & A. M. Ochoa (Eds.), *Bicultural parent engagement: Advocacy and empowerment* (pp. 1–17). New York: Teachers College Press.

Patall, E. A., Cooper, H., & Robinson, J. C. (2008). Parent involvement in homework: A research synthesis. *Review of Educational Research, 78,* 1039–1101.

Payne, R. K. (2005). *A framework for understanding poverty* (4th rev. ed.). Highlands, TX: aha! Process.

Payne, R. K. (2006). *Working with parents: Building relationships for student success.* Highlands, TX: aha! Process.

Pearl, A. (1997). Cultural and accumulated environmental deficit models. In R. R. Valencia (Ed.) *The evolution of deficit thinking: Educational thought and practice* (pp. 132–159). Stanford Series on Education and Public Policy. London: Falmer Press.

Pearl, A. (2011). Engaging bicultural parents for democratic schooling. In E. M. Olivos, O. Jiménez-Castellanos, & A. M. Ochoa (Eds.), *Bicultural parent engagement: Advocacy and empowerment* (pp. 103–119). New York: Teachers College Press.

Pettit, J. (2012). *Empowerment and participation: Bridging the gap between understanding and practice.* Brighton, UK: Institute of Development Studies, University of Sussex. Retrieved June 18, 2014, from: www.un.org/esa/socdev/egms/docs/2012/JethroPettit.pdf.

Pratt, P. S. (1938). *A comparison of the school achievement and socio-economic background of Mexican and White children in a Delta Colorado elementary school.* Unpublished master's thesis, University of Southern California, Los Angeles.

Romano-V, O. I. (1968). The anthropology and sociology of the Mexican-Americans: The distortion of Mexican-American history. *El Grito, 2,* 13–26.

Roser, M. A. (1997, September 11). UT group praises Hopwood ruling. *Austin American-Statesman,* p. B1.

Roser, M. A., & Tanamachi, C. (1997, September 17). Jackson urges UT to fight racism. *Austin American-Statesman,* pp. A1, A10.

Samaras, A. P., & Wilson, J. C. (1999). Am I invited? Perspectives of family involvement with technology in inner-city schools. *Urban Education, 34,* 499–530.

Sheldon, S. B. (2003). Linking school-family community partnerships in urban elementary schools to student achievement on state tests. *Urban Review, 35,* 149–165.

Snider, W. (1990, April 18). Outcry follows Cavazo's comments on the values of Hispanic parents. *Education Week,* pp. 1–2.

Sowell, T. (1981). *Ethnic America: A history.* New York: Basic Books.

Stevenson, H. W., Chen, C., & Uttal, D. H. (1990). Beliefs and achievement: A study of Black, White, and Hispanic children. *Child Development, 61,* 508–523.

Sutterby, J. A., Rubin, R., & Abrego, M. H. (2007). *Amistades:* The development of relationships between preservice teachers and Latino families. *School Community Journal, 17,* 77–94.

Swadener, B. B., & Lubeck, S. (Eds.). (1995). *Children and families "at promise": Deconstructing the discourse of risk.* Albany: State University of New York.

Swanson, M. S. (1991). *At-risk students in elementary education: Effective schools for disadvantaged learners.* Springfield, IL: Charles C. Thomas.

Taylor, M. C. (1926). *Retardation of Mexican children in the Albuquerque schools.* Unpublished master's thesis, Leland Stanford University, Stanford, CA.

Tuck, R. (1946). *Not with the fist.* New York: Harcourt, Brace.

Valdés, G. (1996). *Con respeto: Bridging the distances between culturally diverse families and schools: An ethnographic portrait.* New York: Teachers College Press.

Valencia, R. R. (2010). *Dismantling contemporary deficit thinking: Educational thought and practice.* Critical Educator Series. New York: Routledge.

Valencia, R. R. (2012). Activist scholarship in action: The prevention of a Latino school closure. *Journal of Latinos and Education, 11,* 69–79.

Valencia, R. R., & Black, M. S. (2002). "Mexican Americans don't value education!"—On the basis of the myth, mythmaking, and debunking. *Journal of Latinos and Education, 1,* 81–103.

Valencia, R. R., & Solórzano, D. G. (1997). Contemporary deficit thinking. In R. R. Valencia (Ed.), *The evolution of deficit thinking: Educational thought and practice* (pp. 160–210). Stanford Series on Education and Public Policy. London: Falmer Press.

Valentine, J., & Stark, E. (1979). The social context of parent involvement in Head Start. In E. Zigler & J. Valentine (Eds.), *Project Head Start: A legacy of the war on poverty* (pp. 291–313). New York: Free Press.

Villenas, S. A., & Foley, D. E. (2011). Critical ethnographies of education in the Latino/a diaspora. In R. R. Valencia (Ed.), *Chicano school failure and success: Past, present, and future* (3rd ed., pp. 175–196). New York: Routledge.

Warren, M. R., Hong, S., Rubin, C. L., & Uy, P. S. (2009). Beyond the bake sale: A community-based relational approach to parent engagement in schools. *Teachers College Record, 111,* 2209–2254.

Waterman, R. A. (2008). Strength behind the sociolinguistic wall: The dreams, commitments, and capacities of Mexican mothers. *Journal of Latinos and Education, 7,* 144–162.

West-Olatunji, C., Sanders, T., Mehta, S., & Behar-Horenstein, L. (2010). Parenting practices among low-income parents/guardians of academically successful fifth-grade African American children. *Multicultural Perspectives, 12,* 138–144.

Williams, J. K. (2008). *Unspoken realities: White, female teachers discuss race, students, and achievement in the context of teaching in a majority Black elementary school.* Unpublished doctoral dissertation, Oregon State University, Corvallis.

Young, P. A. (2007). Thinking outside the box: Fostering racial and ethnic discourses in urban teacher education. In R. P. Soloman & D. Sekayi (Eds.), *Urban teacher education and teaching: Innovative practices for diversity and social issues* (pp. 109–128). Mahwah, NJ: Lawrence Erlbaum.

Zarate, M. E., Sáenz, V. B., & Oseguera, L. (2011). Supporting the participation and success of Chicanos in higher education. In R. R. Valencia (Ed.), *Chicano school failure and success: Past, present, and future* (3rd ed., pp. 120–140). New York: Routledge.

9

STUDENT AGENCY AND EMPOWERMENT

It is particularly fitting to close this final chapter of the Three-M Systemic Model with a focus on the most micro stakeholder, the individual student of color. I would like to start this chapter by discussing the concept of motivation. Well more than 50 years ago, psychologist Robert W. White (1959) published a classic article, "Motivation Reconsidered: The Concept of Competence." The basis of his treatise is the growing dissatisfaction at the time with the dominant theories of motivation—namely, Hull's drive reduction theory and Freud's psychoanalytic instinct theory. White contends that drive and instinct frameworks are poorly equipped to explain human behaviors—for example, exploration and the manipulation of one's surroundings. Therefore, he calls for a reconsideration of orthodox theories of motivation by maintaining that "effective interactions" with the environment should be placed under the broad heading of "competence." White continues by arguing that competence should be constructed as a motivational concept—that is, a "competence motivation" or "effectance motivation" (pp. 317–318, 329). He further theorizes that such motivation, especially in children, leads to satisfaction, or feelings of efficacy. Competence motivation, a powerful human need, involves exploration and experimental opportunities, and leads the child to discover how the environment can be transformed and what outcomes ensue from such changes. Such self-determination can be perceived as the quintessence of flourishing in humans (Goodman & Eren, 2013).

Drawing from White's (1959) concept of competence motivation, one can make the case that before a student can gain agency, he/she needs to have curricular opportunities to explore and transform his or her environment in critical ways. For many low-SES students of color attending inner-city schools, this can be an uphill struggle. These students, compared to their economically advantaged White peers enrolled in suburban schools, are more likely to face greater teacher authority in the classroom and on the school campus, have fewer opportunities to fully express themselves, and experience a considerable amount of drill work and test preparation because of failure to meet standards on state-mandated tests. These obstacles to competence and efficacy can lead to students becoming disengaged from school, and expressing this alienation by being antagonistic and/or passive (Goodman & Eren, 2013). Therefore, providing the means for students to become active and engaged agents in their education is essential for their growth.

This chapter is framed around the following topics: (a) student voice, (b) theoretical perspectives on student agency and empowerment, (c) research findings on successful initiatives for student agency and empowerment, and (d) systemic transformations.

On Student Voice

Cook-Sather (2006) has written an insightful essay on "'student voice,'' a term that is relevant to the subject of this chapter on student empowerment.[1] She traces the emergence of the student voice notion to the early part of the 1990s, when educational researchers and school critics began to discuss how students were being excluded from dialogues concerning teaching, learning, and the nature of schooling. For example, in the U.S., Kozol (1991) wrote in his best-selling book, *Savage Inequalities*, "The voices of children . . . have been missing from the whole discussion" regarding schooling and school reform (p. 5; quoted in Cook-Sather, p. 361). In Canada, Fullan (1991) inquired, "What would happen if we treated the student as someone whose opinion mattered?" (p. 170; quoted in Cook-Sather, p. 361). These earlier observations, Cook-Sather notes, were reemerging ways of thought that attempted to reposition students and their voice in various facets of research and reform in education.

This repositioning, Cook-Sather (2006) comments, requests that we not only reach out to those students who speak out with a meaningful and informative presence, but also make connections with students who strive for power to influence schooling practices. Possessing student voice in a democratic context means one has the opportunity and power to speak his or her mind, be listened to, and be able to influence schooling processes and outcomes. Furthermore, having student voice, in its most sweeping form, requires a cultural transformation that brings forth new spaces for students—not only the sound of their voices but also genuine opportunities for students to exercise power for what they deem important changes.

In her treatise, Cook-Sather (2006) also discusses some positive and negative aspects of student voice in the contexts of educational research and school reform. In regard to positive features, one of the most radical, as seen in the scholarly literature, is the growing rich discourse on the need for cultural shifts in altering the imbalances of power between adults in schools and students. Changing the dynamics of power relations between teachers and students within the boundaries of the classroom and beyond establishes the likelihood for students to engage "the political potential of speaking out on their own behalf" (Lewis, 1993, p. 44; quoted in Cook-Sather, p. 366). Another positive aspect of the literature on student voice is that it acknowledges and insists for the rights of students as active participatory citizens—in the classroom, community, and society (e.g., Pearl, 1997, 2002; more on this later at chapter's end). With respect to a number of negative features of literature on student voice, Cook-Sather mentions three that are particularly noteworthy here. First, there might be a tendency by some observers to view student voice in monolithic terms—that is, there is *one* student voice that speaks for all. This perspective creates a risk of overlooking the fundamental differences (e.g., concerns, needs) of varied student groups. Second, some scholars share concerns that the issues and resolutions raised by student voice might lead school officials and teachers to engage in gestures that are tokenistic, cynical, and manipulative. Third, a danger exists that student voice, though well-meaning, could result in oppression of one student group over another. If student voice is guided by the "relations of domination in the name of liberation," then student empowerment is highly compromised (Orner, 1992, p. 75; quoted in Cook-Sather, p. 368).

To sum, given that schools are designed to control and manage students, student voice is very difficult to accomplish (Cook-Sather, 2006). As such, administrators, counselors, teachers, policymakers, parents, and the general public need to understand that value exists in student voice. These stakeholders must become active supporters of providing all students the opportunities to exercise their voice as active participatory citizens.

Theoretical Perspectives on Student Agency and Empowerment

There are a number of discourses in the literature that have been advanced to understand student agency and empowerment. The following theoretical perspectives, as examples, focus on: (a) critical pedagogy (Giroux, 1988, 2011; also, see Ball, 2000), (b) *conscientizacao* (conscientization, meaning critical consciousness; Freire, 1970),[2] (c) transformational resistance (Solórzano & Delgado Bernal, 2001), (d) social capital (Stanton-Salazar, 2001, 2010), (e) positionality (Urietta, 2009), (f) critical youth empowerment (Jennings, Parra-Medina, Messias, & McLouglin, 2006), and (g) democratic education (Pearl, 1997, 2002). For my brief review here, I have selected three frameworks to discuss (transformation resistance; social capital; critical youth empowerment theory), ones that have the most accessible language and demonstrate the most relevance for understanding agency and empowerment among low-SES students of color. The democratic education model has, I believe, the most utility for bringing about comprehensive change. As such, I discuss it in the concluding section on systemic reform.

1. *Transformational resistance.* The model developed by Solórzano and Delgado Bernal (2001) draws substantively from CRT and Latina/Latino critical race theory

(LatCrit).[3] Solórzano and Delgado Bernal introduce the theoretical construct of transformational resistance via an adaptation of the work of Giroux (1983), who asserts that the notion of student resistance has two dimensions that intersect. First, the student needs to identify a critique of socially based oppression. Second, the student needs to be motivated by a concern dealing with social justice. Using these two points as a foundation, Solórzano and Delgado Bernal develop a typology of student resistance (they also refer to it as oppositional behavior). The authors illustrate their typology as a figure (p. 318), but for ease of readability I have adapted it into tabular format.

Table 9.1 shows this modification as a 2x4 matrix. Listed first is *self-defeating resistance*, referring to a type of student who is likely to demonstrate a critique of some oppressive schooling condition, but is not motivated by attaining social justice. Citing Fine(1991), Solórzano and Delgado Bernal (2001) use the example of a student who may have some strong criticisms of schooling inequalities, but he or she drops out of school—a self-defeating behavior. The second type of student resistance is *conformist resistance,* which is characterized by a student who indicates no criticism of school oppression, but is motivated by an interest in social justice. An example the authors provide is that of a student who has little sense of the depth of school oppression, and believes the high dropout rate of students of color can be rectified by tutoring and counseling. The third type of student resistance listed in Table 9.1 is *reactionary behavior.* Such a student lacks both a critique of school and interest in social justice. An example Solórzano and Delgado Bernal offer is the student who exhibits poor behavior in class, campus, or the community and has no sense of the oppressive conditions that contribute to his or her disruptive behavior (i.e., acting out). Finally, there is *transformational resistance*—describing the type of student who has a strong critique of school oppression and is guided by a firm interest in attaining social justice. It is this form of student resistance, Solórzano and Delgado underscore, that leads to student empowerment and has the greatest likelihood of creating social

TABLE 9.1 Types of Student Resistance

Type	*Criteria*	
	Critique of Social Oppression	*Motivated by Social Justice*
Self-Defeating Resistance	Yes	No
Conformist Resistance	No	Yes
Reactionary Behavior	No	No
Transformational Resistance	Yes	Yes

Source: Adapted from Solórzano and Delgado Bernal (2001, p. 318, Figure 1) with permission of D. G. Solórzano and D. Delgado Bernal.

change. In the upcoming section "Narratives on Successful Initiatives for Student Agency and Empowerment," I provide examples of transformational resistance.

Solórzano and Delgado Bernal (2001) comment that the construct of transformational resistance as a theoretical resistance can be further understood by dividing it into two dissimilar forms—internal and external student resistance. Although there is some overlap between them, and an individual can engage the two dynamic notions simultaneously or at varying periods of time, the authors treat the concepts as separate for the sake of analysis. At the surface level, it may appear that a student's expression of internal resistance appears to be conforming to institutional norms. Yet, as Solórzano and Delgado Bernal note, the student maintains the two criteria for transformational resistance—having a critique of social oppression and being motivated by attaining social justice. The authors provide the illustration (which I slightly modify) of a high school student of color who is guided by both criteria. She goes to college, follows the norms of the university (e.g., getting good grades), and meets parental expectations (e.g., working hard), and upon graduation she returns to her community as a middle school teacher in a high-enrollment school of color, well trained in social justice. External student resistance by contrast, is much more overt. The student meets both prongs of the definition of transformational resistance, and his social justice agenda is conspicuous. An example is the protest activities of the high school students who fought against the ban of Mexican American Studies in Tucson, Arizona (see chapter 6).

The transformational resistance model developed by Solórzano and Delgado Bernal (2001) has significant value in understanding agency and empowerment among students of color. It is a framework that needs our attention for two principal reasons. First, as Solórzano and Delgado Bernal note, in the study of student resistance, researchers have been preoccupied with self-defeating resistance.[4] Although these investigations are helpful in that they speak at length to the oppressive schooling conditions that often lead to student alienation, disengagement, and withdrawal, this body of research ignores the types of student resistance that can lead to empowerment and social change. Second, researchers of student resistance can improve our comprehension of student agency and empowerment by more closely incorporating in their methodology how to identify the internal and external forms of resistance. It is vital to make these distinctions because far too frequently "external resistance is romanticized by liberal and progressive scholars while internal resistance is not identified, misidentified, or even ignored" (Solórzano & Delgado Bernal, p. 326).

2. *Social capital.* This framework for helping us understand how to assist low-SES students of color gain empowerment is developed by Stanton-Salazar and explicated in his 2010 article and other publications (e.g., Stanton-Salazar, 1997, 2001, 2004). It is a layered model with a number of interconnected concepts, so I will just summarize the key workings. A chief actor in his framework is the *institutional agent* and his or her role in the empowerment of working-class

adolescents of color. Stanton-Salazar (2010) begins by noting that the study of parental involvement is important, but it is a narrow perspective to understand the socialization, empowerment, and social mobility of youths. He reminds us that middle-SES parents, when advocating for the educational betterment of their children, do not act alone. Rather, these parents' activities are lodged in social networks of the school and its agents, and, in some cases, support agents and organizations in the community—supportive entities seldom available to low-SES parents of color. As such, in his model he focuses on the role of *nonparental adult agents*, which can be, for instance, older brothers and/or sisters, extended kin, nonkin, teachers, and counselors. Stanton-Salazar (2010) comments that there is growing evidence that youths who report an important nonparental adult in their lives have, for example, greater academic success, better completion rates from high school, and better job experiences.[5]

In the social capital model of empowerment of low-SES adolescents of color, the roles of the institutional agent are expressed via a number of actions. For example, the agent serves as an advocate who advances and safeguards the interests of "his" or "her" student. The agent also is an advisor, helping the student to gather valuable information and helping with problem solving. Another role is that of an institutional broker, in which he or she serves as a negotiator of introductions that lead to agreements between the student and other institutional agents (Stanton-Salazar, 2010).[6] These activities of the institutional agent, however, are just the beginning. Stanton-Salazar (2010) notes that the agent needs to have a transformation himself or herself in the form of developing a critical consciousness (see Freire, 1993). Once this mindset is achieved, the institutional agent becomes an *empowerment agent* who now is proficient in discourses that allow for the interrogation of deep societal oppression and the inequalities embedded in schools. At this point, the empowerment agent is competent to assist his or her student develop *counterstratification* dialogues in order to develop key resources and wider social networks so the adolescent can challenge the inequalities, oppression, and hegemony in their lives and their communities, and even in the larger society.

In sum, the social capital framework developed by Stanton-Salazar (2010) is a valuable model to understand how low-SES youths of color can gain agency and empowerment. What is particularly beneficial about this theoretical construction for our knowledge base is that it does what little of the discourse on youth empowerment does: The social capital model highlights and discusses in great detail the empowerment roles of nonparental adults. These significant others—through their apprenticing, scaffolding, and advocating activities—can greatly assist low-SES adolescents of color reach a critical consciousness so they can fight oppression and gain control over their own lives.

3. *Critical youth empowerment.* Building on, integrating, and expanding the theoretical and practical aspects of four existing youth empowerment models,[7] plus their own participatory research endeavors with community-based youth groups, Jennings et al. (2006) have developed the critical youth empowerment

(CYE) model. Based on this fusion, the authors discuss six principal dimensions of the CYE model:

A. *An environment that is safe and welcoming.* Participating youths need to feel that they are valued, shown respect, encouraged, and fully supported. The environment is a physical and psychological space in which youths have ample opportunities for self-expression, creativity, and risk-taking. Given that the environment for such activities is constructed by both young people and adults, it is important that youths truly see these spaces as shared creations.

B. *Engagement and participation that are meaningful.* This feature of the CYE model underscores that engagement opportunities for youths must have some connectedness to their lives—activities that help to foster their competencies, develop their efficacy and self-esteem, and promote intrinsic motivation. Jennings et al. (2006) further add that relevant engagement and participation mean much more than "being present" (p. 44) at a school or community event. Students must engage such activities in highly critical ways that involve dialogue, reflection, and action.

C. *Power-sharing between youths and adults that indeed is equitable.* Considering that power is seldom given away, meeting this dimension of the CYE framework is a difficult task. Jennings et al. (2006) note that for equitable power-sharing to be realized, adult attitudes about power and decision making need to be thoroughly examined and transformed. That is, power-sharing with youths cannot be done in tokenistic gestures. Genuine sharing of power involves confidence on the part of adults that youths can take on leadership roles with strong commitments and efforts. Furthermore, adults should be ready to give feedback to youths in a nonauthoritarian manner.

D. *Interpersonal and sociopolitical processes of engagement need to have critical reflections.* Drawing, in part, from Freire (1970), Jennings et al. (2006) assert that if an individual is not aware of the varying formations and processes that make up the institutions and practices of social organizations, or his or her particular function in such agencies, it is very difficult to become empowered. Jennings et al. also cite Purdey, Adhikari, Robinson, and Cox (1994), who remind us that the word "empowerment" denotes reflexivity, meaning that a person can empower only himself or herself. As such, the CYE model claims it is imperative that youths be provided different learning opportunities and activities involving critical reflections and actions that can lead to social change.

E. *To effect social change there needs to be critical participation in sociopolitical processes.* Jennings et al. (2006) make a sharp distinction between conventional youth civic service and critical social engagement within the bounds of the CYE model. Youth civic service has as its goals the development of competent, mature, and reliable adults. In the CYE model, the objective is to develop youths who are able to interrogate the social arrangements, norms, and sociopolitical processes in their environment that are inequitable and problematic. Such mastery comes about through participating in social actions that are transformative.

F. *Empowerment opportunities need to be integrated at both the individual and community levels.* This dimension of the CYE framework maintains that for true empowerment to occur, youths must be provided opportunities for engagement at two levels: (a) via personal learning and application of navigational skills in the world of adults, thereby improving a student's self-efficacy; and (b) via experiential opportunities with different community sectors. These empowerment activities should be designed so youths have access to valuable resources, contact with diverse groups (e.g., class-, race-, and gender-based), and knowledge of how structures are governed—thus leading to the student's enhanced political efficacy.

In summary, the integration of the preceding six dimensions of the CYE model offers another perspective on how to understand and help create opportunities for student agency and empowerment. Although Jennings et al. (2006) do not specifically mention youths of color as targeted groups in their analysis, they do conclude by noting that the CYE model has the potential to intersect with perspectives that take into consideration inequalities based, for instance, on gender, class, race, immigration status, and language—power differentials that are of concern in CRT and LatCrit.

Narratives on Successful Initiatives for Student Agency and Empowerment

The quest for agency and empowerment among low-SES students of color can be expressed in different forms. One such manifestation is the political demonstration, in which youths of color engage in public confrontations to display their dissatisfaction about schooling conditions, policies, and practices they believe are oppressive. One of the most common types of political demonstrations is the strategy of the "blowout" (or school walkout). I briefly discuss an example, the Mexican American–initiated blowout that transpired in Crystal City, Texas, in 1969. Another way student agency and empowerment can be realized is through a classroom intervention, the most frequent kind of initiative one sees in the literature on student empowerment. As an example, I later discuss a study that involved Black adolescent girls.

As a precursor to the Crystal City blowout, it is helpful to mention the East Los Angeles (California) blowout of 1968 (García & Castro, 2011; Rosen, 1974; Solórzano & Delgado Bernal, 2001). In the late 1960s in East Los Angeles, high school students were teeming with discontent over their schooling—for example, complaints of few Mexican American teachers, counselors, and administrators; no courses on Mexican American Studies; prejudiced White teachers; large class sizes and overcrowded schools; vocational education tracking; and high dropout rates. A key empowerment agent for the students was Sal Castro, a Lincoln High School teacher (García & Castro; Rosen). Between March 1 and 8, 1968, about 10,000 Chicano/Chicana students from several high and middle schools walked out in protest of these oppressive conditions (Solórzano & Delgado Bernal) in one of the largest school reform movements in U.S. history (García & Castro). Although the East Los Angeles blowouts had minimal effect on changing the schools, this landmark political demonstration had significant effects on raising the consciousness of many students by empowering and politicizing them in regard to inequality. As the character of one of the student leaders portrayed in the film *Walkout* said, "The [East Los Angeles] schools might not have changed, but we did" (García & Castro, p. 324).

The story of the Crystal City blowout is a powerful account of empowerment that goes beyond the Chicano/Chicana students themselves. It is also a unique narrative about how an entire Mexican American community took power from the Anglos who dominated race relations and local governance. Similar to California, the educational plight of Chicano/Chicana students in late 1960s Texas was propitious for contestation of oppressive schooling conditions and practices, such as in Crystal City, located in cactus-filled southeastern Zavala County, about 50 miles from the Mexican border (Lenz, 1994). From 1968 to 1970, 39 school walkouts were launched in Texas, with the 1969 blowout in Crystal City being the most successful, well known, and documented (Gutiérrez, 2006; Navarro, 1995; Riley & Brown, 2006). The Mexican American Youth Organization (MAYO), the avant-garde of the Chicano/Chicana movement in the state of Texas, played a significant role in helping high school students organize (Navarro, 1995). Furthermore, a key empowerment agent in the Crystal City blowout was José Angel Gutiérrez, one of MAYO's founders (Navarro, 1995), who later became a prominent civil rights leader (Gutiérrez, 2005).

In April 1969, Gutiérrez—who was born in Crystal City in 1944 and graduated from Crystal City High School (CSHS) in 1962[8]—returned home and found a group of CCHS Chicano/Chicana students organizing. The main issue at the surface appeared to be rather mundane—the process of electing cheerleaders. For many years, they were elected by the students. The procedure changed, however, with the selection now being done by a teacher committee that the principal appointed. Furthermore, although the Anglo student body was the numerical minority, the committee put a quota system in place—one Chicana to three Anglo cheerleaders. It was apparent that the new formula had its basis in placating the Anglo community, who was losing its numerical majority status (Navarro, 1995). In any event, the seeds of protest had been planted.

During the spring of 1969, the students continued to organize, with Gutiérrez serving as their empowerment agent. This incipient activism resulted in the submission of a list of seven demands to CCHS principal John B. Lair. Some of the stipulations were unremarkable (e.g., purchase of new uniforms for the band), but others had a substantive quality regarding education, such as no punishment for free speech and implementation of bilingual/bicultural education. Principal Lair summarily rejected the demands, so the students appealed to the school superintendent, John Billings, who made some concessions (e.g., three Chicana and three Anglo cheerleaders). Yet, in June 1969 the school board, dominated by Anglos, nullified the concessions. Given the lateness of the school term, the approaching summer, and pending student attrition (e.g., many students hitting the migrant trail with their parents), Gutiérrez advised the activist students to work with him over the summer to plan a blowout for the fall term (Navarro, 1995).

By October 1969, the blowout of CCHS was ready to begin, as conditions were auspicious. One event in particular greatly assisted the students in their mobilization. The CCHS Ex-Student Association made a decision to have its own queen at the yearly homecoming football game. The association, however, used a ploy so it could ensure an Anglo would be selected. The eligibility criterion was that the chosen queen had to be from candidates whose mother or father was a CCHS graduate. This requirement, of course, would penalize Chicanas by making them ineligible, as very few had a parent who graduated from CCHS. Gutiérrez, in an adroit move, explained to the students that the criterion for selection amounted to a grandfather clause (a stringent measure designed to disenfranchise or exclude a group; see Robertson, 1995). Subsequently, one of the student leaders, Severita Lara, developed and disseminated a leaflet in which she protested the grandfather clause. Principal Lair suspended her for three days, which raised the ire of her fellow students. They contested the suspension by arriving at school with brown armbands, further setting the stage for an imminent blowout (Navarro, 1995).

What transpired next was a succession of unfolding and reinforcing events. Hundreds of students and their parents confronted the school board over the grandfather clause. Also, the students developed more demands, most of a substantive nature (e.g., firing of racist teachers; hiring of a Mexican American counselor; smaller class sizes). On December 9, 1969, the blowout began, when 200 students assembled with picket signs in the front area of CCHS; by the afternoon, the ranks of protesting students nearly tripled to 550. Of the total CCHS enrollment of 2,200 students, 710 (32%) were absent the next day, December 10. Also, by then the boycott extended to the junior high school. On December 13, 1969, a new dimension to the struggle was added—an economic boycott of the Spears Mini-Max, which was one of the largest Anglo-owned grocery stores in Crystal City. The boycott was triggered by the firing of two Chicano students who were employed part-time there. They had participated in a protest march in the downtown sector. On December 13, 1969, the boycott had reached the elementary schools, and by December 18, 60% of the district's total enrollment of 2,850 students were absent. In order to prevent violence, law enforcement officers were called in (local, state, and the Texas Rangers). The next day, the regional office (Dallas) of the Office for Civil Rights arrived in Crystal City to begin an investigation. The blowout captured widespread attention in the world of politics, as Severita Lara and her peers met with Senators Edward Kennedy and Ralph Yarborough in Washington, DC. On January 6, 1970, the boycott of Crystal City schools came to an end, and the U.S. Department of Justice was called in to serve as mediator (Navarro, 1995).

In sum, the Crystal City school blowout was revolutionary in the history of student-initiated school reform. When this blowout and the East Los Angeles walkouts are analyzed in the contexts of CRT and theoretical frameworks of student empowerment, the transformational resistance model (Solórzano & Delgado Bernal, 2001) is quite informative. Activist students in the East Los Angeles and Crystal City blowouts met both criteria of being empowered—students had a strong critique of school oppression and a firm interest in attaining social justice. The social capital model (Stanton-Salazar, 2010) also has explanatory utility in demonstrating the significant roles of empowerment agents in helping students gain voice and power (Castro in East Los Angeles and Gutiérrez in Crystal City). Both of these events also had favorable educational consequences for the involved Chicano/Chicana students, as many developed a critical consciousness that helped to motivate them to pursue college degrees and, in due course, work for the betterment of their respective communities (García & Castro, 2011; Lenz, 1994). Finally, we can learn from these school blowouts what empowered students and their empowered parents can accomplish when they work together. In Crystal City, what started as a campaign to select an equitable number of Chicana cheerleaders eventually culminated in a political sea change, as evidenced by the dramatic shift in local power when Mexican American citizens of Crystal City soon gained control of the school board and the city council (Navarro, 1998). Furthermore, Severita Lara, quintessential student leader of the CCHS blowout, was elected mayor of Crystal City in 1995 (Gutiérrez, 2006).

In addition to student political demonstrations, a second way in which agency and empowerment can be achieved among students of color is via classroom or school-based interventions. One such example is reported in a study by Thomas, Davidson, and McAdoo (2008). The motive driving the authors' research is that most conventional interventions for youth development frequently fail to be designed around the sociopolitical and cultural worlds of low-SES adolescents of color. Furthermore, girls of color often get ignored in this research—even though it is well known that they face gender discrimination. In light of these issues, Thomas et al. focus on an experimental study in which African American female adolescents serve as the participants. The basic objective of this intervention, referred to as the Young Empowered Sisters (YES!) program, is to help protect the youths from the deleterious effects of racism and to help promote resilience by the incorporation of an empowering, culturally appropriate protocol.

Participants in the Thomas et al. (2008) study attended a public high school situated in a Midwestern semi-urban city. The school, designated by the state as "underachieving," was moderate in size (N = 1,200 students) and multiethnic/multiracial in student composition: 55% African American, 30% White, 8% Latino/Latina, and 7% other. The authors recruited 74 female African Americans, with the majority being freshwomen (57%; 43% sophomores). Other pertinent information about the participants was: mean age, 14.7 years; mean GPA, 2.3; and free or reduced-price lunch program, 58%. In this between-groups, pre-postmeasure experimental design, 36 participants were assigned to the intervention (i.e., experimental) group and 38 to the control group. Participants in the two conditions were matched as closely as possible on the demographic variables (see p. 293, Table 3). The intervention groups received the intervention curriculum over a 10-week time frame; each session lasted for 1.5 hours twice per week; the control group participants merely went on with their daily routine at school.

In order to attain the objectives of the YES! strategy, Thomas et al. (2008) draw from Chipungu et al. (2000) and utilize three broad themes: cultural values, African American history, and contemporary culture. They also frame their curriculum around three philosophical leanings. One orientation is Nguzo Saba (Karenga, 1980), which emphasizes seven values that assist in creating culture, family, and community among people of African origin (see Thomas et al., p. 289, Table 2). A second orientation is critical pedagogy, which draws from Freire's (1970) critical consciousness notion. Third, the authors incorporate holistic learning in the YES! program. Holistic learning, Thomas et al. note, integrates, for instance, critical thinking, a responsibility that is collective in nature, and spirituality (Miller, 1999).

With the foregoing as their theoretical foundation, Thomas et al. (2008) used four different instruments to gather pre- and postmeasure data. These scales measure the following constructs:[9] (a) ethnic identity; (b) racism awareness; (c) collectivism; and (d) liberatory youth activism. This latter notion is especially pertinent to our discussion. To measure it, Thomas et al. had to develop two instruments specifically for their study—the Intentions to Liberatory Youth Activism Scale (ILYAS) and the Liberatory Youth Activism Scale (LYAS).[10] Examples of ILYAS items are: "I would pass out information about a Black cause," and "I would volunteer in a group to help end racism." For the LYAS, examples include: "Got involved in a Black youth rally," and "Talked to a school staff such as a teacher, principal or school counselor about an issue that was important" (p. 297). Thomas et al. report that the students who participated in YES!—compared to the control group participants—scored significantly higher on Black ethnic identity, racism awareness, collectivist orientation, and on the ILYAS and LYAS. The authors conclude that the synergistic structure of YES! offers a framework of empowerment that intensified the participants' intentions for engagement and actual involvement in liberatory activism. These findings, Thomas et al. note, corroborate other research investigations that have incorporated culturally relevant dimensions in their empowerment interventions with African American youths (e.g., Belgrave, Townsend, Cherry, & Cunningham, 1997; Lewis, Sullivan, & Bybee, 2006).

Toward Systemic Transformations

In this section on suggestions for systemic reform, I deviate somewhat from how I structured the concluding segments of the preceding chapters. Rather than discussing a number of ideas, I focus on just one—the notion of "democratic education," which has been developed and explicated by Art Pearl and associates (Laguardia & Pearl, 2005; Pearl, 1997, 2002; Pearl & Knight, 1999; Pearl & Pryor, 2005; Valencia & Pearl, 2010). I have chosen to discuss democratic education because it speaks with great strength to student agency and empowerment, and it has particular utility for low-SES children and youths of color. For the sake of space, I briefly discuss the essential aspects of democratic education.

Current educational theories, Pearl and Knight (1999) argue, are incoherent, elitist, and poorly suited to produce informed citizens. The three major theories of knowledge that dominate education are: essentialism, perennialism, and existentialism (or romantic humanism).[11] Essentialism emphasizes the "basics" as significant knowledge, and has evolved over the last 8 decades, with the most recent rendition being expressed in a curriculum that values competencies (e.g., reading and mathematics, assessed via high-stakes testing; see Valencia & Pearl, 2010, pp. 148–152). This theory is authoritarian and conservative in nature, and it largely treats students as passive learners guided by a precept of disinterested exploration. Pearl and Knight maintain that this theoretical approach to knowledge acquisition is highly questionable in permitting students to develop their identities as moral and social beings. Perennialism focuses on the "great works," allowing students to seek and know "truth." For the perennialist, truth is immutable, and it is sought in a rigidly designed curriculum where students seldom are asked to solve problems. Pearl and Knight note that this theory is framed in elitism, and thus it becomes the crucible in which social reproduction is perpetuated. Existentialism emphasizes "self-awareness" as vital knowledge. This theory of education believes in the facilitation of individual growth, and the principle type of knowledge to attain is self-discovery. Although child-centered education asserts that it is democratic, Barber (1983)—an advocate of "strong" democracy—notes that it practices "thin" democracy, in which students are not prepared to solve crucial social problems, nor are they equipped to balance individual rights with the accompanying responsibilities.

Considering these serious shortcomings of dominant theories of educational knowledge, Pearl and Knight (1999) contend that the only compelling rationale for a general theory of education for public schools is democratic education, which is taught in a democratic classroom, and is constructed to prepare democratic citizens. This comprehensive theory of education applies to all components of schooling (e.g., curriculum; teaching; learning; classroom management; governance) and has four essential requirements:

A. Knowledge should be universally provided to enable all students to solve generally recognized social and personal problems.
B. Students should participate in decisions that affect their lives.
C. Clearly specified rights should be made universally available.
D. Equal encouragement should be given for success in all of society's legal endeavors. (p. 2)

I expound on these requirements by discussing the seven themes that frame democratic education.

1. *Negotiable leadership.*[12] In the eyes of students, the classroom teacher is an unelected authority, and student acceptance of that power generally spans from enthusiasm to active resistance. Authoritarianism in schools—whether it be expressed by teachers, the principal, or general policies—is more frequently seen in high-enrollment schools of color attended predominantly by low-SES students (e.g., Goodman, Hoagland, Pierre-Toussaint, Rodríguez, & Sanabria, 2011). In the bounds of democratic education theory, if students of color are to reach optimal personal and academic growth, then the classroom teacher, school principal and vice-principal, district superintendent, and school board members must use persuasion and negotiation to gain student acceptance of their authority (Laguardia & Pearl, 2005; Valencia & Pearl, 2010).

2. *Inclusion.* A distinguishing feature of a democracy is the extent to which all members are included as equally empowered citizens. In the U.S., the sustaining efforts to develop a democratic society came about as a consequence of its marginalized members' many struggles for inclusion. For example, the elimination of the literacy test and property requirement for the vote, the abolition of slavery, workers' struggles for the right to organize, women's suffrage, the recurring efforts by various immigrants to be included, and the campaign for civil rights all furthered the cause of democracy (Brooks, 1974; Cohen, 1996; Gross, 2002; Johnson, 1998; Klarman, 2004). Today, one of the most devastating forms of exclusion occurs in schools—for example, the vast underrepresentation of students of color in gifted and talented programs (see chapter 1, Table 1.10). Yet, the most visible and injurious type of exclusion is evidenced in curriculum differentiation as seen throughout K-12 education (see chapter 7). In light of the entrenchment of exclusion in public schools, democratic education offers an alternative by drawing upon the principle of full inclusion of all students in all facets of the schooling process. Such an inclusive democratic culture cannot be foisted. Rather, it comes about by a conscious creation, and has a core that has wide appeal for students of color (Laguardia & Pearl, 2005; Pearl, 2002; Valencia & Pearl, 2010).

3. *Knowledge for problem solving.* Democratic education theory maintains that when it comes to the issue of school curriculum, the single most critical question we should engage is: What constitutes important knowledge? Pearl (1997) aptly underscores, "*This is the debate that education has not had*" (p. 216). Indeed, it is an intriguing and controversial query, and leads to related concerns. What knowledge should be valued the most? The least? Why? What knowledge that is excluded should be included? Why? How should this important knowledge be taught and learned? What is the utility of this knowledge for the future of youths? What knowledge is most critical in helping students of color become empowered? Democratic education is by no means silent on these issues.

In the democratic classroom, there is no convenient blueprint to shepherd the teacher in the discourse over what knowledge is important. There are, however, some guiding principles to assist her or him. First, knowledge must not be rationed—as it frequently is in U.S. education—along lines of gender, class, or race. Second, the acquisition of knowledge cannot be decreed. Rather, students must be provided the opportunity—through informed persuasion—of the value and utility of knowledge the teacher deems worthy to be pursued. As such, the instructor needs to understand democracy. Third, and this is the heart of the democratic classroom curriculum, knowledge should be framed around problem solving (Laguardia & Pearl, 2005; Pearl & Knight, 1999).

An example of knowledge for problem solving is the study of history. The conventional approach in learning about history (and other subjects) is the "banking" system (critiqued by Freire, 1970), in which the teacher deposits facts in the passive minds of students. In the democratic classroom, the pupil *becomes* a historian by actively engaging in historical research (Pearl & Knight, 1999). Students learn, under the tutelage of a well-trained teacher, how to do primary and secondary research—and, very importantly, how to conduct an oral history. Depending on his or her interests, the student can interview someone with a significant story to tell—a leader of the Black civil rights movement in 1960s Mississippi, a Chicana who participated in the 1969 school blowout in Crystal City, or a contemporary teenage political refugee from Honduras who made the arduous trek by himself to the U.S. Students who learn how to undertake historical research in the democratic classroom will eventually learn what all historians learn—the difficulties of sorting truth from falsehood, that history is a matter of interpretation, and how to decide what is significant and what is trivial (Pearl & Knight). These acquired skills not only have value in fostering the academic growth of students, but also have positive transfer to the making of an informed citizen.

Although knowledge for problem solving is a key curricular pursuit in the democratic classroom, the subjects, for instance, of reading, mathematics, and science are also vital for developing a democratic citizen. Such a citizen must be proficient in reading, writing, and the skills of argument and oral persuasion. He or she needs to be competent in mathematical computations and measurement in order to understand the mundaneness and complexities of a modern society where numbers and the need for calculations are ubiquitous. To know the nature of science and scientific methods also hold great utility for the democratic citizen in concerns, for example, dealing with crime control, world peace, climate change, and poverty (Pearl & Knight, 1999).

4. *Student rights.* Certainly, there are many ways to define a right. In the context of democratic education, Laguardia and Pearl (2005) offer this definition: "A right is an unabridged activity that does not restrict the activity of others or require from others some special effort" (p. 12). For example, the right of due process for student María does not come at the expense of another student, Ricardo, nor does María have to give away something of substance to receive her right of due process. Entitlements, whether we are talking about student rights

or rights of the everyday citizen, need to be viewed as the anchor of democracy. Without them, we are all imperiled (Pearl, 1997).

Although the U.S. Declaration of Independence decreed unalienable rights to be self-evident, there is little application to school-age students. Ratified in 1791, it took 178 years for the Bill of Rights to have a bearing on students (and teachers). It was not until 1969 in *Tinker v. Des Moines Community School District* that the U.S. Supreme Court extended such rights to students. In *Tinker*, which involved the First Amendment (freedom of speech), 15-year-old John Tinker and two of his peers went to school wearing black armbands in protest of the Vietnam War and in support of a truce. School authorities summarily suspended the students. The U.S. Supreme Court decided for the petitioners, with Justice Abe Fortas, who wrote the opinion in this 7–2 ruling, noting, "It can hardly be argued that either students or teachers shed their constitutional rights to freedom of expression at the schoolhouse gate."[13]

Schools tend to undermine student rights in three distinctive ways (Valencia & Pearl, 2010). First, many schools simply ignore such rights. Second, most schools link rights to responsibilities. This is saying, in effect, that only the responsible can enjoy rights. Thus, the students who need rights the most are the ones most likely to be denied them. The Bill of Rights, however, makes no such discrimination. The rights in the first 10 Amendments are unalienable and available to all, responsible and irresponsible alike. Third, some schools ration rights, typically based on race, class, and gender lines. To sum, these basic and precious entitlements of the Bill of Rights are endangered in schools because they are seldom practiced or discussed.

In regard to student rights in democratic education, there are four that make up a basic minimum: (a) rights of expression, (b) rights of privacy, (c) rights of movement, and (d) due process (Laguardia & Pearl, 2005; Pearl, 2002; Pearl & Knight, 1999). For our discussion, I focus on freedom of expression and due process, as they are particularly pertinent to the subject of this chapter, agency and empowerment vis-à-vis students of color. In the democratic classroom, teachers must help students cultivate voice and self-expression.

Although student criticism of teachers, administrators, and school policies may be unpleasant to hear, adult officials should not suppress such views. If school agents disagree, they should respond in informed, logical ways—not aggressively, condescendingly, and punitively. Students should also be allowed to petition and assemble in regard to some issue. Designated free speech areas, as they exist in many colleges and universities, need to be created in elementary, middle, and high schools. Opportunities for freedom of expression in the democratic classroom represent a valuable preparation for living in a democratic society (Pearl & Knight, 1999).

The U.S. Bill of Rights has as its centerpiece a system of due process entitlements, as described in Amendments IV through VIII. This structure of "fairness" is so fundamental to citizens in a democratic nation that discussions of these amendments of due process are essential to incorporate in the curriculum of the democratic classroom, as well as put into practice on a regular basis (Laguardia & Pearl, 2005; Pearl, 2002; Pearl & Knight, 1999). Considering the growing interest in the theory and practice of school discipline (e.g., Osher, Bear, Sprague, & Doyle, 2010; Theriot & Dupper, 2010) and the overrepresentation of students of color (especially boys) who commit school infractions and receive stern discipline (e.g., Darensbourg, Pérez, & Blake, 2010), the application of due process rights to discipline is particularly germane here. Pearl (2002) comments that for schools to truly become democratic institutions, all students—irrespective of the pupils' school history and background (e.g., race, class)—need to be guaranteed the following: "(a) presumption of innocence; (b) right not to testify against oneself; (c) right to counsel to provide advice and support when accused of rule violation; (d) right to trial before an independent tribunal; and (e) protection against cruel and unusual punishment" (p. 358). These due process rights are designed to promote one objective—fairness. The converse, perceived unfairness of the teacher when it comes to discipline, is one factor that helps to explain the alienation some students of color experience (e.g., Gregory & Thompson, 2010; Thompson, 2008).

5. *Universal participation in decision making.* Democratic education requires that students be provided varied and frequent opportunities to participate actively and fully in decisions that can influence their lives. Such participatory activities offer a solid foundation for eventual engagement in a democratic society, which places demands on its citizens to help create and maintain, for instance, a strong working economy, safe neighborhoods, norms for civility, respect for the environment, and equality for all (Laguardia & Pearl, 2005; Pearl, 2002). The democratic classroom is an excellent forum for students to have these discussions about their present and future roles in participatory democracy.

To achieve self-government, two types of knowledge are necessary. The first form, which I introduced earlier, is applicable to problems of personal and social knowledge. The second type has to do with process, and this knowledge requires the student to be competent in a number of democratic skills. Effective participation means he or she needs to partake in activities that foster the ability to: develop an argument that is persuasive, assume (and even relinquish) leadership roles, negotiate, and implement goals and evaluate their progress. Also, such participatory activities for cultivating democratic decision making in students involve the willingness to: interact cooperatively with a wide spectrum of other individuals, and listen and comprehend the viewpoints of others. Schools that show genuine interest in democratic education have some responsibility to help students attain both of these types of valuable knowledge (Laguardia & Pearl, 2005; Pearl, 2002).

6. *Optimum learning conditions.* This feature of democratic education emphasizes opportunities for students to grow and thrive academically, personally, socially, and politically in the most favorable learning environments possible. Given that optimum learning conditions in K-12 public schools vary considerably across

schools and students—with low-SES children and youths of color having the least favorable and most inequitable circumstances—we cannot underscore enough the importance of the democratic education dimension of optimum learning conditions for all students. The maximization of student potential, which the public school was purportedly designed to do, requires the conscious creation of a very favorable environment for learning and the taking of the necessary steps so all students can benefit (Laguardia & Pearl, 2005; Pearl, 2002; Valencia & Pearl, 2010).

In the bounds of the democratic classroom, what are the characteristics of an optimum learning environment? Based on research on human development and motivation, including their own experiences over 30 years, Laguardia and Pearl (2005) discuss 10 attributes of such an environment: "encouragement to risk, relief from unnecessary pain, meaning, sense of competence, belonging, usefulness, hope, excitement, creativity, and ownership" (p. 20). In the context of agency and empowerment apropos of low-SES students of color, I briefly touch on several of these characteristics that are especially appropriate. First, in regard to hope and meaning, West (1993) notes that they are two essential attributes for Black students to possess (and I would extend this to other students of color) to attain maximum powers. Currently, schools do much to crush both aspects. The more teachers engage students in efforts to shape their own futures, the more the conditions of hope and meaning are met (Valencia & Pearl, 2010). Second, ownership and empowerment go hand-in-hand in an optimum learning environment. In the democratic classroom, students produce things not for the prevailing authority but rather for themselves and in some cases their respective communities. Whatever intellectual process and product they create, students take ownership. When students actually believe they are the primary stakeholder in their educational endeavors, they are much more likely to be motivated to achieve (Laguardia & Pearl; Pearl, 2002). There is persuasive evidence that when students are given opportunities to invest in their schooling and assume ownership over their schoolwork, their achievement motivation is enhanced (e.g., Au, 1997, 2011).

7. *Equality.* All democracies claim equality is vital for a healthy society, but none come close to attaining it. One reason for this is that no agency or governmental instrumentality has the scope and power to bring about equality. Equality cannot be achieved by fiat. Another explanation for this lack of attainment is that there are multiple and sometimes opposing definitions of equality (see Pearl & Knight, 1999; West, 1993). Notwithstanding these concerns, no topic is more significant to a democratic society and nothing is more laborious to secure for marginalized groups than equality (Valencia & Pearl, 2010). In the case of low-SES students of color, their families, and their communities, the quest for equality remains a burning issue (Pearl, 2002). Yet, these struggles have been long and slow, painfully so, and although some gains have been made, deep structural inequality remains in the schools and the larger society.

In democratic education, equality can be operationalized to mean making all the components of a democracy equally available to all students—for instance, equal access to rights, knowledge for citizenship, and being an equally celebrated member of a learning community. As such, equality is closely linked with providing all students with an optimum learning environment (Pearl, 2002; Valencia & Pearl, 2010). With this in mind, in the democratic classroom the meaning of equality takes on a different denotation than how most people view this notion (as fairness). That is, all students are not treated precisely the identical way by the teacher, nor is the objective to have "equal results." Rather, all pupils are deemed equally competent, and therefore are *equally encouraged* (Pearl & Knight. 1999). Yet, in reality many teachers provide unequal encouragement of students—typically along lines of race and class. In chapter 7 (section on "Teacher-Student Interactional Inequalities"), the evidence speaks clearly to this issue. Schools will go a long way toward eliminating this bias if the emphasis is on equal encouragement of all students. Equality viewed in this manner, however, is difficult to implement due to its nemesis, deficit thinking, which is always lurking. Notwithstanding the ubiquity of deficit thinking in education, it can be countered by committed teachers. In any classroom, equal encouragement can commence. "It needs no special mandates or guidelines. It violates no laws or policies. It can be the lived practice of every school [but it] cannot be sustained without the other requirements of democratic education being met" (Pearl & Knight, p. 286).

To sum, the theory of democratic education offers a solid alternative to the oppressive, inequitable schooling of many low-SES students of color. It also provides a sound pathway for these children and youths in gaining agency and empowerment. But does it work? Two such examples come to mind: Sunshine High School (SHS) in Melbourne, Australia, and Central Park East Secondary School (CPESS) in New York City (see Pearl, 1997, pp. 235–236; Pearl & Knight, 1999, pp. 281–282). SHS, located in a working-class sector of Melbourne, began as an experiment in democratic education by Tony Knight and a cadre of young teachers. In this school within a school, the emphasis was on equal encouragement for all students with respect to citizenship, personal development, and culture. Prior to the establishment of SHS, only a handful of students over a 50-year period were admitted to the university. By the time the experiment was over, admission rates were competitive with those of the exclusive high schools (Pearl & Knight).

CPESS, which primarily serves low-SES Black and Latino/Latina students, was founded by progressive educator Deborah Meier. This alternative school draws from some of the principles of democratic education. Emphases are on equal encouragement, competence, experimentation, developing a sense of community, meaning, and hope (Pearl & Knight, 1999). Graduation rates from the school and matriculation rates to college are very impressive (Meier, 1995). On a final note, for democratic education to be successful, teachers need to be fully trained in its theory and practice. This preparation is detailed in Pearl and Knight (chapter 9) and in Pearl and Pryor (2005).

In the Three-M Systemic Model, agency and empowerment constitute a prominent micro-level factor regarding success for low-SES children and youths of color—not only in the realm of academic achievement but also in preparation for democratic citizenship. Considering these positive effects, it is not surprising that the twin topics of student voice and empowerment have generated considerable interest, in both theory and practice, in recent times. A fitting question to conclude this chapter is: What does an empowered student look like? A distillation of what we have covered here informs us that such a student can be characterized as follows: She or he is competent, knows how to negotiate, can work in groups, has opportunities for self-expression, assumes a leadership role, has meaning and hope, receives equal encouragement, has a full set of rights, has a critical consciousness, critiques socially based oppression, and is motivated to engage in liberatory activism. We have also discussed that a robust way to help students of color attain voice and empowerment is via democratic education. We must be mindful, however, that democratic education will not materialize by itself. It requires an advocacy that is inclusive, organized, and creative. Along this line of thought, Pearl and Knight (1999) fittingly close their book, *The Democratic Classroom*, like so: "In order to fashion a democratic classroom, do not think narrowly about democracy and its myriad restrictions and contradictions. Think of it as a way of including everybody in the formation of the future . . . one classroom at a time" (p. 344).

Notes

1. Goodman and Eren (2013), referring to Cook-Sather (2006), note that "voice" and "agency" are synonymous. Goodman and Eren do comment, however, that some scholars make a distinction—that is, voice refers to "self-expression" and agency refers to "decision making" (see Holdsworth, 2000).
2. For further discussion on Freire's notion of critical consciousness, see Mustakova-Possardt (1998).
3. Solórzano and Delgado Bernal (2001) explain, "LatCrit [which is similar to CRT] is concerned with a progressive sense of a coalitional Latina/Latino pan-ethnicity and addresses issues often ignored by critical race theorists such as language, immigration, ethnicity, culture, identity, phenotype, and sexuality" (p. 311). For examples of LatCrit publications, see García (1995); Revilla (2001); Stefanic (1998).
4. Examples of these researchers that Solórzano and Delgado Bernal mention are: Foley (1990); MacLeod (1987); Willis (1977).
5. Stanton-Salazar (2010) cites, for example, Greenberg, Chen, and Beam (1998); McDonald, Erickson, Kirkpatrick, and Elder (2007); Zimmerman, Bingenheimer, and Notaro (2002).
6. See Stanton-Salazar (2010, p. 16, Table 1) for the full list of institutional agent roles.
7. These four models are: adolescent empowerment cycle (Chinman & Linney, 1998); youth development and empowerment program model (Kim, Crutchfield, Williams, & Hepler, 1998); transactional partnering model (Cargo, Grams, Ottoson, Ward, & Green, 2003); and empowerment education model (Freire, 1970).
8. See *Biography—José Angel Gutiérrez*. Latinopia.com. Retrieved July 11, 2014, from: http://latinopia.com/latino-history/jose-angel-gutierrez/.

9. For the names and authors of these instruments, as well as a summary of what they measure, see Thomas et al. (2008, pp. 295–297).
10. See Thomas et al. (2008, p. 296–297) for a discussion of the instruments' psychometric properties.
11. For further discussion of these three theories, see Pearl and Knight (1999, pp. 49–54).
12. Parts of this discussion on the seven themes of democratic education build on, with revisions, Valencia and Pearl (2010, pp. 154–158).
13. *Tinker v. Des Moines Independent Community School*, 393 U.S. at 504 (1969).

References

Au, K. (1997). Ownership, literacy achievement, and students of diverse cultural backgrounds. In J. T. Guthrie & A. Wigfield (Eds.), *Reading engagement: Motivating readers through integrated instruction* (pp. 168–182). Newark, DE: International Reading Association.

Au, K. (2011). *Literacy achievement and diversity: Keys to success for students, teachers, and schools.* New York: Teachers College Press.

Ball, A. F. (2000). Empowering pedagogies that enhance the learning of multicultural students. *Teachers College Record, 102,* 1006–1034.

Barber, B. (1983). *Strong democracy: Participatory politics for a new age.* Berkeley: University of California Press.

Belgrave, F. Z., Townsend, T. G., Cherry, V. R., & Cunningham, D. M. (1997). The influence of an Africentric worldview and demographic variables on drug knowledge, attitudes, and use among African American youth. *Journal of Community Psychology, 25,* 421–433.

Brooks, T. R. (1974). *Walls come tumbling down: A history of the civil rights movement, 1940–1970.* Englewood Cliffs, NJ: Prentice-Hall.

Cargo, M., Grams, G. D., Ottoson, J. M., Ward, P., & Green, L. W. (2003). Empowerment as fostering positive youth development and citizenship. *American Journal of Health Behavior, 27,* S66–79.

Chinman, M. J., & Linney, J. A. (1998). Toward a model of adolescent empowerment: Theoretical and empirical evidence. *Journal of Primary Prevention, 18,* 393–413.

Chipungu, S. S., Hermann, J., Sambrano, S., Nisler, M., Sale, E., & Springer, J. F. (2000). Prevention programming for African American youth: A review of strategies in CSAP's national cross-site evaluation of high-risk youth programs. *Journal of Black Psychology, 26,* 360–385.

Cohen, P. N. (1996). Nationalism and suffrage: Gender struggle in nation-building America. *Signs: Journal of Women in Culture and Society, 21,* 707–727.

Cook-Sather, A. (2006). Sound, presence, and power: "Student voice" in educational research and reform. *Curriculum Inquiry, 36,* 359–390.

Darensbourg, A., Pérez, E., & Blake, J. J. (2010). Overrepresentation of African American males in exclusionary discipline: The role of school-based mental health professionals in dismantling the school to prison pipeline. *Journal of African American Males in Education, 1,* 196–211.

Fine, M. (1991). *Framing dropouts: Notes on the politics of an urban public high school.* Albany: State University of New York Press.

Foley, D. (1990). *Learning capitalist culture: Deep in the heart of Tejas.* Philadelphia: University of Pennsylvania Press.

Freire, P. (1970). *The pedagogy of the oppressed.* New York: Seabury Press.

Freire, P. (1993). *Education for critical consciousness.* New York: Continuum.

Fullan, M. (1991). *The new meaning of educational change.* New York: Teachers College Press.

García, M. T., & Castro, S. (2011). *Blowout! Sal Castro and the Chicano struggle for educational justice.* Chapel Hill: University of North Carolina Press.

García, R. (1995). Critical race theory and Proposition 187: The racial politics of immigration law. *Chicano-Latino Law Review, 17,* 118–148.

Giroux, H. A. (1983). *Theories and resistance in education.* South Hadley, MA: Bergin and Garvey.

Giroux, H. A. (1988). *Teachers as intellectuals: Toward a critical pedagogy of learning.* Westport, CT: Bergin and Garney.

Giroux, H. A. (2011). *On critical pedagogy.* New York: Continuum.

Goodman, J. F., & Eren, N. S. (2013). Student agency: Success, failure, and lessons learned. *Ethics and Education, 8,* 123–129.

Goodman, J. F., Hoagland, J., Pierre-Toussaint, N., Rodríguez, C., & Sanabria, C. (2011). Working the crevices: Granting students authority in authoritarian schools. *American Journal of Education, 117,* 375–398.

Greenberg, E., Chen, C., & Beam, M. R. (1998). The role of "very important" nonparental adults in adolescent development. *Journal of Youth and Adolescence, 27,* 321–343.

Gregory, A., & Thompson, A. R. (2010). African American high school students and variability in behavior across classrooms. *Journal of Community Psychology, 38,* 386–402.

Gross, J. A. (2002). Worker rights as human rights: Wagner Act values and moral choices. *Journal of Labor and Employment Law, 4,* 479–492.

Gutiérrez, J. A. (2005). *The making of a civil rights leader: José Angel Gutiérrez.* Hispanic Civil Rights Series. Houston, TX: Piñata Books.

Gutiérrez, J. A. (2006). *We won't back down! Severita Lara's rise from student leader to mayor.* Hispanic Civil Rights Series. Houston, TX: Piñata Books.

Holdsworth, R. (2000). Schools that create real roles of value for young people. *Prospects, 115,* 349–362.

Jennings, L. B., Parra-Medina, D. M., Messias, D.K.H., & McLouglin, K. (2006). Toward a critical social theory of youth empowerment. *Journal of Community Practice, 14,* 31–55.

Johnson, K. R. (1998). Race, the immigration laws, and domestic race relations: A "magic mirror" into the heart of darkness. *Indiana Law Journal, 73,* 1112–1159.

Karenga, M. (1980). *Kawaida theory: Kwanzaa, origin, concepts, and practice.* Inglewood, CA: Kawaida.

Kim, S., Crutchfield, C., Williams, C., & Hepler, N. (1998). Toward a new paradigm in substance abuse and other problem behavior prevention for youth: Youth development and empowerment approach. *Journal of Drug Education, 28,* 1–17.

Klarman, M. J. (2004). *From Jim Crow to civil rights: The Supreme Court and the struggle for racial equality.* New York: Oxford University Press.

Kozol, J. (1991). *Savage inequalities: Children in America's schools.* New York: Harper Perennial.

Laguardia, A., & Pearl, A. (2005). Democratic education: Goals, principles, and requirements. In A. Pearl & C. R. Pryor (Eds.), *Democratic practices in education: Implications for teacher education* (pp. 9–30). Lanham, MD: Rowman & Littlefield Education.

Lenz, M. (1994, December 6). '69 walkout sparked movement by Mexican Americans. *Austin American-Statesman,* p. B3.

Lewis, K., Sullivan, C., & Bybee, D. (2006). An experimental evaluation of a school-based emancipatory intervention to promote African American well-being and youth leadership. *Journal of Black Psychology, 32,* 3–28.

Lewis, M. (1993). *Without a word: Teaching beyond women's silence.* New York: Routledge.

Macleod, J. (1987). *Ain't no makin' it: Leveled aspirations in a low-income neighborhood.* Boulder, CO: Westview.

McDonald, S., Erickson, L. D., Kirkpatrick, J., & Elder, G. H. (2007). Informal mentoring and young adult employment. *Social Science Research, 36,* 1328–1347.

Meier, D. (1995). *The power of their ideas: Lessons from a small school in Harlem.* Boston: Beacon Press.

Miller, J. (1999). Making connections through holistic learning. *Educational Leadership, 56,* 46–48.

Mustakova-Possardt, E. (1998). Critical consciousness: An alternative pathway for positive personal and social development. *Journal of Adult Development, 5,* 13–30.

Navarro, A. (1995). *Mexican American Youth Organization: Avant-garde of the Chicano movement in Texas.* Austin: University of Texas Press.

Navarro, A. (1998). *The Cristal experiment: A Chicano struggle for community control.* Madison: University of Wisconsin Press.

Orner, M. (1992). Interrupting the calls for student voice in "liberatory" education: A feminist poststructural perspective. In C. Luke & J. Gore (Eds.), *Feminisms and critical pedagogy* (pp. 74–89). New York: Routledge.

Osher, D., Bear, G. G., Sprague, J. R., & Doyle, W. (2010). How can we improve school discipline? *Educational Researcher, 39,* 48–58.

Pearl, A. (1997). Democratic education as an alternative to deficit thinking. In R. R. Valencia (Ed.), *The evolution of deficit thinking: Educational thought and practice* (pp. 211–241). Stanford Series on Education and Public Policy. London: Falmer Press.

Pearl, A. (2002). The big picture: Systemic and institutional factors in Chicano school failure and success. In R. R. Valencia (Ed.), *Chicano school failure and success: Past, present, and future* (2nd ed., pp. 335–364). London: RoutledgeFalmer.

Pearl, A., & Knight, T. (1999). *The democratic classroom: Theory into practice.* Understanding Education and Policy Series. Cresskill, NJ: Hampton Press.

Pearl, A., & Pryor, C. R. (Eds.). (2005). *Democratic practices in education: Implications for teacher education.* Lanham, MD: Rowman & Littlefield Education.

Purdey, A. F., Adhikari, G. B., Robinson, S. A., & Cox, P. W. (1994). Participatory health development in rural Nepal: Clarifying the process of community empowerment. *Health Education Quarterly, 21,* 329–343.

Revilla, A. T. (2001). LatCrit and CRT in the field of education: A theoretical dialogue between two colleagues. *Denver University Law Review, 78,* 622–632.

Riley, K., & Brown, J. A. (2006). The price of dissent: Walkout at Crystal City High School. *American Educational History Journal, 33,* 63–70.

Robertson, H. G. (1995). If your grandfather could pollute, so can you: Environmental "grandfather clauses" and their role in environmental inequity. *Catholic University Law Review, 45,* 131–179.

Rosen, G. (1974). The development of the Chicano movement in Los Angeles from 1967 to 1969. *Aztlán-International Journal of Chicano Studies Research, 4,* 155–183.

Solórzano, D.G., & Delgado-Bernal, D. (2001). Examining transformational resistance through a critical race and LatCrit theory framework: Chicana and Chicano students in an urban context. *Urban Education, 36,* 308–342.

Stanton-Salazar, R. D. (1997). A social capital framework for understanding the socialization of racial minority children and youth. *Harvard Educational Review, 67,* 1–40.

Stanton-Salazar, R. D. (2001). *Manufacturing hope and despair: The school and kin support networks of U.S.-Mexican youth.* New York: Teachers College Press.

Stanton-Salazar, R. D. (2004). Social capital among working-class minority students. In M. A. Gibson, P. Gándara, & J. P. Koyama (Eds.), *School connections: U.S. Mexican youth, peers, and school achievement.* (pp. 18–38). New York: Teachers College Press.

Stanton-Salazar, R. D. (2010). A social capital framework for the study of institutional agents and their role in the empowerment of low-status students and youth. *Youth & Society, 43,* 1066–1109.

Stefancic, J. (1998). Latino and Latina critical theory: An annotated bibliography. *La Raza Law Journal, 10,* 423–498.

Theriot, M. T., & Dupper, D. R. (2010). Student discipline problems and the transition from elementary to middle schools. *Education and Urban Society, 42,* 205–222.

Thomas, O., Davidson, W., & McAdoo, H. (2008). An evaluation of the Young Empowered Sisters (YES!) program: Promoting cultural assets among African American adolescent girls through a culturally relevant school-based intervention. *Journal of Black Psychology, 34,* 281–308.

Thompson, G. (2008). Beneath the apathy. *Educational Leadership, 65,* 50–54.

Urietta, L., Jr. (2009). *Working from within: Chicana and Chicano activist educators in whitestream schools.* Tucson: University of Arizona Press.

Valencia, R. R., & Pearl, A. (2010). Conclusion: (A) The bankruptcy of the standards-based school reform movement; (B) Toward the construction of meaningful school reform: Democratic education. In R. R. Valencia, *Dismantling contemporary deficit thinking: Educational thought and practice* (pp. 148–158). Critical Educator Series. New York: Routledge.

West, C. (1993). *Race matters.* Boston: Beacon Press.

White, R. W. (1959). Motivation reconsidered: The concept of competence. *Psychological Review, 66,* 297–333.

Willis, P. (1977). *Learning to labor: How working class kids get working class jobs.* Lexington, MA: D.C. Heath.

Zimmerman, M. A., Bingenheimer, J. B, & Notaro, P. C. (2002). Natural mentors and adolescent resiliency: A study of urban youth. *American Journal of Community Psychology, 30,* 221–243.

LAST THOUGHTS

Students of Color and the Achievement Gap has covered an expansive terrain of problems and solutions. My intent in these final pages is not to summarize matters but rather to share a few concluding thoughts, points I think will help bring some closure to this tome. These ruminations are, to wit:

1. *Need to think broadly and deeply about how to eradicate TAG.* One of my major concerns about how most scholars approach TAG—in regard to the educational plight of low-SES students of color as well as school reform—is that they lack a coherent, structurally based, and workable theory. Because of this lacuna in much of the literature on TAG, I organized the current book around theoretical frameworks that employ (a) CRT, (b) an assets-based perspective of low-SES students of color (and their families and communities), (c) a class analysis, and (d) a systemic inequality approach. To me, these strategies make so much sense to utilize in order to understand and comprehensively improve the schooling of low-SES students of color. Although some scholars tackle the educational problems of low-SES students of color and school reform along these lines of analysis, most do not. I opened chapter 3, "The 'Other' Gaps: Income, Housing, and Health," with a quote by Horace Mann Bond (1934). In commenting on the educational concerns of Black students, he underscored the importance of synchronizing improvements in "housing, health, wages and working conditions" (p. 460) with reforms in education. If Bond was able to trumpet the need to think broadly and deeply about simultaneous societal and school reform 8 decades ago, surely we should be prepared to do so in contemporary times.

2. *Need to conceptualize TAG reduction as both an educational and economic imperative.* Certainly, providing an optimal education for low-SES students of color is the

right thing to do. For these children and youths, the goals of equal educational opportunity, equal encouragement, voice, empowerment, marked reduction of TAG, and school success are all moral imperatives. Yet, there is also another dimension that should guide us in this quest for the most favorable education—economics, a feature that benefits the common good at the state and federal level.

There is considerable evidence supporting the following scenario: A state that invests in its educational system produces a well-educated workforce, which in turn serves as a key to economic prosperity (Berger & Fisher, 2013). Furthermore, in states with better-educated workers, median wages are considerably higher (see Berger & Fisher, p. 7, Figure D). As such, these higher-paid workers are able to contribute more to the state economy, as seen in tax revenues (Rouse, 2007)—which are used for a variety of public services (e.g., schools; roads; police; recreation). In short, fully funding education is an astute policy for economic development. To support this assertion, Berger and Fisher cite a study by Bauer, Schweitzer, and Shane (2006)—Federal Reserve economists—who investigated the factors associated with interstate economic prosperity. Examining a 65-year period (from 1939 to 2004), Bauer et al. report that a state's attainment rates for high school and college were significant variables in accounting for per capital growth across states. To help bring about greater investment in education, Berger and Fisher argue that states need to focus more, for example, on making available universal preschool education, improving K-12 schooling, and making postsecondary education affordable. This mission of educational investment has particular relevance for the rapidly growing population of low-SES students of color.

At the federal level, one can make a case that reducing TAG is also an economic imperative. Let us take Latinos/Latinas as an example. In 2011, the Latino/Latina labor force in the U.S. numbered 23 million workers (80% full-time), accounting for 15% of the total workforce—and it is expected to increase to 18% by 2018 (U.S. Department of Labor, 2012). Regarding median weekly earnings, full-time Latino/Latina workers made $549 in 2011, compared to $775 for Whites and $615 for Blacks—meaning that Latino/Latina workers' median weekly wage was just 71% of what their White counterparts earned.[1] One key factor that plays a role in this earning differential is educational attainment. In 2011, only 16.7% of full-time Latino/Latinas were college graduates, compared to 36.1% of Whites.[2]

The economic implication of this difference in wages becomes clearer in the context of entitlement programs. Let us take Social Security, which more than any other program of the federal government touches the lives of U.S. citizens. By the end of 2012, 161 million people had paid payroll taxes into the Social Security system, and about 57 million people were receiving benefits (retirement; disability; survivors' payments) at a cost of approximately $786 billion (Desilver, 2013). In 2014, nearly $863 billion in benefits was dispensed to over 59 million recipients.[3] In addition, more and more people will be eligible for Social Security benefits. Largely due to the baby boom generation (people born between 1946 and 1964), currently more than 250,000 individuals per month (well over

8,000 per day) turn 65 years old, of whom most will retire (Casselman, 2014). Mainly because of improved health care (particularly in treatment of cardiovascular disease; Reinberg, 2014), people in the U.S. have longer life expectancy. As such, in 2014 there were 47 million people 65 years and over, and by 2033 it is projected to be 77 million.[4] Another related fact is that in 2014 there were 2.8 workers for each person who received Social Security benefits, and by the year 2033 the ratio is expected to be 2.1.[5]

Clearly, the sharp increase in the number of people retiring and becoming eligible to receive Social Security benefits, coupled with the declining worker/beneficiary ratio, signals some alarm for the nation's most important entitlement system. To sustain the program, it will be critical to assure that low-SES students of color, who make up a larger and larger portion of the K-12 public school enrollment, receive an optimal education. These students of today will be the predominant workers of the future. Fewer well-educated workers will mean a reduction in economic productivity. For low-SES students of color who receive an inferior education, this translates into, for the most part, unemployment, or part- and full-time work in unskilled jobs. Thus, poorly educated workers will have less economic ability to pay into the Social Security fund, which is a safety net for an aging population. Demonstratively reducing TAG indubitably is in the best economic interests of the U.S. and *all* its people.

3. *Need to embrace and support efforts to empower low-SES students of color and their parents.* In my writings, I try to end on an uplifting tone. For closing *Students of Color and the Achievement Gap,* I can think of no aspect more inspiring than empowerment. Although this book provides comprehensive discussions of the need for systemic transformations in society and the schools, we should not forget that the vanguard of this struggle needs to be low-SES students and their parents. Yes, the roles of dedicated schoolteachers, administrators, counselors, school board members, policymakers, and educational researchers are important in helping to reduce TAG. We need to be mindful, however, that low-SES children and youths of color and their parents are the most significant of the stakeholders.

Historical and contemporary events and activities—in classrooms and in the streets—inform us that when low-SES students of color and their mothers, fathers, and relatives gain voice and empowerment, campaigns against educational oppression and for educational equality have made remarkable strides. Considering the importance of agency and empowerment for these stakeholders, it is incumbent on us to value our low-SES children and youths of color, as well as their parents and communities, and to support all efforts that lead to their empowerment and liberatory activism—through our capacities as teachers, principals, scholars, or makers of social and educational policy. To this effect, I find some comfort in the words of John Amos Comenius (1592–1670), Czech theologian, teacher, textbook writer, and educational reformer.[6] Over 350 years ago, he advocated for public and universal education (i.e., for all social classes and boys and girls), a league of nations to discuss politics and government, and world peace. Although Comenius was driven from nation to nation by tyrants and inquisitors, he still had faith in achieving his goals (Ulich, 1945). In 1657, he wrote in his *Via Lucis* (*The Way of Light;* Comenius, 1939),

> For there is inborn in human nature a love of liberty—for liberty man's [and woman's] mind is convinced that it was made—and this love can by no means be driven out: so that, wherever and whatever means it feels that it is being hemmed in and impeded, it cannot but seek a way out and declare its own liberty. (p. 18)

Notes

1. U.S. Department of Labor (2012, p. 1, Table 1).
2. *Id.*
3. Social Security Administration (2014, p. 1).
4. *Id.* at 2.
5. *Id.*
6. This discussion of Comenius builds on, with revisions, Valencia and Pearl (1997, pp. 251–252).

References

Bauer, P. W., Schweitzer, M. E., & Shane, S. (2006). *State growth empirics: The long-run determinants of state income growth* (Working Paper No. 06–06). Cleveland, OH: Federal Reserve Bank of Cleveland. Retrieved August 2, 2014, from: www.clevelandfed.org/research/workpaper/2006/wp0606.pdf.

Berger, N., & Fisher, P. (2013). *A well-educated workforce is a key to state prosperity.* Washington, DC: Economic Analysis and Research Network. Retrieved August 2, 2014, from: http://www.epi.org/publication/states-education-productivity-growth-foundations/.

Bond, H. M. (1934). *The education of the Negro in the American social order.* New York: Prentice-Hall.

Casselman, B. (2014, May 7). What baby boomers' retirement means for the U.S. economy. *Fivethirtyeight.* Retrieved August 2, 2014 from: http://fivethirtyeight.com/features/what-baby-boomers-retirment-means-for-the-u-s-economy/.

Comenius, J. A. (1939). *The way of light* (E. T. Campagnac, Trans.). Liverpool, UK: University Press of Liverpool. (Original work published 1657).

Desilver, D. (2013, October 16). *5 facts about Social Security.* Washington, DC: Pew Research Center. Retrieved August 2, 2014, from: www.pewresearch.org/fact-tank/2013/10/16/5-facts-about-social-security/.

Reinberg, S. (2014, January 6). Americans living longer than ever: CDC. *HealthDay.* Retrieved August 2, 2014, from: http://consumer.healthday.com/public-health-information-30/centers-for-disease-control-news-120/americans-living-longer-than-ever-683595.html.

Rouse, C. E. (2007). Consequences for the labor market. In C. R. Belfield & H. M. Levin (Eds.), *The price we pay: Economic and social consequence of inadequate education* (pp. 99–124). Washington, DC: Brookings Institution Press.

Social Security Administration. (2014). *Social Security basic facts.* Washington, DC: Author. Retrieved August 2, 2014, from: www.ssa.gov/news/press/basic fact.html.

Ulich, R. (1945). *History of educational thought.* New York: American Book.

U.S. Department of Labor. (2012). *The Latino labor force at a glance.* Washington, DC: Author. Retrieved August 2, 2014, from: www.dol.gov/_sec/media/reports/HispanicLaborForce.pdf.

Valencia, R. R., & Pearl, A. (1997). Epilogue: The future of deficit thinking in educational thought and practice. In R. R. Valencia (Ed.), *The evolution of deficit thinking: Educational thought and practice* (pp. 242–255). Stanford Series on Education and Public Policy. London: Falmer Press.

NAME INDEX

SUBJECT INDEX